AMERICAN
DEFENSE
ANNUAL
1985-1986

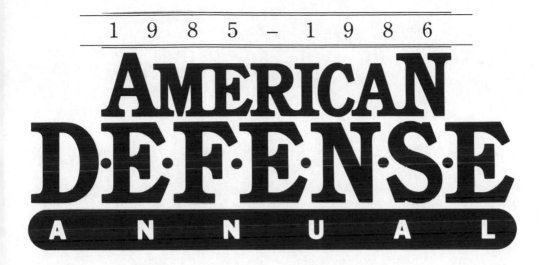

1 9 8 5 – 1 9 8 6

AMERICAN DEFENSE ANNUAL

Edited by
George E. Hudson
and Joseph Kruzel
with a foreword by
Alexander L. George

Mershon Center
The Ohio State University

Lexington Books
D.C. Heath and Company/Lexington, Massachusetts/Toronto

The cartoon on p. 52 is reproduced by the courtesy of Stephen R. Wagner. The cartoon on p. 146 is reproduced by the courtesy of William T. Coulter.

Photo credits:

p. xxii courtesy UPI/Bettmann Archive
p. 18   courtesy National Aeronautics and Space Administration
p. 76   courtesy U.S. Department of Defense
p. 96   courtesy U.S. Department of Defense
p. 114   courtesy U.S. Department of Defense
p. 130   courtesy U.S. Department of Defense
p. 164   courtesy Pete Souza, the White House
p. 186   courtesy U.S. Department of Defense
p. 206   courtesy U.S. Department of Defense

Published simultaneously in Canada
Printed in the United States of America on acid-free paper
Casebound International Standard Book Number: 0-669-09592-3
Paperbound International Standard Book Number: 0-669-09591-5
International Standard Serial Number: 0882-1038

Contents

Figures

Tables

Foreword

Alexander L. George

I n the fall of 1983, faculty members of Ohio State University associated with the Mershon Center recognized the need for an authoritative annual assessment of major issues in American defense policy. No other publication provides a comprehensive analytical survey of this kind. The Annual Report of the Secretary of Defense (the "posture statement") is an invaluable guide to administration thinking on defense, but the report is necessarily a self-serving document aimed at securing passage of the president's defense budget. The International Institute for Strategic Studies' annual publications, *Military Balance* and *Strategic Survey*, provide useful data bases and identify trends, but neither looks in detail at the specific problems confronting U.S. security policy. William Kauffman's critique of the defense budget for the Brookings Institution is a valuable assessment, but it necessarily focuses on budget trends and projections. The *International Security Yearbook* produced by the Georgetown Center for Strategic and International Studies is an excellent survey of global problems, but in assuming a worldwide focus it deals with U.S. defense policy indirectly. Thus, no other publication provides the critique of U.S. security problems and prospects found in the pages of the *American Defense Annual*.

Associates of the Mershon Center also recognized that much of the congressional and public debate about defense issues is preoccupied with the level of defense spending rather than questions of policy. U.S. national security is poorly served by a debate that focuses too narrowly on the second-order question of whether the defense budget should be increased by 3, 5, or 10 percent instead of confronting the crucial question for U.S. defense policy: Are U.S. forces adequate to meet the national security objectives of the country? The Mershon Center hopes that this new publication, the *American Defense Annual*, will help to make the debate about U.S. defense policy more substantive and more meaningful, less organized around the question of the amount of money allocated to defense spending, and more focused on the programs and policies that use defense dollars.

Format

The *Annual* will appear in the spring every year. It will have a standard format, with chapters on defense strategy and the budget, programmatic chapters on strategic forces, theater forces, and seapower and projection forces, as well as chapters on manpower, organization and management, and arms control. Each of these chapters will review briefly the events of the past year and look ahead to the major policy issues that should be on the defense agenda during the year ahead.

In addition, each edition of the *Annual* may have one or more special chapters on topics of particular contemporary significance. This inaugural issue contains two such chapters, one on the Strategic Defense Initiative and the other on low-intensity conflict.

Each year a different set of authors will be commissioned to write the various chapters of the *Annual*. Over time a broad spectrum of views on defense issues will be represented in these pages.

About the Book and Authors

As will quickly become evident from reading the first issue of the *Annual*, no attempt was made to force a consensus from this group of independent-minded contributors. Each author speaks only for himself or herself and is responsible only for his or her chapter. Although most authors could probably be described as moderates on defense issues, they would surely disagree among themselves on the most pressing problems facing U.S. defense and how to go about solving them.

The purpose of the *Annual* is not to present an overall alternative to the administration's defense program but rather to lay out an agenda for debate, to stimulate an informed and productive national dialogue about the legitimate issues in U.S. defense policy. Such a dialogue will improve national awareness of the true costs, the real policy options, and the unavoidable dilemmas that confront defense in the 1980s and beyond. In the end, it will serve to strengthen American national security.

The *American Defense Annual* does not attempt to assess the broader, more complex question of what foreign policy the United States should pursue. A strengthening of the U.S. military posture is essential given the failure of détente and the continued buildup of Soviet forces. Under present and foreseeable world conditions, there is no substitute for a strong, clear, articulate deterrence posture. At the same time, it is incumbent on American policymakers, Congress, and the public to understand that strengthening U.S. military capabilities cannot substitute for a well-conceived, realistically grounded foreign policy. Creating a position of strength or a more favorable balance of forces is only a means to an end. The end itself—the kind of relationship with the Soviet Union and other states that a strong U.S. military posture is designed to help acheive—must be clarified, and appropriate policies to that end must be identified and skillfully pursued. Military power by itself does not automatically or reliably provide appreciable diplomatic dividends. Strengthening the U.S. military posture may be a necessary condition, but it is certainly not sufficient for achieving the limited objective of containment without confrontation in U.S. relations with the Soviet Union or for moving toward the creation of a more stable and viable international system.

About the Mershon Center

The Mershon Center, established at The Ohio State University in 1963, mobilizes faculty and other researchers to investigate issues in national security and public policy. Individuals associated with the center have been responsible for a number of significant volumes over the years. They range from Philip Green's *Deadly Logic* (1966) to Allan Millett and Peter Maslowski's *For the Common Defense* (1984), and from Joel Larus's *Nuclear Weapons Safety and the Common Defense* (1967) to John R. Oneal's *Foreign Policy Making in Times of Crisis* (1982). Under the center's present director, Charles F. Hermann, we can expect the pace of new initiatives from the Mershon Center to quicken. This *Annual* is an important example of these new undertakings.

Acknowledgments

Any edited volume is a collective enterprise, and any inaugural edition of a project such as the *American Defense Annual* necessarily reflects the collective enthusiasm and counsel of many people.

We gratefully acknowledge the research assistance of Bruce Nardulli, who was present at the creation of this project, assisted in its development, and prepared all of the appendixes to this first volume. David Kellogg and Col. James Golden offered helpful advice on the daunting process of bringing the *Annual* to life. Edward Michalski of the Department of Defense provided many of the photographs in the *Annual*, and Tim Kenney deserves full credit for the splendid design of the book and its many attractive graphics and charts.

Charles Hermann, the director of the Mershon Center, as well as our other colleagues associated with the Center, provided great intellectual and practical support to this project throughout its development.

Our publisher, Lexington Books, and in particular our editor, Jaime Welch-Donahue, supplied the perfect combination of enthusiasm, concern, and authoritarianism necessary to convert an interesting academic idea into a practical reality.

Abbreviations

ABM	Antiballistic missile
ALB	AirLand Battle
ALCM	air-launched cruise missile
ARG	amphibious ready group
ASAT	antisatellite
ASEAN	Association of Southeast Asian Nations
ATB	advanced technology bomber
BMD	ballistic missile defenses
C³I	Communications, Command, Control, and Intelligence
CA 90	Counter-Air 90
CDE	Conference on Confidence and Security Building Measures
CENTCOM	Central Command
CINCEUR	Commander-in-Chief Europe
CINCLANT	Commander-in-Chief Atlantic
CINCPAC	Commander-in-Chief Pacific
CINCS	unified and specified commanders
CRAF	Civil Reserve Air Fleet
CVBG	carrier battle group
DOD	Department of Defense
ETI	Emerging Technologies Initiative

FOFA	Follow-on Force Attack
FSED	full-scale engineering development
FY	fiscal year
GAC	General Advisory Committee
GDP	gross domestic product
GLCM	ground-launched cruise missile
HA	Health Affairs
HASC	House Armed Services Committee
ICBM	intercontinental ballistic missile
INF	intermediate-range nuclear forces
IRR	individual ready reserve
ISA	International Security Affairs
JCS	Joint Chiefs of Staff
MAB	Marine Amphibious Brigade
MAD	mutual assured destruction
MAF	marine amphibious force
MAG	marine aircraft group
MAGTF	marine air-ground task forces
MAU	Marine Amphibious Unit
MBFR	Mutual and balanced force reduction
MBR	member
MI&L	Manpower, Installations, and Logistics
MilCon	Military construction
MilPers	Military personnel
MIRV	multiple independently targetable reentry vehicle
MPS	maritime prepositioning ships
MPS	multiple protective shelter
OJCS	Office of the Joint Chiefs of Staff
O&M	operations and maintenance
OMB	Office of Management and Budget
OT&E	Operational Test and Evaluation
PA&E	program analysis and evaluation
POMCUS	prepositioned overseas materiel configured in unit sets
PPBS	planning, programming, and budgeting system
RA	Reserve Affairs
RDF	rapid deployment force
RDT&E	research, development, test, and evaluation

ROTC	Reserve Officers' Training Corps
SAC	Strategic Air Command
SACEUR	Supreme Allied Commander Europe
SAG	Surface Action Group
SALT	Strategic Arms Limitation Talks
SAM	surface-to-air missiles
SASC	Senate Armed Services Committee
SCC	Standing Consultative Commission
SDI	Strategic Defense Initiative
SLBM	submarine-launched ballistic missile
SLCM	sea-launched cruise missile
SSBN	missile-carrying submarine
START	Strategic Arms Reduction Talks
TOA	total obligational authority
USDP/ISP	Undersecretary of Defense for Policy/International Security Policy
USDR&E	Undersecretary of Defense for Research and Engineering
VEAP	Veterans' Educational Assistance Program
VLS	vertical launch system
WEU	West European Union

AMERICAN DEFENSE ANNUAL 1985-1986

Chapter 1

Perspectives

The Domestic Setting
Joseph Kruzel

The portentous, Orwellian year of 1984 was a tranquil one for U.S. defense policy, particularly compared to the tumult of the preceding year, which saw the shootdown of KAL 007, the massacre of U.S. Marines in Lebanon, the invasion of Grenada, great controversy over the deployment of new theater nuclear weapons in Western Europe, and the virtual shutdown of U.S.-Soviet arms control negotiations. By contrast, 1984 saw few international crises, little U.S.-Soviet confrontation, and no overt conflict. Only a handful of U.S. soldiers lost their lives in 1984 as a result of hostile action.

The real action in U.S. defense policy during 1984 was debate about policy and future direction. President Ronald Reagan and challenger Walter Mondale established a long list of apparently irreconcilable differences on defense issues. Reagan claimed that his predecessors had unilaterally disarmed the United States and that the Reagan administration reversed this perilous course and was making the United States strong once again. Mondale charged repeatedly that the Reagan defense buildup was both wasteful and provocative. Favoring real growth in defense spending himself, the Democratic challenger railed against a president who seemed to throw billions at defense without plan or priorities. Even worse, charged Mondale, was Reagan's willful attempt to launch a new cold war against the "evil empire" of the Soviet Union. Mondale never tired of telling his audiences that President Reagan was the first chief executive in a generation who failed to meet his Soviet counterpart.

Yet behind the polarization of the political campaign was a more complex, and a more comforting, reality. The defense buildup that President Reagan proudly claimed to have authored actually began in the late 1970s when the Carter administration pressed the North Atlantic Treaty Organization (NATO) to meet the goal of 3 percent real growth in defense spending. U.S. defense spending accelerated after the Soviet invasion of Afghanistan. As Earl Ravenal and William Van Cleave acknowledge in chapter 2, the last Carter defense budget outlined a military buildup that the Reagan administration basically carried out during its first term in office.

There were, of course, significant differences between the two candidates. Reagan supported the B-1 and MX; Mondale opposed both. Reagan advocated full speed ahead on the Strategic Defense Initiative; Mondale proposed a more tentative approach emphasizing research and development. But the similarities were far greater than the contrasts. Reagan and Mondale both favored real growth in defense spending: Reagan wanted 10 percent, Mondale about half that (and Reagan would count himself fortunate in 1985 to get 5 percent real growth out of Congress). Both supported the deployment of Tomahawk ground-launched cruise missiles and Pershing IIs in Europe; both favored the Trident II missile; both advocated beefing up conventional force readiness and power projection capabilities. Although the campaign tended to draw attention to the differences, it became clear that most of what separated the two candidates on defense was rhetoric, emphasis, and marginal changes in defense programs. Andrew Cockburn spoke for many discouraged liberals when he complained that "Walter Mondale finds little wrong with the policies of the Weinberger Pentagon that could not be put right with a few token gestures."

President Reagan's resounding reelection was nonetheless an impressive mandate for continued growth in U.S. defense spending. While there was overwhelming public support for defense spending in 1985, there was also a growing undercurrent of concern that defense spending was not translating directly into increased military strength. A trillion-dollar defense buildup over four years had not by 1985 produced a defense establishment markedly different from the one bequeathed by the Carter administration after the notorious "decade of neglect." There are still sixteen Army and three Marine Corps divisions, still forty active and reserve wings of combat fighter aircraft in the Air Force. Although the Navy took delivery of over ninety new ships in the first term of the Reagan administration, all but a handful of those were authorized during the Carter administration. There were actually fewer tactical fighter aircraft in the Pentagon's inventory in 1985 than in 1981.

As these facts suggest, the big-ticket items initiated by the Reagan administration were still in the pipeline as Reagan began his second term and would enter the active inventory gradually over the next several years. It seemed almost certain that a painful crunch would occur in the years ahead as the bills came due for the Reagan defense buildup just as Congress struggled to hold down overall spending in order to reduce the federal deficit.

In the mid-1980s public support in the United States for defense spending was undeniably broad but also extremely thin. Americans have traditionally been reluctant to sustain great defense expenditures in the absence of a declared war, and by 1985 there was growing dissatisfaction with the Pentagon's management of its enormous resources. Defense officials spent much of 1984 doggedly knocking down stories about computer chips that would not function, missiles that would not fly, and air defense guns that would not fire. Nothing erodes public support more thoroughly or more quickly than tales of $7,000 coffee pots and $400 hammers. Such stories may be evidence of success by Pentagon auditors, as the Department of Defense claims, or they may be trivial diversions from the real issues of defense spending, as others suggested. It may even be that we need more fraud, waste, and abuse, as some enthusiasts argued, while we endeavor to rebuild neglected defenses. But without public confidence that defense dollars are purchasing real increases in military strength, no administration will be able to sustain for long any real growth in defense spending.

Weinberger-Shultz Disagreement

As the year came to an end, President Reagan's two top national security advisers found themselves embroiled in a curious public debate about the proper use of U.S. military force. In a speech before the National Press Club on November 28, Secretary Caspar Weinberger outlined six conditions that he felt had to be met before U.S. troops should be committed to combat. First, the "vital" interests of the United States or its allies must be at stake. Second, the United States must have "the clear intention of winning." Third, the political and military objectives to be achieved must be clearly defined. Fourth, the relationship between objectives and the U.S. forces committed in support of those objectives must be continually reassessed and adjusted if necessary. Fifth, there must be reasonable assurance of support by Congress and the people. Sixth, combat should be undertaken only as a last resort.

A few days later Secretary George Shultz responded in a speech of his own. The United States must be ready, Shultz said, to use military force to give leverage to U.S. diplomacy. "It is the burden of statesmanship," Shultz added, "to be ready to use force even when there is no prior guarantee of public support." Shultz also cautioned against the United States becoming "the Hamlet of nations, worrying endlessly over whether and how to respond."

The secretary of state playing hawk to the defense secretary's dove may seem like role reversal, but the dispute reflected a long-standing disagreement between the two over the use of U.S. forces abroad. Shultz was a leading advocate within the administration of deploying the marines to Lebanon, of invading Grenada, and of taking a "preactive" approach to combatting terrorism. On each of these policies Shultz was eager; Weinberger and the Joint Chiefs were hesitant.

The uniformed military have traditionally been reluctant to commit U.S. military power to less than all-out war, and Vietnam is the classic case of civilian leaders' enthusiasm for commitment overriding military skittishness about involvement in peripheral conflict. Invariably senior military officials worry that using U.S. troops in such a role could only be a diversion from the central task of preparing for war in Europe with the Soviet Union.

Two facts were troubling about the Weinberger-Shultz contretemps. First was the highly publicized airing of a split within the administration's national security apparatus over the basic direction of defense and foreign policy. The two secretaries had clashed on virtually every important issue on the national security agenda: Central America, arms control, technology transfer, and counterterrorism, as well as the theological dispute about the use of force. Some observers saw in this constant clash of ideas evidence that Reagan's "chairman of the board" model of governance was working. But the analogy was misleadingly comforting. The secretaries of state and defense are not corporate vice-presidents united in a common quest for profit. They are bureaucratic players with very different agendas and very different views of the role of the United States in the world. In the mid-1980s the United States could ill afford the luxury of substituting an interesting academic debate about the basic principles of national security policy for a consistent and coherent approach to defense and diplomacy.

Even more troubling was the prospect that Weinberger's tentativeness about the use of force might carry the weight of conventional wisdom in the Pentagon. Vietnam and Lebanon have left their scars on the U.S. military establishment, but the tragic experience of those conflicts cannot yield the lesson that in the future the United States will commit itself only to risk-free, highly popular skirmishes that threaten vital interests. What conflict in U.S. history has ever satisfied all of Secretary Weinberger's conditions?

More than thirty years separate the Inchon landing, the last unambiguous U.S. military success, from the invasion of Grenada. In those three decades, the U.S. military had few operations to be proud of. The daring raid on Son Tay found an empty prison camp; the rescue of the *Mayaguez* crew cost more lives than it saved; Desert One was a logistical and military humiliation; and the terrorist attack against the marine encampment in Beirut seemed to focus growing military frustration with the use of troops for inappropriate political purposes. But the sad fact is that the future is likely to yield more, rather than fewer, such conflicts.

The fundamental requirement of being a superpower in the late twentieth century means being prepared to join grubby conflicts on the side of less-than-angelic forces in defense of important but less than vital interests in pursuit of political as well as military objectives. Quebec may someday take up arms against the United States, but in the absence of such a conflict, the Reagan administration and its Department of Defense must be prepared for the gloomy prospect of waging difficult wars under daunting circumstances. If Weinberger is serious about his conditions, the Pentagon might as well disband the U.S. Central and Southern Commands, abolish the Special Forces, do away with the Marine Corps, reduce airlift and sealift capability, and cut substantially the number of tactical air wings. These are force elements designed to meet military contingencies that are certain to occur in the complex and unsettled international environment of the future.

American men and women in uniform today enjoy tremendous public support. They deserve every bit of admiration they receive. But respect, admiration, and support are based on the sacrifice that the society knows the military is prepared to make on its behalf. If the military, or its civilian leadership, begins to impose unrealistic conditions on the making of that sacrifice, then public support will quickly erode. We do not spend hundreds of billions of dollars a year to fund a military establishment that will never be used.

Army-Air Force Memo of Understanding

One encouraging bureaucratic event of 1984 was the signing of a Memorandum of Understanding by the Army and Air Force chiefs of staff in May, which committed the two services to cut duplication in weapons programs and to work together more effectively in the field. The two chiefs called the document a "historic agreement." It may be so. Not since the Key West Agreement of 1958 have the services returned to the contentious issue of which military service does what job. "Roles and missions are not the most important thing," said Air Force chief General Charles Gabriel. "Doing the job is."

Gabriel's comment would be unremarkable but for the fact that the services have traditionally held nothing so dear as their roles and missions. Why else would the United States have four separate air forces? While public attention was focused on overpriced coffee pots and wrenches, the Pentagon continued to misspend millions of dollars as a result of interservice rivalry over weapons and programs. Competition among the services may be more than simply wasteful; it may be hazardous to their health. The only problems in the invasion of Grenada apparently came from the inability of Marine and Army troops to communicate with each other because they used different radio frequencies. The desire of all the services to play some role in the Grenada invasion reflected in part the interest of each service in protecting its existing roles and missions.

It is time to revisit the Key West Agreement, to begin the difficult process of making the U.S. military establishment more rational and more efficient. Technology is now giving weapons the accuracy to strike with pinpoint accuracy from great distances, thus tending to blur the traditional distinctions among land, sea, and air delivery. Precision-guided munitions and the growing importance of communications, command, and control have also made it imperative that the services cooperate more closely on the battlefield. The Army-Air Force Memo of Understanding is a start, but the most difficult issues are yet to be tackled. The least accommodating service, the Navy, has yet to be brought into the process, and the most difficult roles and missions have yet to be tackled. No issue is likely to be more controversial than the mission of close air support.

At Key West the Army got helicopters and the Air Force got fixed-wing aircraft, but that division of weaponry did little to resolve the issue of who provided support for the forward line of troops in battle. The Air Force has always considered close air support a less glamorous mission than air superiority, and sensing this lack of enthusiasm, the Army has purchased thousands of helicopters that are a far less efficient and more expensive means of protecting ground forces than slow-moving durable aircraft like the Air Force's A-10.

Generals Wickham and Gabriel deserve credit simply for bringing up the issue of roles and missions; to have begun work on the problem is an act of unusual bureaucratic heroism. The services are instinctively suspicious of joint programs and extremely protective of turf. It will be a difficult task to get them to change their ways, but no other opportunity in the defense arena offers such great potential benefits in improved efficiency.

Congress and Defense Policy

A generation ago the Senate and House Armed Services Committees were enthusiastic and deferential supporters of the Pentagon, operating more as advocates than as watchdogs of defense policy and spending. Members of the two committees defended the defense budget to their colleagues and dispensed bases and defense contracts to themselves in accordance with the ancient tradition of pork barrel politics. Both were seen as rubber stamps for the Pentagon.

Today the Armed Services Committees retain their enthusiasm for defense, but they have lost their deference to the Pentagon brass. A new group of legislators has emerged, favorably inclined to defense spending but eager to challenge what they see as misguided Pentagon practices. In pursuit of a defense establishment that is rational, efficient, and effective, these military reformers and "cheap hawks" have proved to be peskier critics than those who favor across-the-board cuts in military spending.

Much of this new tough-mindedness toward defense was deflected during 1984 into a preoccupation with the details of weapons procurement. The year 1984 may well be remembered as the year of spare parts. Paying thousands for hammers and stepladders was so patently absurd that legislators instinctively seized the issue. It was the sort of outrage that required no detailed understanding of defense policy. It was bipartisan, pro-defense, and a certain headline grabber. The wonder is that more members of Congress did not jump on the bandwagon.

Overpricing of spare parts was simply the most visible part of the larger and more complex issue of weapons procurement. It remained to be seen whether Congress, in 1985 and beyond, would begin to deal with the fundamental structural problem of reforming the weapons acquisition process or be content to settle with the superficial, micromanagerial reforms it instituted in 1984.

As 1985 began, there was growing hope that Congress would begin to exercise real oversight of defense policy. In the House Armed Services Committee, Congressman Les Aspin engineered a startling coup and ousted the aging committee chairman, Mel Price. On the other side of Capitol Hill, independent-minded Barry Goldwater assumed the chairmanship of the Senate Armed Services Committee on the retirement of John Tower. Goldwater was seen as a caretaker chairman, certain to step down at the end of the 99th Congress. Behind Goldwater in terms of seniority were relative youngsters like John Warner and William Cohen, and sitting prominently across the table was Sam Nunn, ranking committee Democrat and hands-down Senate defense authority, eager to take over the Armed Services Committee if his party gained control of the Senate in 1986.

In both committees, power was moving from the generation of combat-tested veterans of World War II to younger Vietnam-era legislators whose military experience was often more analytical than field oriented. This shift may portend a new era of congressional involvement in defense decision making. In the mid-1980s support on Capitol Hill for a strong and effective defense was extraordinarily high—few legislators would describe themselves as antimilitary—but it was accompanied by a new combativeness, an eagerness to ask hard questions, to probe the basis of defense policy in a way that Congress has never done before. At the same time, powerful institutional, procedural, and intellectual restraints worked to keep congressional oversight operating much as it had in the past: weak on policy and force design, heavy on micromanagement.

Defense policy involves the matching of military forces to foreign policy objectives. Shaping defense policy requires making fundamental choices regarding national values, goals, and objectives. It entails a calculation that is moral and political, as well as military and diplomatic. Secretary Weinberger's perennial taunt to critics of the defense budget—inviting them to identify the commitments they would give up in order to accommodate proposed cuts—is in fact the right question. There must be a correspondence between commitment and capability. No amount of verbal acrobatics can long conceal from ourselves, our friends, or our adversaries a fundamental mismatch of foreign policy objectives and military forces.

Grand strategy and force design require vigorous and open debate in which Congress should be an active participant. A strong and assertive Congress does not mean a weak and decisive Pentagon. The nation as a whole will benefit from a defense policy based on a clear conception of goals and objectives and a force posture that can meet those goals and objectives—and that has met the test of responsible congressional oversight. With new chairmen in both the House and Senate Armed Services Committees and with a new willingness on Capitol Hill to look seriously at the complex issues of defense policy, basic reform and genuine oversight may be possible at last.

Arms Control

In his second administration, President Reagan does not have to worry about reelection. As Henry Kissinger has said, the president is now running only for the verdict of history. Almost everyone who knows Ronald Reagan believes that he is genuinely interested in achieving some sort of arms agreement with the Soviets before he leaves office. While few doubt the sincerity of his belief, many wonder whether he knows how to go about the task.

In arms control terms, 1984 ended much better than it began. At the beginning of the year, the United States was still adjusting to the Soviet walkout at Geneva prompted by NATO's deployment of intermediate-range nuclear forces. Many wondered whether anything short of the unacceptable step of withdrawing NATO's Pershing IIs and Tomahawks would ever entice the Soviets back to the bargaining table. By year end, however, the United States and the Soviet Union were preparing to resume negotiations in umbrella talks, a face-saving mechanism that allowed the Soviets to claim they were entering new negotiations, not returning to old ones.

The year-end sense of optimism was tarnished somewhat by the publication of *Deadly Gambits,* Strobe Talbott's disturbing portrait of a chief executive bored by the detail necessary to an understanding of the strategic balance, of cabinet officials with little or no expertise on arms control issues, of midlevel bureaucrats locked in fierce struggle over the basic thrust of the administration's policy. The appointment of Paul Nitze as Secretary Shultz's senior adviser for the January talks was a heartening sign for arms control advocates, but without some fundamental restructuring of the administration's arms control apparatus, it remained doubtful that President Reagan's hope for an accord could be brought to fruition.

First, there were troubling signs of Soviet violations of existing arms agreements: the radar at Krasnoyarsk, the repeated testing of air defense systems in suspect ways, the new generation of ICBMs that may have violated the SALT II rule on new types of missiles. Second, on the U.S. side, there was growing pressure to abrogate the SALT accords, to send a signal to the Soviets that their alleged violations were unacceptable. Unless the administration made some prior adjustment, the launching of the Trident submarine *Alaska* in the summer of 1985 would put the United States in unambiguous violation of the SALT II limit on missiles with multiple warheads.

A third problem was the growing complexity of the arms control enterprise. Even with unbounded goodwill on both sides, the problems of verification, the difficulty of drafting limitations on a vast array of flexible weapon systems, the effectiveness of such limits even if negotiated, and the ability of arms control to keep pace with technology threatened to collapse the entire enterprise. Some pessimists proclaimed the end of traditional arms control and began a search for more meaningful alternatives. The year 1985 promised to be difficult for arms control even if the administration were able to get its bureaucratic house in order.

Air Force Academy Honor Scandal

Over the past three decades, U.S. service academies have been rocked periodically by honor scandals, violations of the honor code by significant numbers of cadets and midshipmen. West Point and the Air Force Academy adhere to the same code: "We will not lie, cheat, steal, nor tolerate among us anyone who does." The honor code at Annapolis is identical, except that it does not proscribe toleration.

In 1984 the Air Force Academy uncovered a cheating scandal of mammoth proportions. Hundreds of cadets were implicated; half of the class of 1984 may have been involved. When academy officials became aware of the scope of the scandal, they realized that the entire honor system had broken down. The superintendent took over administration of the honor system and instigated a full-scale review to determine what had happened and what might be needed to set things right. At year's end the review was still underway, but it seemed inevitable that substantial changes would be made in the honor code and its administration. Very likely the toleration clause would be dropped; possibly officers would be added to the honor boards that determine an accused cadet's guilt or innocence.

Whatever the results of the Air Force Academy review, the incident raised serious questions about the standards expected of future leaders of the U.S. military and about the mores of the military establishment as a whole. The young men and women who attend U.S. service academies are among the best and the brightest of their generation, but they are nonetheless products of a society in which lying, cheating, and even stealing are not unknown and in which toleration is often regarded as a positive virtue. Few labels are more derogatory to a youngster in U.S. society than the epithet "tattletale." Moreover, the honor code is, at least theoretically, an absolute injunction. Stealing a dollar is the same as grand theft; lying to protect the honor of a friend is subject to the same punishment as breaking into a professor's office to steal exams. The honor code imposes absolute standards on the products of a melting-pot society that accepts the gradations of situation ethics.

Yet it seems proper to hold the military, particularly its future leaders, to a higher moral standard than the society as a whole. We ask of those who serve in the military that they be prepared to lay down their lives for their country. It is more than the nation asks of any other group; it is literally the ultimate sacrifice that the state can require of any citizen.

The academies are in the business of training the future U.S. military leaders. An essential component of that training is the holding of these young men and women to a higher standard, to ask of them more than is asked of ordinary citizens. Without this, the academies will have lost a vital part of their mission and will be little more than civilian colleges where students wear uniforms to class.

Economic Security and National Security

In 1985 the United States will spend well over $300 billion on defense. In the same year it will run up a federal deficit of over $200 billion. There is no logical reason to compare these two figures. The amount spent on defense should be determined from an assessment of threats to national interests, not by some arbitrary economic formula and certainly not by measuring the gap between federal revenue and expenditures. If federal deficits are a problem, there are other remedies available short of stripping national defense. Spending on domestic programs could be pared, or taxes could be raised. It is also true that the level of defense spending in the mid-1980s, measured as a percentage of gross national product and compared to other periods in U.S. history, is not an extraordinary burden. The United States spent more on defense during the Eisenhower administration than it does now.

Yet there is a practical connection between national defense and the federal deficit, which is rarely taken seriously by specialists in defense policy. Senator Nunn puts it this way: "The critical national security issue, the principal challenge, that faces us over the next three to five years is deficits." Failure to deal with the deficit could present a threat to the United States just as serious as, if less tangible than, a failure to mount a strong military defense.

There is an ongoing debate within the U.S. defense community over the proper allocation of defense dollars between force readiness and force improvements. The standard lament is that readiness is always sacrificed for future qualitative advantage. There is no strong constituency to protect readiness items—more training hours, more spare parts, more ammunition—while lawmakers and industrialists are certain to protect new, big-ticket weapon systems.

There is a comparable trade-off to be made between current defense spending and the future health of the U.S. economy. Plainly put, in the mid-1980s the United States is paying for its defense buildup out of future revenue, and by doing so, it is jeopardizing long-term national security.

High interest rates and a strong dollar, the direct results of not collecting taxes to pay for current spending, erode the U.S. industrial base. Cheap imports are capturing an increasing share of the U.S. market; more expensive U.S. goods are losing out in international competition. In every successive quarter of 1984, the United States ran a record balance-of-payments deficit. The erosion in U.S. competitiveness is most apparent in mature industries like steel, which suffered a 30 percent reduction from 1980 to 1984, but it also affects new industries like telecommunications and computers. Virtually across the board, in every aspect of manufacture, the United States is losing its market share in the world economy. With lost revenue comes lost profit, and with lost profit comes correspondingly fewer dollars to invest in research and development.

In 1985 the United States thus finds itself in the early stage of a vicious cycle that may lead eventually to the loss of its ability to innovate, to market new products, and to exploit new weapons technologies. For the entire postwar period, this competitive edge in research and development has been the core of U.S. economic and military strength.

Huge deficits threaten national security in another way as well. High U.S. interest rates compound the difficulties of Third World nations struggling to pay off enormous national debts. By adding to the problems of these countries, the United States is unwittingly sowing the seeds of unrest that may one day lead to U.S. military involvement.

If there were a window of vulnerability for the United States, a temporary period of increased peril, then mortgaging the economic future to finance current defense expenditures might make sense, could even be considered a prudent move. U.S. taxpayers could in effect pay off the defense debts they are now accumulating at some point in a more secure future. But the threats that the United States must confront are constant, even growing, and greater defense expenditures will be required in the years ahead. Strong defense is not a static accomplishment; it is a dynamic process that requires the maintenance of a strong industrial base and a continuing commitment to research and modernization.

There is a temptation, not easily resisted, to equate impressive military hardware with strong national defense. But military capability is much more than equipment. Superior morale, strategy, training, and leadership are usually better predictors of combat prowess than fancy hardware. There is a similar temptation to equate strong national defense with strong national security. Defense is certainly a vital component of security, but it is not everything. A credible and confident foreign policy that matches means to ends, a network of alliances that can help shoulder the collective burden of defense, and above all, an economy capable of sustaining a high level of defense spending over the long haul—these are the ingredients of genuine, durable national security.

It is not easy for statesmen or citizens to keep in mind this broad and multidimensional perspective. The military threats are tangible and near term; the consequences of failing to meet them may be felt immediately. The economic threats, on the other hand, are vague, intangible, and distant; they can always be dealt with tomorrow. But tomorrow will come, and any government that accepts the Faustian bargain of short-term military security by mortgaging long-term economic security will have squandered its mandate and done a grave disservice to its people.

The External Environment
George E. Hudson

The Soviet Union

"Will the Soviet Union survive until 1984?" asked the dissident writer Andrei Amalrik. Survive, it did, with a strong military, but also with a continuing problem in its basic political structure: how to choose a successor to the general secretary of the Communist party.

February 1984 brought the death of General Secretary Yuri Andropov, a leader who promised to be forward looking in solving key Soviet economic problems, especially labor productivity. He was succeeded by the ailing Konstantin Chernenko, a throwback to the Brezhnev administration's cadre of conservative bureaucrats and a caretaker who would be unlikely to exert dynamic leadership in either domestic or foreign policy. In December the Soviet minister of defense, Dimitri Ustinov, died and was replaced by a seventy-three-year-old professional military man, Marshal Sergei Sokolov, who had served as first deputy minister of defense for seventeen years. His leadership seemed likely to stress continuity rather than new views in the Soviet military bureaucracy. Significantly this transition occurred shortly after the September firing of Marshal Nikolai Ogarkov, chief of the general staff and a proponent of change in the Soviet armed forces.

Characteristically these leadership changes generated conservatism in Soviet policy. With a weak leadership at the top, the Soviets were in a poor position to challenge the Reagan administration effectively in any new part of the world and could only hang on to areas in which they had already obtained influence—primarily in Eastern Europe, Afghanistan, and Cuba.

Thus the policy inertia generated from past decisions dominated Soviet defense policy in 1984. The Soviet Union remained mired in Afghanistan, one of the poorest nations in the world but evidently one of the toughest. The Soviet Union continued its weapons modernization program by emplacing more SS-20 missiles within striking range of Western Europe, by replacing older-model tactical nuclear weapons with SS-21, -22, and -23 missiles in Eastern Europe, and by stationing cruise missiles in Eastern Europe. The USSR's leadership conveyed the impression that these military activities were a response only to NATO's deployment of Pershing II and ground-launched cruise missiles (GLCMs) in Europe, but it was clear that Soviet policy was at least partly a result of modernization decisions made some time ago (see chapter 5 for a discussion of U.S. theater forces). In addition, the Soviets also were reported to be deploying a new intercontinental missile, the SS-25, and continuing construction of the Krasnoyarsk radar facility. This radar, estimated to be completed in the late 1980s, if used to its fullest would almost certainly be able to operate as a battle management radar, thus violating the 1972 ABM Treaty.

Soviet behavior, coupled with the refusal to discuss strategic and intermediate-range arms limitation with the United States, provided a justification for a higher U.S. military budget and a sterner evaluation of the Soviet "threat." The Soviets appeared to confirm the Reagan administration's assertions about the military danger that the Soviet Union posed and the need to take strong corrective action. The Soviets thereby played into the hands of the president's campaign strategists and helped to increase the appeal of the Republican candidate. Evidently convinced of a Republican victory, the Soviets sent Andrei Gromyko in September to discuss the future of the sour U.S.-Soviet relationship with President Reagan. The timing of the meeting suggested that the Soviets hoped to influence the direction of U.S. policy during the president's second term before it was completely charted. The Soviets did not, however, want to imply an endorsement of Reagan's candidacy and, by implication, his past policies. Thus, Gromyko also met with Walter Mondale to hedge Soviet bets against an electoral upset.

A strong campaign against the U.S. Strategic Defense Initiative (SDI) marked another response to U.S. defense efforts. Albert Carnesale discusses in chapter 10 the difficulties of implementing missile defense. Despite these widely recognized technical problems, the Soviets feared that the United States would make some technological breakthrough that would leave the Soviet Union militarily vulnerable. A U.S. decision to proceed with active research and testing on SDI—even if no successful weapon were developed—would likely lead to more Soviet ICBM deployments in an effort to counteract this defensive system. During 1985 and 1986 the leaderships of both nations have the opportunity to discuss strategic defense limitations and perhaps to halt some forms of strategic defense but at least to control the pace of development of space weapons. This should be a critical item on the U.S. and Soviet negotiating agendas.

Although policy conservatism characterized the Soviet leadership in 1984, some Soviet military writings called for changes that could have an impact on U.S. and NATO force planning in the coming years. Marshal Ogarkov argued for some time that conventional forces needed to be modernized at a rapid pace and should be integrated more fully into a coordinated command-and-control mechanism that would allow some flexibility for commanders in the field. During an interview in May 1984, he repeated these ideas. Although Ogarkov was fired in September, his views still find a strong constituency in the Soviet military. If the Soviets were to place more emphasis on conventional weapons in Europe and develop maneuverable, high-firepower divisions of the type Ogarkov would like, the United States and NATO would have even more of a reason to improve their own conventional forces to deter the Soviets. It is an expensive and perhaps distasteful option, but the military imperatives may demand it.

Europe and Japan

Stationing new-generation theater nuclear weapons and restarting arms negotiations remained major issues in NATO during 1984. There was undeniable success on the part of the United States to implement nuclear deployments in Europe. This success was partly due to continued Soviet missile deployments and ham-handed Soviet efforts to manipulate European public opinion in opposition to Pershing IIs and GLCMs. But the Netherlands continued to refuse to allow the stationing of

GLCMs on its soil unless it were proved that the Soviets had increased their SS-20 deployments over 378 by November 1985. Although the Dutch stance was extreme, it highlighted a major, continuing difference between European and U.S. perceptions on defense. Many Europeans do not sense an immediate threat from the Soviets and believe that U.S. defense policies raise the level of East-West confrontation, thereby increasing the likelihood of war. Europeans also feel caught between the two superpowers and want to find ways to generate more stability than that found in a perilous if durable nuclear standoff.

President Reagan exacerbated these concerns in his Strategic Defense Initiative. Some Europeans thought that SDI was intended to form a protective bubble around the United States that would leave them vulnerable to Soviet missile strikes. In 1984 the Reagan administration attempted to quiet European fears partly by offering to talk with the Soviets on matters of strategic defense, but differences over SDI may continue to plague U.S.-European relations in the years to come.

With increased Soviet-U.S. tensions over the last six years came the decline but not demise of *Ostpolitik*, West Germany's effort to lower tensions between Western and Eastern Europe, in part by allowing more human contacts and communications across that divided continent. During 1984, the effort was revived through Helmut Kohl's invitation to German communist party leader Erich Honecker to visit Bonn. It would have been the first official state visit of an East German leader to the West German capital. Honecker accepted but later cancelled. The Soviet Union likely vetoed the plan because of its lingering fears about German revanchism. Relations between the two Germanies is an issue not only for the Soviets, however. Given the United States' strong support for a reduction in tensions between East and West, *Ostpolitik* could develop over the long term in a way that would undermine U.S. defense policies on the European continent. A relaxation of relations between East and West Germany involving, for instance, considerably more travel and trade between the two nations and between East and West Europe generally could produce pressures to reduce the number of U.S. troops in Europe, even though their main potential adversary, the Soviet Union, could remain at a high level of strength.

The Reagan administration greeted with pleasure the news from the Japanese, who agreed in 1984 to increase their defense spending over the long-standing self-imposed level of 1 percent of GNP. This is a small percentage to spend on defense, but given strong antimilitarist tendencies in Japanese society (and constitutional provisions limiting Japan to self-defense forces), breaking the 1 percent barrier may signify that the Japanese are willing to shoulder more of the defense burden in the north Pacific and take some of the load off the United States—at least so the U.S. government hopes. The Japanese GNP is now larger than the Soviet, giving Japan the second largest economy in the world. Increased Japanese spending on defense could therefore yield considerable amounts for Japan's military. But greater spending could be a double-edged sword, raising questions about a revival of Japanese militarism that could someday threaten U.S. interests in East Asia. Suspicion bred from the experience of World War II still hangs on many U.S. minds. Thus, developments in Germany have their parallel in Japan. Support for current policies could produce results over the long term that could damage U.S. security.

The Developing Nations

With the exception of Central America, the Third World during 1984 did not pose major challenges to U.S. defense. As elsewhere, however, the issues raised during the year had profound implications for the problems the United States is likely to face in the future.

One perennial question that U.S. policymakers encounter revolves about the causes of political instabilities that challenge U.S. interests in developing nations. To what degree are instabilities the result of indigenous forces; to what extent are they the result of Soviet influence? The answer produces a policy that is keyed either to bilateral or regional activity, on the one hand, or to the East-West context, on the other. Whatever the determination, the United States will still need to prepare its armed forces to handle military contingencies in the developing world. But low-intensity conflict, as Robert Kupperman and William Taylor discuss in chapter 11, poses particular problems for using U.S. military forces in confronting indigenous or Soviet challenges. In the absence of sending forces into combat, the United States often uses military aid as a policy tool.

Much of U.S. security policy in the Third World during 1984 remained tied to concerns about the Soviet Union. Pakistan is a case in point. As a result of the fall of the shah of Iran, Pakistan became the only nation the United States could count on to act as a buffer against Soviet activities in Southwest Asia, especially in Afghanistan. In order to create a strong Pakistan and to develop a conduit for surreptitious arms deliveries to the Afghan rebels, the United States decided in 1981 to supply Pakistan with $3.2 billion in economic and military assistance, reversing a suspension of aid in 1979. The aid began to arrive in early 1983 and continued through 1984. This assistance, over half of which is military and includes about $1.1 billion to purchase forty F-16 fighter aircraft, will continue until 1988. But Pakistan could pose problems for U.S. policy in Southwest Asia. President Mohammad Zia ul-Haq refuses to lift the martial law he imposed seven and a half years ago, despite his promises to the contrary, or to allow electoral participation by political parties. This has caused considerable domestic dissatisfaction. He also appears committed to the acquisition of nuclear weapons. The Reagan administration should ponder the lesson of Iran. It needs to ask itself whether the cost of economic and military assistance is worth the risk of dependence on an unpopular ruler. If Zia is overthrown, he could yield to a government unfriendly to U.S. interests and armed with nuclear weapons. Such a situation could endanger regional and even global stability.

U.S. defense efforts in the People's Republic of China (PRC) provided a further example of a policy directed at the Soviet Union. The year 1984 witnessed a flurry of military-related visits between the two nations. In January, Zhao Ziyang made the first official trip by a PRC prime minister to North America; President Reagan returned the visit in April; June brought Chinese Minister of Defense Zhang Aiping to the United States in reciprocity for Caspar Weinberger's 1983 visit; and two delegations of U.S. military personnel went to China in August and October, the latter trip to discuss military training activities. A major deal, the largest to date, was concluded between the two governments in July. The Chinese agreed to purchase twenty-four Sikorsky combat assault helicopters for about $150 million. The Soviet Union naturally, and with some justification, viewed these activities as efforts to strengthen the Chinese military and form a loose military alliance between the United States and China.

But the Chinese proved unwilling to be used merely as a U.S. card in the super-power struggle. During President Reagan's visit they censored some of the president's anti-Soviet remarks from a Chinese television broadcast and throughout 1984 continued talks with the Soviet Union to lower tensions between the communist giants. In addition, the enduring question of U.S. military relations with Taiwan generated Chinese suspicions about U.S. policy in the Far East. There were, then, political limits to Chinese-U.S. cooperation in 1984. These limits are likely to continue as long as the United States is ambivalent about its relations with Taiwan and insofar as the U.S. government views the PRC primarily as a lever to exert pressure on the Soviet Union. A more technical constraint on U.S.-Chinese relations concerns the lack of infrastructure that prevents the Chinese from absorbing large amounts of sophisticated military equipment. Additionally, the United States draws its own parameters about military cooperation. It will not sell the Chinese powerful or sophisticated offensive weapons that might provoke a Chinese-Soviet military confrontation, which could have global consequences.

Events in Central America also demonstrated a propensity to view Third World events in an East-West context. To be sure, the Soviets have interests in Central America, as a yearly $3 billion contribution to the Cuban economy testifies, some of which aids Cuban and Soviet activities in Central America. Soviet policy, such as helping to support the Sandinista government in Nicaragua, is likely responsible, directly or indirectly, for some Central American instability. U.S. policymakers, however, need to assess the extent to which dissatisfaction in that region emerges as a result of indigenous causes, such as inequitable land distribution, that have nothing to do with Soviet efforts at influencing political events. A policy that made this determination could yield relatively more use of U.S. diplomatic and economic elements and less military ones. It might provide a clearer direction for U.S. policy in that troubled area of the world.

There were other events in Third World nations that drew U.S. attention during 1984, but little activity. These situations could demand greater U.S. involvement in the coming years and deserve brief mention here. The Vietnam-Cambodian war is such a case. The Reagan administration appeared to recognize it as a surrogate conflict between the Soviet Union and China, with the Soviets backing the Vietnamese and the Chinese, the Cambodians. As 1984 drew to a close, the Vietnamese launched bloody drives to crush resistance in Cambodia, leading to charges from Cambodian rebels that the Vietnamese wanted to colonize their country. Vietnamese successes may threaten Thailand, a member of the Southeast Asia Treaty (see appendix B for a map of worldwide U.S. security commitments), and then may begin to impinge on U.S. interests. The U.S government should be closely monitoring what occurs in 1985.

The Iran-Iraq war is a second instance of an important Third World event that could produce greater U.S. involvement in the future. The Iraqi bombing of large naval targets (oil tankers) in the Persian Gulf could become highly provocative acts. At an earlier time, they would have been an assault on the economic security of U.S. allies. But during 1984 the conflict did not seem to worry many observers since the key issue, the threat of a cutoff of oil from the Persian Gulf to Western Europe and Japan, did not arise. Plenty of oil was available, at relatively cheap prices, from a multitude of sources. If the Iran-Iraq war begins to affect significantly oil supplies to the West and Japan, then it will raise direct security dangers for U.S. allies. Given that the region is so close to the Soviet Union, U.S.

military moves to halt the war or to guarantee oil supplies could have global, as well as regional, implications. The area will remain a potential hotspot in the years to come, but the Soviet Union appears for the present to want the Iran-Iraq war to remain inconclusive, apparently hoping that it will end without much Soviet assistance and in a way to produce an augmentation of Soviet power or at least to prevent a negative impact on it. The United States has adopted a similarly cautious stance.

In Africa, a coup d'état in Nigeria, a country with which the United States has had strong ties economically and politically, also did not generate a crisis for U.S. security, but continuing instability in that nation could create an opening for anti-U.S. policies. The future of U.S. relations with black African nations depends in part on U.S. policy toward South Africa. During 1984, the United States addressed the apartheid issue through the policy of "constructive engagement," that is, by placing gradual pressure over time on the South African government to alter apartheid. The awarding of the 1984 Nobel Peace Prize to South African Bishop Desmond Tutu helped to generate momentum toward a denunciation of apartheid by many conservative U.S. politicians, including President Reagan, although it remains to be seen whether sufficient U.S. pressure is exerted to institute change in the distribution of political power. So far, there has not been much political change, to the chagrin of many Africans and U.S. citizens. South Africa is potentially important to U.S. security because the military base in Simonstown could be used to defend Western shipments around the Cape of Good Hope. It is unclear whether the middling U.S. policy will succeed. It could satisfy none of the parties concerned by not supporting the South African minority government enough or by not condemning it sufficiently.

Conclusions

The external environment presented few immediate challenges to U.S. security policy during 1984. It allowed the debates during the election year to proceed in a relatively calm international environment. Whether the absence of crises implied a clear reflection on the problems facing U.S. defense is another matter. Many positive things occurred. There was a promise of arms control negotiations with the Soviet Union; Pershing IIs and GLCMs were stationed in Western Europe; Japan appeared more willing to shoulder a defense burden; and the developing nations posed difficulties in only a few areas. These were counterbalanced by negative events. The USSR still had not achieved sufficient stability in its leadership to allow a significant improvement of U.S.-Soviet relations; there were continued strains in the European alliance; and the Third World continued to be unstable.

In 1984 the nature of the challenge to U.S. defense internationally proved to concern itself not about the resolution of current crises but rather the orientation of future policy. How U.S. decisions—ranging from security policy in Europe to the developing nations—relate to the contexts of bilateral, regional, and global affairs in 1985 and 1986 will have enduring consequence.

Chapter 2

U.S. Defense Strategy: A Debate

William R. Van Cleave
Earl C. Ravenal

Opening Statement   William R. Van Cleave

The late Senator Henry Jackson once remarked, "We have no foreign policy, and it is being mismanaged." That remark applies aptly to national strategy and defense policy in the mid-1980s. While certain requirements have been set for components of U.S. military forces and general strategic objectives have been established for various areas of the world, no overall national strategy or comprehensive defense policy exists. Moreover, U.S. military capabilities generally fall well short of the requirements that have been set and the objectives that have been established. That, in short, is the central strategic problem of 1985 and coming years: the mismatch between requirements and capabilities.

Nominally, U.S. policy remains that of containment. But a strategy and the forces to support that policy, and possibly the determination as well, are lacking. As a consequence, containment is failing:

> During the last two decades, the policy of containment failed to prevent the Soviet Union from establishing critical footholds in strategic locations throughout the world. . . . If the trend of Soviet expansion we have witnessed over the last 20 years is permitted to continue, the long-term consequences for the United States would be disastrous.[1]

Soviet imperial urges have long existed, but the military balance that helped contain them has become an imbalance in favor of Soviet expansionism. The Soviet Union has aggressively sought to gain military advantage over the West; it has been willing to devote the enormous resources necessary; and it has been successful. The West, by contrast, while on the defensive, has not been willing to maintain the military strength necessary to an effective countervailing strategy. Nor has it, compared with the Soviets, been willing to think and act in consistent strategic terms. As Lord Carrington has complained, the West lacks both strategic vision and agreed strategies for dealing with the Soviet threat.[2]

That situation must be reversed, or the threat to Western security and way of life will increase. We need a clear affirmative answer to the fundamental question posed a few years ago by Norman Podhoretz: "Do we have the will to reverse the decline of American power and to resist the forward surge of Soviet imperialism?"[3] To date that answer has not been provided, and U.S. military strength remains more in line with a minimal defense posture than one capable of supporting U.S. interests and commitments worldwide. I believe that the choice for the United States is between reaffirming its commitment to containment or resigning itself to strategic retreat and the consequent spread of Soviet totalitarianism. But there is a choice; the latter is not inevitable. To imply the contrary suggests that the United States and its allies, the richest and most technologically and industrially advanced nations in the world, cannot provide the defenses to support their strategic interests as the Soviet Union does its own.

By the time the Reagan administration took office, U.S. defense spending had been declining for over a decade, resulting in an atrophy of U.S. military strength; at the same time, the Soviet military effort had increased annually. U.S. conventional land forces had become no match for Soviet forces anywhere around the periphery of Eurasia. U.S. naval forces, while returning some advantages over Soviet naval forces, had also declined in strength as the Soviet Navy had gained blue-water capabilities. Soviet power projection capability had substantially increased, while U.S. capability had shrunk. U.S. general-purpose forces were stretched very thinly and were suffering major shortfalls in arms, equipment, and training.

Even more ominous, the Soviets had gained clear-cut nuclear superiority and had programs to extend that superiority, while Western nuclear deterrent forces had become dangerously vulnerable. Not only were strategic and crisis stability at risk, but the Soviets had also seized "escalation dominance," thereby weakening U.S. extended deterrence and reducing even further the effectiveness of U.S. nonnuclear forces for containment.

The Reagan administration entered office with a commitment to reverse this decline and to restore military strength across the board. During the 1980 campaign, it had emphasized the following priorities:

1. The formulation and elaboration of a comprehensive U.S. military strategy.
2. Increases in defense spending sufficient to restore vitality to all U.S. military forces and to close the gap with Soviet military capabilities.
3. The immediate strengthening of nuclear deterrent forces, to restore "essential equivalence" and especially to "close the window of vulnerability before it opens any wider."
4. A more realistic arms control policy that put the restoration of strength before the pursuit of agreements.

Since then, there have been modest increases in defense spending and some arrest of the atrophy of U.S. military forces but no real change. U.S. forces remain deficient, and the gap between them and Soviet forces continues to widen in critical areas. To its credit, the Reagan administration has been fairly candid about the situation, but the fact remains that it has not fulfilled its own commitments of 1980.[4] Those four priorities seem to remain the key to U.S. defense requirements.

A Comprehensive Strategy

In terms of basic national security policy, the major issue in 1985 centers around containment—its requirements and its prospects—as it has since George Kennan called for the "firm and vigilant containment of Russian expansive tendencies." Containment officially remains U.S. policy, but it lacks a supporting strategy. If a comprehensive military strategy for the United States has been formulated, it has not been elaborated in any public document. Military strategy has been reduced to separate guidelines for forces, which are not integrated. Once formulated, the guidelines are too often ignored. The resulting gaps between the guidelines and actual force capabilities further confound strategy.

Doctrine governing strategic nuclear forces (SNF) is more developed than that for other U.S. military forces. At least it sets rather clear objectives. Official doctrine requires that SNF be capable of surviving even a well-executed surprise attack with the capacity to retaliate selectively and effectively against a wide range and variety of targets, over a period of time, while maintaining both the capability to extend military-industrial destruction and a postexchange secure reserve force. No major force component should be vulnerable; and the forces, overall, should be essentially equivalent with the capabilities of Soviet forces. But the strategy's applicability is questionable. U.S. forces today manifestly do not meet those standards. And without a higher priority for SNF modernization, it is highly unlikely that U.S. strategic forces will do so in the foreseeable future.

This raises two important strategic questions: should standards and objectives be reduced to fit capability, or should they remain the guidelines for force development; and how should the United States plan (in the long term if the former answer or in the interim if the latter) to target forces far less capable than required by current plans? Despite the rejection of minimum assured destruction by successive administrations, is the United States back to this standard? So far the Pentagon has attempted to avoid the problem of the strategy-force mismatch by best-case planning. For example, the standard of survivability against a well-executed surprise attack appears to have quietly given way to the assumption of effective strategic warning, generated alert, poorly executed attacks, and launch on warning.

For other forces—theater nuclear weapons and general-purpose forces, for example—strategy is even less clear, but it is equally clear that the forces fall short of objective and commitments, even when allied forces are included. In NATO, a strategy formulated twenty years ago has not kept pace with a drastically changed nuclear balance. Doctrinal ambiguities in flexible response have left the alliance with little in the way of strategy. The relationship between escalation—vertical or horizontal—and direct defense, or objective denial, is particularly obscure.

For general-purpose forces, extended deterrence outside NATO, and power projection—all essential to containment—there is no apparent strategy for a wide range of contingencies from low-intensity conflict to assaults on interests declared to be vital to U.S. security. And there is no strategy explaining the relationship of U.S. nuclear forces to these contingencies, if any.

In sum, the United States has not formulated a military strategy to support a policy of containment and to cope with the military threats that it now faces.

Defense Spending

At the center of the defense problems of the United States is inadequate defense spending. For more than a decade and a half, the United States grossly under-funded its defense effort, while Soviet spending steadily increased. For the 1970s alone, the resulting cumulative gap was approximately $700 billion, of which $450 billion was in investment. The consequences of the latter shortfall are not yet fully felt. In SNFs, for the nine-year period between 1975 and 1984, the differential is $250 billion.[5] These enormous differentials cannot be overcome by the modest defense increases of a few years.

U.S. defense spending may be made to seem high when not placed in the context of the Soviet effort, or deficiencies in U.S. forces, or the threat, or even overall government spending. Recent increases may appear substantial when expressed merely in terms of annual percentages, while ignoring the low level to which spending had declined by the time of the increases.

One well-received monograph, typical of efforts to create an impression of excessive defense spending, referred to "the *vast* increase in defense *spending*" under Reagan but then shifts to total budget authority to come up with alleged annual increases of 20 percent, 14 percent, 8 percent, and 18 percent (requested FY85), or a 15 percent average.[6] These seem to be substantial increases. They are also deliberately exaggerated because they are based on current, not constant, dollars. Real increases have been significantly lower. A 1984 Library of Congress report (to use a neutral source) cites increases in obligational authority of 12 percent, 8½ percent, 4¼, and 5¼ percent, for an average of about 7½ percent. Increases in outlays are lower. The report also points out that "after declining in real terms by an average annual rate of 2.2% from FY 1968 to FY 1979, defense budgets grew for five consecutive years," although at rates less than projected in the five-year defense plan of March 1981.[7] What is also often ignored is the fact that the Carter administration finally recognized the need for increases and projected increases very near to those that have taken place during the Reagan administration. In fact, given the likely cuts in requested outlays for FY85, actual spending in four years under Ronald Reagan will be slightly less than projected by Jimmy Carter for the same years.

By any reasonable standard, therefore, increases have been modest, not vast. More is needed and more can be afforded.

The requirements of national security should be determinative of the levels of defense spending—not some contrived or artificial budgetary formula, involving non-defense spending, taxes and borrowing. *There is no question that the American economy is capable of supporting an increased defense effort.*[8]

Surely the requirements of national defense take priority over federal budget deficits, which are not driven by defense spending and cannot be significantly reduced by plausible cuts in defense. At this point, a $50 billion increase or decrease in the deficit would have little economic impact, but a $50 billion increase or decrease in defense spending could make an enormous difference to national defense.

There is also evidence of public support for higher defense spending. A careful poll released in April 1984 showed that although the majority of Americans erroneously believe defense spending to be 20 to 50 percent of GNP, as opposed to about 6 percent, over 70 percent of the public still favor either keeping defense spending at current levels or increasing it.[9]

One ought not to disparage this argument as merely throwing money at defense and citing examples of Pentagon waste and mismanagement. I make no suggestion that increased spending be spent injudiciously or carelessly, and I make no denial that waste and ill-advised programs exist. Prudent allocation of limited resources is essential. (In fact, the Pentagon's record, despite sensationalist allegations by the "military reformers" and others, is better than that of other government departments and agencies and is improving. It is scrutinized annually and far more carefully and skeptically than other government agencies.)

The problem is simply stated: even with the wisest and most careful program planning and money management, there is no way that the force imbalance resulting from fifteen years of highly disparate efforts can be adequately improved without further increases in defense spending beyond those now projected. There are no cheaper ways to compensate for the years of neglect. The defense budget remains inadequate to meet U.S. security commitments. Dean Acheson once wrote:

> The military policy which is outlined here will cost a great deal. We shall be told that we cannot afford it. We never have doubted, or would doubt, if we were attacked that the United States could afford to devote whatever resources might be necessary to preserve itself. Surely, it is folly now to shrink from the effort and close our eyes to the crisis of the world struggle.[10]

Or as a more recent writer has pithily put it: "It is far cheaper to win an arms race than to lose a war."[11]

Strategic Forces

The FY85 *Annual Report* warns that superior Soviet SNF programs "have undercut the stability of the nuclear balance and undermined the retaliatory effectiveness that was at the heart of our policy of deterrence."[12] Taken literally, that is a shocking statement. As much as general-purpose forces have suffered during the underfunding of recent years and as vital to defense as is their restoration, there can be no higher priority than the stability of nuclear deterrence. This is so not only because of the grave risks that attend such instability but also because such a nuclear imbalance magnifies deficiencies in general-purpose forces. Allowing Soviet dominance at the strategic nuclear level thus not only undermines the credibility of the U.S. nuclear deterrent but also erodes the deterrent effect of general-purpose forces; it encourages the Soviets to take risks at nonnuclear levels confident that the United States will back away at the threat of nuclear escalation. "The strategic deterrent is the high ground which overshadows all other use of military force, particularly in situations where the Soviet Union is involved."[13]

The precariousness of the situation at the strategic nuclear level is described by DOD publications, which show that the situation has deteriorated over the past four years, not improved, but even these are understatements of the actual imbalance. A small fraction of Soviet forces have a disarming capability against the preponderance of U.S. SNFs, leaving a very large reserve to deter any U.S. retaliation and an impressive active and passive defense to blunt any that might still occur.

The SNF modernization program, if fully funded, includes worthy force improvements, but it suffers sever weaknesses: it is not being given the priority and budget support it should have, it fails to resolve critical force vulnerabilities, and it lacks a proper sense of urgency. In short, rather than closing the window of vulnerability, it props it open.

If proper priorities for the SNF are not immediately established, the United States faces a long, dangerous period during which U.S. forces will not only be inadequate in terms of established requirements (which is already the case) but will carry high risk as even a minimum deterrent. In the broadest sense, that is the meaning of the window of vulnerability. In a narrower sense, the term refers to the vulnerability of key components of the SNF, particularly the intercontinental ballistic missile (ICBM) force.

Healthy strategic forces and a stable strategic balance are essential to any effective military strategy. Healthy SNFs are impossible without high confidence in their survivability and their ability to fulfill the full requirements of strategic doctrine. The key to that is a survivable ICBM force. Without such force, the entire edifice of U.S. strategic doctrine falls apart, and so does the prospect for any comprehensive military strategy.

The administration's acceptance of the logic of the Scowcroft commission report and the decision to proceed with a vulnerably deployed MX has been a mistake that postpones the resolution of the central problem of the strategic balance: the attractive vulnerability of the strategically most important components of U.S. SNF. U.S. strategic doctrine requires the targeting capability represented by 100 or more MX, but it first requires that improved capability be matched by improved survivability; more capable but more vulnerable forces become more tempting targets. With MX in fixed, undefended silos, the United States is producing targets rather than weapons. At the same time, the Scowcroft commission, pursuing its primary objective (not prudent SNF modernization but deployment of the MX), removed the potentially more survivable small ICBM as an MX competitor by deferring its initial operating capability to the 1990s and recommending against an accelerated program.

There are additional problems as well, but space prevents their elaboration. In essentially all elements of SNF modernization, the administration proceeds at too leisurely a pace. The result will be further erosion of the strategic deterrent before necessary strengthening and exacerbation of the problems already described. Preoccupied with general-purpose forces and relatively disinterested in the strategic force balance, the Office of the Secretary of Defense and the military services share the blame for this lamentable state of affairs.

In contrast, the Soviets continue to assign the highest national priorities to the expansion and modernization of strategic capabilities, and they are now turning increasing attention to three areas in which they are at the threshold of major progress: antisubmarine warfare, missile defense, and space. Space may, in fact, tie the three together; and the scope of the Soviet military space program belies any real Soviet interest in mutual, as opposed to unilateral, space arms control.[14]

Compared to Soviet programs, the Reagan administration's Strategic Defense Initiative (SDI), a highly worthy innovation, is little more than a tentative, long-range research and development (R&D) program. Defensive capabilities have long been a missing link in U.S. strategy, although the evolution of U.S. doctrine would seem logically to require that link (that is, if the United States is serious about nuclear damage limiting, and even for extended deterrence, the case for defensive systems seems to be strong). Both components of the SDI—near-term defense of retaliatory forces and longer-term defense of the nation—deserve the emphasis placed on them by the president, but despite increased funding, the first is receiving little attention and the latter is being treated as long-term R&D most likely to be sacrificed at the altar of arms control.

Realistic Arms Control

The major U.S. arms control mistakes of the 1970s were the belief that arms control could solve, or substantially help to solve, such basic strategic problems as the survivability of U.S. deterrent forces, a consequent overemphasis on arms control at the expense of strategic programs, the erection of arms control as the centerpiece of U.S.-Soviet relations, and the failure to educate the public on the realities of arms control with the Soviet Union.

It may be that the Reagan administration has approached arms control with a new realism. Its efforts began that way.[15] It has also avoided unwise agreements and, along with its NATO allies, proceeded with initial deployment of the European missile systems in the face of intense Soviet arms control propaganda. It also took the unprecedented step of reporting seven examples of Soviet arms control violations to Congress.

On the other hand, the administration has kept arms control on center stage in political importance. Despite the unprecedented release to Congress of two official reports, and one unofficial report, of systematic and expanding Soviet violations of existing arms control obligations, the administration continues to emphasize the importance, utility, and feasibility of arms control. Arms control rhetoric continues to mislead rather than inform the public. And internally, arms control remains a pervasive force influencing programs, planning, and thinking. (It may be instructive to note that the Scowcroft commission report on SNF modernization uses the term *arms control* sixty times in twenty-six pages.)

No one can seriously argue that arms control has placed any significant limitation on the growth of Soviet military capability or contributed in any way to U.S. strategic objectives, including strategic stability. The Soviets have refused to allow arms control to interfere with their achievement of strategic superiority and their deployment of forces that contravene strategic stability. On the basis of the record, it is absurd to believe that the Soviets will now allow arms control to impede either their ballistic missile defense or military space programs.

Arms control, however, has had a dampening effect on U.S. ability to cope with the Soviet threat, and that effect continues under this administration. Plans and programs vacillate between what is needed to meet basic U.S. strategic objectives and what is deemed consistent with arms control. At the same time, the administration weakens the rationale and support for its own programs by its own arms control rhetoric. How can it argue the virtue of reductions and the need to build up at the same time? How can it maintain strategic modernization programs, including the SDI, while stressing the need to "prevent an arms race in space and terminate the one on earth"? Allowing such semantic infiltration merely contributes to a false arms race image of U.S. programs.

In effect, through the internal and public U.S. emphasis on arms control, the Soviets have found and cultivated an effective way to intrude on U.S. strategic planning. The administration's use of arms control rhetoric may seem safer politically than candor, but it dangerously risks trapping the United States in a continuing process contrary to its security interests. The administration would do far better with patient public education.

Conclusion

The success of the United States in containing the Soviet Union and foreclosing to it tempting opportunities for aggrandizement will probably be the most important factor in the political future of the world. Military power is the foundation of the Soviet system and its threat to U.S. interests. If the United States is unable to counterbalance Soviet military power, no coalition of states can do so. Yet the United States has done too little for several years to maintain the necessary military strength. A modest turnaround has begun, but it is not enough, its effectiveness is doubtful, and there are pressures, which might succeed, to reduce even that. If the spread of Soviet hegemony is to be prevented and the risks of war reduced, the United States (and its allies) must undertake a stronger defensive effort, including both strategy and forces.

In this brief review, the issues of direction, will, magnitude of effort, and nuclear planning have been touched upon. They are central, but in fact the West needs a strategy of containment capable of dealing with the full range of Soviet threat, from the strategic nuclear to low-intensity conflicts involving Soviet proxies and Soviet-directed insurgency and terrorism. Otherwise we may validate Jean-Françoise Revel's belief that democracies are not basically structured to defend themselves and their interests against enemies attacking them.

Opening Statement   Earl C. Ravenal

Critiques of elements of the overall or regional strategic balance and discussions of forces or weapons pivot on two fundamental sets of questions:

1. How—against what external requisites of foreign policy or national strategy— are we to measure the balance of these forces and the adequacy of these weapons? With regard to strategic (mostly nuclear) systems, what is their deterrent purpose, and what targets are they to address? With regard to

general-purpose forces, what frontier are they to defend? How far forward? With what allies?

2. To what extent are the requirements that we derive, in the first instance from external challenges and needs, responsive to and limited by constraints arising from within the U.S. domestic social, political, and economic system?

These are parametric questions that inevitably, even if momentarily neglected or ignored, govern the creation, acquisition, and disposition of forces and weapons. The second parametric question, on constraints, is especially important as a corrective to the common approach. To appreciate how slighted still are domestic factors in shaping defense policy, one need go no further than a remark by President Reagan, not just quoted approvingly but—as if to hold the president to his mark—featured as the emblem of the recent report on the military balance presented by the Committee on the Present Danger: "The Number 1 priority of the Federal Government is national security. Therefore defense cannot be looked at as a part of a budgetary solution. Defense must be looked at as to what needs to be done to ensure our national security."[16] One could reply that if defense cannot be looked at as part of a budgetary solution, it will surely become part of a budgetary problem. At the very least, a defense policy—or, for that matter, a foreign policy—that is entirely externally oriented is a one-dimensional exercise.

It seems to me that there are only two important policy positions with regard to U.S. national strategy and defense preparations, and they happen, not entirely by accident, to be the two positions represented in the debate that forms this chapter. The first is the hawkish position, roughly to this effect: the present balance of forces between the United States and the Soviet Union, global and in important regions, is adverse to the United States. The Soviet Union is implacably hostile and expansionist. The United States dares not allow such an adversary to obtain, or retain for long, such a significant advantage or convert it into a permanent advantage, even if it is not precisely sure how the Soviets will use it. Finally, the United States should not care overly how—at what penalty or sacrifice—it will pay for the military capabilities it needs.

Then there is the noninterventionist position. (I will not say "dovish" since that stance could be approximated by a number of less coherent and principled positions.) The noninterventionist position does not quarrel particularly with the hawkish estimates of the size and nature of the threat, or, rather, it need not quarrel with them, since many exponents of the noninterventionist position in fact entertain doubt as to the size and nature of military phenomena emanating from the Soviet state. Rather, as we shall see, noninterventionists typically discount threats; this is not an empirical difference so much as a methodological one. Noninterventionists are sensitive to domestic constraints, that is, in the specific sense that they would allow such domestic constraints to dictate limits to military preparedness and strategic responses. At least they are willing to consider values that inhere in the social, economic, and political system as trade-offs against external security objectives.

Noninterventionists do not tend to consider alliances as good bargains; they are suspicious that the alliances cost more to maintain than the value of any advantages that are derived and that they implicate a guarantor country, as the United States must inevitably be in any alliance relationship, in greater risk than a stance of self-reliance, even if such self-reliance affords a lesser aggregation of power than an alliance or courts other kinds of dangers, such as prejudicing forward strategic positions. Noninterventionists seek for their own country a retracted security perimeter. It is not necessary to the proposal of nonintervention always to be able to specify such a more tightly drawn security frontier with geographical precision or certitude. Such a frontier, generically, would conform to two criteria, characteristics that are in fact mutually reinforcing: credibility and feasibility (or economy). It would be a line that we must hold, as part of the definition of our sovereignty, and a line that we can hold, as a defensive perimeter and a strategic force concept that can be maintained with advantage and within constraints over the long haul.

In this confrontation of the more coherent, though more extreme, positions, the middle, or "liberal," position tends to fall away. The liberal position can be defined thus: the Soviets are not "that" menacing. Their system embodies various weaknesses, and liberals tend to seize avidly, even gratefully, on studies that, by citing such weaknesses, derogate from the threat. Liberals believe, moreover, that the United States has more than enough military and national power to accomplish its strategic objectives, though, curiously, they do not differ much from the hawks in their specification of U.S. essential strategic objectives in the world. But they believe that the United States is spending more than necessary to accomplish these objectives, and they endorse, or invent, certain explanations, some of them myths, to account for why this is the case. Liberals often hold, in one or another foreign policy or military crisis, that the United States could use force more sparingly or even substitute nonmilitary means, particularly diplomacy (which they do not think must be obviously or implicitly backed by force). Liberals also—though here they are not unique—tend to rely on or trust in arms control to constrain or reduce the danger of war, especially nuclear war, and the cost of defense.

I have described the liberal position in some detail, among other reasons because it remains the prevalent position. I will not elaborate a detailed refutation of the liberal position, though I do not think my statement of it is unfair. Suffice it to say that this is not the position I am espousing here, nor is it one that I would recommend, despite its more attractive message.

Strategic Defense

These general and fundamental ideas regarding the structure of the problem and the field of debate can be applied to the issues of current defense policy. (Only the most cursory attention can be given here to each issue.)

First, we have the issue of strategic weapons. The only genuinely new strategic thrust of the Reagan administration (that is, innovation beyond the designs of the Carter administration) might be said to be strategic defense. The most important question is how the U.S. tilt toward strategic defense might affect the integrity of deterrence. Does the prospect of even a relatively impermeable societal defense against incoming nuclear weapons, or of the effective defense of U.S. offensive weapons against a Soviet first strike, make deterrence of nuclear war more certain, by denying entirely or just lowering the confidence of a Soviet countervalue retaliation, in one case, or a preemptive counterforce strike, in the other? Or, on the contrary, does it make the strategic balance more precarious; does it, in the parlance of the trade, derogate from crisis stability by creating the presumption of a now-unanswerable U.S. first strike and forcing our adversary to consider, and offset in various ways, our own preemptive counterforce strike?

My own view is as follows: (1) Strategic defense, insofar as it may be reasonably hoped eventually to substitute partially for strategic offense and as it may serve as an adjunct, not a barrier, to some form of arms control, is a morally worthy and strategically interesting concept. (2) It is not absolutely foreclosed that strategic defense, including some form of boost-phase interception, is technically inaccessible or absolutely beyond the fiscal capabilities or the political will of our society, under some circumstances; but the odds, in those two categories, are much against it. (3) U.S. programs for R&D in strategic defense have been responsible in significant measure for bringing the Soviet Union back to the strategic negotiating table and also could serve to elicit more substantive and satisfactory Soviet proposals to constrain their heavy, counter-force, potentially first-strike missiles (SS-18s and -19s and successors). (4) Finally, a sensible U.S. bargaining strategy must attempt the precise and difficult (because apparently contradictory) feat of keeping strategic defense alive, in order to remain a bargaining chip, and seeming to be forthcoming, at some point and at some responsible price, in trading it away for the proper Soviet concessions, in order that it be a bargaining chip and not a fixed feature in the U.S. strategic firmament.

General-Purpose Forces

The United States is currently entertaining a debate about the role of and the nature and acquisition of its general-purpose forces. There is the Weinberger-Shultz contention about the proper use of force to support diplomacy. Secretary of State Shultz has asserted that we must retain the option of using or threatening force, even in ambiguous cases; Secretary of Defense Weinberger argues for several definitive restrictive conditions to limit the projection of U.S. power. Both positions have disabilities: on the one side, excessive external loss and internal political damage; on the other, default in marginal or undefined cases, and the possibility of cumulative damage to U.S. strategic and political positions in the world. This argument, though overblown, does verge more closely on a true foreign policy and national strategy debate than we have experienced in recent times. Normally such debates are conducted, if at all recognizably, in the guise of minute surrogate issues, such as individual weapons systems, specific cases of intervention, or marginal changes in the size of the defense budget.

As for the nature and equipping of general-purpose forces and the accompanying doctrines for their employment, the military reform movement has increasingly set the terms of this part of the debate. They assert that the United States could achieve more effective and more efficient (not the same thing) translation of resources into military output if it revised the organization of its military establishment; adopted more fluid battlefield tactics; emphasized strategy rather than management in officer training, selection, and assignment; and procured the familiar litany of "weapons that are workable, reliable, and (relatively) cheap instead of overcomplicated, breakable, and wildly expensive."[17]

I am skeptical of the claims and pretensions of the military reform movement. Although it has attracted the allegiance and contributions of a wide range of insightful, intelligent, and knowledgeable defense experts, military reform is unlikely to deliver on its explicit or implied promises. A few military horror stories do not add up to a conclusive critique, and a handful of therapeutic adjectives is not an effective remedy. Those "cheap, sensible" weapons must get at their targets, and maybe get back, in intensive battlefield environments. What is driving up the price of forces and weapons is not, as current mythology would have it, dim-witted generals and grasping defense contractors but rather determined, capable adversaries and the requisites of modern combat.[18] Ultimately we are brought back to our real choice: not whether to have those expensive forces and weapons but whether to fight in those environments and against those adversaries. The military reform movement distracts attention from that harder choice. In the end, because of the means that must be used to protect them, the objects of foreign policy are priced out of reach.

NATO

Another debate is taking shape, on both sides of the Atlantic, about the role of U.S. forces, both strategic and general purpose (a category that includes tactical nuclear weapons), in the defense of Western Europe. As one might expect, the debate typically takes surrogate forms: recriminations about burden sharing, demonstrations over the introduction of intermediate-range nuclear weapons into European territory, and so forth.

What is implicitly being discussed is not just the U.S. role but the future of NATO as a multilateral, trans-Atlantic alliance. The past two years have seen the recrudescence of the debate about U.S. first use of nuclear weapons in Europe. Although the option of first use, in response to an overwhelming Soviet conventional attack, remains official U.S. and NATO policy, some authoritative figures from former high national security positions (notably McGeorge Bundy, George Kennan, Robert McNamara, and Gerard Smith) have challenged this recourse to nuclear weapons in the defense of Western Europe.[19] And some reaches of Western European politics and public opinion (the left wing of the German SPD and the Greens and the British Labour party) also would forgo the use, and even the presence, of nuclear weapons. All still—and this is the logical and strategic rub—insist on the integrity of NATO and the efficacy of joint defense of Western Europe.

The condition that might reconcile such an apparent contradiction is the strengthening of NATO's conventional defense. Indeed, the requisite is a high-confidence, self-contained conventional defense of Western Europe in the face of even a large-scale, determined Soviet offensive. Two points emerge, neither of which has been ignored by European governments and articulate commentators in Europe.

The first is the empirical unlikelihood of attaining sufficient conventional defense of Western Europe—unlikely because of the predictable failure of the

Western European allies, and even probably the United States, to rise to the level of expenditures necessary to repair NATO's conventional weaknesses; and because, even if such an objective level of defense could be attained, the question of a Soviet breach of that level, and the recourse NATO would then have, cannot be exorcised. European governments have failed to meet even the 3 percent annual real increments commonly agreed in 1977, and even the United States is hardly funding its present conventional contribution to NATO's defense, let alone providing the additional forces and weapons systems, including the new generation of high-tech weaponry, to reach the extremely high level of conventional confidence necessary to validate abjuring the first use of nuclear weapons.

Indeed, if the United States were to set for itself and its allies the task of providing a confident conventional defense against Soviet arms, principally on the central front of Europe, the costs of this in terms of U.S. defense spending would be far higher than most proponents of this course are willing to concede. A rough estimate of the entailed costs has been given by Leonard Sullivan, Jr. Part of his estimate is relevant to the staunch conventional defense of NATO:

> Expanding our conventional forces by 20% over the next 10 years to offset the numerically, qualitatively, and geographically expanding threat requires that defense outlays rise another full percentage point, to 9-1/2% of the GNP . . . (about 1/2% more in TOA [Total Obligational Authority]).[20]

That 10 percent, applied to the probable 1986 GNP of $4.17 trillion, would mean a defense budget authorization of $417 billion, not the $314 billion requested. The defense of NATO in 1986 would cost $179 billion instead of $134 billion.[21]

The second point about the proposal to abjure U.S. first use of nuclear weapons in Europe is the fact that this action almost by definition would decouple the United States from the defense of Europe and thus collapse the strategic foundation of the Atlantic alliance. Ironically, this would be true especially if the substituted conventional defense of Europe looked as if it might be sufficient. For it is the very fear of inevitable escalation of a local European conventional war to a global conflagration that constitutes the essential element in the coupling of the U.S. strategic nuclear arsenal to the local defense of U.S. allies. To be successful, extended deterrence (that is, the extension of the U.S. nuclear umbrella over objects beyond its own territorial and political integrity), the escalatory chain, from conventional war to theater nuclear weapons to the use of the ultimate strategic weapon, must seem to be unbroken. Bundy, McNamara, and others propose to break that chain at the point of the first use of tactical nuclear weapons in Europe.

The commitment to Europe presents the United States with a choice between unsupportable costs, associated with the confident defense of Europe with conventional forces, and unassumable risks, attributable to reliance on the earlier use of nuclear weapons. The direction in which this tension is resolved by any particular U.S. administration is not rigidly determined. To some extent, cost can be transmuted into additional risk, and risk can be transformed into mere cost. (That is what is meant by raising or lowering the nuclear threshold.) But as long as the United States is committed to Europe, the choice itself is inescapable. And this this situation, with its underlying—if not always acknowledged—logic, will continue to generate proposals, however disguised, or incomplete, or inconsistent, for breaking the U.S. tie to the defense of Europe.

Rapid Deployment

Another significant area of change in recent defense policy, and an area of some contention, is the development of U.S. capabilities and intentions for intervention at long range in peripheral areas of the world—that is, not Europe or its immediate flanks. Notably, the Persian Gulf, or Southwest Asia, has become over a decade not only a new area of strategic concern but also the fulcrum for the first major force creation since the drawdown of forces from Southeast Asia in the Nixon administration and the first specific identification of a major new unified command: U.S. Central Command (CENTCOM).

The acquisition of a new area of defense raises an obvious question: whether, and by what criteria, it is worth it to acquire defensive responsibilities for this area. To do this exercise—to construct a sort of algorithm—we must identify the asset relevant to ourselves that is at risk in the area. In the case of the Persian Gulf, besides such incidental assets that inhere in the geostrategic position itself, there is the oil of the region. Although Persian Gulf oil accounts for less than 3 percent of U.S. energy requirements, it is of great importance to countries of Western Europe and Japan, whose economies affect the United States indirectly. These allies' dependence on oil from this region is much more abject than that of the United States.

To take on the defense of additional regions eventually requires tangible dedicated units, with airlift, sealift, and logistical sustenance. In the case of the gulf, since the overall U.S. force structure since 1976 has been increased only by one aircraft carrier and by the two light army divisions created in fiscal years 1985 and 1986, the additional forces for the gulf must come from forces previously allocated to Europe and, to a lesser extent, to Asia.

Does it make sense to propose and prepare to defend the gulf? How does the United States decide this question? The feasibility of this proposition can be assessed only by presenting a calculus in terms of expected losses, of contrasting courses of action or inaction: to protect access to this region by U.S. armed intervention or to "let" it slip into the hands of the Soviets, their proxies, or independent local revolutionaries.

Taking the comprehensive cost, in the FY86 budget, of defending the gulf at $49 billion a year, to prepare over ten years to fight a war to defend Persian Gulf oil would cost, cumulatively, $797 billion.[22] In addition, we might increase the chance of a regional war—say, a Vietnam-size war—by 5 percent, and the 1986 cost of such a war would be some 3.38 times more expensive than the $350 billion it had come to by 1975; and that yields an expected loss of some $59 billion. Further, we would court the risk, say even 1 percent, of a general nuclear war in which the United States might lose one-third of its annual gross national product (at its 1986 value of $4,172 billion), or $1,391 billion, for ten years—an expected loss of $139 billion. The total of these three cost factors is $995 billion. All this must be thrown into the balance against the consequences if the United States failed to defend and if some sequence of events resulted in deprivation of oil. The United States might lose 10 percent of its gross national product for as many as ten years, or a total of $4,172 billion, and this eventually might become as much as 20 percent more probable, yielding an expected loss of some $834 billion.

Although this kind of exercise cannot be conducted with even a semblance of precision, it supports a certain intuition: some national interests cost more to defend than they are worth.

Grand Strategy of the Reagan Administration

Consideration of the major two general-purpose force commitments of the United States, NATO and the Persian Gulf, raises the question of the strategy of the Reagan administration, an issue enveloped in partisan argument and polemics. The contention is widely aired that the administration has no strategy. In fact, critics of the Reagan administration have been leveling two kinds of attacks, which are oddly contradictory. The first is that the administration has vastly expanded U.S. international goals and added some novel strategic elements, such as horizontal escalation, including assaults on Soviet naval forces in their ports and nuclear war winning through developing the capacity to wage protracted nuclear war. On the other hand, the critics charge that the Reagan administration has no strategy at all, indeed that it does not even have a foreign policy—that it is just throwing money in the general direction of national security.

That is certainly a case of critical overkill. Both of the critiques cannot be true. In a sense, neither is. First, questions of foreign policy and national strategy are always answered, more or less explicitly, in the actions, orientations, and dispositions of nations. And national strategies are derived from—and are, in the longer run, consistent with—foreign policies. A nation has both, whether or not a presidential speech has enunciated them or a blue-ribbon commission has defined them.

Second, the Reagan administration has much the same foreign and military policies as the Carter administration, both in size and substance. For all its increased defense budgetary requests, the Reagan administration has added hardly any manpower or force structure. At most, it has fleshed out some skeleton air wings and upgraded one carrier battle group from a sort of cadre status to a more fully active one, and starting in 1985 it is developing existing army units into a few more, lighter, divisions.[23]

If we are willing to screen out much of the noise at intermediate levels of government, we find that the Reagan administration has implemented the programs and strategies of the Carter administration (at least after Afghanistan, in what could be called the second Carter administration). In every consequential aspect, the Reagan administration has displayed remarkable continuity: in the strategic dimension, counterforce, war fighting, and the MX missile (the exception is the Reagan administration's novel emphasis on strategic defense); in the general-purpose force dimension, the reinstitution of global defense and direct U.S. involvement in regions, featuring the U.S. Central Command (the unified command that replaced the Rapid Deployment Joint Task Force), and the acquisition of stepping-stone bases; in the Middle East, the policy of active intrusion;

with regard to China, the reinforcement of alignment; and in the area of arms control, after a late start, a negotiating posture of deep cuts. Only in Central America has the Reagan administration seemed to go considerably beyond the Carter limits, but by January 1981, Carter's policy had not yet been tested by an evolving Marxist regime in Nicaragua and a polarized political and military situation in El Salvador.

I find nothing particularly novel in the utterances of various figures in the Reagan administration to the effect that the United States must design its forces and doctrines so as to prevail in a nuclear war. There is nothing even alarming about those statements beyond what is irreducibly alarming about nuclear confrontation and mutual deterrence themselves. Better to keep one's eyes on nuclear posture and doctrines of targeting and precedence of use. Those are the elements that constitute the U.S. nuclear strategy and the ones that might make a difference in the propensity of the United States to go to war or to escalate to nuclear war. When we examine the U.S. nuclear strategy in this light, we find that the Reagan administration is simply affirming the requisites of a traditional U.S. strategy of extended deterrence: the use of nuclear weapons to deter all kinds of threats, conventional or nuclear, to allies as well as itself, and to strategic objects and positions of less than truly vital interest to itself. This strategy of extended deterrence in turn has necessitated its move to counterforce targeting, which is bound up with its retention of the option of first use of nuclear weapons.

What, then, of the preparations for protracted nuclear war, specified in the famous Defense Guidance issued by Secretary Weinberger to the military services?[24] Here, even the proviso that U.S. nuclear forces must "prevail and be able to force the Soviet Union to seek earliest termination of hostilities on terms favorable to the United States" has a familiar ring to anyone who has worked and planned in the Pentagon during the past twenty years. But it is particularly redolent of the years of Jimmy Carter and his secretary of defense, Harold Brown, who advanced the concept of prolonged, multiphase nuclear war, with the disabling of Soviet leadership and the sinews of the Soviet state. Also, in the development of counterforce weapons, such as the MX, Trident II, and intermediate-range cruise missiles, Carter was the precursor of Reagan. PD-59, the August 1980 presidential directive that codified nuclear war-fighting stance, was, in a sense, the first strategic act of the Reagan administration.

Yet the Reagan administration's creation of CENTCOM and its tangible implementation of the Carter doctrine have engendered a more specific debate about its strategy: how to characterize that strategy and whether it is well advised. This debate can be described in the terms of the title of a book by Robert Komer, former third-ranking official in the Carter administration's Department of Defense: *Maritime Strategy or Coalition Defense?*[25] The second option, coalition defense, was the NATO-first, Central Europe emphasis of the Carter administration; the first, maritime strategy, represents the thinking of Reagan's secretary of the navy, John Lehman (and is also associated with Secretary of Defense Weinberger and the present third-ranking defense official, Fred Iklé), and has also been dubbed horizontal escalation.

Although in my view this antithesis is overdone in its delineation of opposing positions, its identification of the horizontal sea-lane and gulf emphasis as the unprecedented creation of the Reagan administration, nevertheless there is a germ of truth in the characterization of the alternative strategies. The Carter administration was the high-water mark of the tangible emphasis on NATO in terms of the percentage of the general-purpose force structure, and insofar as the horizontal strategy is not just a ploy to rationalize Secretary Lehman's 600-ship navy, it does represent the spreading of U.S. forces and the shifting of its forces, not precisely to a new area of strategic concern, but to the gulf at the relative expense of Europe.

Rank ordering of U.S. military commitments is not the point and does not express what is interesting and possibly troublesome about the shift in national strategy in the Reagan administration, however slight I might consider it to be: the assumption of excessive simultaneity of commitment. In his FY86 posture statement, Secretary Weinberger states:

> Our forward-defense strategy dictates that we be able to conduct concurrent deployments to widely separated areas of the globe. Our present goal is to achieve the capability to deploy forces to a remote theater such as Souhwest Asia, while maintaining an acceptable capability to reinforce NATO and key areas of Northeast Asia.[26]

The intention to deploy forces simultaneously raises the issue of double counting. A close reading of the force allocation embodied in the secretary's statement indicates that, to some extent, the Pentagon intends a double assignment of certain units—characteristically for the Persian Gulf and also for Europe or East Asia and the Western Pacific. This not only violates the First Law of Thermodynamics but raises the question of the strategic overextension of general-purpose forces. In fact, in more general terms, it suggests an imbalance of commitments and resources.

This problem did not originate with the Reagan administration. It has characterized U.S. force planning since the two-and-a-half-war doctrine of the Kennedy-McNamara administration and the reduced (on both sides of the equation) one-and-a-half-war doctrine of the Nixon-Kissinger-Laird administration; and before either of those the Eisenhower-Dulles-Radford-Wilson administration. But the Reagan administration has somewhat exacerbated the contradiction with its implication of a wider strategic scope of simultaneous responses to Soviet aggressions and with its more tangible implementation of the commitment to defend the Persian Gulf and Southwest Asia, without significantly increasing the force structure or overall military manpower.

Paradigm Change

What the United States faces after four years of the Reagan administration's conduct of foreign relations and military policy is a crisis of solvency, in several pertinent senses of the word: not merely fiscal solvency, though this is perhaps the most pressing and obvious, but also a gross misalignment between the country's strategic objectives in the world and its manifest willingness to pay for them.

The problem of solvency presents itself with peculiar poignancy to the Reagan administration as it begins its second term. This, after all, is the president who said in his 1980 campaign "[When Jimmy Carter says he] simply cannot balance the budget, provide for the national security and reduce the high tax load on the American people, I say, 'Stand aside—because we can! And we will.' "[27]

Of course, the Reagan administration did not invent its problems. Actually this administration has been trying to implement the defense objectives it inherited. As Secretary of Defense Weinberger put it in his maiden presentation to Congress in 1981, the Carter administration had grossly underestimated the demands that Soviet challenges were making on the tangible military responses of the United States. Above all, it had systematically underfunded its own defense programs, leaving a cumulative shortfall of several hundred billion dollars for its successor to make up. Taken as a relative or conditional judgment, there is a certain wry justice in Weinberger's statement. If you ignore the rhetoric, overlook some of the nuances, and leave out of the calculation those policy objectives that have little consequence for military forces or defense costs, you could judge that Reagan's foreign and military policies are not much different from Carter's. The Reagan administration is just the latest in a long line, Democratic and Republican, from the beginning of the cold war, to promote the U.S. paradigm of large-scale deterrence and extensive forward defense or alliance. All it has tried to do is spend enough to implement it.

The national strategy of the Reagan administration is a variant on the traditional U.S. national strategy. Thus, what is wrong with it is not what is peculiar about it but what has been wrong with the U.S. paradigm itself for the past forty years—at first only latently or incipiently but by now grossly and obviously. The framework of deterrence and alliance is increasingly unstable because its foundations are being eroded by objective factors in the world and in the U.S. domestic system. In the world, there is the changing shape of the international system: an increasing diffusion of power, frustrating U.S. intervention and making the extension of its nuclear umbrella more riskly. At home, there are revolts against taxes and conscription and resistance to the enlarged governmental authority necessary to sustain an ambitious foreign policy.

At stake is the entire U.S. stance of containment of the Soviet Union and Soviet-inspired communism, the stance it has maintained over the four decades since the beginning of the cold war in the late 1940s. If the United States is to—and if it were to—make significant cuts in its defense program, both of the cardinal elements of the present U.S. strategic paradigm would have to change. Instead of deterrence and alliance, it would pursue war avoidance and self-reliance. Security would depend more on its abstention from regional conflicts and, in the strategic nuclear dimension, on what I would call "finite essential deterrence."

These are not rhetorical terms. Unfortunately, an extensive definition of their meaning and their implications for U.S. forces is not possible here.[28] Suffice it to say that the U.S. military program would be designed to defend the most restricted perimeter required to protect its core values. Those core values are political integrity and the safety of citizens and their domestic property. That is a much smaller perimeter than the one the United States is now committed to defend.

The concomitant is that the United States would encourage other nations to become self-reliant, to hedge. In fact, other countries that are foresighted already discount U.S. protection in a wide range of possible cases, despite its formal obligations to come to their assistance. This does not imply that all these countries face imminent threats; simply that some are impressed more by U.S. defaults than by U.S. reassurances and have drawn the appropriate conclusions.

War avoidance invokes primarily, though not exclusively, the strategic nuclear component of the U.S. counterparadigm. It will always need a strategy that discourages direct nuclear attacks on its homeland or intolerable coercion of international political choices by nuclear threats. But today, given the parity between the nuclear arsenals of the two superpowers, safety depends on maintaining a condition that is called crisis stability, wherein both sides have a strong incentive to avoid striking first with their nuclear weapons.

The two elements of war avoidance and self-reliance constitute a new paradigm. They amount to a principled policy of nonintervention that is consistent enough to merit the status of a major alternative. We would no longer consider peace to be seamless and indivisible. There might well be continuing troubles in the world, including cases where a Soviet-sponsored faction perpetrates a forcible revision of the local military balance. If the United States were to intervene, it might win a few rounds (witness the obvious example of Grenada in November 1983). But the list of feasible interventions is far shorter than the list of desirable ones and even shorter than the list of necessary ones.

Rejoinder   William R. Van Cleave

Earl Ravenal begins his opening statement by posing a basic and relevant question: against what requirements does the United States assess the adequacy of its military power? It is clear that we disagree on the answer. It seems to me that broadly, if not always specifically, those requirements are established or implied by the continuing contours of U.S. foreign and defense policy as set forth in numerous documents. Ravenal, however, would substitute a totally different policy of his own highly subjective preference. It is an alien policy.

He would also have it seem that his policy is based on and in harmony with domestic considerations, while what I suggest is not. Nothing could be further from the truth. Since what I have suggested is essentially to take our established policies seriously and develop the military capabilities required by them, it is clear that those policies do take domestic constraints, as well as an assessment of external threats, into account. I agree that domestic factors will influence national policies, whether decision makers will it or not.

It is Ravenal's policy that is not consonant with domestic realities any more than it is with international and threat realities. What he recommends would not receive the support of the public, of Congress, or of any electable administration, Democrat or Republican. In fact, he offers no realistic alternative. There is no real choice between what he pejoratively calls interventionism, which is merely the continuation of a general foreign policy followed by Republican and Democrat administrations alike for forty years, and what he normatively terms noninterventionism, which is nothing more than isolationism and retreat. This is not a constructive or acceptable basis for U.S. policy.

In general terms, Ravenal makes it clear that he is for international disengagement (isolationism) and against both "selective intervention" and "more comprehensive versions of containment."[29] But what does that mean? What does it tell us to defend? When? Where? Are interests worth defending restricted to our own territorial integrity? Do we have no other strategic, economic, and political interests worth defending? Do we defend strategic positions that could decrease or increase threats to those interests and to our own national security? Does a true concept of national security transcend physical security and include the defense of a way of life against the encroachments of a totalitarian communist system? Ravenal seems to say no to all but our own territorial integrity, but he is not all that clear, and we know that even that narrow interest can be progressively threatened piecemeal and over time.

Five deceptively simple propositions summarize the Ravenal view, but they raise deeply disturbing questions.

The U.S. military program would be designed to defend the most restricted perimeter required to protect its core values. (What is that?)

Over time, we would accommodate the dissolution of defensive commitments, including NATO, that obligate us contingently to overseas intervention. (Over time? All commitments?)

This is not necessarily a prescription for instantly dismantling our formal alliances. (It isn't?)

As for the United States, in this proposal we would defend against military threats directed against our homeland. (Only when direct and unambiguous? Only after actual attacks?)

In a program of nonintervention, the United States would defend against an umbrella of direct threats to those values that are so basic that they are part of the definition of state and society, and against a penumbra of challenges that are indirectly threatening but are relevant because of their weight, momentum, direction, and ineluctability. (Now I am confused, besides wondering how to defend against the ineluctable, which seems even more hawkish than I.)

Ravenal believes that the United States is overextended and has excessive commitments, leading to a mismatch between objectives and capabilities. He further believes that the United States cannot, and should not, bring capabilities more in line with commitments. Here is the core of our disagreement. I agree that the United States cannot fulfill present commitments or adequately improve the military balance with the Soviets at present and projected rates of defense expenditure. My answer, however, is clear: the United States should retain its commitments and international objectives—indeed, pursue them more vigorously—and increase its capabilities accordingly. To argue that it cannot afford to do so is nonsense.

Ravenal bases his case for disengagement largely on an assertion that is erroneous and a choice that is as spurious as it is unreal. The assertion is that defense spending based on its present foreign policy will render the United States "insolvent." We are already, he asserts, facing a "crisis of solvency." Our (spurious) choice, then, is between bankruptcy and solvency through Ravenalian isolationism.

I find the proclamation staggering. It is not national solvency that is at issue; it is national security. Why national solvency is at stake in any of the range of defense policies and budgets being debated by responsible groups—from the Senate Budget Committee to the Pentagon to the Committee on the Present Danger, to take a range—he does not explain.

The differences being debated are perhaps a couple of percent of the U.S. gross national product. What does that have to do with national solvency? For most of the time since World War II, the United States has borne defense budgets at higher percentages and has prospered, with periods of the greatest prosperity often coinciding with periods of higher defense spending. The percentage of GNP going to defense is lower than it was in any year between 1951 and 1972. It is a mere 6 1/2 percent of GNP. The last year the United States had a balanced federal budget, FY69, it was spending 9 percent of GNP on defense—beyond anything being suggested at this time. The administration plans a continued slow increase in defense spending to peak at 7.5 percent of GNP by 1990. That is a rate of spending lower than any year during the Eisenhower or Kennedy administrations. There is no vast increase in defense spending under the Reagan administration, and the increase that has taken place has not been at the expense of output available for nondefense spending, which, private and public, increased during the Reagan administration about seven and a half times the increase in defense spending.[30]

Ravenal attempts to create a false image of the magnitude, the increase, and the domestic consequences of U.S. defense spending as an apocalyptic rationalization for a radical policy. His argument won't wash. The real issue is whether the United States is spending enough given the magnitude of the threat. I do not believe that it is.

I take it as axiomatic that U.S. security rests on the maintenance of a stable global balance of power that permits the flourishing of independent states (to the extent possible, free economy democracies), and I take it as axiomatic that the Soviet Union aims to upset that balance of power, spread instability, extend its hegemony, and establish an international order of dependent states under Soviet control.

The Soviet Union cannot be contained by any force other than U.S. power; without it, no other coalition of states could resist Soviet coercion and encroachment. The disengagement that Ravenal recommends would be no less than a strategic retreat that would radically destabilize any global balance of power and only encourage the advance of the Soviet empire. It would concede to the Soviets all of Eurasia, and it could not possibly leave the Western Hemisphere unaffected. It would fan the flames of Soviet-directed insurgency right up to the U.S. southern border. It would ultimately be a prescription for war, not a means for avoiding war.

To prevent this, we need a resurgence, not a retraction, of U.S. power and determination to defend allies and strategic positions. As a home-grown American philosopher, Eric Hoffer, put it in common language:

> We are a learning people. We learn from experience. We know how third world wars start and how to prevent them, see. And the way to prevent a third world war is to pick the bully and get as close to him as possible and breathe down his neck until he settles down. You do not start a world war when a democracy throws its weight around facing a bully. World wars are started when the democracies are too unprepared, too cowardly, too frightened, too reasonable, or too tired.[31]

Ravenal's "new isolationism" is based not on strategic or economic logic, although it may be borne of a disenchantment with alliances and foreign troubles. Rather, as Charles Krauthammer notes, it is based on a prior value judgment that America's only security interest resides in defending its territorial integrity against direct attack, and no one or nothing else. Ravenal believes that we should defend basic political values, but he limits that defense to the shores of the United States. Such a narrow assessment of political and strategic interests is not at all persuasive.

I believe neither that U.S. physical security can be preserved by overseas disengagement nor that the definition of its national security should be limited to its own territorial integrity; but rather that "in the last analysis, national security transcends the traditional concerns with territorial integrity and national sovereignty" and extends to "the defense of a way of life."[32]

There are many problems with a policy of containment. It does have costs and it does involve risk. It requires a sustained vigilance, for which democracies are ill equipped; it requires military presence in much of the world; it tends to be defensive and reactive; it is not clearly a winning strategy. Yet, as Eugene Rostow has pointed out, no one has yet offered a viable or "plausible substitute for the creative ideas President Truman propounded nearly forty years ago."[33] That policy itself, of course, does not define the conditions for the use of military force. Ravenal believes the so-called Shultz-Weinberger disagreement over those conditions is an important debate. On this I agree, although we clearly come down on different sides of that debate as popularized by the press.

Ravenal criticizes the Shultz approach since it would use or threaten force "even in ambiguous cases." But that is what is wrong with the Weinberger (and Ravenal) approach; it requires an immediacy and clarity of threat and a unanimity of support for action that would be provided by virtually nothing short of a direct attack on the United States. To wait for threats to meet those conditions is most likely to wait too long; it greatly risks losing friends and allies, strategic position, strategic materials, and relative strength; it would encourage further threat and aggression. The need to act in ambiguous circumstances is strategic and political reality; it is the essence of strategy and statesmanship.

Curiously Ravenal cites as disabilities of the Weinberger position "default in marginal or undefined cases, and the possibility of cumulative damage to U.S. strategic and political positions in the world." I cannot imagine more cumulative damage to U.S. strategic and political positions than a policy such as Ravenal recommends. If those are disabilities in the Weinberger approach, they become fatalities in the Ravenal approach.

I do agree that U.S. allies should contribute more to the common defense. Their military contributions in varying degrees have lagged for several years and are rising more slowly than U.S. expenditures. (But they are rising.) They could also do more to support, at least politically, U.S. actions outside alliance boundaries that are in U.S. security interests, and ultimately in their own as well. But to suggest that allies do not contribute to U.S. security and that alliances are a form of U.S. philanthropy is nonsense. U.S. military forces are not abroad simply to protect other nations but to protect U.S. interests.

Ravenal attempts to divide the U.S. defense budget among alliances or theaters, as if each were a discernible cost that need not be borne if the United States simply disengaged. Aside from the frailty and disutility of his methodology, he ignores or disparages the very real allied contributions to the success of U.S. foreign and defense policy. (He would, of course, fundamentally change that policy so that allies are by definition superfluous, but he apparently needs first to disparage the contributions of allies as a rationalization for changing that policy.)

It is, in fact, fortunate that the United States does not have to rely solely on its own forces and resources. As the 1985 DOD *Annual Report* concludes, the security benefits resulting from these alliances "are far greater than we could obtain from comparable unilateral endeavors and expenditures."[34] Allies also supply an asset of incalculable strategic value: their own territory as a forward extension of U.S. military power.

Ravenal, at least in my view, takes a more sensible approach to the SDI, which he correctly identifies as the "only genuinely new strategic thrust of the Reagan administration," and moderately endorses it. He regards it as "morally worthy and strategically interesting," as do I, and opines that it is "not absolutely foreclosed that strategic defense, including some form of boost-phase interception, is technically inaccessible [*sic*]." The point I believe he means to make is that it may be technically feasible, which I believe to be clearly true in one worthwhile form or another. Ravenal, however, views the SDI primarily as a means "to some form of arms control," a disturbing phrase.

The SDI ought not to be treated merely as a bargaining chip in arms negotiations, much less sacrificed for "some form of arms control," even though a combination of bureaucratic inertia and arms control dynamics is likely to make it so. Both its more modest objectives (such as defending land-based deterrent forces) and its more ambitious aims (thick area defense) are highly worthy strategic objectives that should be pursued with vigor. In that vein it would do well to recall the words of a great British scientist responding to arguments in 1934 that there could be no defense against attacking bombers:

> That no method can be devised to safeguard great centres of population from such a fate appears to me to be profoundly improbable. . . . To adopt a defeatist attitude in the face of such a threat is inexcusable until it has definitely been shown that all the resources of science and invention have been exhausted. . . . All decent men and all honourable Governments are equally concerned to obtain security against attacks from the air and to achieve it no effort and no sacrifice is too great.[35]

Arms control has supposed to have had the purpose of promoting national security by improving strategic stability and enhancing the survivability of deterrent forces. U.S. willingness to accept "some form of arms control" without close enough attention to whether that form promotes or detracts from those objectives, or is merely irrelevant to them, is part of the explanation for the strategic problems and the manifest failure of arms control that we face today.

Ravenal avers that the United States can reduce its defense effort not only through disengagement abroad but also through arms control agreements that would truly limit our adversary and thus reduce the threat. He does not tell how to achieve that ever-elusive end or to resolve the central, simply stated dilemma of arms control: that, because of the Soviets, provisions that would truly limit our adversary and thus reduce the threat are also nonnegotiable.

Ravenal would have us add the deception of disengagement to the deception of arms control as a means of cheap national security. He somehow believes that experience and reality support his point of view. To the contrary.

Rejoinder   Earl C. Ravenal

The crux of the contention between William Van Cleave and myself is whether the United States can afford even its present level of defense, let alone the more rigorous, demanding, and consistent version of the Reagan administration's defense program proposed by Van Cleave. (This is aside from questions of the risk of certain defensive arrangements and the morality of certain weapons and doctrines.) How can we pay for it and in what ways, for surely it must be paid for?

Van Cleave sees this not as a problem, just a test of the collective will. Economics is dismissed in two sentences: "Surely the requirements of national defense take priority over federal budget deficits, which are not driven by defense spending and cannot be significantly reduced by plausible cuts in defense. At this point, a $50 billion increase or decrease in the deficit would have little economic impact, but a $50 billion increase or decrease in defense spending could make an enormous difference to national defense." This kind of argument is a radical confirmation of the fiscal conduct of the Reagan administration itself. The passion for defense, whatever the cost, is supposed to pass in our era for conservatism. One wishes that Van Cleave were as rigorous, demanding, and consistent about fiscal as about military matters.

It does not help for Van Cleave to obscure the issue of costs by impugning others' numbers. Van Cleave mistakenly cites my own analysis, in my 1984 book, *Defining Defense: The 1985 Military Budget*, as "typical of efforts to create an impression of excessive defense spending." First of all, the "alleged annual increases" that I cited were calculated precisely from Secretary of Defense Weinberger's FY85 defense report (published February 1, 1984), and they were clearly stated in terms of current dollars and budgetary authority. (The administration's 1985 request was later trimmed in the give and take with Congress.) But the point is that whether such increases in defense spending are vast or not is irrelevant. I once said that "defense is not obscenely expensive, just prohibitively expensive."[36]

Defense spending is what it is, without adjectives and beyond public misperception. Its real effects, on economy and society, are what they are, not what they are wished to be. (Just try to spend that 20 to 50 percent of GNP that Americans supposedly "favor" and see whether they still favor the real effects.)

In fact, Van Cleave's rather abstract dismissal of the problem—"There is no question that the U.S. economy is capable of supporting an increased defense effort"—is itself typical of arguments (usually liberal) for the affordability of high defense spending. Most of these are implicit appeals for more taxation. Couldn't the nation simply "decide" to assume the burden of substantially increased taxes (and perhaps also that moral equivalent of taxation, conscription)? One commentator puts the matter thus: "Under John Kennedy in 1961, this country spent 9 percent of its gross national product—half the federal budget—on defense. Today we allocate only a bit more than 6 percent of GNP, a quarter of the federal budget, to defense. . . . What has changed in this country over two decades is the addition of so many other costly activities and income-redistribution programs."[37] This may be historically true, but the United States is situated in a web of economic and political factors, and its choices are where it finds them now, not where they might have been two decades ago. The fact that domestic social welfare expenditures have overtaken, and putatively preempted, defense expenditures does not mitigate the situation; it certainly does not make defense more affordable. Quite the contrary, it makes it even less affordable. If anything, it argues for reducing both social welfare spending and defense spending. It simply means that the fiscal sins of the past era are finally catching up.

The fact that there are options, such as greatly increased taxes, does not make them more desirable, even if they were politically feasible. There are costs, though in the case of taxation they are diffused. Higher taxes reduce productivity and incentives while distorting price relationships among competing economic factors. Among other things, taxes reduce the marginal efficiency of the nation's capital by depriving it of part of its returns. Indeed, all but the most confiscatory increases in tax levels or inventions of new imposts would hardly close the budgetary gap.

But even if the government could, in theory, balance its books by exacting more resources in the form of taxes and conscription to support a large defense establishment and extensive commitments, that would be just the end of one problem and the beginning of another. Solvency means that the external and internal stances of this country comport with each other. Resources (and support) are not automatically granted; to be available to the state, they must be mobilized from society, which is the base and context of the state. An extensive, engaged foreign policy and a large, active military posture require big, intrusive, demanding government. If, as we are promised, the Reagan administration is supposed to be a more reserved, less extensive government, then we must have a more detached, disengaged foreign policy. The dilemma is especially cruel for the conservative president who said in this first inaugural address that "government is the problem."

But where is the money in the defense budget? The important question is not whether you think the defense budget "should" be cut or even how this might be done, practically or politically, but the basis on which the defense budget can or should be cut: whether it can or should be cut only if we make commensurate alterations in our national strategy; or whether we can cut defense spending by some sleight of hand, such as "fiscal guidance," leaving the poverty to be spread around somehow; or whether there is so much fat in defense programs that cuts of significant magnitude would not necessitate any change in forces or strategy.

Therefore, before we arrive at an anatomy of the defense budget, it will be useful to dispose of several misleading approaches to identifying, and eliminating, portions of defense spending. These incorrect analyses rest on pseudo-theories, some of which have acquired the status of myths, about where the money is and why defense spending might be excessive.

These "devil theories"—usually the province of liberal commentators on defense—include the ministrations of right-wing ideologues, mindless bureaucratic momentum or mindful bureaucratic self-serving, paranoid obsessions with "threats," or the incubus of a military-industrial complex whose suboptimizations somehow become preemptive national policy.

Their preferred remedies spring from their false analyses. Some would cut support and overhead without cutting combat units, causing unbalanced forces unfit to fight or at least to fight for long. Some impugn inferior weapons systems or systems unsuited to the environments in which they would be likely to fight but usually without proposing substitutes, except a collection of national characteristics that amount to sheer verbalisms. Some would stretch out weapons purchases, not realizing that this drives up unit costs since weapons eventually must be bought. Some would simply eliminate a "hit list" of troublesome or notorious weapons, not understanding that something quite similar must be substituted as long as the United States retains the forces that must be equipped. Some prescribe across-the-board cuts—percentage reductions—without admitting that these might have effects on military readiness, the ability to project force, or the capacity to support alliances. Others urge selective commitment or deployment, without, however, relinquishing the situations that might require the main elements of U.S. forces. Some would change U.S. foreign policy formulas, stressing certain areas of the world instead of the present ones—usually, in the contemporary setting, "concentrating" on the Persian Gulf or the sea-lanes, but not giving up the other military missions and so actually adding force requirements to those the United States already has. Such commentators, for the most part diplomatists rather than strategists, think that foreign policy is essentially a cost-free exercise that consists of signaling intent, establishing presence, shifting emphasis from one region to another, or enunciating doctrines without creating the forces to deal with the additional contingencies that such doctrines would invite.

Arbitrary measures conceived in ignorance and desperation to cap the rise of defense spending cannot be efficacious. What is needed is analysis that is capable of deriving a true bottom line—that is, deriving defense dollars and military manpower from major weapons systems, forces, and doctrines and tactics; then, in turn, from military strategies for various regions and situations; then from national strategies or grand strategies (that is, large-scale ways of relating to a strategic environment); and finally from foreign policies.

Two widely credited explanatory fallacies, however, stand in the way and should be dealt with. One of these is well captured in the remark of David Stockman, director of the Office of Management and Budget, that the Pentagon is "a swamp of $10 to $20 to $30 billion worth of waste that can be ferretted out." In fact, for many months now, we have been treated by the media to a daily soap opera of waste, fraud, and mismanagement in the Pentagon. Journalists have been literally rummaging through military parts bins, and they have finally found a defense issue worthy of their talents. They have come up with $400 claw hammers and monkey wrenches, and—the greatest of horrors so far—a plastic cap for the leg of navigators' stools, from Boeing, Inc., that cost the Pentagon $916. These procurement practices are ridiculous, indeed outrageous. But we have to put them in perspective. The Reagan defense budget request for 1986 is $314 billion. It takes a pile of stool caps, claw hammers, and monkey wrenches to total $314 billion, even if they are gold plated or made of titanium. In short, I agree with Van Cleave that waste is not at the heart of the defense issue.

Moreover, waste, in any strict sense of the word, amounts to only a few billion dollars a year. And despite some commendable efforts in and out of the Pentagon, waste in the procurement and deployment of forces and weapons is virtually a constant over time. First, a certain level of incompetence and malfeasance is built into any human activity, even private organizations, let alone public institutions, which produce no real goods, serve no real customers, and strive for no real profits. Second, the waste that exists is not easily recoverable. It is not all in one convenient place but is distributed almost randomly over a myriad of programs and activities. Therefore one cannot expect to make surgical excisions of fat, sparing the bone and muscle of the programs themselves. Ironically, those who are serious about retaining defense programs must plan to fund the waste along with the substance or they will end up cutting the substance along with the waste.

The second illusion is that of military reform. This movement was discussed earlier in the context of general-purpose forces. The overall point about military reform is the problem of sufficiency. In other words, these critiques beg a further question: even if we were to adopt the proposed reforms, would they save enough to allow the United States to renew its lease on the world? Military reform ultimately distracts from considering the feasibility of the global mission of the United States. In their obsession with the details, the military reformers overlook the more comprehensive logic of the defense problem the United States faces. Defense is expensive. Here again I agree with Van Cleave.

Where is the real money to be found in the defense budget? It is in the large aggregate combat forces and, in turn, the broad missions of those forces in the world. To understand this, an anatomy lesson is in order. The dollar figures in the following examples are slices of the Reagan administration's requested 1986 defense budget authorization (not the outlay, which trails the authorization in a period of rising expenditures). That requested authorization is $314 billion. Strategic nuclear forces (including, as they should, their full share of military support costs and Pentagon overheads) come to about $73 billion, or 23 percent of the requested authorization. All the rest, about $241 billion or 77 percent, is dedicated to general-purpose forces: land division, tactical air wings, and surface naval units. Some specific costs of major components of the general-purpose forces are as follows: An average army division will cost over $4.8 billion, and there will be eighteen of them. A wing of tactical aircraft will cost about $2.1 billion, and there will be the equivalent of forty-four of these. The Marine Corps will cost $22 billion. The full cost of deploying one aircraft carrier battle group forward, in the West Pacific or the Indian Ocean or the North Atlantic or the Mediterranean, will be over $13.5 billion, and U.S. strategy requires that four or five groups be kept forward.

But to put the defense budget in the sharpest perspective, we need to move beyond the cost of elements of the force structure to a geographical cross-section.[38] My preliminary judgment for FY86, derived from the current Defense posture statement presented to Congress by the secretary of defense on February 4, 1985, is that, for FY86, the Reagan administration intends the following regional attribution of a total of twenty-one active ground divisions: NATO/Europe, eleven and two-thirds divisions; East Asia, three and two-thirds divisions; other regions and the strategic reserve, five and two-thirds divisions.

Applying these fractions to the total cost of the general-purpose forces, $241 billion, we can calculate the rough cost of these three regional commitments. Europe will continue to be the main beneficiary of U.S. defense resources in 1986, accounting for $134 billion. Asia will absorb $42 billion. And the expanding requirement for rapid deployment forces will take $65 billion, of which about $49 billion is for the Persian Gulf.

What this lesson ought to demonstrate is that defense budgets are not for nothing; they are for something. The dollars buy forces; the forces have missions; the missions are in regions where the United States has defensive commitments or supposed strategic interests; the strategic involvements, in sum, are practically equivalent to the nation's foreign policy. Therefore, defense budgets cannot be cut significantly—on a scale, say, commensurate with the federal deficit problem—without consequences for their objects: alliances and foreign policies.

Conversely, the objects of U.S. military protection cannot be significantly expanded or the intensity or level of confidence with which the United States plans to protect them cannot be significantly heightened without commensurately increasing defense budgets, well above the levels proposed by the Reagan administration. This is a point made by Van Cleave with which I entirely agree.

If there is an imbalance, it is not ultimately between "Soviet expansionism" and U.S. "strategy and the forces to support [the] policy . . . of containment" but rather, as Van Cleave says, between U.S. "capabilities" and the objectives that it has established. Two points emerge. First, the real antithesis, underlying "capabilities versus objectives," is resources versus foreign policies and national strategies. Second, foreign policies and national strategies, far from being absolutes, dictated precisely and rigidly as matters of necessity by the Soviet threat, are actually matters of national choice. As such, they can be changed, more easily than resource constraints, which are parametric.

The defense budget is the fulcrum on which these questions rest. The precise point of objective balance may not be entirely clear, and the actual point that will provide a political equilibrium may not be predetermined. But one thing is certain: resource constraints cannot be willfully set aside, as Van Cleave and a flock of superhawks would like to do and would like the rest of us to believe.

Concluding Remarks   William R. Van Cleave

> The ideas that the defense program is enormous, is the principal cause of the deficits, and is a great burden on the American economy and the American people seem to resist all factual information.
>
> Committee on the Present Danger,
> *Defense and the Deficit*

The areas of agreement and disagreement between Ravenal and myself are clear. We agree that there should be a strong cohesion of policies, strategies, and capabilities, which is now lacking. We agree that the United States cannot with confidence meet current commitments and officially established defense requirements with present programs and levels of spending. We are both very concerned about this mismatch between objectives and capabilities. Ravenal, however, argues that we are overcommitted and overspending on defense. The principal question to him is: Can this nation afford its present level of defense, let alone the more rigorous, demanding, and consistent version of the Reagan administration's defense program proposed by Van Cleave? I do not believe the question to be one of affordability, except in this sense: Can we afford *not* to do so?

I repeat that it is not national solvency that is at stake, but rather national security, and that few if any would share Ravenal's view that defense spending is

causing any crisis in solvency. The image of Reagan defense spending as prohibitively expensive is a false one. To the contrary, as James Schlesinger has
recently pointed out, U.S. "rearmament has been derailed" and we are witness-
ing "a substantial collapse of the administration's defense goals."[39] At this
writing, the FY86 defense budget is likely to end up some $75 billion under what
was deemed necessary in 1981, and some $20 billion under Carter projections.
The military imbalance has not been fundamentally altered in the first Reagan
term, and in some respects—such as the strategic and theater nuclear
balances—it has, if anything, worsened. Our national security and global interests are being threatened by failure to do enough, not by spending too much
on defense.

Ravenal also believes that we can safely abandon the policy of containment
and disengage from abroad, presumably to avoid insolvency. Is this because he
believes Soviet expansion unlikely, or because he sees no threat to U.S. interests
and values from Soviet expansionism? Surely he does not entertain the notion that
an expansionist Soviet Union could be contained by any coalition of states lacking
the United States.

Ravenal would have the United States withdraw to a very restricted defense
perimeter, which is not described but seems by implication to be very close to a
"fortress North America." (I assume from the general tenor of his remarks that
he would oppose U.S. "interventionism" intended to prevent the Sovietization of
our Central American neighbors, should that be threatened.)

Our defense requirements are demanding precisely because we are facing an
enormous threat to our interests and to international stability. Doubt about U.S.
purposes, determination, and defense capabilities would most likely worsen the
situation dangerously. I do not believe that U.S. strategic, political, and economic
interests and values can be protected by Ravenal's disengagement, for all of the
reasons that have been persuasive to successive U.S. administrations from Truman's to Reagan's. Fortunately, as I have observed, disengagement is not a realistic choice. Therefore, our focus should be on the defense capabilities necessary to
support our policy.

Let me conclude by summarizing the defense tasks that I believe remain
before us:

We must reaffirm U.S. determination to contain Soviet expansion and to use
military force in timely fashion when required by challenges to our interests.

We must provide the funds and programs to bring our military capabilities
in line with the requirements established for them and in line with the
threat.

We must, as a matter of urgency, tackle the numerous nuclear deterrent force
vulnerability problems, particularly of the ICBM force. While providing
greater survivability, higher priority should go to correcting the strategic nuclear imbalance and to modernizing SNF to give them more flexible and dis-
criminating targeting capability, penetrability, and endurance.

In both plans and programs, we should proceed vigorously with strategic
defenses, including near-term capabilities.

Theater postures and plans must be improved, both for NATO and elsewhere; there are too many gaps and contradictions at present.

The combat capability and readiness of theater and mobile general-purpose forces must be improved, but the effectiveness of such improvements will be reduced without the improvements above.

Our means of dealing with Soviet proxies, Soviet-sponsored terrorism and insurgency, and other low-intensity or indirect Soviet threats must be improved by both executive and legislative action.

We must adopt a realism about arms control and prevent it from interfering with our capability to deal with threats when arms control itself does nothing to reduce those threats.

Such exhortation, of course, does not do justice to practical, political, and budgetary constraints, as Ravenal would point out, nor to the need to establish priorities and effect compromises, nor to the analysis involved in all of these matters. The subsequent chapters in this book, however, will add much more detail to the issues involved in the defense debate.

Concluding Remarks   Earl C. Ravenal

Limitation of space is the reason for not cataloging, let alone exposing, Van Cleave's rhetorical slights, invidious appeals to authority, misapprehensions of my argument, and assertions of the self-evident nature of his argument. Suffice it to say that they do not enhance his case.

The pervasive problem with Van Cleave's argument—or, I should say, brand of argument, since his is amply representative of a large group in the foreign policy bureaucracy and the "foreign policy community"—is that he, and they, think that their function is and should be autonomous. They believe, moreover, that its sole referent is external: the state of the world, the condition of various regional balances of power—in a word, "threats." I believe that such an attitude toward foreign and military policy represents not its unique validation but its pathology. For it is clear that our domestic system places constraints on our power, not only its projection but its generation. Furthermore, a foreign policy that is lopsidedly responsive to threats and challenges, and that *incurs* such pressure through its multiplication of foreign commitments and its assumption of foreign interests, will encounter more of these domestic constraints.

Policy practitioners have on occasion taken extraordinary pains to insulate their function from its domestic inhibitions. Yet, if our experience, of the past several decades at least, tells us anything, it is that we cannot indefinitely entertain strategies that are at odds with the requisites of national solvency; nor, as we have seen from such political traumas as Watergate, can any discrepancies be resolved by means that would suppress or subvert the peculiar liberties that this country was organized to promote.

A further word about threats. No pile of facts—say, about the military capabilities or the intentions of the Soviet Union—no matter how high or deep, leads by itself to any conclusion, particularly a policy conclusion. What is essential in disposing a nation's response to some challenge or state of affairs is the *"major* premise," which is always an "if-then" proposition—in other words, a general policy statement. (Indeed, a nation's "policy" can be considered to be a summation of the important major premises relating to possible events or occurrences across geographical areas or in functional areas of national activity.) Thus, it is well to take seriously the facts of the Soviet state and leadership. But such sobriety in itself neither disposes the factual determination nor dictates the policy conclusion. Odd as it may seem to Van Cleave, there is no necessary connection between taking threats seriously and doing something about them. We could even grant most of the evidence of the hawks and still argue for nonintervention.

Moreover, Van Cleave, and virtually all proponents of a broadly interventionist position, fundamentally misconceive the nature of the noninterventionist case. A debate about foreign policy and national strategy should not be a beauty competition of attractive values, a parade of wish lists for the United States and the world. And so, my case for nonintervention is not a pure prescription of a state of affairs that is inherently and universally attractive. Prescription is mingled with prediction. Nonintervention is proposed as an adjustment to the world as it is shaping up and to the constraints of our polity, society, and economy. Worthy causes are not free. As in all things, there is a price to be paid; and that price has been growing higher. The multidimensional costs of intervention (the specific acts and the general stance of perpetual preparedness) should be, and are, weighed against the consequences of not intervening and not preparing to intervene. Part of the prediction is that our country, taken as a decision-making system, will not pay those costs.

To illustrate that my case is objective, substantive, and consequential, I propose a comparison of costs. We can make large cuts in the defense budget *if* we severely limit our foreign policy objectives. But large cuts in the defense budget can be made *only if* there is a fundamental change in American foreign policy. We could defend our essential security and our central values with a much smaller force structure than we now have. Such a force structure would provide the following general purpose forces: 8 land divisions (6 Army and 2 Marine Corps), 20 tactical airwing equivalents (11 Air Force, 4 Marine Corps, and 5 Navy), and 6 carrier battle groups. With the addition of a diad of nuclear forces, submarines and cruise-missile-armed bombers, this would mean manpower of 1,185,000 (370,000 Army, 315,000 Air Force, 365,000 Navy, and 135,000 Marine Corps). The total defense budget at the end of a decade of adjustment would be about $158 billion in 1986 dollars. In contrast, the Reagan administration has requested, for 1986, 21 land divisions and 44 tactical airwing equivalents, with 13 carrier battle groups; this force requires 2,178,000 men and a budget authorization of $314 billion.

These differences will multiply greatly unless we change our course. The way we are headed, the defense budget will be close to $750 billion by 1995, and cumulative defense spending during that decade will be over $5.1 trillion. Under a noninterventionist policy, the 1995 defense budget would be 68 percent less, and the cumulative cost over a decade would be under $2.7 trillion.

Let me recapitulate how I conceive of my alternative: first, as an accounting, a costing out; second, as a choice, a presentation of the conditions and consequences of attaining this alternative stance; third—and only third—as a decision to make that choice, to accept that alternative, with its comparative costs and its particular consequences. Each of these phases is conceptually separate. One can take or leave the third phase, the decision, and still understand and recognize the validity of the first two phases.

To say, as does Van Cleave, that such an alternative is unrealistic because it appears to be a political nonstarter is actually to reinforce what *I* have been saying: that the public, and most foreign policy elites, too, prefer to choose their goals and directions without a calculation of costs and consequences. But the nation's inevitable choice is not among ideal programs and states of affairs, unencumbered by their entailed requirements and effects. Without confronting those hard conditions and results, we would be opting for illusions. What makes solutions probable is not their attractiveness or political acceptability. What makes them likely, even historically inevitable, is that the other attempted courses will fail.

STEPHEN R. WAGNE

Chapter 3

The Defense Budget

Leonard Sullivan, Jr.

O n February 4, 1985, President Reagan submitted to the Congress his proposed federal budget for fiscal year (FY) 1986. The total request for $974 billion includes $314 billion in total obligational authority (TOA)—$278 billion in outlays—for the Department of Defense (DOD). It also includes an estimate that the federal government will spend $180 billion more than it will take in as revenue. Clearly the defense budget will be subjected to both intense scrutiny and substantial unwarranted abuse as the U.S. Congress, the media, and the informed public debate the many contentious issues imbedded in federal spending trends and priorities.

Characterizing the Defense Department

The primary purpose of the DOD is to provide ready operational forces of sufficient stature to deter any potential adversary from resorting to war against the United States, its allies, or its friends as a means of attaining national objectives. To accomplish this fundamental objective, the U.S. military has evolved into a vast, complex conglomerate of active and reserve forces totaling over 3.25 million military and 1.1 million civilian personnel, operating weapons and other equipment costing over $2.8 trillion to replace (in FY86 dollars), from facilities with a replacement cost of over $400 billion, excluding land.

These U.S. forces are the world's third largest in personnel (after the People's Republic of China and the Soviet Union) and the second largest in terms of weapons, equipment, and facility holdings (after the Soviet Union). Roughly one-quarter of all U.S. forces are permanently stationed abroad, about the same fraction as the Soviets deploy beyond their borders (including 105,000 in Afghanistan).

Table 3–1. Deployment of Superpower Forces Abroad (End FY84)

	U.S. Forces	USSR Forces
Europe	324,600	686,500
East Asia/Pacific	103,400	83,300
Africa/Near East/South Asia	4,900	122,800
Western Hemisphere	17,400	4,600
"Afloat" worldwide	69,300	55,200
Total abroad	519,600	952,400
Total active forces	2,123,400	3,625,000
Percent abroad	24.5	26.3

These overseas deployments are expensive and require the retention of a suitable rotation base at home. Comparative U.S. and Soviet overseas deployments are shown in table 3–1.[1]

Attention to the defense budget is more often focused on the hardware holdings than on personnel requirements. In fact the personnel requirements for both the Navy and the Air Force are established in terms of the weapons and equipment they will use. Only the army and marines tend to set their force levels in terms of personnel, whom they then equip as best they can. In either case, the total equipment holdings for the DOD are very large indeed, as shown in table 3–2.

Table 3–2. U.S. Military Equipment Inventories, 1985

Tanks/tracked vehicles	60,000
Trucks/road vehicles	600,000
Tactical missiles	70,000
Antitank missiles	200,000
Helicopters	9,300
Fighter/attack aircraft	7,500
Patrol/transport aircraft	1,900
Other aircraft	6,500
Aircraft carriers	13
Attack submarines	100
Surface combatants	230
Amphibious/logistic ships	124
Auxiliary support ships	52
Ships under construction	(94)
Bombers	300
Strategic submarines	38
ICBMs and SLBMs	1,640
Tactical nuclear missiles	6,000

Annual defense funding falls into two major areas: the continuous and recurring costs of training, operating, and maintaining the current (and past) active and reserve forces and the continuous and recurring costs of modernizing both the facilities and the weapons and equipment that establish the hardware performance potential of those forces. The former are generally referred to as current operating costs; the latter represent investment costs for future capabilities. Currently defense expenditures are almost evenly divided between current and future capabilities. As pressures mount to constrain defense spending, the tendency, as in the past, will almost certainly be to mortgage future potential rather than reduce current capabilities.

The FY86 defense submittal provides the fourth consecutive defense budget fully representing the conservative tendencies of the current administration. The FY82 budget was prepared by the Carter administration after President Jimmy Carter's election defeat and after the Soviet invasion of Afghanistan. It was modified by the new Reagan administration to add supplemental funds that would be spent within FY82 ("fast-spending" dollars not representative of a totally balanced budget). For comparative purposes, then, it is most revealing to compare the FY86 Reagan budget requests with the last "normal" Carter budget five years prior. Table 3–3 provides this comparison in both current ("then-year") dollars and in constant FY86 dollars, with the impact of past inflation removed.

Table 3–3. Comparison of FY81 and FY86 Defense Appropriations

(billions of dollars)

| | FY81 | | FY86 | Percentage |
	FY81$	FY86$	FY86$	Increase
Appropriation				
Procurement	47.8	60.9	106.8	75
Research, development, test, and evaluation	16.6	21.2	39.3	86
Family housing, military construction, other	5.9	7.5	11.7	56
Total investment	70.3	89.6	157.8	76
Operations and maintenance	55.2	70.3	82.5	17
Military personnel	36.7	46.8	54.8	17
Retired pay	13.7	17.5	18.6	7
Total operating budget	105.6	134.6	155.9	16
Total budget	175.9	224.2	313.7	40
Military personnel		2,082,000	2,178,000	5
Civilian personnel		1,019,000	1,107,000	9

It is clear from table 3–3 that the major beneficiary of the Reagan defense spending increases has been the investment accounts, which have increased 76 percent (in constant dollars); the operating accounts have increased only by 16 percent. Within the investment appropriations, the procurement budget has grown by 75 percent, while the budget for research, development, test, and evaluation (RDT&E) has increased 86 percent. On the operating side, the operations and maintenance (O&M) budget has gone up by 17 percent—primarily to increase readiness—while the military personnel (MilPers) account has risen 17 percent. The MilPers increases are a combination of a 5 percent increase in military force levels and a 12 percent increase in real wages to make up for prior decreases during the years of double-digit inflation. These budget increases can also be related to the major defense program categories, as shown in table 3–4.

Table 3–4. Comparison of FY81 and FY86 Defense Programs

(billions of dollars)

	FY81		FY86	Percentage
	FY81$	*FY86$*	*FY86$*	**Increase**
Strategic forces	12.7	16.2	29.9	85
Tactical forces	68.3	87.0	132.1	52
Intelligence and communications	11.2	14.3	27.9	95
Airlift and sealift	2.9	3.7	8.0	116
National Guard and reserve	9.9	12.6	16.9	34
Research, development, test, and evaluation	14.2	18.1	30.4	68
Central support and maintenance	17.6	22.4	26.5	18
Training, medical support, and personnel support	35.0	44.6	35.6	– 20
Other	4.3	5.5	6.4	17
Total budget	176.1	224.4	313.7	40

Since 1980 the greatest percentage budget increases have been bestowed on U.S. airlift-sealift forces (in support of the newly organized rapid deployment force), strategic forces (as President Reagan attempts to close the "window of vulnerability"), and intelligence and communications operations, which are essential to the operation of all U.S. forces. Spending on general-purpose tactical and lift forces remains more than four times as great as that on strategic nuclear forces.

Perspective: Long-Range Defense Spending Trends

Despite the tendency of the Congress and the media to look at defense spending on an isolated, annual basis, virtually all of DOD's major programs and forces can be maintained only by continued stable, long-term funding. RDT&E programs often take ten years to completion. Production programs often go on for as long as twenty years. It takes two or three years to form and train a new operational unit, and it can often take two or three years of disruption and multiple personnel transfers when a unit is disbanded. The best test for the adequacy of defense spending, then, is to look at the longer-range trends.

Operational costs are overwhelmingly linked to active force levels and cannot readily be changed (either up or down) to meet budgetary exigencies. Hence, when budgets were cut in the aftermath of the Vietnam war, the investment accounts absorbed the greater share of those reductions. Similarly, the largest share of the increases in the Reagan budgets has been applied to force modernization through the investment accounts. Although there has been a modest buildup in the size of U.S. forces since 1981 (a larger navy, one new active and one new reserve division, and few more tactical air squadrons), the biggest increases have gone to RDT&E and procurement.

Figure 3–1 indicates the level of defense and nondefense spending since 1955 (in constant FY86 dollars). Excepting the Vietnam war costs of $410 billion, the

Figure 3–1. Federal Defense Spending Trends, FY55–FY90

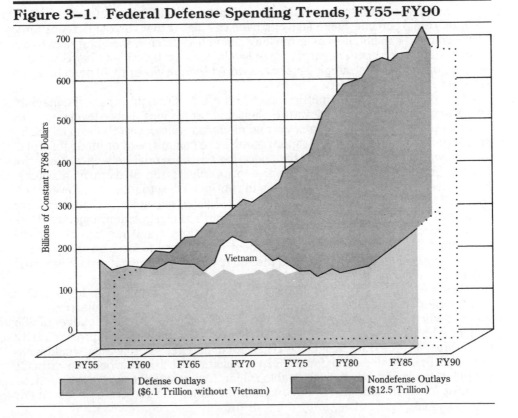

DOD has spent $6.1 trillion over the past thirty years. Nondefense federal outlays have totaled $12.5 trillion over the same period.

What has been frequently described as the biggest peacetime defense buildup in the history of the United States has actually amounted to a very small buildup in force levels but a massive make-up for underinvestment throughout the 1970s, during which time capital stock in U.S. weapons, facilities, and equipment depreciated substantially. The U.S. government was not buying enough aircraft to replace peacetime accidents or enough ships to replace retirements. The FY79 and FY80 investment budgets were sufficient only to permit a rollover of major weapon systems once every thirty years; the Great Reagan Buildup has now reduced that turnover rate to once every twenty-four years.

The defense buildup of the 1980s, amounting to an increase of 39 percent in constant dollars, is dwarfed by the buildup in entitlement programs during the 1970s. In fact, from 1965 to 1980, when non-war-related defense spending stayed flat in constant dollars, nondefense spending increased by 136 percent. As a result, the share of federal spending devoted to defense has dropped substantially since the pre-Vietnam period, and defense spending as a share of the GNP dropped from about 12 percent in 1964 to a low of 4.9 percent during the Carter administration. The changing shares of federal spending are shown in figure 3–2.

The FY86 defense proposal, if enacted intact, would bring defense spending back up to 6.6 percent. Some analysts have calculated that current defense force levels cannot be maintained over the long run unless defense spending rises to approximately 8 percent. The larger force levels believed by some to be required to support current U.S. strategic objectives would require closer to 10 percent of the GNP on a continuing basis.

One of the most costly inefficiencies in the U.S. fiscal process is the inability to make meaningful midrange future plans and projections. Force-level decisions (such as the move to a 600 ship navy) and modernization decisions (such as the introduction of a new strategic weapon) require the commitment of funds for a decade or two into the future. Since the operating costs are relatively uncontrollable, budget projection uncertainties devolve primarily to the investment accounts. Since research and development seems to continue close to a constant level of effort and since certain military construction (MilCon) expenditures are necessary to keep the physical plant up to national standards and regulations (such as those of the Occupational Safety and Health Administration and the Environmental Protection Agency), most of the investment uncertainty focuses on the procurement account. Figure 3–3 illustrates the range of defense budget projections that have existed during the past decade.

As an example, the FY86 defense budget requests $107 billion for procurement authority in this fiscal year. In FY76, a reasonable forward projection of the planned Ford defense budgets would have produced a procurement budget of $88 billion. The final year of Carter's FY81 five-year plan would have provided only $65 billion. On the other hand, the FY83 Reagan defense projection would have provided over $140 billion for FY86. Acquisition decisions would be difficult enough to make with a relatively stable rolling five-year defense plan as practiced by most Western nations. An environment in which the projected procurement account has varied by a factor of two within ten years makes a mockery of U.S. defense planning.

In addition, there has been a characteristic growth pattern in each of the major appropriations from year to year, well beyond inflation. This growth appears to corrrespond to the quality index recognized in the civilian sector. The quality index is a measure of the rate at which products tend to become more expensive due to the addition of various new quality features. The military parallel appears to be the rate at which additional sophistication must be added to counter the opposition's new weaponry. It is likely that the essence of the arms race is imbedded in this technological competition.

This growth factor results in each new weapon system's being more expensive to build than its predecessor by about 5 percent annually, compounded across the years between the successive designs. Similarly, and possibly for the same reasons, the O&M account has been growing at a rate in excess of 3 percent per annum per military person. To the extent that past planning has not recognized what amounts to an annual loss in purchasing power, aspirations for maintaining and modernizing future forces are significantly overstated in the defense five-year plan. In fact, this has resulted in the Reagan force "buildup" being significantly smaller than originally hoped for by the military departments—and promised by the Reagan administration.

Figure 3–2. Defense and Nondefense Program Shares of GNP, FY55–FY90

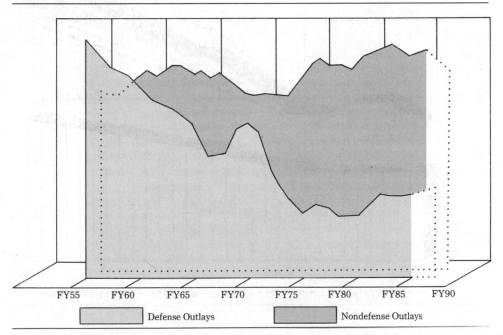

FY55   FY60   FY65   FY70   FY75   FY80   FY85   FY90

Defense Outlays   Nondefense Outlays

Military Personnel Appropriations

The most basic DOD appropriations are those that provide the salaries, benefits, and allowances for U.S. uniformed personnel. The FY86 request is up $6.2 billion from FY85, to $57.4 billion, plus an "undistributed contingency" to cover the proposed wage increases during FY86. About 70 percent of this appropriation goes directly for pay, including bonuses for duty in certain high-risk or less attractive assignments. Twenty percent goes for subsistence and housing allowances and the remainder for FICA payments, travel to new duty stations, and the like. Table 3–5 indicates the number of military personnel in each service on active and reserve duty, the increases over FY 81, their FY85 average pay, and their approximate length of service.

It should be clear from the tour lengths that the U.S. military forces represent a level of commitment unmatched in other countries. In most of the military forces of Europe, on both sides of the iron curtain, the military is composed primarily of recruits who serve for fewer than two years. While this may result in somewhat higher average pay scales for U.S. forces, it also results in substantially more professional forces, with a far greater capacity to handle sophisticated military equipment.

Figure 3–3.   Changing Defense Budget Projections, FY75–FY90

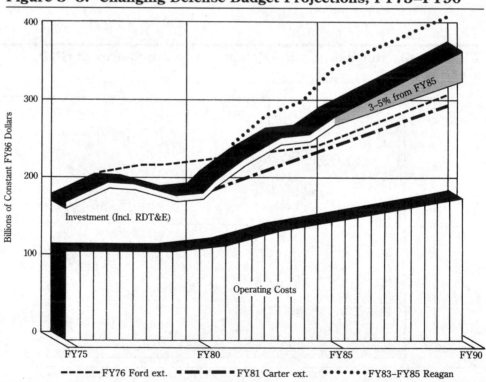

Table 3–5. Military Personnel Levels, Pay, and Tour Lengths

	FY81 Personnel	FY86 Personnel	Personnel % Increase	FY85 Average Pay[a]	FY85 Average Tour (years)
Army					
Active	781,000	781,000	0.	$14,100	9.7
Reserve/National Guard	614,200	751,000	22.27	3,700	15.6
Navy					
Active	540,200	586,000	8.48	14,500	6.3
Reserve/National Guard	87,900	142,000	61.55	4,400	13.4
Marine Corps					
Active	190,600	199,000	4.41	12,500	5.8
Reserve/National Guard	37,000	43,000	16.22	2,800	5.5
Air Force					
Active	570,300	612,000	7.31	15,100	10.9
Reserve/National Guard	159,900	188,000	17.57	4,200	19.9
Department of Defense total					
Active	2,082,200	2,178,000	4.60	14,300	8.1
Reserve/National Guard	899,000	1,124,000	25.03	3,800	14.8

[a]Does not include housing, subsistence, FICA, or travel.

The U.S. defense budget is unique among the budgets of the U.S. federal government—and of the rest of the Western world—in that it provides the funds to pay retirement benefits for prior service. In FY86, retired pay will increase $1.1 billion to $18.6 billion and is growing at just under 3 percent annually as the retiree population continues to increase. It is expected to peak out at approximately 1.5 million people by the year 2000. Average benefits in FY86 will amount to some $12,800 per retiree. This appropriation also amounts to an entitlement program in that the pay schedules are set by existing legislation over which the DOD has virtually no control. Repeated attempts to move this appropriation out of the defense category have been unsuccessful; instead it is now being folded into the MilPers appropriation.

The major budgetary questions related to the MilPers account deal not with the pay and allowances provided but with the numbers of personnel. As the economy continues to improve (making military service somewhat less attractive) and as the U.S. demographic facts of life continue to evolve (reducing the number of available teenagers), the military eventually may have to consider ways to get along with fewer uniformed personnel. The FY85 allocation of military personnel is shown in table 3–6.

Table 3–6. Allocation of Defense Manpower, 1985

	Active	Reserve	Civilian
Strategic forces	93,000	24,700	11,400
Tactical and mobility forces	1,029,300	814,400	63,100
Auxiliary activities[a]	109,700	23,500	95,500
Support activities[b]	642,400	196,300	913,800
Individuals[c]	311,500	44,500	
Total	2,165,800	1,103,700	1,084,800

[a]Intelligence, central communications, RDT&E activities, geophysical activities.

[b]Base operations, medical support, personnel support, training, logistics and management.

[c]"Transients," patients and prisoners, students, cadets, and trainees.

Table 3–6 shows that only about 60 percent of current military personnel are directly involved in the operation of combat forces. Another 25 percent are involved in support activities (such as supply, training, and maintenance), and another 15 percent are either moving or being trained. It has been estimated that over 520,000 military personnel and 770,000 civilian employees are involved in equipment maintenance either in operational units or at the central depots. It is in these latter areas where some economies eventually will need to be effected.

No other very large, complex organization is staffed by employees averaging less than thirty years old, operating equipment worth over $1.2 million per capita, who start out with essentially no job training. The magnitude of the training task for FY85 is outlined in table 3–7. The equivalent of some 214,000 student-years were required in FY85, using 132,000 military and 61,500 civilian personnel as trainers. In short training requirements in U.S. forces involve over 400,000 military and civilian personnel. The cost of this training will reach approximately $19.5 billion in FY86.

Operations and Maintenance Appropriations

Almost two-thirds of current force operating costs are paid for out of the O&M budget. The FY86 request is up $4.2 billion to $82.5 billion, continuing a growth pattern of almost 5 percent annually in constant dollars. This account pays for current operations and exercises and maintains equipment, bases, facilities, and personnel. Well over 90 percent of the 1.1 million DOD civilians are engaged in support activities paid for from this appropriation. Table 3–8 indicates the distribution of O&M spending among the services by major functional areas, based on FY86 shares.

Direct operating costs are those associated with consumption of fuel and other commodities during flying hours, steaming hours, and field maneuvers. About 18 percent of O&M spending is directly related to these levels of activity, with the Navy alone consuming over $5 billion annually in its operations. Navy ships each average from 100 to 130 days per year at sea. The 4,500 Navy and 5,900 Air Force active aircraft will each average over 400 flying hours per year. Army operations, with relatively low flying costs for their more than 9,000 helicopters

Table 3–7. Military Training Requirements, 1985

	Military Trainees	Course Length (hours per year)	Military Trainers	Civilian Trainers
Recruit training	342,000	62	9,200	300
1-station unit training	83,000	106	8,600	600
Officer training	18,900	617	3,200	2,500
Special skill training	1,250,000	39	50,000	9,200
Flight training	14,600	182	15,900	1,800
Professional development	18,000	243	2,400	2,100
Training base support			42,600	45,000
Total	1,726,500	56	131,900	61,500

($250 per hour versus $1,400 per hour), will cost about $4 billion in FY86. Each of the 375 Army and Marine battalions will average about 155 training days in the field.

Support of combat force operations will almost double the direct operating costs. Administering the forces requires about 1.3 percent of uniformed personnel and about 4 percent of the DOD civilian payroll. Operating the several dedicated communications systems such as the worldwide military command and control system and the long-haul communications system, as well as operation of the Defense Communications Agency, requires over 20,000 civilians and 68,000 military personnel. Another 5 percent of the DOD O&M budget is spent in the supply system, where 92,000 civilians and 6,500 military personnel move 20 million tons of materiel through the supply depots in almost 60 million separate supply actions, coupled with another 50 million actions at the inventory control points. Over 5 million separate procurement actions will be processed. Finally, over 9 million tons of materiel will be moved by DOD transportation assets: 10 percent by air at a cost of over $2,000 per ton and the rest by sea at a cost of about $150 per ton.

Maintaining and supporting operational equipment will continue to require almost 30 percent of the total O&M appropriations for defense, varying by service from a low of 15 percent for the Army to almost 48 percent for the Navy. This involves both depot maintenance and existing equipment upgrading, as well as some smaller catch-all categories of logistics management. Depot maintenance is by far the largest O&M activity and has been growing at almost 9 percent annually. It will cost about $6 billion for aircraft and another $5 billion for ships alone. Equipment is often modernized at the same time that depot overhaul is accomplished; these costs will add another $2.5 billion in FY86. Vast as these sums may appear, they represent less than 1 percent of the estimated replacement cost of the equipment.

Table 3–8. Estimated Distribution of FY86 Operations and Maintenance Spending

(millions of dollars)

	Army	Navy	Marine Corps	Air Force	DOD Total	DOD Percentage
Operations	$3,943	$5,339	$344	$4,324	$14,462	17.5
Operations support	3,918	3,092	303	3,655	13,033	15.8
Equipment support	3,258	12,755	164	5,003	24,004	29.1
Facility support	5,913	3,202	747	3,879	14,681	17.8
Personnel support	3,047	1,645	125	1,428	7,934	9.6
Other miscellaneous and fixed expenses	2,497	719	46	2,635	8,376	10.2
Total	22,576	26,753	1,729	20,924	82,489	100.0

Facility support includes both base operations and real property maintenance. Base operations is the second largest O&M activity and will require about $11 billion in FY86. The funds will be used to operate all of DOD's 794 active force installations, including 350 overseas, and 31 reserve force installations. Facility support encompasses everything from security functions and quality-of-life improvements for barracks to garbage removal and grass cutting. Base operations utilize 194,000 military personnel and 208,800 civilian personnel (including foreign hires). Although base operating costs have not been rising rapidly, real property maintenance costs have been increasing at almost 8 percent per year, requiring about $5 billion in FY86 plus the skills of some 21,000 military and 47,400 civilian personnel.

Support of military personnel will demand over $8 billion in FY86, including recruiting, training, and medical support. Recruiting will require over half a billion dollars in FY86. Based on past experience, it will cost about $1,800 to bring in and process an army recruit, $1,300 for a marine, $1,000 for a sailor, and $800 for an airman. Reserve and National Guard recruiting requires another $400 to $800 per enlistee. Training costs have been rising at more than 9 percent annually (in constant dollars) and will require over $3.5 billion from the O&M account in FY86 (plus almost $11 billion from MilPers). Medical support costs have been growing at more than 7 percent annually and will require over $4 billion in FY86. This equates to roughly $400 per year for each eligible person, including 2,178,000 active personnel and 1,480,000 retirees, plus 2,800,000 dependents of active personnel, and 3,700,000 dependents of retired and deceased personnel. Roughly 300,000 people of the 10 million eligible are expected to require hospital stays, averaging fewer than nine days each.

The DOD civilian work force, engaged primarily in depot and shipyard maintenance, is paid primarily from the O&M account. The DOD provides a remarkably stable, highly skilled infrastructure. For the past thirty years, DOD has employed almost exactly one civilian for every two persons in uniform. In FY86, the DOD civilian payroll will probably reach $33 billion, for an average wage, including DOD contributions to health and life insurance and retirement benefits, of about $30,000.

Military Construction and Family Housing

The FY86 defense budget request contains almost $12 billion for military construction and family housing at the various bases, facilities, and installations around the world. This is $1.9 billion more than the FY85 appropriation. About 75 percent of the funding request will be for military construction, and about one-third of that will be spent on projects overseas. The MilCon budget typically contains over 900 construction projects across virtually all of the states and another 300 projects overseas.

DOD operates some 5,500 installations on 41,000 square miles of land. The replacement value of the structures (not including contents) and other land improvements (roads, runways, and so forth) is set at over $350 billion. Only about 1 percent of replacement value was spent annually during the 1970s on new construction, resulting in substantial depreciation of fixed assets. The Reagan administration has raised this figure to over 2 percent, producing a more realistic forty-five-year rollover rate for DOD's physical plant.

Projects vary from new maintenance and test facilities for MX and Trident II missiles, to child care centers, schools and dental clinics for American dependents, and hardened ground-launched cruise missile (GLCM) facilities in several NATO countries. A special emphasis in the Reagan administration has been placed on improving enlisted barracks at overseas sites. Some barracks still date from the late 1940s. New construction costs are approaching $25,000 per barracks space, and over 300,000 spaces are needed.

The family housing appropriations for the military departments, on the other hand, are a combination of construction and housing improvements (about 20 percent) and operating and maintenance costs (about 80 percent). The Army will spend over $1 billion in FY86 operating and maintaining its family housing units; the Navy Department will spend about $600 million; and the Air Force about $800 million. One of the obligations to a more professional, lower turnover military force is accommodating a substantially higher proportion of married personnel.

Research, Development, Test, and Evaluation

The FY86 Defense RDT&E budget request is for $39.3 billion, up $7.8 billion from FY85. These appropriations, which have run close to 10 percent of the overall DOD budget since the early 1960s, is the surcharge on the procurement account by which the United States strives to maintain a technological edge in its weaponry over the Soviet Union. The current surge to 12.5 percent of a growing budget stems primarily from the very high costs of strategic RDT&E, mainly for the Air Force and "Star Wars" strategic defense systems, plus several large and growing classified projects.

To the extent that an arms race is underway between the two superpowers, it tends to be focused in this area, since neither side can readily afford to increase its quantitative standing force levels very much. In fact, the qualitative competition has become substantially more intense. Many defense analysts have begun to doubt whether the West's remaining technological advantage is sufficient to offset Soviet numerical superiority in virtually all weaponry categories. The proposed allocation of RDT&E funding for FY86 is shown in table 3–9.

Table 3–9. Allocation of FY81 and FY86 Defense Research, Development, Test, and Evaluation Funds

(millions of dollars)

	FY81		FY86	Percentage
	FY81$	*FY86$*	*FY86$*	Increase
Technology base	2,600	3,313	3,525	6.4
Advanced technology	593	756	5,461	622.6
Intelligence and communications	1,632	2,080	5,031	141.9
Strategic programs	3,440	4,384	8,556	95.2
Tactical programs	6,130	7,812	12,395	58.7
Mission support	2,238	2,852	4,312	51.2
Total	16,633	21,197	39,280	85.3
Division of FY81 and FY86 Defense RDT&E Funds				
Army	3,124	3,981	5,280	32.6
Navy Department	5,025	6,404	11,264	75.9
Air Force	7,134	9,092	15,579	71.4
Department of Defense total	16,633	21,197	39,280	85.3
Percentage of Department of Defense budget		9.4	12.5	

Approximately two-thirds of RDT&E spending is devoted to full-scale development of operational weapon systems and equipment in the areas of intelligence and communications, strategic programs, and tactical programs. During the 1970s, the primary focus was on the development of a new generation of conventional force equipment—ships, aircraft, helicopters, missiles, and tanks—on the heels of the Vietnam war. During the 1980s, the emphasis has shifted to the development of a new set of strategic weapons across the nuclear triad (nuclear-armed strategic bombers, missile-carrying submarines, and land-based ballistic missiles) in an attempt to reverse the perceived shift toward Soviet nuclear superiority. In addition, substantially increased emphasis has been placed on technological advances in U.S. intelligence-gathering capabilities (primarily from space) and on improved connectivity (communications) for essential strategic forces. The 1990s are likely to bring a return to greater emphasis on nonnuclear weapons.

About one-quarter of the RDT&E budget will continue to be devoted to the development and demonstration of new military technologies suitable for incorporation into the weaponry of the next century. The technology base efforts are devoted to basic research that cannot be derived from the civilian sector due to the lack of commercial prospects.

There is considerable management concern that funding in basic and applied research may not be increasing rapidly enough, although a determination of how much is enough is virtually impossible to make. On the other hand, there has been a substantial growth in the funding for advanced technology. This is where the eventual applicability of new technologies to defense needs is first demonstrated. Much of the experimental stealth technology is presumably included in this funding category, although its specific applications are highly classified.

The final 10 to 15 percent of the RDT&E budget is devoted to mission support. Most of these funds are spent on test facilities and ranges where the technical and operational suitability of new military equipments is proved prior to full rate production. Continuing congressional concern over insufficient proof testing ensures that this category of spending will continue to grow apace.

Procurement Appropriations

It is possible for the United States to maintain a substantial technological lead over its adversaries in laboratories and on test ranges and still have fielded forces that are inadequately modernized to match the threat. Ultimately the pace of modernization is controlled by the spending in the procurement appropriations, not in RDT&E. Hence, although strategic modernization programs demand relatively higher RDT&E expenditures (because production quantities are so small), the ratio of procurement spending to RDT&E spending has not improved and remains less than 3:1. The allocation of these large procurement increases is shown for FY81 and FY86 in table 3–10.

The FY86 procurement request is for $107 billion, almost the same as that requested in FY85 but $10 billion over that appropriated by the Congress in FY84. Since FY81 there have been substantial increases in procurement of most weapon systems. Aircraft procurement continues to demand almost 40 percent of all defense procurement, while electronics, communications, and "other" consume another 20 percent. The Navy's buildup from 500 to 600 ships has required less than 20 percent of the procurement budget annually.

A modest continued growth in procurement funding should permit acquisition of the 2,000 to 2,500 tracked vehicles needed per year to maintain a total inventory of 60,000. Continued procurement of about 22 to 25 ships per year will permit attainment of the 600 ship deployable battle force before 1990 and maintain it at the level thereafter. The ability to buy the 1,200 to 1,500 aircraft and helicopters needed annually to maintain a total inventory of almost 25,000 seems considerably more dubious. For instance, the FY85 procurement request asked for only about 980 aircraft and helicopters at an average cost of almost $28 million apiece. The FY86 budget request asks for about 1,080 more at an average unit cost close to $26 million.

The total replacement cost of DOD's weapons and operational equipments is somewhere between $2,500 billion and $3,000 billion in FY86 dollars (around 75 percent of the GNP), and is growing (like the GNP) at roughly 4 percent annually. If this inventory is to be turned over once every twenty-five years, roughly 3 percent of GNP will be needed in the procurement accounts alone. The combination of RDT&E and MilCon adds another 1 percent of GNP to the investment side of the ledger.

If operating costs continue to demand at least 50 percent of total defense spending (including retired pay), then the United States appears to have estab-

Table 3–10. Allocation of FY81 and FY86 Defense Procurement Funds

(millions of dollars)

	FY81		FY86	Percentage
	FY81$	*FY86$*	*FY86$*	Increase
Aircraft	17,755	22,627	42,122	86.2
Missiles	7,616	9,706	19,878	104.8
Ships	7,617	9,707	11,412	17.6
Combat vehicles	3,374	4,300	5,739	33.5
Ordinance and support equipment	2,165	2,759	4,362	58.1
Electronics, communications, and other	9,341	11,904	23,244	95.3
Total	47,868	61,003	106,757	75.0
Division of FY81 and FY86 Defense Procurement Funds				
Army	10,622	13,537	21,367	57.8
Navy Department	20,145	25,673	37,431	45.8
Air Force	16,779	21,383	46,567	117.8
Department of Defense total	47,868	61,003	106,757	75.0
Percentage of Department of Defense budget		27.2	34.0	
Procurement/Research, development, test and evaluation ratio		2.88	2.72	

lished a military force with a permanent lien on the U.S. economy of 8 percent of GNP. If the Congress declines to allocate sufficient revenues for military forces, then eventually the United States must shift toward smaller or less well-equipped active forces.

The full costs of defense modernization in FY86 are understated by approximately $7 billion, the funding appropriated to the Department of Energy for the development and procurement of nuclear warheads, including the maintenance of a modern industrial base and suitable nuclear materials. This $7 billion is allocated approximately as follows: RDT&E, $2.0 billion; procurement, $2.5 billion; industrial base, $1.0 billion; and nuclear materials, $1.5 billion.

Controllability of Defense Spending

The magnitude of the federal deficit, projected at $180 billion in the president's FY86 budget and $210 billion by the more independent Congressional Budget Office, has forced exceptional congressional scrutiny of this year's DOD budget.

In response, DOD will try to explain that its budget, even though appropriated on an annual basis, has many of the characteristics of the entitlement programs. In fact, only a small percentage of defense spending is controllable—in the year that the funds are appropriated. The myth that defense spending is truly discretionary in the near term has proved virtually impossible to dispel.

There are fundamental differences between congressional appropriations, which represent obligational authority (promises to pay when the bills come due), and outlays, which are actual government payments from the treasury for bills that have come due. For instance, before the Navy can order an aircraft carrier from a shipbuilder, Congress must grant the TOA required to build it, although construction and outfitting may require seven years. The government need not raise the actual money to make progress payments (outlays) until they come due. Thus, although the Congress appropriated funds for two nuclear aircraft carriers in FY83, both now under construction at Newport News, Virginia, the final bills will be paid by taxes collected in FY89 and FY90.

Each appropriation has its own characteristic spend-out rate. The operating cost accounts tend to be fast spending: 99 percent of FY86 retired pay will be transferred by government check to the recipients within the fiscal year; 97 percent of military pay and benefits and 79 percent of O&M funds spend out within the year. On the other hand, only 58 percent of RDT&E funds spend out within the year; the rest is spent over the following three years. MilCon takes five years and spends only 16 percent in the first year. The procurement account is the extreme: spending about 14 percent in the first year and the remainder over the next five or six years (ships having the longest spend-out time).

These fiscal realities present budget cutters with two difficult situations: the FY86 fast-spending funds are largely for military and civilian personnel and must be paid continuously and on time; while the slow-spending investment funds come primarily from prior-year appropriations and involve work already in progress under firm government contract. As contract obligations, these expenditures are almost as sacrosanct as the entitlement programs, in which the payout is regulated by existing legislation. Thus social welfare payments are statutory and not subject to the annual appropriation process; meeting long-term U.S. national security obligations is treated as an optional annual decision.

On this basis, it is not surprising that well over 70 percent of the congressional cuts to the first four Reagan budgets came from the investment accounts. Furthermore, in times of steadily rising budgets (since FY80), investment outlays lag appropriations by a substantial amount and cause almost unavoidable out-year increases. For instance, the increase in spend-out of FY85 procurement appropriations in FY86 is bigger than the entire first year spending of the FY86 procurement. Only the drop-off in outlays from FY83 and FY84 appropriations prevents an inescapable increase. In fact, FY86 outlays will match those of FY85 even if no new FY86 procurement is appropriated.

These slow-spending accounts also make it appear that the Pentagon has amassed billions of unspent dollars. Almost every year, someone suggests that the Pentagon should live off its backlog for a year or so. While this statement may have public political appeal, it is a deceptive misrepresentation of financial realities. As table 3–11 shows, in FY86 the Pentagon will have committed itself to paying eventually bills not yet due of $213 billion. Only $171 billion of the $314

Table 3–11. Appropriation Source for FY86 Outlays

(billions of dollars)

	Year of Appropriation			
	FY81	**FY82**	**FY83**	**FY84**
Retired pay				0.0
Military personnel				0.1
Operations and maintenance				1.4
Family housing				0.2
Military construction	0.1	0.3	0.4	0.9
Research, development, test, and evaluation	0.0	0.0	0.3	1.6
Procurement	0.6	3.6	8.5	23.7
Total	0.7	3.9	9.1	27.9

billion appropriated in FY86 will be spent in that year. The remaining $106 billion is from prior years. In this case, FY86 procurement outlays will be comprised of $12 billion from FY86 appropriations, $35 billion from FY85, $24 billion from FY84, $9 billion from FY83, and $4 billion from FY82.

In short, it is the annual appropriation process itself that makes the defense budget seem virtually uncontrollable. If the president decides, for instance, to hold military and civilian personnel levels constant in FY86 and the Congress does not pass its appropriations until the beginning of FY86, then it is too late to effect any savings within that year from personnel cuts other than failing to grant raises or replace attrition. Even in that case, the resulting rejuggling of assignments to compensate for the shortfalls can eliminate any anticipated savings. Yet the Congress has no binding authority to control the following year's budget content.

Beyond pay freezes, cutting personnel creates havoc with stable and ready forces without saving money in the near term; O&M cuts produce lower readiness of the personnel and depreciate their equipment and fixed plant. Retired pay cannot be touched without new legislation. New RDT&E program starts can be delayed, but generally the savings amount to no more than 1 or 2 percent of the RDT&E budget; ongoing programs can be stopped at 58 cents on the near-year dollar or stretched out at increased future costs. Procurement and military construction can be deferred or cut at 15 cents on the dollar and thereby increase the "bow wave" of future modernization programs (as was done in the 1970s).

Unless and until Congress comes to realize the long-range nature of defense force commitments and negotiates with the administration to establish an agreed affordable force posture, anything beyond superficial near-year budget cuts will not be practical and will not provide the desired fiscal relief. If no funds at all are appropriated for defense in FY86, there would still remain a substantial budget

Year of Appropriation		Total FY86 Outlays	To Be Spent 1987–1990	Prior Years' Total
FY85	FY86			
0.0	18.5	18.5	0.0	0.0
1.1	52.7	54.0	2.1	1.3
14.6	63.0	78.9	20.1	15.9
0.8	1.9	3.0	1.8	1.0
2.6	1.1	5.3	8.7	4.2
10.6	22.1	34.5	19.3	12.4
35.0	11.7	83.2	161.2	71.4
64.7	171.1	277.5	213.2	106.3

deficit in FY86. Even a freeze in defense outlays would cause turmoil since extensive personnel and/or O&M cuts would be required to offset the statutory increases in retired pay (about $2 billion) plus the $16 billion dollar increase in bills coming due for MilCon and procurement work-in-progress.

Major Determinants in Defense Spending

It is easy to justify very large and increasing expenditures for U.S. military forces. In fact, it can be shown that the budget is not large enough to ensure continued modernization of the active force levels now planned. Unless the budget increases well beyond the 4 to 5 percent needed to compensate for the rising quality index, U.S. forces will continue to spend too much on operating costs and too little on investment.

Heavy congressional budget cuts, which seem likely, are almost certain to exacerbate the gap between what is needed and what is appropriated. Furthermore, the imbalance between spending for modernization (too low) and for operations (too high) is likely to grow worse. In short, we seem destined to face a continuing structural imbalance between the real needs of the Reagan military machine and the willingness of either the administration or the Congress to raise the revenues required to build and maintain it. This mismatch is far larger than can ever be rectified by management efficiencies. Instead structural changes in U.S. military forces will probably be required to avoid returning to the "hollow" and "aging" forces of the 1970s. The ten major determinants of the overall size of the defense budget (which must continue to grow at the rate of the GNP to stay even) are as follows:

1. About 75 percent of defense spending is proportional to the total force levels themselves. Consideration eventually may have to be given to reducing the

total number of fully manned, fully ready divisions, air wings, or naval battle groups.

2. Active force levels probably cannot be reduced unless there is a corresponding reduction in forward deployed forces since a rotation base must be maintained at home. Prime candidates would be land, sea, and air forces assigned to the North Atlantic Treaty Organization (NATO).

3. The current structural imbalance, which favors operating costs at the expense of modernization costs, can be rectified by the shift of some active force elements to the reserves, with a corresponding reduction in total force readiness.

4. It is possible to keep the active forces at current levels but to underman them somewhat during periods of deep peace, using reservists and transients to fill the ranks during crisis and mobilization periods.

5. Conceivably current high readiness levels actually exceed those required for forces so unlikely to be committed to combat in the near future. Lower activity, training, and exercise levels could produce substantial personnel and O&M savings while increasing dependence on using a mobilization phase.

6. Substantial savings could accrue from switching some current unit equipment to war reserve status, making those units that much smaller but more sustainable. There are some compelling reasons for shifting the balance toward somewhat smaller active forces with longer nonnuclear staying power.

7. Modernization costs can be significantly reduced by procuring a somewhat less sophisticated mix of equipments, at some reduction in total force capability. Many defense critics believe the high-low force mix is now much too high. Some new development programs would have to be cancelled.

8. It is possible to make some reductions in modernization costs by greater use of product improvement in lieu of new designs. This would require substantially greater discipline in the weapons acquisition process.

9. There may be some opportunities to reduce full-scale engineering development costs in RDT&E by greater use of prototypes. Premature commitment of this sort generally results in substantial development and production program overruns.

10. There are significant costs associated with modernization program stretch-outs due to lower than expected out-year funding. Enforcing a congressionally approved five-year defense plan is by far the best way to improve defense spending efficiency.

Dividing Military Responsibilties between the United States and Its Allies

There is no more contentious subject in national security circles today than the issue of the division of labor between the United States and its allies. Despite a truly gigantic international political and military constituency dedicated to maintaining the status quo, the incontrovertible consequence of the Reagan defense buildup is that, by the end of FY86, the United States will be spending twice as much of its national product on its defenses as the rest of the Western world combined. Were it not for the massive failure in U.S. leadership over the past two decades, the "Reagan build-up" should have taken place in the military forces of our Western "allies" across the Atlantic and Pacific. Instead, we have elected to provide more of their defenses in the name of our own.

It is not difficult to estimate the share of the FY86 defense budget request that is directly related to the defense of NATO. As shown in table 3–1, 72 percent of U.S. forward deployed nonnuclear forces are in the European theater. It is not unreasonable to estimate that the same fraction of active and reserve forces in the continental United States is intended as reinforcements to that theater. Similarly, the allocation of defense programs suggests that 84 percent of defense spending is for tactical, mobility, and National Guard and reserve forces. Combining these percentages, it is reasonable to conclude that 60 percent of U.S. defense spending is related to the defense of NATO. That equates to 4 percent of U.S. GNP and roughly 17 percent of all U.S. federal outlays.

There are many ways to contribute to the burden of preserving the West's security. Contributions are needed politically, economically, and ideologically, as well as in the defense sector. Even within the defense sector, there are secondary issues of base and overflight rights, host nation support, real estate and facilities for garrisoned forces, and others. Nevertheless, the two dominant factors remain each nation's commitment relative to its total manpower and its fiscal resources. Table 3–12 provides an estimate of the six major nations' contributions to their own defenses and indicates the departures of each from the ideal (and doubtless unachievable) average.

The message in the table is clear: among the six major NATO nations, the United States represents 57 percent of the GNP and 48 percent of the population but contributes 70 percent of the defense spending and 55 percent of the active military and civilian personnel. An equal split in these two categories would reduce U.S. spending by $53 billion and its manning levels by 442,300 personnel. At the other extreme, if the rest of the NATO nations and Japan are also equalized, then the United States exceeds its spending share by $93 billion and its personnel share by 741,500 personnel. Although such equalization will never be reached, substantial gains can be made by moving in that direction.

In order to achieve substantial economies, there would have to be some major realignments in the NATO divisions of responsibility and in the strategy for its conventional defense if the nuclear threshold is to be raised. Several fundamental new guidelines would need to be accepted by both military and political leaders of the alliance:

> Some U.S. active forces now committed to NATO would have to be replaced by European reserve formations. U.S. forces would focus instead on contingencies elsewhere.

> NATO planning would have to concentrate on developing new types of initial defense forces, stressing high conventional firepower and low active manning.

> West Germany would have to place a higher premium on hardening its borders against massed armor attacks and a lower premium on the symbolism of open borders, borders now open to tanks and defended in part by the United States.

> NATO would have to redeploy some of its limited forces in order to turn Soviet strategic imperatives into vulnerabilities while reducing premature losses of its counterattack forces.

Table 3–12. Defense Burden Sharing Estimates for FY86

	Gross Domestic Product (billions of dollars)	Population (millions)	Defense (billions of dollars)
United States	3,899	232.1	277.5
Federal Republic of Germany[a]	851	61.6	36.9
France	696	54.2	28.4
United Kingdom	608	56.0	33.1
Italy	447	56.6	11.5
Canada	375	24.6	8.0
Other NATO countries	585	100.5	12.5
Japan	1,448	118.0	14.2
United States as a percentage of:			
Major NATO countries[b]	56.7	47.8	70.2
All NATO countries	52.3	39.6	68.0
NATO countries plus Japan	43.8	33.0	65.8

[a]Including Berlin costs and rent for U.S. bases.

[b]United States, Federal Republic of Germany, France, United Kingdom, Italy, and Canada.

Weapons, equipment, and munitions for the NATO defense of Europe should be primarily developed, produced, and maintained by Europeans, even if to be used by Americans.

Possibly these fundamental shifts in NATO defense strategy could eventually reduce the U.S. defense burden by at least 1 percent of U.S. gross domestic product (GDP). This could permit the U.S. version of the Soviet threat to NATO to be deterred by conventional forces within funding levels acceptable to NATO allies. Those allies collect almost 38 percent of their GDP in federal, state, and local taxes (compared to 31 percent in the United States) but spend on average only 3.8 percent of their GDP on defense while the United States spends almost 7 percent. These anomalies will make it increasingly difficult for the Congress to support Reagan budget requests in FY86 and thereafter.

Defense Manpower, Active Plus Civilian (thousands)	Defense as a Percentage of Gross Domestic Product	Defense Manpower, Active Plus Civilian, as a Percentage of Population	U.S. Decrease If Equalized	
			Defense Spending (billions of dollars)	Defense Manpower (thousands)
3,270	7.1	1.4		
666	4.3	1.1		
722	4.1	1.3		
562	5.4	1.0		
568	2.6	1.0		
122	2.1	0.5		
1,490	2.1	1.5		
265	1.0	0.2		
55.3			− 53.32	− 442.3
44.2			− 64.37	− 337.0
42.7			− 92.79	− 741.5

Chapter 4

Strategic Forces

Walter B. Slocombe

I n 1984, President Reagan's strategic program began to hit its stride. Despite substantial criticism of a number of aspects of the administration's strategic force programs, there were, even under the pressure of an election year, no permanent alterations in those programs. And in the election President Reagan won four more years in which to carry out his program. As a result, although a few specific weapons, notably the MX missile, have an uncertain future, the perspectives, policies, and even the prejudices that the Reagan administration brings to U.S. strategic policy and to the nuclear relationship with the Soviet Union are likely, given the long-lived character of strategic weapons systems and the growing momentum behind these costly and complex developments, to continue to have an impact for many years to come.

Intercontinental Ballistic Missiles

If public and congressional attention are the measure of significance, the year 1984, like many of the years before it, could be called the "Year of MX." U.S. strategic force policy has been overshadowed for many years by the problem of what to do about building a new generation of land-based intercontinental range ballistic missiles as a successor to the existing 1,000 Minuteman missiles housed in fixed silos across the upper Midwest. First deployed in the 1960s, the Minuteman system was extensively modernized in the 1970s with the deployment in 550 of the launchers of a three-warhead, multiple independently targetable, reentry vehicle (MIRVed) version, the Minuteman III, and with major warhead and accuracy improvements. These 1,000 intercontinental ballistic missiles (ICBMs), with 2,100 warheads, constitute about 20 to 25 percent of total U.S. warheads and nearly half of the day-to-day alert force. They pose a threat to a considerable number of the 818 hardened Soviet MIRV silos, the degree of the threat depending on whether the number of missiles equipped with the new, more powerful Mark 12A warhead, remains at the current 300.

The Minuteman force is less famous for its power than for its potential vulnerability to a first strike by the much larger and even more powerful Soviet ICBM forces. The eventual vulnerability of Minuteman to Soviet attack has been anticipated since at least the late 1960s. Since fixed ICBM silos have a known location and hardness, it was long expected that in time the Soviets would reach the necessary combination of accuracy, yield, and weapon numbers to make an attack on the U.S. ICBM force theoretically possible. By the late 1970s, during the Carter administration, the defense community, if by no means all its outside critics, judged that technically the Minuteman was vulnerable. The sustained Soviet program of reequipping a larger ICBM launcher total (1,400 silos) with MIRVed missiles with some 6,000 warheads and the requisite yield and accuracy to threaten U.S. silos was nearing completion.

The Carter administration, after an attempt in March 1977 at an arms control solution to the Minuteman vulnerability problem, reluctantly but definitely concluded within its first year in office that no plausible SALT II agreement would eliminate this threat. The SALT II Treaty, finally signed in June 1979 and observed but not ratified since then, certainly left the Minuteman force vulnerable, although advocates argued it made solving the problem easier by limiting growth in Soviet warhead numbers and permitting mobile ICBMs.

For a combination of reasons—some strategic, some geopolitical, and some having to do with a concern to demonstrate firmness as a means of winning support for the SALT II Treaty—the Carter administration decided to go forward to build the long discussed, very large, ten warhead MX missile, and—far more controversial and consequential—to base it in a so-called multiple protective shelter (MPS) system. Under this shell game plan, some 200 MX missiles would have been shuffled among some 4,000 hardened shelters, presenting too many targets even for the large Soviet ICBM force.

The Reagan administration came to office very nearly as strongly opposed to the Carter MX program as it was to his SALT II Treaty. Although there was no lack of candidate alternatives to the Carter MX scheme, finding one that met both strategic and political criteria proved immensely difficult. The bulk of the first Reagan term was spent in advocating a series of alternative MX proposals. In the process, the administration demonstrated again, as its predecessors had done before, that there is no perfect solution to this problem. In 1981 Secretary of Defense Caspar Weinberger overrode a recommendation by the first of three Reagan MX study groups, the Townes commission, that the MPS system be kept alive while alternatives were studied. The commission proposed deploying 100 MXs in reconstructed, harder Titan II or Minuteman silos while researching a number of more survivable alternatives, including an aircraft-based option. When the Republican-controlled Senate decisively and immediately rejected that proposal, a reconstituted Townes commission, cleansed of sympathizers with MPS, was reconvened in 1982. This group recommended the so-called *Dense Pack* system in which fixed silos for MX would be placed so closely together that an attack on one would interfere with attacks on others. This idea, too, not only failed to arouse the necessary political support but was promptly rejected by Congress soon after being proposed in late 1982.

In an effort to broaden the debate beyond the choice among relatively unattractive technical solutions to the MX basing question narrowly construed, yet another commission was formed in early 1983. It was headed by retired Air Force Lieutenant General Brent Scowcroft, who had been national security adviser for President Gerald Ford and a supporter of the SALT II Treaty. His commission report, published in April 1983, took a far broader perspective on the ICBM vulnerability problem; unlike its predecessors, it was drafted with a clear eye on congressional reaction.

The Scowcroft commission report—and its acceptance by the administration and, initially at least, by a congressional majority—represented a pulling toward the center of the debate. Analytically the technical susceptibility of U.S. fixed-silo ICBMs to a sudden Soviet surprise attack was acknowledged as a technical possibility. But the resulting window of vulnerability was discounted as a major near-term threat to deterrence or to U.S. political interests. The Scowcroft report pointed out that the threat, however real from a technical point of view, affected only the land-based missile part of the U.S. strategic force, leaving submarines unscathed and giving important additional warning to the bomber force. This observation, made many times in the past by opponents of MX as well as by supporters who took a less alarmed view of the general importance of ICBM vulnerability, was now finally accepted by an administration battered by its earlier MX failures. The administration may have been less inclined in office to denigrate the U.S. deterrent than its members had been in opposition.

With the strategic problem reduced to more manageable terms, the Scowcroft commission advanced a multipart program, pragmatically designed to appeal to a broad range of opinion. Its basic theme was long-term emphasis on more survivable and more stable strategic forces, featuring the development of a new, much smaller single-warhead ICBM, promptly dubbed Midgetman, which would be designed to be small enough and light enough for mobile basing. The commission also called for renewed emphasis on arms control as an element of U.S. strategic policy, pointed out that single-warhead ICBM systems like the Midgetman might provide both sides a path away from the instabilities introduced by high-accuracy, multiple-warhead ICBMs.

The Scowcroft commission, however, loyally supported the concept of building the MX. It called for a force of some 100 MX missiles in fixed silo ICBMs. Acknowledging that such a force would be not significantly, if at all, more survivable than the Minuteman it would replace, the commission argued that an interim MX deployment was important to augment U.S. prompt counterforce retaliatory capabilities, to demonstrate an ability to carry through on a controversial strategic program, and to give negotiating leverage in future arms control negotiations. In 1983, the administration won funding for twenty-one MX missiles and for the commission-endorsed concept of their deployment in former Minuteman silos.

In 1984, the MX controversy continued and indeed sharpened. The administration requested funds for forty-one more missiles and pointed to the successful initial flight tests of the missile and to the Soviet tests of new follow-on ICBMs of their own as evidence of the validity of the military requirement. Moreover, it argued, the Soviet walkout from START (Strategic Arms Reduction Talks) illustrated the importance of maintaining effective bargaining leverage through continuing the MX program.

MX Missile Deployed in Minuteman Silo

This artist's concept depicts the deployment of the MX missile (dubbed the "Peacekeeper" missile) in an existing Minuteman missile silo. Modification of the existing silo would be minimal; the installation of a new shock isolation system would be the primary new addition. Some internal electronic components would be changed also. The Minuteman silo would not be hardened above current levels, but better protection for the MX would result from the new shock isolation system and the launch canister that holds the MX prior to launch.

Source: U.S. Department of Defense

Critics contended that the Scowcroft commission, while nominally endorsing the MX program, had in fact destroyed its rationale by discounting the significance of ICBM vulnerability. In any event, they emphasized, deploying a bigger and better missile in equally vulnerable silos did nothing to solve the problem of ICBM vulnerability. In fact the increased capability that the MX would give the United States to attack Soviet silos could mean that even a limited deployment would be highly destabilizing because it might tempt the Soviets to attack first in a crisis out of concern for MX's threat to their ICBM force, a far larger part of their total strategic nuclear arsenal. The interruption of the START negotiations and the allegations of foot dragging on Midgetman made many MX critics argue that the administration was not supporting all parts of the Scowcroft commission package. Indeed, for some, opposition to MX was viewed as bargaining leverage against the administration to force greater arms control efforts.

With the MX a major symbolic issue for both sides and with the House and Senate split on the issue, debate over MX was a continuing obstacle to agreement on the FY85 defense program. In the end, after prolonged maneuvering, Congress temporized. Funds for a range of fifteen to twenty-one MX missiles were approved, but actual spending was delayed until March 1985 and even then would require affirmative votes by both houses.

Meanwhile the Midgetman part of the program continued. In the budget presented in February 1984, the Air Force proposed that almost half a billion dollars be spent on long-range planning for the missile and alternate basing modes. Many supporters of Midgetman—both those who argued that it should entirely replace MX and those who believed that it should be taken seriously as a successor—expressed concern that the Air Force, either deliberately or out of habit, was overdesigning the missile so that it was becoming heavier and heavier and thereby less consistent with the objective of mobility. In 1984, however, $461.5 million was appropriated. During the year successes were claimed on tests of system components, and the program seemed to be going forward with a firm decision on basing scheduled for the end of 1986 and deployment in the early 1990s.

The future of the ICBM force was second only to the Strategic Defense Initiative program (SDI) as the most controversial defense program of the mid-1980s. A major struggle over whether to build even a few more MX missiles seemed likely in 1985. A reelected President Reagan is unlikely to find the new Congress significantly more enthusiastic about MX than the old one, especially as the program has become something of a symbol of the alleged excessive scale and lack of focus of the Reagan defense buildup. MX opponents claimed they had made small gains in the 1984 congressional elections, and some prior supporters expressed doubts as the session began.

But it would be premature to reckon MX as dead. The resumption of arms control talks will surely give new vigor to the bargaining chip argument, and there was little in the 1984 election campaign to encourage Democrats, much less possible Republican defectors, to believe that a clear-cut victory over the president on a big defense program issue would bring great political payoffs. Given the general success of presidents who choose to make national security and defense decisions a matter of top priority, the prospects are that President Reagan can succeed in obtaining some limited continuation of MX construction.

If current schedules are followed, the first MX will be deployed by 1987. The real issue is how far the program will go beyond initial deployments and where land-based missiles will fit into future U.S. forces. One fact is certain: the deployment of a handful of MX missiles in Minuteman silos will do less one way or the other than the passionate controversy about the program indicates. MX is much criticized on the grounds that it poses a dangerously provocative threat to the Soviet ICBM force. A Soviet Union that has deployed some 600 or 700 missiles of its own equivalent to the MX and is vigorously pursuing a mobile ICBM program to give it a survivable land-based force whatever the United States does seems unlikely to be greatly impressed by 100 U.S. MXs, either from the point of view of making concessions in arms control negotiations or of being pressured into potentially suicidal overreaction in a crisis.

In the longer term, the United States will have to make more fundamental decisions about land-based missiles. One option is to carry out the Scowcroft commission program to deploy 100 or so MXs in silos, treating the action as an important but strictly interim measure, while planning in the longer term to maintain a viable land-based ICBM force via the Midgetman. Even deployed in fixed silos, the single-warhead Midgetman would be a significant contributor to a stabilizing strategic force. Silos holding missiles with only a single warhead, being individually less valuable, would not present nearly such tempting targets as silos holding multiple-warhead missiles. A single-warhead, silo-based Midgetman could look particularly attractive in the context of substantial restrictions on warhead levels achieved through arms control, for such limits would make attacks using more than one warhead to destroy a warhead still less feasible. Indeed, unless there are considerably fewer warheads available for a first-strike than with today's heavily MIRVed focus, the number of silo-based single-warhead ICBMs would have to be large for the force to contribute much to stability.

That Midgetman will prove deployable in some mobile mode seems at least doubtful. Continuous roving patrols in peacetime on roads not controlled by the military have in the past consistently been rejected as unacceptable to the U.S. population, a conclusion whose accuracy (whatever its technical validity) is reinforced by each nuclear accident controversy. Therefore any mobile Midgetman system would almost certainly have to be confined to military reservations. This requires the missile carriers to have considerable hardness since the areas in which they could move would be relatively restricted. In general hardness increases weight and reduces mobility, perhaps to an unacceptable degree. (It is, ironically, not entirely out of the question that the MPS concept, no doubt suitably renamed, might be revived for Midgetman.)

Other alternatives are obviously possible. (There exists an almost endless variety of proposed MX basing schemes, each more survivable than MX in silos and almost all with fewer complications than active defense. Improbable though it now seems, it is always possible that one or another would acquire sufficient backing to revive the idea of retaining the long-term U.S. land-based missile force on the basis of a survivable MX. Indeed, at the end of 1984 there were reports of revived interest in one of the more fanciful schemes: burying the MX (or a smaller missile) far underground, to dig itself out after attack to serve as a "reserve" force for a protracted war.) In the discussion of the strategic defense initiative program, there has been much consideration of defense of land-based silos as the most feasible objective technically, at least for the next generation or so. Defense of ICBMs does not raise either the feasibility or the doctrinal problems associated with defense of cities. Defense to increase survivability would be consistent with traditional deterrence concepts. Opponents argue, however, that if ICBM survivability is the aim, there are cheaper options with fewer potential destabilizing side effects.

A proposal to save ICBMs by such a defensive deployment would, in effect, bring the ABM-ICBM debate back to where it began in the late 1960s, when the Nixon administration proposed to deploy the so-called Safeguard ABM system to defend Minuteman. Such a program would imply a substantial continuing commitment to the MIRVed MX and would be less consistent with an emphasis on Midgetman.

Finally, the United States could, in the long run, abandon a land-based missile element of the deterrent. As submarine missiles improve in accuracy and, hence, in countersilo capability, the ICBM potential as a hard target killer loses its uniqueness. Whether the other advantages of the ICBM—confident communications, high alert rate, low operating costs—can be duplicated at sea is more doubtful. And abandonment of a land-based form, political considerations aside, would permit the Soviets to concentrate added resources on bomber defense and antisubmarine warfare.

A bellwether of the future of the ICBM force is the decision, which must be made during 1985, about whether and how to comply with the requirement of SALT II that the United States have not more than 1,200 operational MIRV missile launchers. In 1984, Congress adopted a nonbinding resolution calling for continued adherence to the Carter and Reagan policy of not undermining the SALT II Treaty but did not specify the measures to be followed to that end.

In late 1985, when the seventh Trident submarine goes to sea, bringing U.S. MIRVed missile launchers over the total unless older launchers have been retired, the United States will have to have decided what to do. At the end of 1984 the administration's declared intention was to dismantle a corresponding number of submarine-launched ballistic missile (SLBM) tubes in Poseidon boats. Some conservative spokesmen argued that, especially since the Soviets have not reduced their launchers to the 2,400 required by the treaty, the United States should not feel itself under any obligation to reduce MIRVs at all. Still a third view argued that a reduction should be made by retiring vulnerable three-warhead Minuteman IIIs rather than dismantling highly survivable eight to fourteen-warhead Poseidons.

Strategic Bombers

The bomber force, consisting largely of B-52s, remains a mainstay of the U.S. strategic force. Some eighty older B-52s were retired during the first four years of President Reagan's term as part of a general policy of eliminating older systems (including the Polaris force and the Titan II). The strategic program, which the Reagan administration inherited from the Carter administration, put considerable stress on using 1970s technology air-launched cruise missiles (ALCMs) to permit the B-52 to remain viable until it could be succeeded by the advanced technology bomber (ATB, or Stealth) that is much more difficult to track by radar than either the B-52 or B-1.

The Reagan administration promptly resurrected the B-1 in an improved B-1B version with lower radar visibility and greater resistance to efforts to destroy it during takeoff. Critics claim this decision was made partly to make funds available for the revived B-1. The Administration insisted that its only motive was to reflect the judgment that a cruise missile employing Stealth technology would be available relatively soon. The ALCM program has been cut back to about 1,800 missiles, only about a third of the original plan. In any event, the ALCM program is continuing on a reduced scale and some 90 B-52Gs equipped with ALCMs are operational. By 1988, the full complement of about 200 ALCM-equipped B-52s will be in the force. The plan is for an eventual air-launched cruise missile force of some 3,000 missiles, of both current and advanced varieties.

The new B-1B bomber has become the centerpiece of the Reagan administration's program. Along with MX, it continued to be one of the weapons most often singled out for elimination from the defense budget. The program took a publicity blow during 1984 from the accidental crash of a prototype B-1A bomber in August. Despite the controversy, the B-1B program seems to be very near, and probably past, the point at which controversy can bring the future of this large and expensive defense project into serious doubt. Efforts to cut back funding for the B-1 program were readily overcome in Congress, with appropriations only $31 million less than the $7.1 billion requested.

The roll-out of the first B-1B in October 1984 may well have signaled the assurance of survival of the program. It surely symbolized the decisive reversal of presidential attitudes toward the plane from President Carter, who tried to kill the bomber, to President Reagan, who was a proud onlooker at the ceremony. The first B-1B squadron is due to enter service in 1986, and the full 100 are planned to be in the force by 1988.

The Stealth program remains shrouded in secrecy further obscured by controversy about the relationship between the prospects for the ATB program and the continued requirement for B-1. Deployment is not expected before the mid-1990s. The program continues to receive funding, though an effort was made to reduce funds in 1984. A potential setback was avoided in late 1984 when an employee at a major Stealth subcontractor was arrested as he was seeking to pass important data related to the program to his Soviet intelligence controllers.

Although the exact shape of the future bomber program seems likely to continue to be a matter of controversy, if only because of the large costs of manned aircraft, the place of manned bombers in the strategic program seems secure for the indefinite future. Equipped with cruise missiles, B-52s will remain a significant part of the force for many years to come. Their substantial reequipment with new weapons and electronics will overcome the age of the airframes themselves. With a clear further four years' lease on life, it seems almost inevitable that at least 100 B-1Bs will join the Strategic Air Command (SAC) in the coming years. The more controversial issue is likely to be whether the B-1B program will stop in 1988 when the projected 100 have been built, a decision with a large economic impact on the extensive B-1B contractor structure. The central question is whether the B-1B will be followed as planned by a single-minded focus on the Stealth bomber or rather, for technical reasons or in order to maintain the momentum (and contractor base) of the B-1 program, additional B-1 bombers will be built beyond the 100 now projected. Should Congress (or the Air Force) seek to continue the program without impact on contractors, action would be needed in 1985 to forestall some subcontractor lines from closing.

Ballistic Missile Submarines

The nuclear-powered ballistic missile-carrying submarines (SSBNs) are the least controversial of the three elements of the nuclear triad. The submarine modernization program continued apace in 1984. The retrofitting of older Poseidon submarines with Trident I (C-4) missiles is now complete, with twelve submarines so fitted. All of the first-generation Polaris submarines have been retired from the operational SSBN force, though two have been kept as "unconventional warfare" ships with their (actually deactivated) tubes continuing to count against the SALT limits. As a result, the dependence of the U.S. SSBN force on overseas bases has been substantially diminished. U.S. submarine bases at Rota, Spain, and Guam have been closed, and the base in Scotland will continue to decrease in importance for SSBN operations as Poseidon (C-3) missiles are retired. The large, new base for Trident submarines at Bangor, Washington, on Puget Sound, is now operational.

During 1984, the very large new Trident submarines *Florida, Michigan,* and *Georgia* joined the fleet, bringing the total in commission to four. A fifth, the *Henry M. Jackson,* was on sea trials in early 1985. With the approval of the additional new Trident submarine requested in the FY85 budget, the total now authorized is twelve, with a still-growing total target of about twenty. Often-discussed plans for a next generation, presumably smaller, missile-carrying submarine remain strictly at the study stage.

Supplementing the submarine construction program, work continues on the Trident II or D-5 submarine-launched ballistic missile. This missile is now contemplated as having very high accuracy and, in at least one of its several configurations, a sufficient combination of accuracy and yield to make it a serious threat to Soviet silos and other hardened targets.

There has been some controversy over the D-5 on the grounds that the development of an SLBM capable of attacking ICBM silos would represent a serious new threat to stability. High-accuracy submarine missiles with a short time of flight (if they are fired close to their targets) could, it is claimed, add to pressures to launch ICBMs preemptively. Supporters of the D-5 respond that because the submarines themselves are likely to remain invulnerable to attack, high-accuracy SLBMs in fact offer an extremely stabilizing response to strategic challenges. Their capability acts as an inhibition on the Soviets, and their survivability means that the Soviets can gain nothing by preemption against them. A considerably more esoteric controversy about the D-5 has to do with the trade-off between antisilo capability and increased range. Heavier, high-yield warheads require a sacrifice in range and reduce the operating area of the submarine. Smaller warheads would increase the operating area and thus raise a hedge against improved Soviet antisubmarine capabilities.

In the longer term, missiles on submarines seem likely to be an increasingly important part of the U.S. deterrent posture. Their accuracy and their capabilities will increase as the D-5 is deployed, an event scheduled for the end of 1989. Despite various warnings, there seems no immediate prospect of a serious threat to the missile-carrying submarines' survivability. Problems with both the ICBMs and the bombers tend to make submarines a relatively more attractive option.

Perhaps the most serious concern relative to the submarines is communications with them. In general, communications, command, and control, although the least discussed aspect of U.S. strategic forces, is probably the most problematic. In 1984, as for several years previously beginning under the Carter administration, substantial amounts of money were made available for programs to improve the ability to receive warning of an impending attack and to ensure that a decision to retaliate, once made, would be effectively and properly communicated to the forces.

Sea-Launched Cruise Missiles

One development in 1984, though of marginal military significance, might, some of its critics claimed, appear in years to come as a fateful, even irreversible step toward losing control of the arms race. That was the deployment by both sides of nuclear-armed sea-launched cruise missiles (SLCMs) with long ranges. The United States has been developing a so-called Tomahawk nuclear land attack missile for deployment on naval vessels for some years. The SALT II Treaty barred its deployment before the end of 1981 but permitted development work to proceed.

Extensive and rapid deployment of the SLCMs for various missions—conventional land attack, conventional anti-ship attack, and nuclear land attack—became a prominent feature of the naval expansion superintended by Reagan's secretary of the navy, John Lehman. Plans called for deployment of SLCMs on special armored platforms on surface ships, initially the newly recommissioned *Iowa*-class battleships, and, more significant, on attack submarines. Some 4,000–5,000 SLCMs of all kinds are planned; about 750 are planned to be nuclear-armed. The military mission of these nuclear land attack weapons has never been very clearly defined.

The range limitations of SLCMs is such that few of the ships carrying them could be both in range of nuclear targets and properly positioned for their primary conventional naval mission. The stated mission of the SLCMs is to serve as an auxiliary nuclear force. They could, for example, provide an intermediate-range theater nuclear force in areas where land-based or carrier aircraft or other delivery systems were unavailable. They could also serve as a supplement to theater nuclear forces in other areas and as an element in strategic nuclear reserve forces, available even after a massive exchange. Even some in the Navy question whether these somewhat marginal military missions justify the reduction in conventional capability entailed in removing torpedoes from submarines to make room for SLCMs.

Many critics made a much more fundamental argument: that because SLCMs were deployed on platforms in ways that were virtually indistinguishable from conventional forces, they were immensely difficult to verify and threatened to make the problem of monitoring nuclear forces indeterminate. In some respects these claims are clearly exaggerated, since SLCMs, like other nuclear forces that are hard to count in detail, still require characteristic support systems. which should provide a way of monitoring the numbers deployed with acceptable uncertainty. Moreover, the Soviet Union has deployed SLMs, albeit of lesser capability and range, for many years, so the verification problem is not wholly a new one.

These arms control concerns coupled with the limited military utility of SLCMs lay behind congressional efforts to defer U.S. deployment. The Democratic-controlled House called for a moratorium on SLCM deployment. The Republican Senate rejected such a delay, and the conference agreed only to require a presidential report on nuclear SLCM verification problems. Amid the congressional maneuvers, the Department of Defense, in June 1984, announced that the United States had, as previously planned, begun deploying long-range nuclear-armed cruise missiles on submarines.

In October 1984, the Soviets announced that as part of their program of responses to the U.S. deployments in Europe of Pershing IIs and GLCMs, the Soviet Union would begin deploying long-range SLCMs on submarines of its own. From a military point of view this development was less than revolutionary. The Soviets had deployed older SLCMs for many years and had been reported earlier in the year to have at least two new, much improved SLCMs under development. However, because of both the verification problems and the explicit intention of the deployment to reduce U.S. warning time, the Soviet step seemed to confirm to critics that a further area of dangerous competition was being opened up.

Antisatellite Weaponry

Effectively part of the strategic program though oriented far more toward command and control than to the forces themselves was the question of antisatellite (ASAT) systems. There were congressional efforts on arms control grounds to hold off an imminent U.S. step. The House proposed a year's delay in any tests of the U.S. ASAT system against actual targets. As with SLCMs, the Senate declined to impose the restraint on an unwilling executive, and the conference committee agreed to permit three tests, after March 1, 1985, conditioned on presidential certification that the tests will be consistent with the ABM Treaty and that he is seeking an ASAT agreement with the Soviet Union.

Since the mid-1970s, the Soviet Union has had a deployed ASAT system. The system is relatively primitive, requiring that the interceptor be placed in orbit with the target in a relatively time-consuming process that offers a properly prepared target opportunity for evasion. Nonetheless, the Soviet system has the capability to reach many important U.S. satellites, notably photographic satellites.

Since the mid-1970s, the United States has been vigorously deploying its own ASAT system. This system, in contrast to the co-orbital Soviet system, would rise directly to attack its target as it passed overhead. For this reason the system would be harder to evade.

Many arms control concerns have been expressed about ASAT weapons. They relate to the general question of introducing active weapons into space, to the threats to stability posed by increased ability to attack command and control and intelligence resources in a crisis, to the difficulty of verifying the number of ASAT systems deployed (which on both sides used fairly common launch platforms, F-15 aircraft in the U.S. case and space boosters in the Soviet case), and to the connection between ASAT and ABM capability.

The Soviets proposed a moratorium on further ASAT testing in late 1983, timing likely related to the beginning of U.S. testing, which occurred in 1984. Congressional initiatives in 1984 deferred until 1985 any full-scale testing in the U.S. ASAT system, but such tests would probably not have occurred before then in any event.

The question of ASAT systems seems likely to be a major issue in the arms control negotiations, whose resumption was agreed on at the beginning of 1985 when the Shultz-Gromyko meetings in Geneva added a new, third forum—weapons in space—to the earlier Intermediate-Range Nuclear Force (INF) and START talks. Soviet agreement to start space weapons talks without a prior U.S. moratorium on tests was a concession, for that had been a condition of the Soviet ASAT talks proposal made in the summer of 1984.

In some respects the issue of ASAT systems has acquired a public role that probably goes beyond its military significance. Satellites as systems, including their delicate ground control equipment and the mechanisms needed to communicate with the satellites, are susceptible to a variety of kinds of interference and attack. Of these threats, physical destruction of the satellite itself is only one. The effort to contain the impending ASAT race draws adherents from a number of perspectives. Some oppose the general idea of extending the arms race to outer space. Others argue that the United States, being far more dependent on space than the Soviet Union, has an affirmative interest in doing whatever possible to reduce Soviet threats to those assets. Indeed in one curious piece of byplay during the year, the Navy—whose interest in dealing with a Soviet radar satellite supposedly capable of tracking ships at sea had been one of the claimed main utilities of the U.S. ASAT system—let it be known that it did not wish to be regarded as sponsoring the Air Force's ASAT program. Others emphasized the special dangers of high-confidence attacks on satellites as a form of action that could appear both safe and effective in a crisis but that would, by reducing information and threatening key military systems, be a major escalation.

Both the shape of the ASAT programs on the two sides and the prospects for any arms control agreements seem likely to be heavily affected by the close relationship between ASAT capabilities and ABM capabilities. Both sides would likely insist on having a well-tested ASAT system before embarking on high-confidence attacks on critical satellites as a supposedly low escalation measure in a crisis. Many ballistic missile defense systems, however, would have significant ASAT potential. In many respects the technical tasks of an ASAT system resemble those of a ballistic missile defense system. At the most basic level, each involves placing an interceptor in a location where it is able to destroy a noncooperating target. Indeed, the administration's unwillingness to pursue an ASAT system moratorium seems likely to derive at least as much from a desire not to constrain what could be done in ballistic missile defense experimentation as it does from any real dedication to ASAT systems as such.

Strategic Defenses

By far the most significant initiative of the Reagan administration's first four years is the Strategic Defense Initiative initially announced by the president in March 1983. This proposal (discussed by Albert Carnesale in detail in chapter 10) was important for other strategic forces because more than any other program, including MX, it raised basic questions over what the purposes of U.S. strategic forces should be.

Many of the military and technical advocates of increased work on strategic defenses envision quite limited goals for such defenses. They argue, with considerable evidence to back them up, that whatever might be said about the technical

obstacles to city defense, limited defenses of critical military targets, such as
ICBM silos, would be both technically feasible at affordable cost and entirely consistent with a strategic policy based on deterrence, for it would increase the survivability of retaliatory forces.

This argument for ballistic missile defense falls clearly within the conceptual
framework of deterrence. Many proponents of deterrence nonetheless oppose
reliance on active defenses, arguing that there are easier ways to insure survivability of retaliatory forces and that any ballistic missile defenses pose threats to
stability even if they are supposedly intended only to enhance the survivability of
retaliatory forces. For example, it is notoriously difficult for the side facing a
defensive system to have a realistic sense of the system's limitations. Accordingly, it is argued, a defensive system that has only relatively limited capability
may seem to the other side to require substantial increases in offensive forces to
overcome or frustrate it.

A second, somewhat more ambitious argument for defenses suggests that the
ability of ballistic missile defenses to defend various kinds of critical military
targets could be important in denying the Soviets the opportunity for relatively
small-scale but militarily very significant nuclear attacks. Such a deployment is
somewhat more demanding technically and, even more than an ICBM defense,
faces the technical problem of the susceptibility of being overwhelmed by the simple tactic of increasing the size of the attack. Technical issues aside, from the
point of view of gaining political support, the explicit nuclear war-fighting aspect
of this argument for SDI has little popular appeal.

In his personal statements, if not always in formal statements issued in his
name, President Reagan, however, consistently talks about SDI as something
quite different: protecting the population of the United States from nuclear attack. From his initial announcement in which he spoke of making nuclear
weapons "impotent and obsolete" through his campaign discussions of a switch
from "assured destruction" to "assured survival" to his inaugural remarks about
defenses as a "security shield" to "render nuclear weapons obsolete," the president has shown that he definitely has in mind a system for high-confidence defense of the bulk of the U.S. population against nuclear attacks. No matter how
much some of his advisers seek to limit the goals they espouse as feasible in implementing the president's program, the fact that he presses the concept of population defense has profound implications for strategic policy far beyond issues of defensive systems as such.

The president's proclaimed goal is nothing less than replacing the threat of
retaliation with the assurance of being able to insulate U.S.—and perhaps allied
and even Soviet—societies against nuclear attack. The theoretical attraction of
this objective—the ground on which the president prefers to frame the debate—is
hardly open to dispute. But focus on the abstract desirability of making nuclear
weapons impotent sidesteps vastly more difficult issues.

First is the question whether such a system can ever be built at any price,
given the immense destructiveness of nuclear weapons and the difficulties of
building a perfect defense. The technical difficulties of population defense, which
would necessarily have to achieve near-perfect levels, are immense. Even
defenders of SDI for ICBM protection, negotiating leverage, or war-fighting
potential shy away from claiming any realistic hope of protecting cities, against

which a leakage rate of even a few percent is quite literally fatal. The attacker seems simply to have too many opportunities for countermeasures, surprise, or saturation.

At a more fundamental level, the implications of attempting to build such a near-perfect defense remain very much to be thought out and debated. For realistic analysis, one must assume the Soviet Union will, within a relatively short period of time, be able to match any U.S. technical developments. Certainly their own efforts in ballistic missile defense suggest that they would do so, however much those efforts underline the hypocrisy of Soviet professions of dismay that Americans should contemplate greater efforts on missile defense.

A missile defense system good enough to give its possessor any hope of reducing the force of a first strike would likely be far more effective in protecting the initiator against retaliation by an already grievously disabled opponent. Many responses to preserve retaliatory capability are theoretically possible, but at minimum, the impulse to expand offensive forces in an effort to overcome defenses seems likely to be very strong. Reliance on complex, and probably vulnerable, defense systems would also put a premium on shooting first, before the other side had a chance to weaken the effectiveness of the defense.

These concerns for stability, coupled with technical doubts and fears of embarking on an immensely costly program without fully understanding its implications, have created a good deal of congressional caution, despite the general popular appeal of defense. In 1984, Congress cut about 20 percent from the administration request for SDI and expressed concern at the effects of the project on allied interests.

A key issue for 1985 and beyond will be the degree to which the administration is compelled to state clearly the real objectives and purpose of its missile defense programs. In the short term, a combination of matching Soviet efforts, the need for serious U.S. programs in a period of negotiation, and the generally conceded desirability of doing enough research to know what might be possible should be more than enough to secure substantially expanded spending on ballistic missile defense. But the issue of ultimate goals cannot be avoided entirely even at the initial stages.

Whatever the technical merits of less ambitious goals, President Reagan's advisers would face a major problem if they sought to persuade the most astute U.S. national politician in a generation to tailor his proclaimed goals to fit their view of technical feasibility. Politically the hope of population defense has immense public appeal, for it offers the prospect of a way out of the dilemma of deterring war by threat of mass holocaust. Hitherto, as a theory for a national policy to avoid nuclear war, deterrence has had to face competition only from the still less popular idea of trusting the Soviet Union to join in massive disarmament. SDI (sometimes called "Star Wars"), grandly conceived, holds out a hope of a third course. It is this hope, even if illusory, that gives the idea its political appeal.

Accordingly advocates of a serious commitment to missile defense face the problem that what is probably feasible technically—limited defense geared to a limited war theory—if honestly presented, is unlikely to prove sufficiently salable to Congress or the public to secure the vast funding and arms control uncertainties entailed. By contrast, what is politically popular—city defense—is almost certainly impossible technically for many, many years and in all probability forever. The administration seems likely to seek to straddle the issue: pointing to the hope of "assured survival" as the image toward which currently feasible efforts, first for research and then for limited defenses of ICBMs and other military targets, are merely necessary early stages.

Unless there is a revolution in technology, that hope will remain essentially impossible. And proclaiming an unrealistic objective for a fundamental part of U.S. strategic programs could carry profound dangers. Urging support for Star Wars by proclaiming the immorality of deterrence, or at least the moral imperative of supplementing it, is likely to prove shortsighted. Maintaining deterrence and stability in a world in which neither the Russians nor nuclear weapons will go away takes public willingness to accept a heavy dose of unpleasant reality, never an easy task. Holding out, even as an ultimate goal, the chimera of a technological defensive miracle to rescue us from the painful complications, costs, and contradictions of deterrence is, in its way, as dangerous as suggesting that it takes only Western goodwill to break through to a fundamental agreement with the Soviet Union that would rid humanity of the specter of nuclear war. Thus, an initiative, conceived in part as a way to deflect unrealistic hopes of agreements with the Soviet Union on simple, comprehensive solutions to the problems of deterrence, could well end up being turned on deterrence itself.

The question of whether deterrence will remain a viable policy (as well as whether there are any alternatives to it) is likely to remain an issue of debate, transcending questions of particular programs for many years to come. The traditional concepts of deterrence are under assault from both sides: on the one extreme from those who argue that active defenses provide a way out of the threat of retaliation as by the principal reliance for security and on the other from those who argue that deterrence is inherently unstable and only radical reorientation of U.S. foreign and arms control policies offers a hope of avoiding a nuclear war in the relatively near future.

Nuclear Winter

A development that attracted a good deal of public attention—and even a certain amount of rethinking of assumptions by experts—was the announcement in late 1983 of important new work on the nuclear winter effects of a large-scale nuclear war. The basic argument of this analysis was that a general nuclear exchange would not only produce terrible effects of immediate blast and lingering radiation but would also produce profound and long-lasting climatic effects, mostly because of fires set off by the initial detonations. The immense clouds of smoke and debris produced by a large-scale exchange would, the analysis predicted, generate a significant drop in temperature in the northern hemisphere, and possibly the southern as well, with immense effects on crop production and on any prospect for the survivors' reconstituting an enduring society.

As with any other projection of the effects of large-scale nuclear exchanges, the nuclear winter analysis depends on a series of uncertain and debatable assumptions, as well as the degree to which cities—the greatest source of fires—were attacked. One effect of the initial announcement was to stimulate a series of further analyses, some conducted by the U.S. government itself. Congress required a major study of the issue in the FY85 defense bill. An important issue was whether, as the initial reports claimed, these catastrophic effects would follow not only very large-scale exchanges using the bulk of the arsenals on both sides but also much smaller nuclear wars using something like a few hundred weapons per side.

The National Academy of Science published a report late in 1984, which while generally confirming the assessment that a major nuclear war would likely have profound climatological effects, underscored the uncertainties and unknowns associated with the issue. The conclusions, if any, of the internal DOD and Department of Energy studies intended to clarify the uncertainties will be some time in coming. The general tone seemed to be to take the problem seriously.

Overall Perspective

As in many years past, public debate over strategic programs during 1984 was more vociferous than the dollar cost of these programs justified. Relative to the overall defense budget, strategic forces absorb only a comparatively small percentage—10 to 20 percent, depending on how indirect costs are allocated. The big nuclear programs are publicly debated not only because of their individually very high prices but also because they are a symbol of policies the United States is following with respect to nuclear forces. It is easy to get lost in the details of the specific programs, their costs, and their alleged relative impact as enhancements or obstructions to negotiations and to stability. But the fundamental issue for public policy is why the United States possesses nuclear weapons and how well and how safely they carry out the critical missions assigned to them.

The stated U.S. policy under the current administration, as in the past, remains the deterrence of attack on the United States, its vital interests overseas, and those of its major allies. This objective is said to require not only an ability to retaliate on a very large scale against large attacks on the United States itself but to carry out smaller, more flexible responses to nuclear and, in principle, nonnuclear aggression. In particular, the United States continues to extend a nuclear guarantee to its NATO allies and to other countries as well.

In a sense, the most important development in 1984 was that deterrence was maintained for another year. That this should be so is scarcely a surprise. The United States maintains very large, very secure strategic forces. On a typical day, half the submarine force, say 18 submarines with almost 300 tubes and nearly 3,000 weapons, is at sea. Twenty to thirty percent of the B-52 and other strategic bombers are on alert, adding close to a thousand weapons. The 1,000 ICBMs, with more than 2,000 weapons, even in their now vulnerable silos, contribute to deterrence of a bolt-from-the-blue attack, if only because, as noted by the Scowcroft commission, it is extremely difficult to carry out a successful simultaneous attack on both bombers and ICBMs. Thus, nearly 6,000 weapons are in the alert force. (In a crisis, the level of alert could be significantly increased.)

While it is always possible to construct scenarios in which parts of this force are caught napping or events take place so quickly and so destructively that no decision to retaliate can be made or effectively transmitted to the force because of weaknesses in the communication system, it seems reasonable to conclude that the United States maintains a very high level of security even from a sudden all-out attack.

With respect to smaller attacks, U.S. forces, despite various weaknesses, would be able to carry out a range of limited attacks in response to a more limited aggression. There is, of course, a real question about the ability of such an exchange to be kept limited, but that is a different issue.

Considering the overall strategic balance, there has been relatively little change in four years. The total number of U.S. missile warheads and bomber weapons rose about 1,100 (due to commissioning of three new Trident submarines and deploying ALCMs on 90 B-52s); the Soviet number by about 800 (due to MIRVing of SLBMs). This left the United States with a weapon lead of some 3,000, up somewhat from four years before. The Soviets retained a lead of about three to two in their traditional area of advantage, throw weight, a rough measure of the destructive power of the force, even with bombers counted. In terms of launchers, the Soviet force was essentially unchanged, while the U.S. force declined by about 160, with additions of 72 Trident is offset by retirement of 22 older Titan II ICBMs, 79 B-52Ds, and 128 Polaris SLBMs. A summary of the strategic balance is portrayed in figure 4–1. Overall the effect of these changes was to leave the balance essentially unchanged. More important than the simple

Figure 4–1. Composition of U.S. and Soviet Forces, 1985

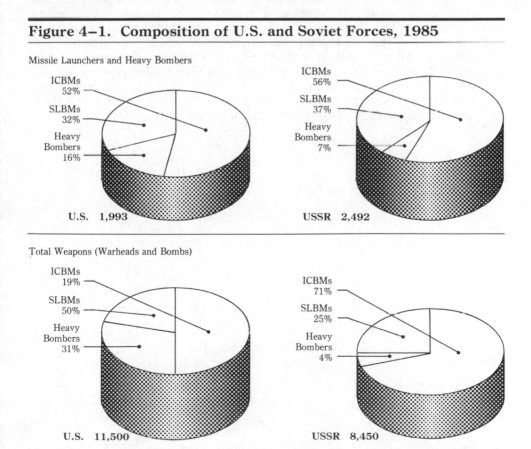

Missile Launchers and Heavy Bombers

ICBMs 52%
SLBMs 32%
Heavy Bombers 16%
U.S. 1,993

ICBMs 56%
SLBMs 37%
Heavy Bombers 7%
USSR 2,492

Total Weapons (Warheads and Bombs)

ICBMs 19%
SLBMs 50%
Heavy Bombers 31%
U.S. 11,500

ICBMs 71%
SLBMs 25%
Heavy Bombers 4%
USSR 8,450

numbers, nothing in the active buildup on the two sides during the last few years has changed the basic proposition that neither side could attack the other without risking a counterblow that would utterly destroy its society, economy, political structure, and military power.

U.S. strategy after four years—and indeed after nearly forty years of the nuclear era—remains in a state of flux. Formally U.S. policy remains based on traditional deterrence. But there are a variety of challenges and questions about that policy. The Reagan administration has dropped a good deal of its earlier rhetoric about prevailing in protracted nuclear war, even as it stresses the counterforce capability of MX and D-5 and searches, at least in its rhetoric, for a technically and politically viable concept of assured survival.

The public perspective is more complex. Traditional deterrence has never been well understood by the public. This is hardly suprising for it has many paradoxes and many contradictions to conventional military wisdom and even to common sense (except for the very basic idea that people, even those who lead the Soviet Union, are likely to avoid actions that will lead to the certain destruction of themselves and their state). Moreover, like all other strategies, deterrence depends on judgments and uncertainties. Poll data indicate that the public regards deterrence as unattractive in principle but effective in practice. Defenses are attractive in theory; there is in particular a typically American unwillingness to be too critical of the hope that technology will find a way out. Nonetheless, in the continuing debate, the public seems likely to remain fairly tolerant of the idea that drastic alterations in national strategy must offer improvements in stability and security, relative to current deterrence policies and that new doctrines that are attractive in principle must also be grounded in technical feasibility.

Chapter 5

Theater Forces: U.S. Defense Policy in NATO

James A. Thomson
Nanette C. Brown

The year 1984 closed on a positive note for U.S.-European relations and NATO. Initially the year was marked by increased tension over NATO conventional defense and burden sharing, but, with the conventional defense improvement package approved at NATO's Defense Planning Committee meeting in December 1984, the year ended in seeming alliance cohesion. Assistant Secretary of Defense Richard Perle described the session as "the most satisfying and most successful" in recent years.[1]

As in the past, U.S. policy in NATO was confronted by many political and military challenges. On the political front, the traditional American way of doing business with European allies was disrupted by both international and domestic pressures. In Europe, U.S. dominance of NATO decision making was brought into question by two issues: the revival of the once-dormant European defense organization, the West European Union (WEU), and increased Franco-German defense cooperation. In the United States, dissatisfaction with NATO's status quo and demands for increased European contributions to the common defense dominated the debate. As part of what seems almost a cyclical trend, Congress and other political actors sharply criticized the European allies for their unwillingness or inability to meet their defense commitments to NATO. Some within the United States favored dramatic structural changes in NATO, mostly focused on an increased and more cohesive European role in Europe's defense. In March, Henry Kissinger proposed that a European should be NATO's supreme allied commander and that Europeans have a greater voice in arms control forums in order to "reinvigorate allied cohesion by defining clear responsibilities for each side of the

Atlantic."[2] On a less radical but more important note, Senators Sam Nunn and William Cohen proposed to reduce the level of U.S. troops in Europe unless the Europeans moved to improve their defense capabilities, an idea reminiscent of Senator Mike Mansfield's proposed amendment in the late 1960s and early 1970s.

In addition to these challenges, U.S. policy in NATO was also confronted by a growing trend on both sides of the Atlantic to reduce reliance on nuclear weapons for deterrence of conventional attack. If 1983 was the Year of the Missile, then 1984 can be seen as the Year of the Conventional Defense Alternative. The initial deployment of Pershing II and GLCMs in Europe caused political leaders in both the United States and Europe to look for a way to reduce NATO's nuclear dependence and thus calm the political unrest that resulted from the Euromissile deployment. Conventional defense alternatives such as the various deep strike initiatives gained attention in the United States and Europe.

Europe's Place in U.S. Defense Planning

Despite a vigorous public debate about U.S. defense policy, the defense requirements set by recent U.S. administrations have stayed within a spending pattern established in the 1970s. This overall consistency in U.S. defense priorities is partly related to Western Europe's continued preeminent place in U.S. strategic priorities. Since World War II, Europe has been the main driver of U.S. defense planning because of the United States' historical preoccupation with containing Soviet power there. The U.S. strategic nuclear guarantee and the presence of U.S. forces have become an essential part of NATO's deterrent. This link between U.S. and European security has thus provided continuity for U.S. policy.

The most significant indication of the U.S. commitment to Europe is the presence of U.S. forces. Over the past decade, the United States has stationed the equivalent of five divisions in Europe as part of its overall commitment to NATO.[3] At present, it is second in size and combat capability only to the West German *Bundeswehr*. The United States currently maintains four army divisions, two separate brigades, two armored cavalry regiments, and twenty-eight air force squadrons in Europe.

In addition, the United States also contributes significantly to NATO's overall conventional and nuclear force. Figure 5–1 compares total quantities of NATO and Warsaw Pact conventional weapons systems deployed in Europe, indicating the U.S. contribution. Table 5–1 shows U.S. nuclear weapons in Europe. At the end of 1984 approximately 5,700 nuclear warheads were stationed there, although this figure was scheduled to be reduced by 1,400.

The U.S. defense commitment to Europe overshadows any other regional commitment. In budgetary as well as programmatic terms, the United States does more to protect against Soviet aggression in Europe than in the Middle East, Southeast Asia, or Central America. Despite the centrality of Europe in U.S. defense planning, a gradual broadening of U.S. strategic interests has occurred since World War II. Originally Western Europe was the United States' primary, if not sole, military and commercial focus. As the Soviet Union obtained the ability to project power to regions outside Europe and as U.S. commercial interests diversified, the U.S. list of priority interests grew. Thus, over the years, Europe's position has increasingly been challenged by the diversion of U.S. attention and resources to other regions.

During this period, each decade has brought its own set of challenges. In the late 1950s and 1960s, China and the possibility of a Sino-Soviet pact threatened

U.S. interests and security. To adjust to this threat, the United States adopted a conventional strategy and force structure based on a two-and-a-half war theory: having the ability to deal simultaneously with a European war, a war in Asia, and

Figure 5–1. U.S./NATO–Warsaw Pact Conventional Force Comparison, 1985

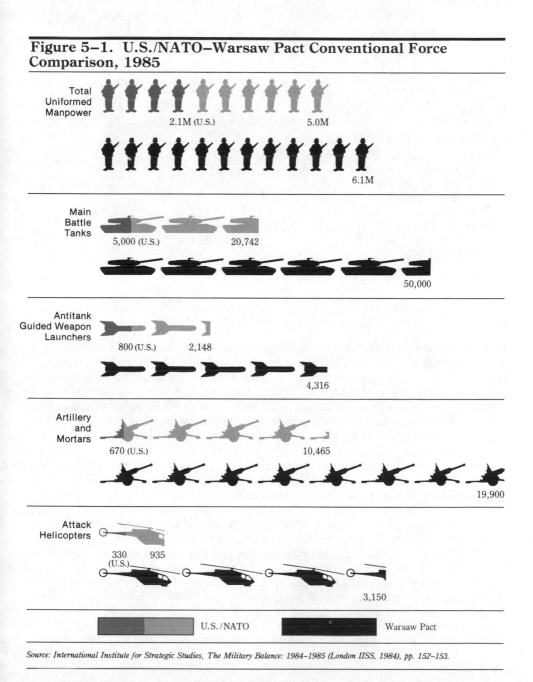

Total Uniformed Manpower: 2.1M (U.S.), 5.0M, 6.1M

Main Battle Tanks: 5,000 (U.S.), 20,742, 50,000

Antitank Guided Weapon Launchers: 800 (U.S.), 2,148, 4,316

Artillery and Mortars: 670 (U.S.), 10,465, 19,900

Attack Helicopters: 330 (U.S.), 935, 3,150

U.S./NATO   Warsaw Pact

Source: International Institute for Strategic Studies, The Military Balance: 1984–1985 (London IISS, 1984), pp. 152–153.

Table 5–1. Nonstrategic Nuclear Force Warheads, 1984

Weapon (Warhead)	United States	Europe U.S. Use	Europe NATO Use
GLCM/Pershing II (W-84, W-85)		150	
Bombs (B-28,B43,B-57,B-61)	1,210	1,415	320
Depth bombs (B-57)	560	130	60
Pershing IA (W-50)		180	100
Lance (W-70)	587	325	370
8-inch artillery (W-33,W-79)	500	505	430
155mm artillery (W-48)	160	592	140
Honest John			200
Nike Hercules (W-31)		110	390
Atomic demolition munitions (W-45,W-54)	220	370	
Terrier (W-45)	64		
ASROC (W-44)	224		
SUBROC (W-55)	110		
Total	3,635	3,777	2,010

Source: William Arkin, Thomas Cochran, and Milton Hoenig, "Resource Paper on the U.S. Nuclear Arsenal," *The Bulletin of the Atomic Scientists* 40 (August–September 1984):10s. Copyright © 1984 by the Educational Foundation for Nuclear Science. Reprinted by permission.

a minor contingency elsewhere. Although following the Sino-Soviet split and the U.S. recognition of China, the United States redefined its planning strategy to a one-and-a-half war strategy—preparing for a European war and a minor contingency elsewhere—the Vietnam war was a drain on U.S. defense personnel and resources, including those in Europe. The high costs involved in fighting that war caused many force improvement programs oriented toward NATO, proposed or approved in the 1960s to be postponed until well into the 1970s.

Following the withdrawal of U.S. forces from Vietnam, the United States intended to refocus its attention on Europe. However, the theme of the Year of Europe in 1973 was quickly forgotten as U.S. attention was drawn toward the Middle East and Southwest Asia, first by the 1973 Arab-Israeli War and later by the revolution in Iran. The identification of this region as a U.S. military problem ultimately resulted in a significant planning change in 1979–1980: the development of the rapid deployment force (RDF) to provide the means to carry out missions there.

This trend affected U.S. forces committed to Europe because the growth in military commitments was not matched by a proportional increase in the size of the overall defense budget. The problem became one of allocating limited resources to more commitments and caused the European share of the defense pie to be reduced. In order to minimize the negative effects of this trend, most U.S. administrations were careful to pursue a strong European policy as well. For example, the Carter administration balanced its Southwest Asia interests and its RDF initiative with one of the largest force improvement initiatives for NATO, the long-term defense program. Thus, until the end of 1980, Europe's position was not significantly threatened by other U.S. strategic interests.

The Reagan administration marks a milestone in the trend toward broadened U.S. strategic interests. This administration's strategic outlook has caused defense resources to be spread even more widely. As described in Secretary Weinberger's FY83 annual statement to Congress, "Our long-term goal is to be able to meet the demands of worldwide war, including *concurrent* [emphasis added] reinforcement of Europe, deployment to Southwest Asia, and support in other potential areas of conflict."[4] The set of priorities also now includes reestablishing, in the administration's view, U.S.-Soviet strategic parity, preparing for Soviet threats outside Europe (particularly in Southwest Asia), coping with communist threats in the Western Hemisphere, and establishing new military and commercial policies in the Pacific region.

As a result of the administration's interest in planning for multiple contingencies, U.S. defense policy toward NATO has been affected in two ways. First, although Europe is still the central focus for defense planning, the defense budget emphasizes force improvements not directly linked to Europe. For example, many strategic programs, such as the B-1B and the MX, have been revived or accelerated. In addition, among the three services only the Navy, with its 600 ship goal, will see any significant growth in force structure in the coming years.[5] Second, an apparent casting about for new strategies for Europe is occurring. With this search has come renewed debate about horizontal escalation, reducing NATO's nuclear reliance, and conventional defense alternatives.

1984 in Perspective

As the Reagan administration enters its second term, it is possible to see two significant implications of these patterns: the administration has initiated a limited number of weapon programs directly related to U.S. forces in Europe, and the search for new strategies has caused confusion regarding U.S. policy toward defense improvements in NATO, both at home and in Europe.

The Reagan administration took office in 1981 with the primary defense objective to "correct the major weaknesses in our defenses that have resulted from a decade of neglect." To meet this goal, it immediately and substantially increased defense spending. This trend culminated in the FY85 proposal that sought defense budget authority of $305 billion, an increase of $46.8 billion from the total Congress approved for FY84. After adjusting for inflation, the request represented a 13 percent increase. The overall real increase in defense spending has resulted in significant gains in all areas of the U.S. defense program, including funds for programs directed for U.S. European forces.

Perhaps the only area for which this has not been true is land-based, nonstrategic nuclear forces for Europe. Although U.S. and West European governments are continuing the Pershing II and GLCM deployments, neither side is anxious to rekindle the nuclear weapons controversy with further nuclear modernization programs.[6] Thus, any needed nuclear improvements, such as modernization of short-range forces, will probably not be considered in the near future.

As a result of the political stalemate in theater nuclear modernization, the Reagan administration has emphasized conventional force improvements, specifically in the areas of readiness, sustainability, and force modernization. Among the programs currently underway, the effectiveness of U.S. forces in Europe has been augmented by an increase in strategic lift capability to reinforce U.S. troops more rapidly and by an expansion of the U.S. strategic reserve force. The NATO Infrastructure Program signed in 1984 will help in solving, among other things, the long-recognized problems of lack of aircraft shelters.

Other conventional force modernization programs also had an impressive year in 1984. The Reagan administration boosted funding for the M-1 Abrams tank, the Bradley fighting vehicle, antitank weaponry, various attack helicopters, short- and long-range air defense systems, and advanced tactical air fighters. Despite the emphasis placed on conventional force modernization in 1984, the major weapons now being procured are extensions of previous programs. In looking to the future, the Reagan administration has sought to engage European allies in joint ventures aimed at shoring up conventional defense with new weapons programs.

The new conventional defense initiatives that have emerged in the past four years suggest important programmatic and doctrinal changes for NATO. Among the most prominent are the Emerging Technologies Initiative, Follow-On Force Attack, AirLand Battle (and its futuristic progeny, AirLand Battle 2000), and Counter-Air 90. All of these proposals bear a U.S. stamp. While many of them were introduced in 1981–1982, they received renewed attention in 1984 as a result of growing political interest in improved conventional defense.

All of these initiatives are generally grouped together under the conventional deep strike defense concept. The term *deep strike* has come to describe different methods that NATO could employ to attack and thus destroy, disrupt, and delay the Soviet–Warsaw Pact second-echelon forces moving toward the line of battle. These alternatives focus on NATO's inability to stop the reinforcement of Warsaw Pact troops and not the problem of holding the initial pact thrust. The solution to this problem, as prescribed by the initiatives, is to exploit the West's technological superiority to offset the Warsaw Pact's superiority in conventional forces.

Among the four, the Emerging Technologies (ET) Initiative is the broadest, for it is a grab-bag of technologies that the other initiatives can draw upon. It was first suggested in May 1982 at a NATO summit meeting in Bonn. Subsequent ET studies build upon modern technology—for target acquisition, situation assessment, precision guidance, and munition lethality.[7]

Follow-On Force Attack (FOFA) and AirLand Battle (ALB) provide different doctrinal guidelines for the employment of these advanced technologies. FOFA is a concept developed at Supreme Headquarters, Allied Powers Europe (SHAPE), in the early 1980s under the direction of General Bernard Rogers. His interest was in constructing a method to target Warsaw Pact follow-on forces throughout the depth of pact territory with highly accurate conventional weapons. By 1981, the Army had already been moving in a similar direction with its adoption of the ALB doctrine. ALB is current U.S. Army doctrine that extends the battlefield by advocating aggressive use by corps commanders of deep strike operations. ALB 2000 is different; it is a futuristic projection of army needs in the year 2000 and beyond. Thus it draws on even more unproved technologies and asserts bold ideas on how to win the war.

Counter-Air 90 (CA 90), although not technically a deep strike concept, is often associated with ET, FOFA, and ALB/ALB 2000. Unlike the other deep strike concepts that emphasize attacking second-echelon forces, CA 90 focuses on improving the survivability of NATO's air forces. It includes a package of defensive initiatives aimed at blunting the effect of Warsaw Pact missile and air attacks on NATO air bases, as well as offensive programs. For the latter, CA 90 calls for the deployment of conventionally armed ballistic missiles to attack Warsaw Pact airfields. It is this offensive component that allows CA 90 to be considered a deep strike initiative.

All of the initiatives have been criticized on the basis of concept and technology. A number of objections have been made by U.S. allies, among them that deep strike would appear offensive and would be interpreted by the Soviet Union as a nuclear attack. It would be seen as shifting NATO's attention away from the modernization of existing forces to launching costly new weapons programs. In addition, the political costs of changing NATO's doctrine or placing more weapons in Europe are also seen as high. Referring to the proposed ballistic missiles for CA 90, General Billy Minter of the U.S. Air Force commented, "With all the trouble we're having getting a 1,600-lb. missile into the theater, what kind of trouble do you think we're going to have getting 200,000-lb. missiles in here?"[8] Finally, these problems are compounded by the question of who will develop the advanced technologies. Western Europe feels itself falling further behind the Americans and Japanese in technology. Given past failures to build a two-way street between the United States and Europe, these initiatives appear to many Europeans as bearing the "buy American" stamp.

The concern within NATO over the various deep strike initiatives has also been heightened by the president's SDI. As part of the larger investigation to develop defenses for the United States, both the White House and the Pentagon have suggested a similar program for Europe. While little serious programmatic work has been done on how to defend Western Europe as part of the SDI program, the U.S. government has assured the Europeans that they will not be forgotten. These reassurances have not quelled overwhelming European objections, and it is likely that SDI will continue to be a topic of alliance debate.

Prospects

Thus, NATO enters 1985 with a number of competing conventional defense initiatives. While a political consensus exists that NATO should do more toward improving its conventional defense capabilities, there are divisions over how to accomplish that goal. The United States, despite its dominant position, cannot decide unilaterally this important issue. Because the European allies provide the bulk of ready forces, inevitably it will be addressed as an alliance issue.

The numerous initiatives for improving NATO's conventional defenses and the heightened political expectations left by the conventional defense debate of 1983 and 1984 raise the question of how the United States and its NATO allies will address the long agenda. Three broad approaches have been under discussion. The first is substantial increases in U.S. and NATO defense resources to accommodate the agenda. General Bernard Rogers's suggestion of 4 percent real growth in NATO defense spending might also fit this category. Second is the emergence of a strong independent European defense effort, an idea that was near the top of the European political agenda in 1984. The third approach is efforts within NATO to make difficult choices about which improvements should be given priority.

Defense Resources

The route of increased NATO defense resources appears to be closed, at least in the short term. As 1984 ended, the ever-present mismatch between defense requirements and available resources was growing in NATO. Political pressures on the U.S. defense budget combined with the already large procurement agenda to pose more difficult programmatic choices than in previous years. In this sense, the United States began to experience the same resource pressures that its allies felt over the previous four years.

Clearly the Pentagon will have to settle for less growth than it had been requesting. Although the political debate over defense spending cuts intensified after the 1984 presidential election, the Pentagon had already seen its budget requests slashed by Congress in the previous three fiscal years; Congress tended to cut in half the more than 10 percent real growth requested by the president. For a time, it appeared that a national consensus had formed around 5 percent, but in the face of continued projected large deficits, even this consensus began to unravel.

Thus the Pentagon will face increasingly difficult choices in the areas of defense investment—research and development, procurement, and construction. These categories of defense spending contain the key programs oriented toward NATO conventional force improvements. These effects could be offset, of course, if U.S. allies in Europe begin to increase their defense efforts and satisfy the growing congressional demands for European action. This seems unlikely. The European economic recovery was not so robust as that of the United States, and European governments have been less willing than the Reagan administration to make resource trade-offs between social welfare and defense spending. Far more than in the United States, both categories are seen as essential components of national security.

Consequently European defense budget growth has fallen behind that of the United States. The NATO goal of 3 percent real budget growth, established in 1977, has been ritually repeated in NATO communiqués since but openly ignored by some European governments recently. For example, in 1983 (the last year for which NATO data are available), European defense spending grew by only 2 percent in real terms, while U.S. defense spending grew by nearly 8 percent (see table 5–2).

This decline has occurred in the face of political changes in Europe that seemed at the time to portend increased European defense spending. In both Britain and Germany, in 1979 and 1982, respectively, parties came to power that were committed to substantial defense increases while out of power. Despite Britain's economic woes, Margaret Thatcher's government boosted defense spending during the early 1980s, but now the Thatcher government has said that Britain will no longer meet the NATO 3 percent goal.[9] By the same token, Chancellor Helmut Kohl's Christian Democratic Union leveled heavy criticism at the defense efforts of the Schmidt government before its fall in 1982. But the Kohl government has had little effect on the growth rate of German defense spending, which, if anything, is declining.

German ability to devote more funds to defense, especially in defense investment, will be further circumscribed as Germany comes to grips with its looming manpower shortage. The declining cohort of draft-age youths is projected to cause a shortage of 104,000 out of the needed 252,000 draftees in the *Bundeswehr* by 1990

Table 5–2. Real Increases in NATO Defense Outlays

	1980	1981	1982	1983
Belgium	1.9%	0.9%	-3.3%	-3.0%
Canada	5.1	3.1	4.9	5.0
Denmark	0.7	0.6	-0.3	-0.2
Germany	2.3	3.2	-0.8	1.9
Greece	-9.4	22.8	0.1	1.3
Italy	4.9	-0.5	3.2	1.1
Luxembourg	16.3	4.8	3.9	3.5
Netherlands	1.8	2.7	4.1	2.8
Norway	1.8	2.7	4.1	2.8
Portugal	6.0	0.9	0.5	0.4
Turkey	2.0	1.8	4.6	1.9
United Kingdom	2.8	1.4	6.4	3.0
United States	4.9	4.7	7.6	7.6
Non-U.S. NATO total	2.6	2.8	2.3	1.9/2.1
NATO total	4.0	4.0	5.7	5.6/5.7

Source: Department of Defense, *Report on the Allied Contributions to Common Defense* (1984) as cited in William Drozdiak, "Conventional Buildup Troubling NATO," *Washington Post*, November 21, 1984, p. 9.

Note: Percentage change from previous year in constant prices (excluding inflation).

unless remedial steps are taken soon. Although Defense Minister Manfred Woerner suggested some steps in October 1985, including lengthening the period of military service for draftees from fifteen to eighteen months, these have not been approved and in any event would not come cost free. The manpower problem will thus combine with a recognized crisis in German defense investment. Procurement of the current generation of weapons, such as the Tornado aircraft and Leopard II tank, is already straining the defense budget. There is no room for the new NATO conventional initiatives. As a result of the twin manpower and procurement crises, German armed forces may begin to shrink in the late 1980s and early 1990s.

Almost regardless of the politics of the parties in power, European defense growth will probably continue to be restricted. Europe's economic prospects are not as bright as those of the United States and Japan. As the experience of the Kohl government in West Germany shows, the commitment to social welfare as a key component of national security is not tied to a single political party or bloc but is a historical, social, and cultural fact. Given this situation, a report by Karsten Voight, foreign affairs spokesman for West Germany's Social Democratic party, predicts European defense spending growth of around 1 percent through 1990.[10]

European Defense Cooperation

Both the United States and its European allies have supported increased European defense cooperation from the beginning of NATO. Little progress has been made, largely because of conflicting interests among the European countries. Recently, however, the issue of Europeanization of defense has moved to the forefront of the European political debate.

There were two principal aspects to this development: Franco-German defense cooperation and the revitalization of the WEU. One impetus for this development included long-standing European unhappiness with U.S. dominance of the defense market, but the chief driving force was the perceived need among European governments to reduce the appearance of Europe's overwhelming reliance on the United States for defense in the aftermath of the INF controversy. A reduction in this reliance would be welcome; a stronger European partner would be a more efficient provider of defense and could bear more of the defense burden. The key question, however, is whether the current initiatives are likely to bring about either of these results in time to affect the agenda NATO now faces. The answer seems to be that achievement of these results is a distant prospect, at best.

Franco-German cooperation probably has the better chance of making progress. Although the two countries have cooperated closely in a number of areas for years, serious discussions of defense cooperation began only when President Francois Mitterand and Chancellor Kohl promoted them in 1982. Now French and German foreign and defense ministers meet twice a year to discuss security matters, with the agendas prepared by bilateral working groups composed of high officials from both countries.

The original French motive for opening these discussions has receded, however. In 1982, French officials were deeply worried that the INF debate in the Federal Republic meant that Germany was drifting away from the Atlantic alliance into a kind of neutralism. With the Kohl government's successful management of the 1983 INF crisis, France has turned its attention to long-standing French economic and commercial interests in cooperative research, development, and production in the armaments field.

While France has increasingly focused on the economic and commercial agenda, West Germany sees Franco-German cooperation in strategic terms. The Germans hope to induce France to closer military cooperation with Germany and with NATO, in both the conventional and nuclear fields. In particular, they hope to secure a stronger French commitment to early engagement in the forward defense of the central front. From this German perspective, the recent agreement to develop jointly an attack helicopter will provide the new French *force d'action rapide* with the means to reinforce the central front quickly.

The helicopter agreement notwithstanding, the West Germans have reservations about cooperation with France in armaments. The Germans regard French nationalized industry as inefficient and are wary of French efforts to gain a disproportionate share of the economic benefits generated by such projects. More important, West German industry has strong interests in cooperating with the United States in order to gain access to U.S. technology and know-how. Such concerns have contributed to German reluctance to join France in its proposed joint development of a reconnaissance satellite.

France has reservations about Germany's agenda too. Because French nuclear forces are the political symbol of France's independence and special global status, it is unlikely that France will agree to any significant cooperation in that arena. With its pro-NATO leanings, the Mitterand government would probably be inclined to cooperate more closely on conventional defense, but even here, French domestic politics would still apply a strong brake. The legacy of Charles de Gaulle—his strong emphasis on French independence and his decision to withdraw from NATO's integrated military structure—has been internalized in French domestic politics. Any politician seen moving back toward NATO would risk adverse political consequences.

Thus, progress in Franco-German defense cooperation is likely to be long term and incremental. Not only do both countries have somewhat different objectives, but they are also nervous that European defense cooperation might be interpreted as antagonistic toward the United States and thus might fuel rather than assuage U.S. domestic political pressures for troop reductions.

If progress in Franco-German defense cooperation will be slow and incremental, the same will certainly be true of the revitalization of the WEU. The French have been the main architects of this effort, which they have seen chiefly as a way to pursue their arms cooperation agenda in a European framework outside NATO. Both France and Germany saw the WEU as a way to wrap their bilateral cooperation in a wider political blanket.

The other five WEU members—Britain, Italy, and the Benelux countries—went along with the French initiative with varying degrees of enthusiasm. Italy was most interested, primarily because it hoped for a larger role in European arms production. The Benelux countries saw the WEU as a way to ensure that they were not left out of the Europeanization process. With its special position and relationship to the United States, Britain was most skeptical but was also concerned about being excluded.

The result has been a good deal of political activity associated with the WEU but little of substance. At an October 1984 meeting, the WEU foreign and defense ministers agreed to some organizational changes, including the revival of a defunct defense consultative group. They pledged to meet twice annually to discuss a range of security issues, including arms control. But the principal focus of the WEU's work will be the development of an "effective and competitive European arms industry." Whether this will amount to anything, after all earlier efforts have failed, is doubtful.

Setting NATO Priorities

With prospects for substantial defense resource growth or the emergence of a strong independent European defense effort bleak, the United States will have to work within NATO to shape a priority action program. Unfortunately neither the United States nor NATO has a good track record in setting and holding to priorities.

The NATO force planning process creates a six-year multilateral program on a two-year cycle. It is not a true multilateral process, however, but rather a collection of processes in which the national programs are combined into a NATO program, and the resulting seem more or less rubber stamped by the NATO authorities. No clear priorities are set. NATO has no ability to enforce the program, aside perhaps from the grumbling of NATO's military commanders.

It is easy to lay the failure to set priorities at NATO's door, but the problem stems from the United States. After all, as the dominant voice in the alliance, the United States could, if it wished, shape the NATO agenda. The United States obviously does this; it is the source of the many initiatives now on the table. Yet it rarely enunciates priorities to its allies, telling them what it would like to see done and not done. Indeed this is the current situation. The Pentagon's legendary inability to set priorities within and among the services is the reason that the United States comes forward with long lists of required programs. The United States must address this problem before too much blame is heaped on NATO.

With a long menu of potential conventional force improvement actions and a small amount of discretionary funds to address those actions, priorities are what the United States and NATO need now.

Priorities

An understanding of priorities ought to stem from an appreciation of NATO's current strategic situation—that is, the current balance of forces.[11] Then proposed improvements can be tested against the balance to see which yield the greatest benefit to NATO, and thus a rough idea of priorities can be constructed.

U.S. assessments of the force balance examine a wide spectrum of potential military campaigns in the central front, encompassing a variety of different but plausible assumptions about conflict initiation and the performance of military forces in conflict. Such analyses are richer from the standpoint of understanding the balance of forces than the traditional balance assessments, which often simply tote up weapons counts in various categories. This sort of analysis can identify situations in which NATO's forward defense would collapse catastrophically. These are the cases we are interested in, for at the top of our priority list ought to be measures to avoid catastrophic collapse.

We summarize the main points of our assessment as follows: If NATO can obtain and make reasonable use of strategic warning, can resupply its forces without serious interruption, and can survive the "Day-1" air battle, then the outnumbered NATO front line has a reasonable chance of conducting a successful forward defense.[12] A successful forward defense means that a Warsaw Pact attack grinds to a halt without a serious penetration of the forward defense area. If forward defense is successful, then Soviet concern for internal security in Eastern Europe and even in its homeland should grow. These concerns can become objects for NATO military or political action, potentially opening the way for termination of the war on NATO terms. If the Soviets see such a situation, they ought to be deterred.

In the three "if" statements and the "reasonable chance" lie the priorities for force improvements. The gaining and use of warning is potentially the most important if clause, for warning provides time for many of the essentials of a successful forward defense: the forward deployment of forces, the organization of prepared defenses, the mobilization of rear area security, and the deployment of combat aircraft from the United States. Steps that increase the chances of obtaining warning information, increase the likelihood of political decisions to react to the information, or decrease reliance on warning should have the highest priority.

The first category includes all means of intelligence, especially of the Warsaw Pact force readiness and disposition, the most tangible indication of war preparation. Programs that help collect information of ground force dispositions will be helpful. The more crucial problem is the analysis of the numerous pieces of information likely to be available in a crisis into a coherent picture of evolving Warsaw

Pact capabilities. In recent years, U.S. programs in this area of situation assessment have suffered technical and financial setbacks, although work continues under the Joint Tactical Fusion Program.

The second category includes politically sustainable options for reacting to ambiguous warning signals so that NATO can ratchet up its readiness in step with changes in the Warsaw Pact posture. Reportedly the Reagan administration has given greater emphasis to the development of these options.

The final category is probably the most important of the three. It includes such steps as modest peacetime defense preparations (strong points, barriers to inhibit maneuver) and redeployment of some of NATO's malpositioned brigades. It also requires a high level of day-to-day staffing of the forward defense forces so that they do not rely unduly on mobilization or postmobilization training; however, significant permanent fortifications have been ruled out by West Germany on political grounds. And although NATO has made some progress in capabilities to construct barriers rapidly in a crisis and in the deployment of scatterable mines that provide greater ability to delay or channel the movement of enemy forces, this area has traditionally been at the short end of the funding stick. Germany has moved slowly on U.S. proposals to restation some badly maldeployed units because the necessary real estate is not available. While U.S. combat units are maintained at high levels of manning, many allied units, especially Benelux forces, have significant peacetime shortages.

The second if clause refers to the sustainability of the NATO forces—both the availability of material and the ability to get it to the forces that need it. If NATO forces do well in the first few days of a forward defense only then to have to ration ammunition, the defense will collapse. The need to sustain forces has long been a tenet of both U.S. and NATO defense planning. U.S. allies, however, have historically not invested in sustainability to the same degree as the United States, apparently with the view that any major conflict would quickly become nuclear (and, in this view, quickly end). The result has been a growing concern in the United States that European forces have many logistical shortages, especially in the more advanced (and more costly) conventional munitions.[13] Fortunately, both U.S. and NATO authorities, including the new NATO secretary-general, Lord Carrington, have turned their attention to the sustainability matter.

Another feature of sustainability is the ability to get supplies to the forces. This means that NATO rear areas need to be kept relatively secure. Territorial defense forces, such as the German Territorial Army, and beefed-up local security are needed to thwart Soviet special operations attacks against supply depots-points and lines of communications. Most of these NATO forces depend heavily on warning time to mobilize. In addition, air superiority is needed over NATO's rear area. NATO needs to win the "Day 1" air battle to accomplish this.

The third if clause reflects the growing Warsaw Pact threat to NATO's air forces, which have two vital jobs in the conduct of forward defense: air superiority is needed over the NATO rear area for the security of the resupply operation, and NATO's air forces can help make up (though not overcome) the Warsaw Pact's numerical ground force superiority; NATO air forces have a superior ability to destroy ground forces. Both of these jobs are threatened by Soviet plans to mount a multiwave air assault on NATO air bases at the outset of conflict. The modernization of pact air forces over the past decade, particularly through the increase in ground attack capability, has made this threat of greater concern. The threat may increase if modern Soviet ground-based missiles obtain improved conventional munitions or are able to conduct chemical attacks. The former can be used to pin in NATO's air defense aircraft by attacking runways and opening the way for an annihilation of NATO's air forces on the ground with follow-on waves of air attacks. The latter can substantially degrade NATO's ability to generate sorties by forcing support personnel to operate in protective gear. With their so-called counterdeployments of SS-21s, -22s, and -23s (counters to the Pershing II and GLCM), the Soviets have begun the process. It is only a matter of time until they obtain the requisite delivery accuracy for this capability.

Although the threat is growing, it can be counteracted in a number of ways. The construction of several additional takeoff and landing strips on NATO air bases can multiply the aim points the Soviet missiles must attack, thus raising the cost of a successful attack; an alert posture for conventional fighter aircraft (similar to NATO's nuclear aircraft alert posture) can help ensure that NATO gets its fighters in the air before pin-in attacks arrive; and more aircraft shelters or, absent those, more sensible parking of unsheltered aircraft can substantially reduce the effectiveness of Soviet air bases attacks. Most of these steps, however, are not included in current programs or in the CA 90 initiative. The primary one—aircraft shelters—faced difficulty in obtaining the needed funds from the U.S. Congress and from the NATO Infrastructure Program until the December 1984 agreement to boost the NATO Infrastructure budget. Passive measures in the chemical arena, such as planned improved detection equipment and protective gear, can also reduce the effect of Soviet chemical attacks on air bases.

If NATO's air forces can survive the initial Soviet air attack, they can undertake their own counterair operation against Soviet air bases, as suggested in the CA 90 initiative. Currently NATO's air forces must penetrate Warsaw Pact air space all the way to the targets and then deliver relatively ineffective "dumb" munitions. How to improve counterair capability has become a matter of substantial debate in the West with advocates of ground-based ballistic missiles on one side and those who prefer improved air-delivered, precision-guided munitions with standoff capability on the other side.[14] Because NATO already has these aircraft in its inventory, the latter is likely to be the more cost-effective approach. At the end of 1984 the debate continued, and neither capability was yet programmed.

If the West could feel more certain about the three if clauses, it could turn to the question of the "reasonable chance." Even with the if clauses, this remains a chance, not a certainty. The sheer weight of a multiecheloned Warsaw Pact ground force attack could still wear down NATO's front line and achieve a penetration. If exploitation of the penetration were successful, NATO's forward defense could collapse catastrophically; West Germany has little strategic depth. Soviet operations aimed at strategic objectives along the Rhine could divide NATO forces and conceivably knock West Germany out of the war. Soviet operational groups on the loose in NATO's rear could disrupt or cut the resupply operation and lead to the collapse of the forward defense.

This specter has been the impetus to the development of many of the so-called deep strike NATO initiatives, specifically those like General Rogers's FOFA that aim to prevent or delay the advance of Warsaw Pact follow-on (or second-echelon) forces. These fresh reinforcing forces pose the threat of wearing down the NATO forward defense. Under this concept, Soviet mobile forces would be detected behind the battle line and struck with ground- or air-launched missiles.

Much has already been said and written about deep strike.[15] Recently such analysts as Steven Canby have raised serious issues of cost and operational effectiveness—that it may cost an order of magnitude more than estimated by the advocates and still not work or be easily overcome by cheap Soviet countermeasures.[16]

The uncertainties associated with this concept raise the question of whether it is the best way of preventing a successful exploitation of a Warsaw Pact breakthrough. One of the reasons for concern about exploitation is the shortage of NATO's operational reserves—forces that can be held out of the main battle and committed when needed for counterbreakthrough or other operations.

An alternative approach to the various deep strike concepts would guard against the exploitation of penetrations by increasing NATO's operational reserves. The addition of French forces to the operational reserve of the Supreme Allied Commander in Europe (SACEUR) would help a great deal, but they are not committed to NATO and thus SACEUR cannot count on them. Since the additional forces would not be initially committed to the forward defense, they can rely more on the mobilization of manpower than the forward defense forces and might even be cadre units in peacetime. Robert Komer has suggested that twelve additional allied reserve brigades (or four equivalent divisions) would substantially raise the chances of a successful forward defense.[17]

Such force structure additions would not be cheap or easy to develop. Komer gives an estimate of $3 billion to $4 billion for investment. Twice that is probably closer to the mark (at $2 billion per armored or mechanized infantry division). Cost would be lower for infantry divisions, but those are not appropriate for the counterattack role. Moreover, the burden of these additional forces would have to fall on the Federal Republic of Germany. Even if these forces could be maintained at a cadre strength, the additional manpower needs would run smack into the impending German manpower shortage.

Obviously it would be preferable to buy both the deep strike capability and operational reserves, but one must be placed above the other in a priority ranking. In this context, operational reserves are preferable because the military value of ground force formations is reasonably well understood and certain. By comparison, the military value of deep strike systems may be questionable because of the associated technological uncertainties. Moreover, the deep strike systems must be able to destroy far more Warsaw Pact divisions than the number of additional NATO operational reserves needed to achieve the same military effect.[18]

Other questions could and have been raised about the various deep strike concepts. These concepts are not new but are variations on air interdiction strategies that air forces have planned since the advent of air power. Concepts such as FOFA seek to extend the range of interdiction operations deep into the enemy's rear by the application of new technologies that can see and then shoot at ground formations with great accuracy. The technological challenge and organizational complexity of operations over such an expanse of terrain have contributed to criticism of the deep strike concepts. Alternative concepts that are not so technically or operationally challenging include the so-called interdiction belt. With this interdiction strategy, aerial bombardment, delivered by aircraft and ballistic missiles, would be directed against lines of communications and forces in a narrow zone directly behind the front lines. Preliminary studies indicate that this concept, which does not rely on the sophisticated intelligence required by FOFA, is feasible with some modest expansion of NATO Air Force capabilities.

In any case, the priority choice between operational reserves and the deep strike concepts is complicated by its multinational nature. In the main, the United States controls the technology associated with deep strike, and the United States is likely to buy some of it, if only to modernize its interdiction capabilities. The ground force formations associated with operational reserves must come from U.S. allies, Germany in particular. Although the Federal Republic has made strides in recent years in increasing the capability of the combat formations in its Territorial Army, continued progress is doubtful because of the fiscal and manpower constraints.

Yet even with the if clauses addressed and improvements made in the areas of operational reserves or deep strike, NATO would still not have a certain conventional defense capability. Thus, nuclear capability would still be needed for deterring a conventional Soviet assault.[19]

Conclusions

In the coming decade, NATO will increasingly face important decisions regarding how to improve its conventional defense capabilities. A beginning has been made. In 1984 the United States proposed alternative initiatives for reducing NATO's reliance on nuclear weapons for deterring conventional Warsaw Pact attacks. In 1985, U.S. and European officials must begin to sort out the various proposals in order to start designing a concrete program for conventional improvements for NATO. In constructing such a program, however, NATO decision makers will inevitably find that requirements are in excess of available defense resources. This mismatch of resources and strategy will mean difficult choices.

Three alternative methods to solve this problem were considered in this chapter: increased defense spending, greater European cooperation, and establishment of defense priorities. In the near future, it is unlikely that the first two alternatives can occur. Both the United States and Western Europe are currently operating on constrained defense budgets, and cuts in some cases seem more likely than increases. Also despite the political momentum surrounding the Europeanization of defense, increased European defense cooperation is unlikely to bring about an increased European defense effort. Thus, the U.S. and NATO must do more toward establishing a system of priorities.

Historically, this has not been an easy task within NATO, largely because the United States itself is unable to suggest priorities. Our analysis indicates that the best way to do this is to identify the necessary military means to avoid early catastrophic defeat. The possibility of early NATO defeat could provide the Soviets with great political and psychological leverage over NATO, and the West Europeans in particular. In the coming years, NATO could reduce the likelihood of this prospect by emphasizing improvements in three areas: reduction of reliance on warning time, greater sustainability, and improved air base survivability. The recommendations laid out in this chapter are within reach of NATO resources and could assist in meeting NATO's first priority requirement.

Of second importance to defense planners is providing NATO forces with the means to stop the Warsaw Pact's massive follow-on forces from overrunning West European territory. This problem has been the chief preoccupation in the current debate over conventional defense improvements. The deep strike initiatives seek to destroy these forces before they can reach the forward battle. However, according to our analysis, it might be better for NATO to increase the number of operational reserves because of the great strategic and technological uncertainties associated with the deep strike concept.

In 1984, U.S. policy in NATO focused on one part of the priority issue: stopping the overrun of NATO territory through alternative deep strike tactics. In addition to the political and military problems associated with initiatives such as FOFA and ET is the problem that such a U.S. policy focuses on only one aspect of a two-part problem. Thus, the United States and NATO must establish priorities and cope with the highest priority first. Without redirection, NATO could be planning to fight the second battle without having prepared itself to win the first.

Chapter 6

Seapower and Projection Forces

Harlan K. Ullman
R. James Woolsey

O f the many complex defense and security issues facing the United States,
two challenges have proved particularly vexing. Both are relevant to the
entire U.S. force posture but are particularly pertinent to U.S. seapower
and projection forces.The first issue concerns the division between nuclear and
nonnuclear forces and the manner in which this division influences the choice between strategies that seek to deter conflict and strategies aimed at the waging of
war should deterrence fail. The second deals with the balance between capabilties
for a European war and forces designed for out-of-area contingencies.

These two problems interact. Out-of-area or Third World contingencies, with
or without Soviet involvement, are far more likely to occur than war in Europe.
But Third World contingencies are not likely to prove as dangerous because direct and automatic linkage with nuclear weapons is less likely, especially when
the Soviet Union is not involved. Finding a balance between forces required in
Europe and forces required elsewhere has been an enduring problem for the United
States and its allies. Striking a balance between deterrence and war fighting has
been another central aspect of the security debate since 1945. Clearly seapower
and projection forces play a crucial role in both sets of issues.

Also important is the threat raised by unconventional attack and unconventional forces. Unconventional attack involves more than the terrorist threat; it
could well include technologically advanced weapons and at some stage even the
threat of chemical, bacteriological, and radiological agents. Unconventional threats
posed by small but politically significant forces could put at risk large and powerful conventional forces that, under certain circumstances of surprise and stealth,

could be severely damaged or even defeated. U.S. power projection forces must be prepared for unconventional threats such as the bombing in October 1983 that claimed the lives of 241 U.S. Marines in Beirut. This is a difficult requirement to meet because unconventional forces can strike without warning.

These two sets of issues and challenges, modified by the implications of unconventional threats, frame several key choices between military forces and between political and military solutions. Even with policies specified in a clear-cut manner, determining the appropriate force structure remains difficult. For example, if political decisions are made that stress deterrence and European priorities over war-fighting and out-of-area regional priorities, the choices for force structure are not necessarily eased. One must still choose between maintaining prepositioned forces in a forward defense posture along the inner German border and resupplying and reinforcing through mobile, rapidly transportable projection forces. Similarly difficult choices are necessary when political decisions dictate other directions and priorities.

In many ways, projection forces, such as aircraft carriers and U.S. Marines, have the quality of fitting not only contingencies in Europe (at least on the flanks) but also conflicts or crises elsewhere. In addition, such forces serve both deterrent and war-waging capabilities, although they are no longer a centerpiece of the U.S. nuclear arsenal. This flexible and multifaceted nature of projection forces does have a negative side, however. Some observers have argued that forces that are not intrinsically rooted in European defense may not reassure European allies and indeed may have the opposite effect. They have contended that spending on such forces erodes the political cohesiveness of the alliance. Furthermore, even such a traditionalist as the late Senator Richard Russell worried that projection capabilities could breed use and that limits on projection forces might be desirable in order to keep force from being employed where national interests were not fundamentally involved. Both concerns are arguable. Nonetheless, defining the balance between European and out-of-area requirements forms a major part of the debate about U.S. projection forces. The second issue—balancing and distinguishing between deterrent and war-waging objectives and strategies—remains a key dilemma of the nuclear age; however, it is discussed elsewhere in this book.

Complicating these future choices concerning seapower and projection forces is the emergence of two possibly contradictory trends. First, new technology in the form of "attack of follow-on forces" may make conventional defense in Europe a more plausible and attractive option. If such technology continues to show promise, then predeployed forces can and will have greater utility in deterring and defeating Soviet attack. Concurrently the potential for regional instability and the increase in the number of regions where contingencies might arise—Central America, for example—suggest that out-of-area requirements are likely to increase. This means, presumably, that more U.S. projection forces will be needed in the future.

Reconciling these diverging trends will not be made any easier by likely constraints in defense budgets and available manpower levels. In fact, continued debate over the balance between largely prepositioned forces for a European contingency and projection forces for out-of-area operations will likely be sharpened. These are issues that have persisted for nearly forty years, but recent history will make them harder, not easier, to resolve.

The categories of seapower and projection forces suggest a distinction that may be artificial and misleading rather than helpful. Naval and marine forces are seapower forces in the purest sense. They are also fundamentally power projection forces. Yet the converse is not always true: ground and land forces that have a projection mission may never contribute directly to maritime operations. Thus, although the distinctions of seapower and projection are used in this chapter, readers should bear in mind the obvious restrictions to this use. Further, the air and sealift necessary to support seapower and projection forces cannot be neglected or its importance downgraded. Space precludes complete discussion of air and sealift, but this does not diminish the vital importance of such forces.

Events of 1984

Aside from routine deployments, three regions assumed particular importance for U.S. projection forces in 1984: the Persian Gulf, the Red Sea, and Central America. In particular, the Iran-Iraq war threatened to spill over into the rest of the gulf as attacks against local shipping mounted. Such an escalation would have presented grave problems for the United States, especially if either country had attempted to blockade the gulf.

Even in a time of oil surpluses, the results of such any blockade, threatened or imposed, would be significant. First, any blockade, or even the threat of one, could cause another oil shock, particularly in Western Europe and Japan. Although the United States itself is more insulated, existing oil-sharing agreements would make it likely that the effects of any shortage would be shared. Hence, an economic crisis, or at least the threat of crisis, would be very real. Second, the United States might be forced into some form of direct action, perhaps even military intervention. Such action would encounter both military and domestic political impediments, depending on the amount of military power needed and how quickly and in what manner the War Powers Resolution was applied. Although it is technically feasible to keep the gulf open for shipping by preventing direct military attack, including mining, an operation of some duration would be politically difficult to sustain. Any thought of direct U.S. attacks against Iranian or Iraqi military capabilities to relieve a threatened blockade would raise the issue of the degree of commitment. A single strike would probably be insufficient for such a purpose, and it seems unlikely that the United States would commit itself to sustained military action.

As a result of potential contingencies and regional crises, U.S. seapower and projection forces have to be prepared for a variety of uses, the location and specific nature of which may be highly uncertain. This is an inherent problem for all projection forces. Being prepared to deal effectively with uncertain contingencies requires a high state of readiness and a large degree of flexibility. Although the Iran-Iraq war did not appear as threatening at the end of 1984 as it did earlier in the year, preparation for possible contingencies arising from the Persian Gulf and other regions remains a central requirement for U.S. seapower and projection forces.

Incidents like the mining of the Red Sea in the summer of 1984 pose other requirements for U.S. projection forces. The minesweeping operation was not a classic case of power projection, but it did demonstrate that U.S. forces not normally stationed in a region can be required at short notice. It is possible that such operations will be needed more often in the future.

Central America is also a region that could pose new requirements for projection forces. The question of dealing with Nicaragua is likely to involve a range of politico-diplomatic instruments, including the show of force. Speculation over Nicaraguan receipt of Soviet MiG-21s (or other destabilizing weapons) gave rise in 1984 to suggestions that the United States might respond with direct attacks against those aircraft should they actually be stationed in Nicaragua. U.S. military maneuvers on land and at sea have been conducted in Central America with increasing frequency. Whether or not the Soviets will ever attempt to ship MiG-21s to Nicaragua, it is likely that U.S. projection forces will continue to undertake deployments and exercises in Central America.

Current and Projected Strategy

Although the maritime strategy of the Reagan administration has some unique aspects with respect to seapower and projection forces, it has much in common with strategic planning of the Carter administration, although with a higher budget. The strategy has wartime, peacetime, and crisis elements.

Wartime strategy in part focuses on the following scenario: war is started by the USSR and its allies and begins with Soviet attack into northern Iran. This is followed by an offensive in Korea and ultimately by attack into Europe. U.S. and allied forces are postured in a forward defense. They must stop the initial attack, restore prewar boundaries, and establish an end to conflict on favorable terms.

In this scenario, U.S. power projection forces must bring force to bear both in geographical regions where predeployed U.S. forces are already operating and in regions where they are not, such as the Persian Gulf and Southwest Asia. Most critically, U.S. power projection forces will be used to reinforce and resupply U.S. and allied forces in Europe and the Pacific (Korea and Japan). Such a plan would call for approximately ten U.S. divisions and sixteen fighter wings to be in Europe within two weeks of the start of conflict.

Conflict is more likely to occur in the Third World than in Europe, at least such has been the history of the last generation. Here the strategy is slightly more difficult to interpret because the situations that would arise might well occur with little warning and under uncertain conditions. In such an out-of-area crisis, the United States has a wide range of seapower and power projection forces at its disposal. These include much of the U.S. Navy, the U.S. Marine Corps, Central Command (CENTCOM), and airlift and sealift.

CENTCOM, originally known as the Rapid Deployment Joint Task Force (RDJTF), is perhaps the most publicized of U.S. projection forces. The Carter administration initially intended the RDJTF to be used for two purposes: to deter any Soviet encroachment into Southwest Asia that would threaten Western access to Persian Gulf oil and to support and defend littoral regimes threatened by subnational groups or local radical states such as Syria, Iraq, and Iran.

In other regions of the world, the United States can respond to a crisis or contingency with a variety of projection forces. The U.S. Navy and Marine Corps are perhaps the most well known and most utilized. The advantages of maritime power include flexibility, sustainability, and containability. The flexibility of such forces is obvious. They are readily mobile, can be kept at the ready over the horizon, and brought to bear with immediacy. They do not require extensive land bases. They arrive fully provisioned and are self-sustainable for a month or more.

Seapower forces include the requisite land, air, and sea capabilities so they can function independently and in a self-contained fashion. These capabilities do not in themselves constitute a strategy, however.

A combination of experience and preparedness is required so that such seapower forces are sufficiently ready and deployed to respond to the unforeseen. No strategy can anticipate all of the uncertainties of crises or contingencies. While this is less a strategy than an option for responding to uncertain needs, having substantial forces that are reasonably mobile and deployable on short notice provides U.S. decision makers with effective foreign policy instruments that can prevent crises from occurring or from escalating into broader conditions of conflict. The future is unknown; given such uncertainty, it is difficult to elaborate an effective strategy in advance that will fit every possible contingency. The flexibility offered through power projection forces is essential and necessary insurance for any U.S. administration.

Seapower

U.S. Navy

The general-purpose striking power of the future U.S. navy is derived from the approximately 600 ships that will be in service at the end of the 1980s. In the mid-1980s about 525 ships are in active service. The 600 ship navy will center on 15 carrier battle groups (there were 13 in 1984), 100 nuclear attack submarines, 100 surface ship escorts (apart from those normally in a carrier battle group), amphibious lift for assault echelons of one marine amphibious force and one marine amphibious brigade, and supporting logistics and mine warfare ships. Because navies are inherently flexible and mobile, the substantial capabilities accruing from seapower forces have clear application to a broad range of uses and roles.

The Carrier Battle Group (CVBG) nominally consists of an aircraft carrier, its airwing, five to eight surface combatants, a supporting logistics group with fuel, ammunition, and materiel, and a supporting nuclear attack submarine. The airwing has about ninety aircraft, including two fighter squadrons of twelve aircraft each, three attack squadrons, one antisubmarine squadron, plus helicopters, utility aircraft, airborne tankers, and early warning aircraft. The battle group has a striking range possibly in excess of 500 miles, depending on the tactical situation. Where appropriate, these forces will be supported by land-based aviation.

The Surface Action Group (SAG) consists of one battleship and three or four surface combatants. These units will normally be complemented with tactical aviation from either carrier or land bases. The SAG has application to a variety of naval warfare roles. As more vertical launch systems (VLS) enter the fleet and permit cruise missiles to be carried in very large numbers, VLS ships such as the *Ticonderoga* class cruiser may become the centerpiece of future SAGs.

Like the CVBG and the SAG, the Amphibious Ready Group (ARG) is a flexibly organized naval task unit nominally with three to five ships. The ARG is usually associated with a Marine Amphibious Unit of 2,500 men. The ships in the ARG include an amphibious assault ship, an amphibious transport dock, an amphibious cargo ship, a dock landing ship, and a landing ship tank. Special supporting units for reconnaissance, combat service support and combat engineers are normally embarked.

Table 6–1. Projected Composition of U.S. Naval Forces, 1985–1999

Ships	1985	1986	1987	1988	1989	1990
Strategic[a]	43	44	44	45	45	46
Battle forces[b]	437	440	452	458	468	464
Support	56	56	53	55	57	59
Mob Cat A[c]	18	22	28	34	38	48
All ships	554	562	577	592	608	617

Note: These are estimated figures derived from current statements of the secretary of defense, the secretary of the navy, and the chief of naval operations.

[a]Strategic nuclear ballistic submarines and their tender supporting ships.

[b]Carriers, battleships, cruisers, destroyers, frigates, attack submarines, amphibious warfare ships, mine warfare ships, and replenishment ships.

[c]Ships in the Naval Reserve that are partially manned by active duty crews and can become fully operational at short notice.

The projected composition of U.S. naval forces is shown in table 6–1.

U.S. Marine Corps

The U.S. Marine Corps is the only U.S. service to have its structure defined by law. The National Security Act of 1947 (as amended) specifies that the Marine Corps will consist of three active duty divisions and three associated airwings and one reserve division and airwing. Active duty strength in FY84 was 196,600.

Each active duty division has about 17,000 assigned personnel and is organized around three infantry regiments, one artillery regiment, and five to six separate battalions, including tanks, engineers, reconnaissance, amphibious assault, and headquarters. In FY86 light armored vehicles will be added to the divisional structure. The associated airwing includes three fixed-wing (fighter and attack) Marine Aircraft Groups (MAGs), one helicopter group, plus supporting air control, electronic warfare, reconnaissance, tanker, and light antiaircraft missile capabilities.

The cutting edge of the Marine Corps lies in its operational organization into Marine Air-Ground Task Forces (MAGTF). The MAGTF, as in naval organization, combines flexibility and mobility and is specifically organized for each task. The three basic elements of the MAGTF are the Marine Amphibious Unit (MAU), the Marine Amphibious Brigade (MAB), and the Marine Amphibious Force (MAF).

The MAU is the smallest but most responsive. It is organized around a battalion landing team and includes a supporting air squadron of about eight Cobra Attack helicopters or six Harrier fighter-attack aircraft and twenty medium- and heavy-lift helicopters. A MAU numbers 2,500 men and can be transported in three to five ships. MAUs carry about two or three weeks of logistic support with them.

The MAB is organized around a regimental landing team and includes an MAG. The MAB consists of about 18,000 personnel. The supporting air group includes about ninety fixed wing aircraft and over one hundred helicopters. The MAB is embarked in about twenty ships and deploys with about a month's supplies.

1991	1992	1993	1994	1995	1996	1997	1998	1999
47	48	46	34	30	24	23	23	24
466	457	464	469	474	486	480	487	482
55	51	52	53	54	57	56	57	58
52	52	52	52	51	51	51	51	51
620	608	614	608	609	618	610	618	615

The MAF is organized around a marine division and marine airwing and consists of about 50,000 to 58,000 personnel. The airwing includes about 250 fixed wing tactical aircraft and over 300 helicopters. A MAF is embarked in about 30 to 40 ships and deploys with as much as 60 days of supply.

The Marine Corps currently has three MAFs. One is located on the West Coast (I MAF) and is charged with planning for Southwest Asia contingencies. The second is on the East Coast (II MAF) and deploys units to the Caribbean, Mediterranean, and Atlantic. A third force is forward deployed in Japan (III MAF) and includes the Near-Term Pre-positioned Force at Diego Garcia in the Indian Ocean.

The seapower forces provide a broad range of capabilities to respond to a host of missions. The flexibility and sustainability of these forces make them particularly relevant to coping with an uncertain future.

Projection Forces: CENTCOM

Activated on January 1, 1983, CENTCOM is responsible for contingencies in nineteen countries in the crescent from the Horn of Africa through Southwest Asia to the edges of Pakistan and Afghanistan. Forces available to CENTCOM include elements from all four services. The Army has earmarked four divisions and an air cavalry combat brigade; the Marine Corps contributes a full MAF and an MAB. The Air Force has assigned to CENTCOM seven tactical fighter wings and two strategic bomber squadrons to be used in a conventional role. The Navy has committed three CVBGs, one SAG, and five maritime patrol squadrons.

By 1989, these forces are slated to be increased to ten tactical fighter wings, two MAFs, and five Army combat divisions. This will bring total personnel to about 440,000 from the 222,000 assigned to CENTCOM in 1985.

Supporting the MAF, as well as Army and Air Force units in CENTCOM, are the seventeen ships on the Near-Term Prepositioning Force at Diego Garcia. Ultimately plans call for prepositioning equipment and supplies for three MABs. This support will be provided by thirteen maritime prepositioning ships (MPS).

In addition to the forces noted, other important units such as special operating forces, reconnaissance, electronics, and support have been earmarked for commitment to CENTCOM.

Airlift and Sealift

Central to any projection force must be the accompanying capability for airlift or sealift. Airlift has the unassailable advantage of rapid response but the liability of usually requiring a benign environment. Lift of heavy equipment in large numbers is extremely difficult to sustain by air because carrying capacity is limited. One C-5A, for example, can carry only one M-1 tank. Air transport of fuel in quantities required for combat operations is virtually impossible. During the October 1973 Arab-Israeli war, the fuel consumed was five to six times the weight of actual cargo hauled.

Sealift will carry all unit equipment, including oversized materiel that cannot be shipped by air. In war, normally 95 to 98 percent of all equipment goes by sea. Sealift is clearly days slower than airlift and also entails more demanding requirements for embarkation and disembarkation facilities. Hence, trade-offs between and among airlift and sealift capabilities will always be required.

U.S. strategic airlift assets consist of 64 C-5As and 215 C-141s. In addition the Civil Reserve Air Fleet (CRAF), a DOD-subsidized program in which U.S. airlines would provide their aircraft for military airlift of U.S. personnel, can provide additional lift. CRAF can generate 52 wide-body and 58 narrow-body aircraft for equipment transport and over 200 aircraft for personnel transport. U.S. in-theater or tactical airlift is built around 512 C-130 aircraft.

U.S. strategic sealift assets include the ships shown in figure 6–1.

Future Issues and Implications

The major issues facing U.S. seapower and projection forces can be categorized under four general headings: implications of likely changes in the operating environments, structural replacement decisions concerning future U.S. forces, tactical and technical operational challenges, and sealift and airlift.

The operating environment is likely to change in ways that suggest greater threat and danger for U.S. projection forces as the diffusion of high technology weapons continues. Currently there are few operating areas in the world that cannot be considered high threat in nature. As the British learned in the South Atlantic conflict during 1982, the threat of the cruise missile can be very real even operating against a nation with little indigenous military industry or technology. The presence of highly capable weapons in the hands of Third World adversaries would be keenly felt by U.S. projection forces; however, inventories of these weapons held by Third World states are likely to be limited, suggesting that conflict in which high technology weapons are utilized is likely to be short. Further, access to high technology weapons is not the sole determinant of how Third World nations will fare against major powers. The United States enjoyed complete military technological superiority over North Vietnam in a conflict that ultimately proved successful to the technically inferior party.

A second problem is U.S. capability for dealing with simultaneous crises. In 1958 President Dwight Eisenhower could deal comfortably with crises occurring simultaneously in the Taiwan Straits and in Lebanon. In the future, crises could occur simultaneously in three, four, or more areas. But U.S. forces, however capable, cannot be in two places at once.

A third problem is that some crises may have enormous political significance although involving military forces of only modest size. If the Desert One raid in 1980 to free U.S. hostages held in Teheran had been successful, the position of the United States in the world, and possibly the outcome of the 1980 presidential election, could have been affected. If the U.S. intervention in Grenada in 1983 had met stiff resistance or if there had been public executions of U.S. students, popular outcry in the United States could have had a major negative international political effect and a decisive impact on the 1984 U.S. election. Neither eventuality occurred, but that does not eliminate the possibility that in the future contingencies that involve comparatively minor uses of military force may have enormous political significance, especially in an age of almost instantaneous media coverage. These environmental factors must clearly be understood and applied to the manner in which the United States designs, procures, and operates its projection forces.

Figure 6–1. U.S. Strategic Sealift Assets, 1985

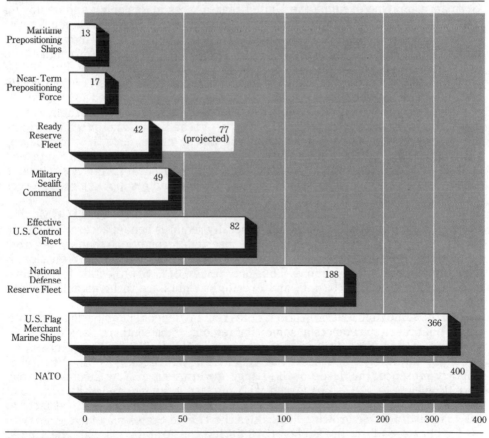

Source: Office of the Chief of Naval Operations (Strategic Sealift Branch).

Of the key structural decisions facing the United States, one of the most important has to do with replacement of power projection forces. In the Navy, for example, decisions will have to be made before the end of the 1980s about what, if anything, should replace the large deck aircraft carriers. By the end of this century, aging U.S. aircraft carriers will begin to leave the fleet inventory. If less than planned defense spending occurs, those carriers may leave the inventory even sooner. If the United States plans to maintain fifteen carrier battle groups into the future, replacement ships will have to be on the building ways in the 1990s and ready for operational service by the end of the century. With long lead times for construction—often more than a decade elapses between authorization and operation—decisions on carrier replacement will soon be facing U.S. defense planners.

The second structural decision concerns the role and design of light or highly mobile forces. If low-intensity conflict imposes greater requirements for U.S. military forces, then the forces added for those contingencies should be lighter and more mobile than those designed to conduct armored warfare on the North German plain. One dilemma the United States faces in designing and deploying light forces is that these forces may well find themselves up against much heavier adversaries. Even using the most advanced weaponry, light forces may have only limited utility against traditionally armor-heavy Soviet forces. Although these light forces could be quickly deployed in the event of war in Europe, it would be very difficult to ensure that they could acquit themselves successfully in conditions of conflict against heavy forces that they were not designed to engage.

The third structural decision involves access, basing, and overflight rights. For U.S. projection forces to be effective, overseas basing and overflight rights are essential. Without overflight rights and basing agreements, it would be virtually impossible for the United States to resupply its military forces in Southwest Asia by air. And even relying on maritime forces, if basing were not available along the likely ocean deployment routes, refueling and resupplying these forces would be exceedingly difficult.

Part of the access question has to do with forceable entry. CENTCOM, with the important exception of the MAF, generally requires benign access. The Eighteenth Airborne Corps could certainly be inserted in conditions that are far from benign, but immediate resupply, which is vital to the success of such a mission, is difficult under hostile conditions. Thus, any review of U.S. projection forces must also detail how access, basing, and overflight rights are to be established and maintained.

At the same time that projection forces remain dependent on basing and overflight, political circumstances in some vital regions in the southern flank of NATO, in Australia and New Zealand, and perhaps in the Philippines raise questions about the future of U.S. access. The coolness of the Greek government to U.S. military presence, the desire of the Lange government in New Zealand to deny port privileges to U.S. ships armed with nuclear weapons, and the prospect of domestic instability in the post-Marcos Philippines are current political facts of life that testify to the growing difficulties the United States may have even with ostensibly close allies. In October 1973 during the Arab-Israeli war, the United States was not allowed to use NATO bases in the resupply of Israel. Similar conditions could apply in the future.

If the Philippines in the post-Marcos era were to move away from the United States, U.S. bases at Clark and Subic could be lost or their use severely restricted. The United States would have to look elsewhere in the region for some form of basing so that if forces had to be projected either in the western Pacific or Southwest Asia, logistics would be available. There are alternatives to the Philippines. Australia and members of the Association of Southeast Asian Nations (ASEAN) are possibilities, although greater use of Guam and some parts of Micronesia could be somewhat easier politically. Predeploying or prepositioning of equipment through MPS (maritime prepositioning ships) or POMCUS (prepositioned overseas material configured in unit sets) sites in the Southwest Asia littoral are also possibilities. But political implications are crucial for any prepositioning and it may be very difficult to secure agreement of littoral states for such initiatives.

The third major issue has to do with tactical and technical challenges facing the operation of projection forces. One of the most interesting and difficult technical issues has to do with command, control, communications, and intelligence. The establishment of CENTCOM with headquarters at MacDill Air Force Base in Florida provided an additional unified commander with responsibilities inside Southwest Asia in general and in the Persian Gulf specifically, but the organization raises questions about the overall chain of command. CENTCOM's leading element forward deployed inside the gulf is Commander Middle East Force, who in part is responsible to Commander-in-Chief Pacific (CINCPAC), from whom he draws his resources and logistics. Deployed forces to the Middle East Force are assigned by Commander-in-Chief Europe (CINCEUR), who in turn receives those forces on a six to eight month deployment basis from Commander-in-Chief Atlantic (CINCLANT) in Norfolk, Virginia.

Should CENTCOM be activated into the region, it will be supported by both CINCEUR and CINCPAC. The CINCEUR lines of responsibility begin and end on the Mediterranean side of the Middle East. CINCPAC's responsibilities begin at sea east of the north-south line drawn between Iran and Oman through the Strait of Hormuz. CENTCOM would operate inside the Persian Gulf and ashore. This is a cumbersome administrative arrangement. Although it could operate successfully, there is a distinct possibility of administrative overload. Too many senior commanders are involved in the region, each with critical responsibilities. Examining these command interrelationships and the manner in which CENTCOM might actually operate is an important priority.

In a larger sense, it is fair to ask whether U.S. strategy for Southwest Asia as currently structured will continue to advance U.S. interests. In the event of Soviet encroachment into northern Iran, if U.S. forces were directed to drive out Soviet forces, given the current regime in power in Teheran, it is likely that the United States could find itself in conflict first with Iran before reaching the line of battle with the Soviet Union. The United States must have a strong declaratory policy that makes it clear to the Soviet Union that interruption of Western access to Southwest Asian oil is unacceptable. But there may be better ways to demonstrate purpose than through the possibility of direct hostilities with Iran, which might occur if the Soviets were to occupy or invade the northern regions of Iran. For example, greater involvement of NATO in the region might make possible a larger role for Turkey and Turkish bases in the event of hostilities in Iran.

There are also the issues of time, distance, and access to Southwest Asia. Figure 6–2 portrays the relative distances by sea from the United States to other areas of the world. With the exception of polar regions, Southwest Asia is perhaps the most difficult part of the world in which the United States could be required to project force. Access and basing rights are essential. Without access to the Suez Canal, U.S. supply lines would stretch nearly 12,000 miles; the resources necessary to support the five divisions and the MAF engaged in conflict in Southwest Asia would be enormous. Current sealift assets are perhaps sufficient for the task but would still require a monumental effort. For those reasons, reexamination of the implications and requirements of the Southwest Asia strategy would be well advised. If major changes in this strategy are indeed forthcoming, the budgetary resources to be saved from that review would be relatively minor. The forces already designated for Southwest Asia are also earmarked elsewhere, and, if the Southwest Asia requirements were indeed altered, those forces could be readily reassigned. The maritime prepositioning ships and other capabilities

Figure 6–2. Distances of Sealanes from United States

U.S. defense commitments and interests take U.S. forces many thousands of miles. From New York, it is over three times farther to the Persian Gulf via the Cape of Good Hope than to Amsterdam.

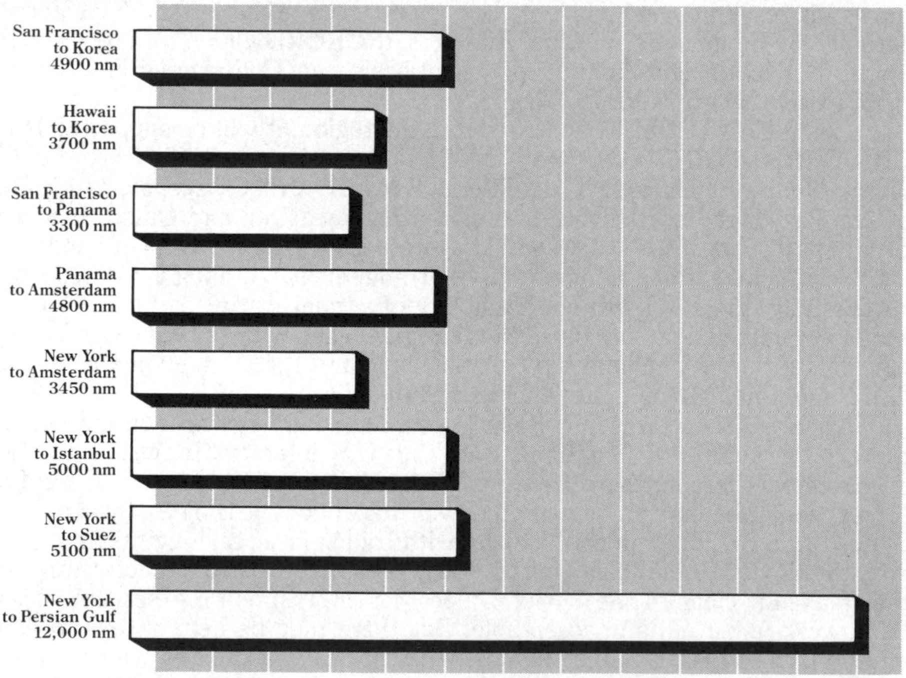

San Francisco to Korea 4900 nm
Hawaii to Korea 3700 nm
San Francisco to Panama 3300 nm
Panama to Amsterdam 4800 nm
New York to Amsterdam 3450 nm
New York to Istanbul 5000 nm
New York to Suez 5100 nm
New York to Persian Gulf 12,000 nm

Source: John M. Collins, U.S.-Soviet Military Balance Concepts and Capabilities, 1960-1980 (New York: McGraw-Hill, 1980), p. 278.

related to Southwest Asia basing have already been funded. Nonetheless it is perhaps time to review U.S. strategy for Southwest Asia.

Central to the foregoing and to U.S. seapower and projection forces is the lift capability required to support them. Comparatively little emphasis has been placed on stratgic lift. Only recently have attempts been made to identify existing shortfalls.

For economic reasons, U.S. commercial merchant fleet assets are declining. By 1989, U.S. flagships may decrease from the mid-1980s level of 536 to as few as 300. With respect to the lift needed early in hostilities, this does not affect sealift as much as the numbers would suggest because the DOD has initiated compensating programs. If the projected decline in the U.S. merchant fleet occurs, however, there may not be sufficient total U.S. flag sealift for both military contingencies and normal economic requirements.

Airlift, particularly in-theater, remains a serious problem because airlift is severely restricted in lifting heavy equipment. Technology can never compensate for this outsize haulage limitation. And over time, lift has not received the same priority as forces that provide immediate combat power. A major defense issue of the next decade may well be how to develop innovative and imaginative ways of enhancing lift as a force multiplier.

Other factors also bear on U.S. seapower and projection forces. To cite two examples, the contribution of U.S. allies to their own military capabilities both in and out of area and U.S. arms transfer policies are both important factors. It was not long ago that the Nixon doctrine established as one criterion that the United States would provide a strategic umbrella, while local countries would provide for their own direct defense. Both factors are still worthy of emphasis.

Regarding the contribution of allies to their own defense both in and out of area, several trends are emerging. Largely as a result of its experience in the Falklands, Britain is putting together a small, rapidly deployable force of about 10,000. These forces could have great utility in small-scale crises. The French have always maintained a sizable presence in Djibouti in Southwest Asia. They are also in the process of fielding their own rapid action force.

The French force is not designed for Third World use, although there are contingencies in the Third World in which it could probably be brought to bear. The fundamental purpose of this 50,000-man French force is to be readily transportable within a 500 kilometer radius from France in Europe. Such a force would be projected in the event of war in Europe against Soviet operational maneuver groups for two purposes: to blunt the attack and to demonstrate clearly and convincingly to the Soviet Union that France is serious in its efforts to stop aggression. If the rapid action force is unsuccessful, French nuclear weapons would be used. The rapid action force is one more flexible instrument in French deterrent strategy. It demonstrates how serious the French would be in the event of war with the Soviet Union. For that reason expectations about the utility of that force and its application to Third World situations should not be overdrawn.

Concerning increased direct budgetary contributions of allied states to their own defense, it is unlikely that much in addition to current allocations will be forthcoming in the absence of a crisis. NATO has committed itself to a $7.8 billion increase over five years for modernization of member states' forces. In East Asia, the United States continues to press for increases in Japanese defense spending. While the Japanese are likely to increase spending at a modest pace, it is unlikely that they will spend to the limits that would satisfy the United States. Additionally Japanese defense efforts are likely to be centered within the western Pacific region and not in terms of projecting force thousands of miles away from home waters.

Arms transfers will remain a persuasive policy instrument but one that has two sides. As the United States learned in Iran, transferred arms can be turned against the supplying state. Indeed the Soviet Union has learned that same unhappy lesson from several of its own experiences.

Conclusion

U.S. seapower and power projection forces face many new and uncertain challenges. The most important of these challenges is the prospect of simultaneous future crises in the Third World. It is also likely that the political significance of such crises may far outweigh the military forces brought to bear. Such crises are further complicated by the diffusion of high technology weapons. Crises will also take place in conditions that favor unconventional threats and unconventional attacks that use stealth and surprise to achieve their purposes.

Deterrence and stability in Europe probably will remain basically unchanged in the future. That is not the case in the areas outside Europe. As a result of these trends, U.S. seapower and projection forces are likely to be needed even in larger numbers than at present. Given the prospect of only modest growth in U.S. defense spending, such forces are likely to be overstretched. Doing more with less will become inevitable.

If this line of reasoning is correct, then the United States must investigate alternative means of designing its projection forces. Highly capable units that are flexible and mobile and also equipped to accomplish specific missions and requirements are needed. This does not mean wholesale restructuring of U.S. projection forces, but it does point to careful consideration of new options and alternative force design packages. Indeed the entry into service before the decade's end of sufficient MPS for three MABs can provide exceptional flexibility and capability. This is one area where considerable innovation can be achieved. The question of access, basing, and overflight rights remains central. Answers to access questions will depend on the availability of local states and their relationships with the United States. The challenge facing the United States is to maintain sufficient capability so that when and if forces have to be projected in the future, they will be sufficiently ready, skilled, flexible, capable, and supportable to guarantee success.

Chapter 7

Manpower

Martin Binkin

In November 1983 Secretary of Defense Weinberger proclaimed that the volunteer force was no longer experimental. "We know now that an all-volunteer force can succeed," he said, "and we know what it takes to make it succeed. We need only the will, the perseverance—and the commitment to quality."[1] If 1984 was any indication, his unbridled optimism was justified. By the most common yardstick for measuring the vitality of the volunteer force—the quality of new army recruits—FY84 was a resounding success: unprecedented proportions of new soldiers had a high school diploma and scored average or above on the enlistment test.[2]

This improvement continued a trend, begun in 1981, toward upgrading the qualifications of people serving in the nation's armed forces. The record of the past few years stands in marked contrast to the late 1970s, when the qualifications of military enlistees had dropped to postwar lows. By the end of the decade, the alarming decline prompted many legislators and policymakers to question seriously the viability of raising armed forces by strictly voluntary means.

The dismay of the late 1970s has been replaced in the mid-1980s by a sense of confidence. Indeed the many concerns that dogged the volunteer force throughout the 1970s—the questionable quality of enlistees, the heavy losses of experienced specialists and technicians, the social composition of the force, the low morale of troops, the unusually high training washout rates, and shortages in reserve manning—have all but disappeared.

At the same time there are good reasons to ask whether recent successes can be sustained over the long haul. Several trends, each with adverse implications for military recruitment, are likely to converge within the next decade or so. The military services are likely to be squeezed between a dwindling population of prospective volunteers and a growing requirement for skilled people to operate and maintain high technology systems. If a return to the problems of the 1970s is to be avoided, it is important that options be devised for dealing with shortfalls should they develop, or better yet, that policies be implemented for preventing them from developing at all.

1984: A Banner Year

Approximately 310,000 recruits entered the nation's armed forces in fiscal year 1984: of these, about 290,000 (93 percent) were high school graduates, and roughly 205,000 (66 percent) ranked in the top half of the youth population in terms of enlistment test scores. Although the Air Force and Navy, which have been least affected by the end of conscription, have typically attracted volunteers of this high quality, the Army has not. In 1984, however, 91 percent of the Army's recruits had high school diplomas and over 63 percent scored at or above the fiftieth percentile on the enlistment test.

These record-setting achievements were all the more impressive since they occurred just four years after the Army's poorest recruiting year. In FY80 roughly 54 percent of the Army's enlistees had completed high school, and only 28 percent scored in the top half of the youth population. Worse yet, about half scored below the thirty-first percentile—a cohort that, by past experience, requires disproportionately more training and accounts for more than its share of disciplinary problems (see figures 7-1 and 7-2).

The Army's fortunes turned in 1981 on the heels of a deepening recession and substantial increases in military pay. Also contributing to the turnaround were improvements in military educational benefits for certain Army recruits that coincided with anticipated reductions in federal student loan programs. The more positive public image of the military attributed by many to the patriotic theme of the Reagan administration helped as well. The separate influences of these factors cannot be measured precisely, but together they resulted in a steady improvement in qualitative characteristics over the period 1981 through 1984.

Not only were there gains in recruitment, but the military also became a more attractive career alternative for many people. In contrast to the late 1970s, when skilled specialists, technicians, and supervisors were leaving the military in droves, reenlistment rates among experienced personnel have improved significantly in the recent past. Particularly comforting for the military services has been the rise in the rate of reenlistment among careerists—those who have demonstrated by reenlisting after an initial enlistment an interest in pursuing a military career. Although career reenlistment rates in FY84 were slightly below the previous record-setting year, they nevertheless represented a substantial improvement over those rates recorded during the late 1970s.[3]

The posture of the nation's reserve forces also improved in FY84. Total strength in the selected reserve increased by about 40,000 during the year to a record-breaking 1.046 million, or close to 33 percent above the FY78 level.[4] At that strength, selected reserve units were manned on average at close to 85 percent of their wartime requirements. Progress in filling the ranks of the army's individual ready reserve (IRR), however, has been slower. The IRR is composed of people who have served fewer than six years in active or reserve units (and thus have a residual obligation) but are not members of units and generally do not train or get paid. They are liable to call-up and, along with members of the selected reserves and certain retired personnel, constitute the pool of pretrained individuals earmarked to fill out active units either upon mobilization or as combat replacements in the early days of conflict.

The Pentagon was reporting a reserve shortage as high as 270,000 in 1979; the Army now pegs it at roughly 117,000.[5] The smaller estimate has resulted from increases in the size of the Army's selected reserves and the number of pre-assigned retirees and a growth of about 50,000 in the IRR. Since Congress increased the total service obligation from six years to eight years for volunteers entering the armed forces after June 1, 1984, a substantial increase in the IRR can be expected, but not before 1990. In the meantime, concerns about the Army's mobilization potential persist and mar the otherwise rosy assessment of 1984.

Figure 7–1. Percentage Distribution of Army Recruits, by Aptitude Test Scores
Selected Fiscal Years, 1971–1984

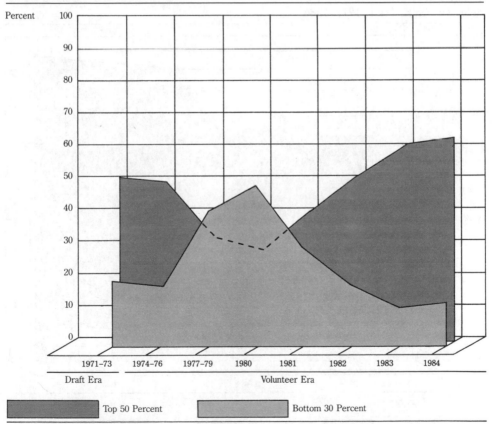

Source: Derived from data provided by Defense Manpower Data Center. Figures are rounded.

Finally, in FY84 the racial-ethnic composition of the armed forces remained essentially unchanged, with minorities constituting about 29 percent of the enlisted ranks and 11 percent of the officer corps. For the Army, which of the military services has always had the highest concentration of minorities, the proportion of recruits who were black remained at roughly 23 percent in 1984, considerably higher than the proportion of blacks in the eighteen- to twenty-four-year-old population (13 percent) but down from the peak of 37 percent in 1979.[6] The relative decline in the black enlistment rate is attributable to an increased interest in the military on the part of white youths that resulted from worsening conditions in the job market, large increases in entry-level pay, and enlistment incentives that tend to favor whites (such as supplemental educational benefits available only to those with above-average aptitude scores).[7] Despite the smaller number of black recruits in recent years, blacks still comprise about 31 percent of the Army's enlisted force, down just 2 percentage points from 1979.

Figure 7–2. Percentage Distribution of Army Recruits, by Level of Education

Selected Fiscal Years, 1971–1984

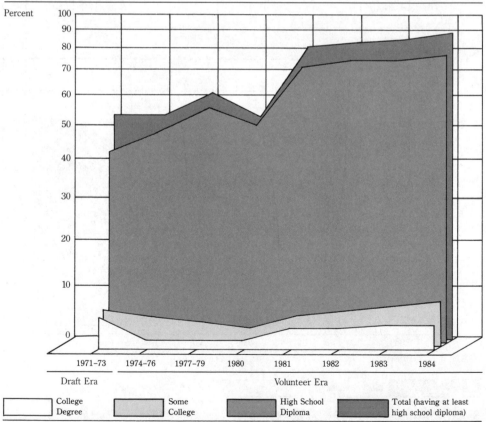

Source: Derived from data provided by Defense Manpower Data Center. Figures are rounded.

Manpower Legislation, 1984

With the manning situation seemingly under control, the Reagan administration's budget for FY85 contained no major manpower initiatives. A modest increase in active duty manpower strengths of roughly 30,000, later scaled down to 23,000, was requested as part of a longer-range plan to expand the size of the Navy and Air Force. In addition, an initial request for an increase of about 50,000 in the average strength of the selected reserves was revised downward to just over 45,000. The administration also requested an increase of close to 29,000 in the Army's civilian strength. An across-the-board pay raise of 5.5 percent was sought for military personnel and 3.5 percent for federal civilians. On the thorny issue of retirement system reform, the administration deferred any proposals, pending the outcome of a DOD review being conducted as a part of the Fifth Quadrennial Review of Military Compensation.

Congress made only minor modifications to the administration's active and reserve manpower requests. In cutting about 13,000 from the administration's request for active duty strength, Congress provided an increase of 10,000 over the previous year. Similarly, while reducing by about 10,000 the administration's request for selected reserve strength, Congress provided an increase of 43,000 over the previous year. Finally, Congress waived the requirement for a civilian personnel end strength authorization for FY85. Regarding compensation, the administration's proposed 5.5 percent pay increase was reduced to 4 percent, with recruits excluded for the second consecutive year.[8]

The major piece of defense manpower legislation enacted in 1984 was a new educational assistance program. Although opposed by the administration as unnecessary and costly, the new program was a compromise between House and Senate versions that had been tacked onto the 1985 defense authorization bill.

Under the House-Senate compromise, all recruits entering the armed forces between July 1, 1985, and June 30, 1988, except those who choose not to participate, would take a reduction of $100 a month in their basic pay for the first twelve months of service, receiving in exchange educational assistance ranging from $250 to $300 per month for thirty-six months. By comparison, participants under the basic post–Vietnam era Veterans' Educational Assistance Program (VEAP) now contribute up to $2,700 during their enlistment period, which the government matches on a two-for-one basis.

The new legislation also authorizes the secretary of defense to increase the rate by up to an additional $400 per month for individuals enlisting in certain critical skills. Further, the secretary is authorized to provide supplemental assistance of up to $300 a month for service members who complete the initial service required for the basic benefit and serve either an additional five years on active duty or an additional two years on active duty and four years in the selected reserve. This supplemental benefit could be increased by up to an additional $300 per month for those reenlisting for the specified period in designated critical skills.

The net benefits under this program thus could range from $9,600 under the basic entitlement to as high as $45,600 for an individual serving in designated critical skills either for eight years on active duty or five years on active duty and four years in the selected reserves.[9] By contrast, the current maximum basic benefit under VEAP is $5,400 and the maximum net entitlement is $23,700, now provided under the Army College Fund to high school graduates scoring at or above the fiftieth percentile and volunteering for four years of active duty in a designated skill. The new law extends benefits to reservists on a noncontributory basis; those extending their obligation by six years would be entitled to $140 a month for thirty-six months. The relative merits of the new program will be difficult to assess until a clearer picture emerges of the number and qualifications of participants and of the extent to which such benefits are needed to attract them.

To some observers, enactment of a broader program of educational incentives at a time when the armed forces were setting new recruitment records and the nation faced serious deficit problems appeared frivolous or at least unnecessary. Although the motivations of the bill's various sponsors differed, the common thread of support in Congress for some form of new education bill was a concern that additional incentives would be needed in the future when, as many expect, recruitment trends reverse. In fact, based on testimony by Army officials in 1984, some legislators were fearful that the corner had already been turned.

Army Manpower Quality: Issue for the Mid-1980s

Generally lost amid the celebration over the record-high qualifications of recruits who entered the armed forces in 1984 was the decline in the number of volunteers who actually signed up in 1984. Under the services' delayed entry program, many of the recruits who put on uniforms in one year actually enlisted during the previous year. In terms of new enlistment contracts negotiated in FY84, a more current gauge of recruitment success, the Army was about 8,000 short of its overall goal and 6,000 short of its goal for high-quality males. Thus the Army started FY85 with about 18,000 high-quality males awaiting entry against a 1985 recruiting goal of 60,500. By contrast, at the beginning of FY84, there were about 24,000 high-quality males in the delayed entry pool against a goal of 58,000. Army officials expressed concern that "the first small piece of bad news . . . may be a harbinger" of worse things to come.[10]

To counter this development, the Army raised the maximum educational benefit offered under the Army College Fund program in October 1984 from $20,100 to $26,400 (including the participant's $2,700 contribution) and increased the maximum enlistment bonus from $5,000 to $8,000. Under a new program (called Hi-Grad), the Army also offered volunteers with two years of college up to $20,100 in educational assistance for completing two years of military service in designated occupations. Upon resumption of their college program, these individuals would also be enrolled in the Reserve Officers' Training Corps (ROTC), graduating as second lieutenants. The cost of these initiatives was estimated at $28 million for FY85.[11]

The causes of the decline in enlistment contracts in 1985 and the extent to which it constitutes a problem are matters for debate. In some respects, it should have been anticipated, given the drop in the unemployment rate during FY84 (from 9.1 to 7.3 percent).[12] Moreover, since military pay raises had been capped at 4 percent in both 1983 and 1984 and recruit pay levels were frozen in 1984, military pay, especially at the entry level, dropped substantially relative to civilian pay.

Whether the Army's inability to maintain its current high-quality mix should even be a cause for concern raises questions that have important implications in both the near and long term. The fundamental question is: How many high-quality male recruits does the Army need, and how many can it afford?

Specifications concerning the quality mix of recruits are fairly arbitrary since there are no rules for judging how smart or how well-educated individuals must be in order to function effectively in the armed forces. It is no secret, nor is it par-ticularly surprising, that in the absence of this capability, the services seek to at-tract as many high school graduates with above-average aptitude as possible.

Thus the Army, buoyed by its recruitment record of the last several years, is budgeting "funds for maintaining high-quality recruiting levels in the competitive labor market projected for the late 1980s."[13] The Army's recruitment goals for FY86 and beyond—at least 90 percent high school graduates, at least 65 percent with enlistment test scores that rank in the top half of the population, and not more than 10 percent in the lowest test score category—have been rationalized on the grounds that the increased sophistication of Army weaponry and the adoption of a maneuver warfare doctrine demand soldiers who are better qualified than their predecessors. DOD manpower officials, however, are reported to be skep-tical; some apparently feel that the high-quality recruits being sought by the Army would not be worth what it would cost to attract them.[14] With respect to the Army's quality goal, Lawrence J. Korb, the Pentagon official responsible for man-power issues, stated in November 1984, "It has not been approved by the Depart-ment of Defense or me."[15] Thus the issue appears far from settled.

There is an inadequate understanding of the impact of new technology on the occupational distribution and on the qualifications of the military work force. Some argue that the effects of complexity have been overdrawn. A top military commander in Europe wrote that critics of technology do not understand "the fact that technology can and normally does make things simpler to operate." He cited as one example the M1 Abrams tank's relative simplicity of operation when com-pared to the M4 Sherman tank of World War II.[16] Technology will create a range of jobs, so this argument goes, for which psychomotor skills, demonstrated by the younger generation's deftness with video games, may be at least as important as the cognitive skills measured by the current standardized entry tests.

Another senior Army officer was more skeptical that new technology simpli-fies operations in the field. He contended that new weapons demand increased specialization and intelligence to operate. A six-page checklist just to check the thermal sight on the M1 tank makes it "clear that the age of 'Willie and Joe' walk-ing down a dusty road with their rifles is over."[17]

Congress has also expressed an interest in the question. In reporting out the FY85 defense authorization bill, the Senate directed the Pentagon to report by March 1985 on the quality needs of the armed services.[18]

Military Manpower and the FY86 Budget

In its defense budget request for FY86, the Reagan administration planned to hold down growth in manpower costs by proposing a 5 percent pay cut for federal civilian personnel, a freeze on cost-of-living adjustments for military and civilian retirees, and an apparent freeze on military pay. All of these proposals seemed likely to encounter difficulties from members of Congress concerned that the ad-ministration was attempting to reduce the deficit on the backs of the defense work force, while expensive weapons programs went virtually untouched.

In truth, however, the proposed freeze on military pay was not a freeze at all, inasmuch as military personnel were scheduled to receive an increase of 3 percent in July 1985. Under this gambit, members of the armed forces would appear to be sharing the cut with their retired and civilian counterparts, but in fact, by receiving a 3 percent increase three months early, they would gain the equivalent of a 4 percent increase for FY86.

Although this proposal, if enacted, would widen the gap between military and civilian wages (as measured by the government's employment cost index), the effects on recruitment and retention would not likely be substantial. Whatever impact there might be, however, would be greatest on the Army and could hamper its ability to achieve the service's quality goals over the longer term. This risk could be offset by more efficient means than by granting larger across-the-board increases in military pay. The evidence is impressive, for example, that targeted increases, such as enlistment and reenlistment bonuses, are a more cost-effective means than across-the-board raises for attracting high-quality people to the armed forces.

In addition to its pay proposals, the administration requested an increase of 25,600 in active duty strength and 47,000 in reserve strength, thus continuing a trend toward assigning more responsibility to the reserve forces. Finally, although the administration proposed to alter the civilian retirement system, it made no similar proposal, long awaited, to reform the military retirement system. Apparently the Fifth Quadrennial Review of Military Compensation was completed, but its recommendations were not embraced by the military services. Congress could devise its own reform, as it previously threatened, but the military retirement issue is extremely complicated, and efforts to change the system in any fundamental way are likely to be characterized by long debates. This status could make simpler changes—such as permanent reductions in cost-of-living increases—more tempting. Reducing such increases for retirees under a certain age or above a certain income would yield substantial savings, but at least part of the savings would have to be reapplied in the form of bonuses or other special pay, if the force profile is to be maintained.

Future Prospects

Although the administration's FY86 budget request appears to take little notice of army recruitment problems, the situation has the potential to worsen and perhaps spread to the other services in the coming years as the pool of qualified youths shrinks, the need for more and perhaps better recruits expands, and competition with the nation's colleges and universities intensifies.

Changes in the Youth Population

The armed forces will confront a declining supply of prospective volunteers over the next ten years as the nation's youth population dwindles. In contrast to 1985, when close to 3.7 million Americans turned eighteen, only 3.2 million are expected to reach that age by 1995 (see figure 7–3). This decline of over 13 percent in the age group from which the military traditionally seeks its volunteers will make recruitment more difficult. And since the smaller population will be composed of a larger proportion of minorities (31 percent in 1995 compared to 26 percent in 1985), the decline in the number of qualified youths will be even sharper because of differences in eligibility based on enlistment tests. In 1984, for example, 71 percent of white youths could have been expected to meet the Air Force's minimum education and aptitude standards compared to 22 percent of blacks and 33 percent of Hispanics.[19]

A useful perspective of the demographic influence on the recruitment task is provided by calculating the proportion of qualified and available males who in the long run would have to volunteer for military service before reaching age twenty-three if the active and reserve forces are to meet their annual recruit needs.[20] This can be done by following one age group through time, excluding those who, based on past experience, are not likely to volunteer (third- and fourth-year college students) and those who cannot volunteer (those mentally, physically, or morally unqualified).[21] Table 7-1 shows that during the 1984-1988 period an average of 1.8 million noninstitutionalized males will be turning eighteen each year. If history is a guide, 525,000 would enter the college track and another 526,000

Figure 7–3. Projected U.S. Eighteen-Year-Old Population by Sex and Race, Selected Years, 1984–1994 *(In Thousands)*

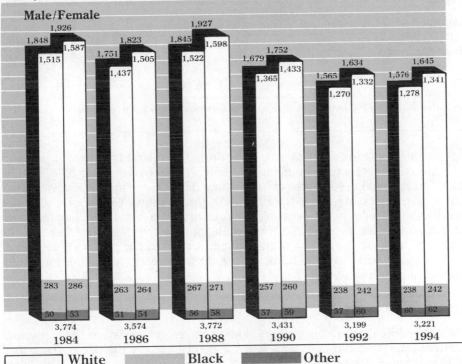

	1984	1986	1988	1990	1992	1994
Male	1,848	1,751	1,845	1,679	1,565	1,576
Female	1,587	1,505	1,598	1,433	1,332	1,341
White M	1,515	1,437	1,522	1,365	1,270	1,278
White F	1,926	1,823	1,927	1,752	1,634	1,645
Black M	283	263	267	257	238	238
Black F	286	264	271	260	242	242
Other M	50	51	56	57	57	60
Other F	53	54	58	59	60	62
Total	3,774	3,574	3,772	3,431	3,199	3,221

☐ White   ▨ Black   ▧ Other

The number of Americans turning eighteen will decline between 1984 and 1994. This will present recruiting difficulties for the nation's armed forces.

Source: U.S. Bureau of the Census, Current Population Reports, series P-25, no. 952, "Projections of the Population of the United States: 1983 to 2080" (U.S. Government Printing Office, 1984), pp. 41–61. Figures are rounded.

Table 7-1. Qualified and Available Males Required for Military Service, Selected Periods, 1984-1995

	1984-1988	1991-1995		
		A	B	C
	Annual Average (thousands)			
Total noninstitutionalized eighteen-year-old males	1,800	1,612	1,612	1,612
Minus: college enrollees less first- or second-year dropouts	525	464	464	464
Minus: mentally unqualified	337	291	291	486
Minus: physically or morally unqualified	189	170	170	131
Equals: qualified and available male pool	749	687	687	531
Total male recruit requirements	376	376	413	413
Active forces	278	278	297	297
Reserve forces	98	98	116	116
Percent of pool required	50	55	60	78

Source: Derived from Martin Binkin, *America's Volunteer Military: Progress and Prospects* (Washington, D.C.: Brookings Institution, 1984), pp. 31-39.

would not meet minimum standards. Thus during this period the pool of prospective male volunteers would be filling by about 750,000 a year, out of whom the armed forces would need to attract half—about 376,000—to meet planned recruitment requirements. By the early 1990s, the figure grows to 55 percent as the noninstitutionalized eighteen-year-old cohort drops to about 1.6 million (scenario A in table 7-1). Not factored into this calculation, however, are the effects of the anticipated increase in the size of the armed forces and the possible adoption of more stringent entrance standards, as the Army's recent proposals to attract higher-quality recruits suggest.

Military Buildup

Although the Reagan administration, bowing to budget pressures, has appeared to retreat from its initial intentions to expand substantially the size of the armed services commensurate with its military buildup, modest increases in active strength are still planned for the Air Force and Navy. Additional Air Force manpower would support the deployment of cruise missiles to Europe, the MX, and the expansion in tactical fighter wings; the Navy increase would support a 600 ship fleet. The Army, for its part, scrapped earlier plans to expand its active component and now plans only to increase the size of its reserve components. All other things equal, adding roughly 200,000 to the active and reserve military rolls as planned could be expected to increase the average annual requirement for male recruits by approximately 27,000, raising the total to 413,000 or 60 percent of the qualified and available population in the early 1990s (scenario B in table 7–1).[22]

Quality Factor

In addition to the prospect that the military services may have to attract more recruits is the possibility that they may have to seek better recruits—that is, those possessing aptitudes for absorbing more complex technical training. The changes that will be required in the quality mix are difficult to predict, but the potential effects can be illustrated. For example, assuming that the Army adopts higher standards to achieve its ambitious goal for quality recruits, fewer young males will qualify for military service. At the extreme, if the Army adopted the minimum standards now used by the Air Force, the pool of qualified and available male youths would shrink by over 20 percent, and three out of every four would eventually have to enlist to meet projected military requirements in the early 1990s (scenario C in table 7–1).[23]

Competition from Higher Education

The decline in the youth population will affect not only the military but all youth-dependent institutions, including higher education. To offset expected enrollment losses from the traditional student pool, many colleges and universities are expecting to attract greater numbers of adults and foreigners.[24] If these strategies prove to be unsuccessful, however, many higher education institutions will try to attract more traditional college-age youths, perhaps by lowering admission standards. To the extent that the college participation rate of this group increases, the pool would shrink further, and the recruitment task would become even more challenging.

Options

Whether the armed forces can continue to attract a sufficient number of volunteers meeting appropriate quality standards is uncertain, with a great deal depending on the state of the economy, how much the nation is willing to invest in the military payroll, and, perhaps most important, how the concept of appropriate quality is defined. The prospect of a slowdown in the rate of economic recovery in 1985—bad news for the nation but good news for military recruiters—would tend to offset the effects of the less than comparable increase in military pay that the administration proposes. On balance, although the Army might be unable to meet its goals for high-quality males, serious recruitment shortages should not develop in 1985. It is important, nevertheless, to hedge against the possibility of future problems. A variety of practical measures are available to reduce the demand for high-quality male recruits (the most critical resource) or to increase their supply. The major options are: to increase recruitment incentives, to curtail the planned growth of the active forces, to utilize more uniformed women or civilians in jobs now done by military men, to reduce turnover by retaining people longer, to accept lower-quality recruits, or to expand the recruitment market.

Increasing Recruitment Incentives

When and if the armed forces begin to experience problems in attracting recruits with the desired qualitative characteristics, they can be expected to call first for increases in financial incentives. Among their top priorities will be general increases in military pay levels, which because of recent pay caps, the Pentagon reports to have fallen behind comparable private sector salaries by about 12 percent as of January 1985. To restore that difference by means of across-the-board increases would cost roughly $5 billion a year in actual outlays and tack over $7 billion a year onto the defense budget (to account for accrued retirement costs). Neither the administration nor the Congress would be likely to support this restoration, given concerns over the federal deficit.

Targeted pays, such as enlistment bonuses, would be more cost-effective, but their widespread use is generally resisted by those who worry about the compression of pay between the upper and lower ranks and those who contend that differential pay contributes to morale problems. Moreover, a small but influential group of legislators, who oppose enlistment bonuses in principle as contributing to the mercenary image of voluntary forces, find the recently enacted GI bill a more palatable approach. But the extent to which the recently enacted GI bill will serve those purposes remains to be seen.

Curtailing the Manpower Expansion

Congress has already put pressure on the administration to rethink its plans for expansion. Congress cut Pentagon requests for additional active military manpower in each of the last three years while encouraging a larger role for reserve forces. Whether the net effect on the recruitment task would be beneficial, however, would depend on the extent to which a reserve buildup could be accomplished by a greater dependence on signing up veterans leaving active duty rather than by attracting new recruits. If not, the recruitment problem would merely be transferred from the active to the reserve forces, and the overall task would remain essentially unchanged, unless it proves easier to attract high-quality youths to the reserve forces than to the active forces.

Expanding the Role of Women

The services have been under continued pressure to widen opportunities for women. Although the expansion over the last decade in the number of military women has been quite dramatic, there remains a widespread feeling that more can be done, especially by the Air Force, which is least constrained by existing laws and policies regarding combat exposure. In fact, the FY85 defense authorization bill included a provision requiring that 19 percent of Air Force recruits in FY87 and 22 percent in FY88 be female.[25] These represent substantial increases over an average of 13.7 percent during the 1981–1984 period and the 14 percent goal for FY85.

Since the Air Force has traditionally had little difficulty in filling its ranks with high-quality males, forcing it to take in more women appears to have greater social than military merit. If preliminary research results hold up, however, the Army can expect to attract one high-quality male recruit for every two that the Air Force foregoes.[26]

The possibilities to expand the role of women are narrower in the other military services, but the issue deserves further consideration. The nation has yet to come to grips with the basic question of whether the laws and policies that constrain further expansion are justified by valid national security concerns or instead remain anchored in sexual stereotypes of an earlier era.

Substituting Civilians

The possibility for substituting civilian for military personnel in appropriate jobs also deserves attention. While some progress has been made over the last decade in the utilization of civilians (federal and contract), there is ample evidence that the potential has not been fully exploited. One analysis suggests that the Navy could fill at least 17,000 and perhaps as many as 45,000 shore billets with civilians without degrading fleet capabilities.[27] Overall it has been estimated that roughly 300,000 positions now filled by military personnel conceivably could be filled by civilians, even after allowing for overseas deployments and job rotations.[28] Moreover, advances in military technology should open even more opportunities for civilians. With the greater emphasis on replacing failed equipment with easily substituted units (so-called black-box replacement) at the operational unit level, for example, a greater share of the equipment maintenance burden should be absorbed at the civilian-manned depot level.

Reducing Personnel Turnover

The retention of a larger proportion of military personnel is another means for reducing the requirement for new recruits. This approach, moreover, would also provide an effective corps of specialists and technicians more closely matched to the technological needs of the modern military. The appropriate mix of career and first-term members is a controversial question, influenced by the military's accent on youth and adherence to the traditional pyramidal rank structure. To realize the full potential of a more seasoned military force, however, would require a restructuring of the military compensation system. Reform of the military retirement system should be an integral part of that restructuring.

Assessing the Quality Mix

Since the recruiting task is so sensitive to the level of manpower quality being sought, it is important that the services' quality requirements be scrutinized. In the face of technological advancements it may well be that soldiers of the future will have to be better qualified if they are to be effective. But if the Army's goals regarding quality carry too high a price tag, proposed weapons systems should be reexamined with a view toward making them more compatible with the capabilities of the people whom the Army can realistically expect to attract and retain. This is not to say that the Army should eschew high technology; rather it suggests that greater emphasis be placed on reliability and maintainability, even if some capability must be sacrificed.

Penetrating New Markets

In addition to the possible measures for decreasing the demand for high-quality males, the armed forces could look to new markets to expand the supply of prospective volunteers. Among the candidate groups are the over 1 million males enrolled in the nation's two-year community colleges and vocational training schools. To date, the military services have targeted most of their recruiting resources to the familiar ground of the nation's high school campuses. They have appeared hesitant to move into the postsecondary market out of concern that college students might require a premium, such as entry at a higher grade or the promise of accelerated promotion, which would disrupt normal promotion flow and probably diminish morale. Yet the army's new Hi-Grad program is a step in this direction and, if it proves cost-effective, could become a model for an expanded program.

Summary

The vitality of the nation's volunteer forces today stands in sharp contrast to the dismal state of military manpower in the late 1970s. Indeed, after suffering their worst recruiting year under the modern volunteer concept in 1980, the military services—aided by the deepest recession in the postwar era and substantial increases in military pay—rebounded dramatically and since 1981 have posted unparalleled recruitment statistics.

But there were signs in 1984 that the golden age of military recruiting may be drawing to a close as the Army and, to a lesser extent, the Navy signed up fewer recruits from the top half of the youth population than they had the year before. This downturn should not have come as a surprise since military recruiters were not only drawing volunteers from a shrinking youth population but from an economy with expanded civilian job opportunities. Also the fact that since 1982 military pay was permitted to erode relative to civilian pay probably caught up with recruiters. On top of this, the Army tried to attract the best-qualified recruits in its history.

Despite the infusion of additional incentives by the Army in late 1984, 1985 probably will not be any better unless the economy falters beyond reasonable expectations. A failure of the Army to meet its requirements in 1985, however, is unlikely to prompt serious concern among defense policymakers or legislators, inasmuch as the Army's goals appear to be based at least as much on judgment as on technical merit.

The question will not disappear, however, and in fact looms as the most important contemporary military manpower issue. As the youth population continues to dwindle later in the decade, the Army will find it increasingly difficult—and expensive—to recruit competent volunteers, especially if the U.S. economy remains healthy.

Early attention to the question of the Army's quality mix is important. If the Army is seeking more quality than it needs, it should lower its sights lest it squander limited defense resources or unnecessarily prompt a return to conscription. But if the Army's quest for quality is legitimate, options need to be investigated, analyzed, and decided on before serious shortfalls develop. The longer action is postponed, the less effective it will be. Given the potential financial, social, and security implications of the issue, it deserves a place high on the national agenda in 1985 and 1986.

Chapter 8

Organization and Management

Philip Odeen

I n many ways, the defense debate during 1984 followed a traditional pattern. The DOD budget was the prime topic, with the argument focusing on the rate of real growth: 3 percent, 5 percent, 7 percent, or something more. Little attention was devoted to examining the purposes for the proposed capability or even the cost-effectiveness of planned forces and programs. The DOD's ability to manage the acquisition process also became an issue, with the focus primarily on the cost of spare parts. ICBM modernization, and the MX in particular, continued to be a knotty, controversial problem. But a new issue also drew some attention: the organizational structure of the DOD.

The organizational issue surfaced in 1982 when General David Jones, then chairman of the Joint Chiefs of Staff, proposed a series of reforms to strengthen the chairman's role and give the Joint Staff more independence and competence. The debate was stimulated further when General Edward C. (Shy) Meyer, Army chief of staff, made an even more sweeping set of proposals. A spate of articles and conferences resulted, and the Senate and House of Representatives held hearings and drafted legislation to implement certain of the changes. This debate has continued and has broadened well beyond the question of how the Joint Chiefs of Staff (JCS) are organized.

Major Developments during 1984

Presidential Campaign

Defense organization and management was not a significant issue in the 1984 presidential campaign or even in the Senate and House races. Both presidential candidates endorsed continued growth of defense spending (although at different

147

rates of increase), and clashes between the two over specific issues failed to generate much interest. The real differences were more in the foreign policy realm on such issues as arms control, Central America, and the Middle East.

Walter Mondale felt President Reagan was vulnerable in the areas of the risk of nuclear war and lack of progress in arms control negotiations with the Soviets. But these issues never developed to the point where they made much of a difference in voting behavior. Mondale's occasional attacks on the administration's management of defense—charges ranging from neglect of readiness to failure to manage the acquisition of spare parts—also failed to strike a responsive chord. Therefore the campaign debates and speeches shifted to bread-and-butter issues, especially taxes or broad foreign policy and arms control questions. Defense management was not an issue of consequence in the election.

Organization

The debate over defense organization during 1984 took place largely in the halls of Congress. The initial focus was almost entirely on the JCS issue, spurred by the reforms proposed by Generals Jones and Meyer. Critics cited a number of shortcomings in the persent organization and related procedures. First, the chairman of the JCS had too many constraints on his ability to provide independent, cross-service advice. Furthermore, the service responsibilities and loyalties of the chiefs of staff made it difficult for them to provide independent advice in areas where the vital interests of their respective services were at question. Additionally the JCS was tied up in complex procedures that gave the services a virtual veto over recommendations and led to compromised positions and vague, verbose advice. Finally, the quality of officers assigned to the Joint Staff was spotty since it did little for their careers. Moreover, they risked their future if they failed to support their service's position on important issues.

In the light of the interest generated by Jones and Meyer, the House Armed Services Committee (HASC) held hearings during 1983 on JCS reform. Responding to requests from Congress, the Reagan administration proposed the following modest changes: (1) inserting the chairman in the operational chain of command, in place of the Joint Chiefs; (2) eliminating the 400 officer ceiling on the size of the Joint Staff; and (3) relaxing restrictions on the length of Joint Staff tours and repeat tours. Following the hearings, the HASC passed a bill to strengthen the chairman and Joint Staff, which was later approved by the full House. The Senate did not act on the House bill that year, but HASC persisted, raising the issue again in 1984, this time with modest results.

The House bill put pressure on a reluctant Senate at least to consider the issue. Senator John Tower, chairman of the Senate Armed Services Committee (SASC), scheduled a series of thirteen hearings, which began in September and lasted until December 1983. A total of thirty-four witnesses were heard, including senior administration officials (Secretary Weinberger, the service secretaries, and chiefs), as well as a range of outsiders, mostly former civilian and military officials. As the *Armed Services Journal* noted, all but one felt that reform was needed.[1] The hearings broadened the debate well beyond the JCS question, encompassing the Office of the Secretary of Defense (OSD), the service secretaries and staffs, the unified and specified commanders (CINCs), and the Congress.[2]

Following these extensive hearings, the committee staff prepared an exhaustive report for the members. Although it has not been released, it apparently covers a broad spectrum of possible reforms, including changes that affect the OSD, the service secretariats, and the JCS. A series of diversions, including the Lebanon crisis and the never-ending battle over the budget, as well as the reported reluctance of Chairman Tower to take on the controversy that the JCS issue was certain to arouse, kept the full SASC from formally reacting to the report. Thus the SASC did not address the House bill or even openly debate the report that its staff prepared.

The HASC persisted, appending its JCS reform bill to the FY85 defense authorization request and thereby forcing the Senate to consider the issue in conference. The House bill accepted the three changes proposed by the secretary of defense and added other major provisions.[3] The chairman: would be given the right to provide advice in his own right (as opposed to speaking for entire JCS) and to manage the Joint Staff, would be a permanent member of the National Security Council, would be permitted to set the agenda for meetings of the Joint Chiefs and select officers for assignment to the Joint Staff from lists submitted by the services; and would be directed to supervise the CINCs and be their spokesman in Washington.

The authorization conference proved to be an impossible place to consider such complex and controversial matters, especially in 1984 when there were major differences in funding levels between the two houses, as well as sharp disputes over key weapons such as the MX. The Senate side, led by Chairman Tower, was adamantly set against accepting the House bill and agreed to only a few minor changes.[4] These changes permitted the chairman to select Joint Staff officers from nominees offered by the services, establish the timing of JCS decisions, and act as the CINC's spokesman in Washington on operational matters. In addition, the legislation eased certain limits on the length of Joint Staff tours (increased from three to four years) and the time between repeat tours (two versus three years). The goal was to provide more continuity and experience to the staff.

More important than these modest changes was the apparent commitment of both houses of Congress to address reorganization in 1985. The report pledged both the HASC and SASC to study JCS and DOD reform "with the intent of enacting legislation during the next legislative year." They agreed those issues will receive "high priority," while stating that JCS reform "cannot be treated in isolation" from other problems within the Pentagon.[5]

In addition, the report addressed a series of questions to the key players in DOD, including the secretary of defense, the JCS chairman, the service chiefs, and the CINCs, that were to be answered by March 1, 1985.[6] The questions covered virtually every issue regarding the organization of OSD, the services, the JCS, and the CINCs, as well as questions regarding defense planning, weapons acquisition, and programming and budgeting.

Despite the apparently clear commitment in the conference report and any debate that the Pentagon's response to its list of questions may provoke, the likelihood of results in 1985 is still unclear. New leadership on both armed services committees adds a note of uncertainty but also increases the probability that action will be taken. Perhaps more important is the question of whether Secretary Weinberger is interested in change or even willing to support a few modest initiatives. To date the secretary's focus has been on the budget; he tended to see organizational issues as a diversion. Whether he will change his stance during a second Reagan administration is uncertain. Thus, 1985 has the potential, but not the certainty, of being the biggest year for defense organizational change since 1958.

The issue of how Congress addresses the defense budget and program was also raised during 1984. Ask a senior defense official about the source of the Pentagon's problems, and Congress is almost certainly raised as one, if not the primary, culprit. Although this reaction is almost certainly overdrawn, few observers doubt that the Congress must bear some of the blame. Its review of the DOD program and budget seems interminable; three sets of committees (Budget, Armed Services, and Appropriations) in each chamber call a wide range of defense witnesses and submit countless questions for information to the department. During 1983, for example, DOD witnesses appeared some 1,300 times before 96 committees and subcommittees. Some 400,000 pages of materials justifying the budget were submitted to the relevant committees. In addition, DOD reports receiving 85,000 written inquiries from the Hill and some 600,000 telephone calls. The problem, however, goes well beyond attendance at hearings and answering inquiries. The committees made thousands of changes in programs. Most were minor, but even small changes can disrupt program execution, raising costs and slowing deliveries.

Many of the program changes may be justified. Indeed the sharp increase in them over the last few years reflects the role Congress has played in limiting DOD budget increases to levels that Congress, at least, believes can be sustained in the light of large deficits. The Congress has made unprecedented reductions in the DOD authorization and budget requests, ranging from 5 to over 7 percent in the last four years. Given the reluctance to kill major programs, the reductions have been accomplished by making literally thousands of smaller cuts, affecting virtually every appropriation line item. In a sense, Congress is playing the role usually played by the OSD comptroller or the Office of Management and Budget. Nonetheless, few people would dispute the charge that congressional micromanagement has increased exponentially in recent years. In part this is a function of the sharp increase in staff who are looking for ways to serve their members and make a mark. Measuring the extent of this growth is difficult, but one knowledgeable ex-official estimates that staff have increased between four and ten times over the past twenty years. Other factors include the proliferation of specialized subcommittees looking at particular aspects of the DOD program and the weakening of the control once exercised by the committee chairmen.

Many congressional leaders are troubled by the situation, and there is a growing interest in reform. A number of studies, committees, and internal groups are discussing ways to simplify the committee structure and streamline procedures. Among the more encouraging developments are the following:

In 1983 and 1984, there were numerous legislative proposals to establish a biennial budget. None of these proposals was acted on during the Ninety-eighth Congress.

During 1984, Congressman Anthony Beilenson chaired a House task force on the budget process. The report, which recommended some changes in the

1974 Budget Reform Act, was referred to the Government Affairs Committee. The committee held a hearing on the report but took no further action.

Senator Daniel Quayle chaired a task force on Senate procedures. The bulk of this group's report dealt with committee assignments. An appendix called for implementation of a biennial budget cycle, which was not taken up by the Senate.

Congressman Jim Wright introduced a bill late in 1984 to establish separate capital and operational budgets. No action was taken, but it seemed likely that Wright would reintroduce his bill in the Ninety-ninth Congress.

Budget

The defense budget was clearly the most time-consuming issue during 1984, with the FY85 budget absorbing the attention of senior defense management and the Congress from January through September. The FY86 budget was the major issue within the executive branch for the rest of the year.

The Reagan administration was successful in getting its way on the budget in its initial year. In particular, major additions to the FY81 budget were accepted, almost without debate or change. But since then substantial reductions have been made each year by the Congress, as shown in table 8–1.

Table 8–1. Congressional Reductions in Defense Budget, FY82–FY85

	Requested (billions of dollars)	Congressional Reductions (billions of dollars)	Percent Reduction
FY82	226.5	12.7	5.6
FY83	257.5	18.9	7.3
FY84	273.4	15.3	5.6
FY85	305.0	20.3	6.7

Despite these substantial cuts, DOD is receiving significantly more funding than was contemplated during the Carter administration. Moreover, despite some claims to the contrary, the Reagan administration has largely fulfilled its pledge in 1981 to provide substantial increases to the defense budget. Comparisons with the Carter plans and even with the initial Reagan proposal are not easy to make due to significant changes in actual and prospective inflation. The five-year budget numbers include an inflation factor, and these factors have changed significantly since 1981. Thus, most easily made comparisons are not meaningful since the earlier numbers assumed very high inflation. This is the basis for recent DOD claims that they are budgeting less for defense than the Carter administration planned.

Secretary Weinberger's strategy in the budget battle is to ask for very large increases and refuse to compromise. Some argue that this strategy is faulty. If he worked with the Congress and requested more realistic increases, the results would be even more dollars for DOD. There is considerable evidence that such an approach would have been successful with the 1985 budget at least. A deal with Congress for a 7 percent real growth increase seemed within reach in the spring of 1984 but was rejected by the administration. (DOD eventually received 5 percent.) But for the other years, the case is less persuasive. Regardless of the correctness of the strategy, one thing is clear: the result has been the biggest congressional cuts in the defense budget in post-World War II history. The cuts in the past four budgets have ranged from 5½ to over 7 percent, figures that dwarf cuts in other years. In 1980, for example, President Carter's defense request of $139.3 billion was only cut $1.5 billion or 1 percent. During the tight budget days of the 1950s and 1970s, cuts of as much as 2 percent were rare (indeed, during the late 1950s, Congress often added to the budget).

The most serious issue regarding Secretary Weinberger's strategy is whether it results in increments of real output in military capability to match the higher input of funds. In effect, this approach lets Congress play the role of the Office of Management and Budget (OMB), making major cuts and in the process establishing or changing priorities and deciding which programs move ahead or lose ground. Moreover, congressional cuts follow a pattern that can adversely affect readiness and sustainability, crucial aspects of overall defense capability. For example, major weapons programs are almost never killed (unless they are foreign-produced items) since such hard choices run head on into local employment needs and the lobbying clout of the aerospace companies and unions. Weapons delivery schedules are often stretched, that is, the United States buys fewer weapons than planned during a year, stretching the purchase over more years (for example, sixty per month in lieu of seventy). Although this reduces the need for funds in the near term, it leads to higher unit costs and greater total program costs (assuming DOD eventually buys the planned number). It also delays the modernization of U.S. forces. Cuts are frequently made in those accounts that provide quick reductions in outlays. These are also the accounts that directly affect readiness for combat and the ability to sustain a conflict after it starts. Most vulnerable are funds for operations and maintenance and miscellaneous procurement (such as spare parts, ammunition and combat consumables such as wing tanks). There is little constituency for these programs, other than the combatant forces and a small group of enlightened senators and congressmen. Finally, if cuts are made in construction funds, they are for overseas projects (such as barracks for troops in German or maintenance facilities for forces deployed in the Far East), not projects in the United States.

Readiness

The readiness issue did get some attention in 1984, in part due to a HASC report that sharply criticized the Reagan administration's record in this area. The report stated that readiness funding had been sacrificed to buy new weapons. It pointed up wide differences in readiness levels between the services as well as within individual services. Moreover, by some measures, readiness levels had barely improved since 1980. In short, the Reagan buildup had failed in one of its major objectives.

Defense reacted strongly, with senior military leaders attesting to the great progress made over the last four years, especially in the areas of the quality of manpower and the modernity of U.S. equipment. A flurry of press conferences, speeches, and statements ensued to rebut the House report. The result was essentially a standoff. But there is agreement on some issues. First, readiness programs have not received the priority or funding given modernization. Second, readiness is poorly defined (for example, does it include such matters as the ability to sustain a conflict?) and is hard to measure precisely. Third, the existing measures and reporting systems leave much to be desired and need improvement if the issues are to be addressed rationally.

Test and Evaluation

Another organizational issue that clouded relations between DOD and the Congress during 1984 was the form and influence to be given the operational testing function. The need for an independent testing staff has been recognized for well over a decade. Such a staff was proposed by Secretary Melvin Laird's Blue Ribbon study panel in 1970. In response, an Operational Test and Evaluation (OT&E) office was created and headed by a senior, respected military officer. Its role was to oversee service OT&E efforts and advise the secretary on the readiness of weapons to move into production. The office was placed under the direction of the undersecretary of defense for research and engineering (then called the director of defense research and engineering).

Critics objected to this organizational structure, feeling that objectivity and independence were compromised by placing OT&E under the control of the chief weapons developer who presumably was an advocate for new technology. Given these concerns, Secretary Harold Brown considered placing the office under the assistant secretary for program analysis and evaluation (PA&E). This shift was not made, however, and the OT&E function continues to be part of the Research and Engineering Office.

In late 1983, Congress mandated that the OT&E function be taken out of the R&E office and that the director be made to report directly to the secretary of defense. DOD fought this provision, trying to get it dropped from the defense authorization bill. After it became law, senior OSD officials tried to get Congress to rescind the provision, although it soon became clear that this would not happen. The battle then shifted to the nature of the office's charter, staffing, and other bureaucratic considerations. At the end of 1984 a permanent director had still not been selected.

The Congress continues to be critical of DOD's lack of response on this matter and seeming resistance to a clear mandate. DOD counters by saying that the issues of organization and relationship to other parts of OSD and the services are complex and require thoughtful resolution. Moreover, it was difficult to attract a strong candidate for the director position given the obviously controversial nature of the job and the upcoming election. Regardless of where the truth lies, the status of the OT&E function is still confused. There should be some clarification during 1985.

Acquisition Process

The question of spare parts costs was the 1984 defense issue that received the most attention by the media and had the greatest impact on the public. Strategic deterrence theory and ICBM vulnerability are difficult for the lay public to comprehend, but $7,000 coffee makers and $400 hammers are easy to understand and therefore had real consequences for public views on defense spending.

The press and congressional outcry generated far more heat than light, but it did force DOD to give the problem greater priority. A number of remedial actions were taken. First, DOD mandated greater competition in the purchase of spares, as well as efforts to buy in larger quantities (in some cases the problem was caused by a decision to buy a few items, which led to costly production setup and a short production run). Second, procedural changes were made, such as providing descriptions and pictures to ensure that buyers actually knew what they were purchasing. In some cases the purchasing officer had no idea that he was paying an outrageous price for an item since he was merely dealing with a part number. Third, higher-level approval of purchases was required where prices increased more than 25 percent over past prices. Scant attention was often paid to sharp, unjustified increases. Fourth, certifications were mandated from suppliers that the prices charged the government were the lowest charged anyone else, thereby putting a legal burden on the seller.

In addition, a new staff element in OSD was established to oversee service spare parts programs. Headed by a deputy assistant secretary in the manpower, installations and logistics office, the staff is developing new management initiatives

"HEY, BUDDY, COULD YOU SPARE 1,500 BUCKS FOR A CUP OF COFFEE?"

and oversight mechanisms. But given the scope of the DOD spares purchasing, it is unlikely the problem of excessive prices will be solved.

A related acquisition reform effort launched by Deputy Secretary William Taft late in 1984 may also help with the spare parts problem. It involved a program to reduce the heavy use of military specifications. At present DOD frequently uses long, detailed specifications to spell out what it wishes to buy (for example, a four-page specification for men's underwear). The goal is to make the buying process objective and to ensure that the various bidders are proposing the same item, making it possible to use price as the basis for decisions. In fact the heavy use of specifications often has perverse effects. Available and perfectly adequate commercial items may not meet the specs exactly and therefore may not be proposed— or if they are, modifications have to be made that drive up costs without increasing serviceability or performance. In other cases, a product may meet the spec precisely but suffer other shortcomings since given the volume of specs to be written, they often have weaknesses or inadvertent errors. By taking judgment out of the process, we get less from our dollar. Overly detailed specs also make it more costly to produce spare parts. Special production runs may be needed to produce the item. Moreover, specs make use of less costly substitutions difficult, if not impossible.

Steps to Strengthen DOD Organization and Management

Historical Background

Since the end of World War II, the central issue with regard to how the U.S. defense establishment is organized and managed has been the degree to which the distinct military capabilities of the Army, Navy, Air Force, and Marine Corps need to be centrally directed and integrated if the United States is to plan, prepare for, and conduct effective military operations.[7] That some integration is required was amply demonstrated during World War II itself. In the words of President Eisenhower, "Separate land, sea, and air warfare is gone forever." Modern warfare requires not only unity of operational command but also integrated and coordinated means to prepare strategic plans and to develop and procure forces and equipment. On several occasions since 1945, U.S. presidents, military leaders, and defense officials have sought to implement measures designed to integrate the defense establishment more closely and provide stronger central management over the military departments.

The National Security Act of 1947 established the secretary of defense as the primary agent of integration in the defense establishment. The secretary is the principal adviser to the president for matters of national defense and has the primary responsibility for translating guidance from the president and the National Security Council into specific policy directives for the armed forces. The secretary must ensure that U.S. military capabilities are able to accomplish the president's national strategic purposes. A crucial element of this effort is the allocation of resources among the various missions and major organizational components of DOD. Thus the secretary must play a crucial role in decisions on the services programs and budgets to ensure they are buying the capability required to meet the president's and secretary's vision of security goals and priorities.

To support the secretary in these roles, a range of staff organizations and management processes have been created. The desire of the military services to retain their historic autonomy, as well as the institutional conflict between the executive and legislative branches, have ensured that these mechanisms develop slowly through a process of evolutionary rather than revolutionary, change. Radical realignments, such as disestablishing the military departments or creating a single service, were rejected during congressional debate over the 1947 National Security Act and have received little support since. Instead, beginning with the 1949 amendments to the National Security Act, greater integration of the defense establishment has been sought by creating a single Department of Defense encompassing all three military departments and by balancing the influence of the services with two central organizations—one civilian and one military. On the civilian side, the OSD was established to support the secretary in his integrative role of coordinating the plans and programs of the military departments. On the uniformed side, the joint military structure—consisting of the JCS, the Joint Staff, and the CINCs—was strengthened to provide integrated military advice for the secretary and joint direction of military operations.

Subsequent reforms during the Eisenhower administration strengthened the role and the authority of OSD and the joint military structure. Building on these reforms in the early 1960s, Secretary of Defense Robert S. McNamara instituted the planning, programming, and budgeting system (PPBS) to link defense planning to specific program and budget decisions. The reforms initiated by President Eisenhower and Secretary McNamara concentrated on three objectives:

1. Increasing the ability of the existing joint military structures to provide realistic, relevant, and integrated military advice, planning, and operational direction.
2. Reinforcing the ability of OSD to assist the secretary in integrating and managing the plans, programs, and budgets of the military departments.
3. Establishing force development and acquisition processes designed to ensure that defense resources are linked to overall national strategic priorities.

Since the early 1960s, a series of experts and official studies have criticized the defense organization, but virtually no significant changes have been made in the formal structure by which the DOD conducts its business. Moreover, changes to key management processes have been limited. In the view of many observers and participants, the postwar period of defense organizational evolution is still incomplete. This stagnated structural evolution is seen as an important cause of the range of problems that confront the United States in managing its national defense efforts.

Key Problems

Both the structure and management processes of DOD have shortcomings. Four structural problems stand out. First, responsibility and authority are not clearly spelled out. Everyone—the services, OSD, Congress, JCS, even the OMB and the National Security Council—tends to share responsibility for virtually all aspects of the defense program. And when everyone is responsible, in fact no one is. Second, there is little effective joint or cross-service military advice available to the secretary of defense, the president, and the Congress. Both individual and collective views are valuable, but sound cross-service advice is essential when choices must be made regarding strategy, force structure, or weapons. Third, the CINCs, who have responsibility for fighting wars, have inadequate authority or capability in peacetime to plan and prepare for potential conflicts. Last, OSD, the secretary's staff, is not well structured to provide clear policy direction and priorities or to exercise the oversight role necessary to ensure that programs are well implemented.

In the area of defense management processes, five problems deserve attention. First, the process for allocating resources, PPBS, is seriously deficient. The planning phase receives little attention; the programming and budgeting processes are disjointed and often redundant. The resulting instability undercuts the management and execution of programs. Second, far too little attention and focus go to the execution of programs or subsequent evaluation of whether and why programs were successes or failures. Third, the Congress spends far too much time reviewing the defense program and budget, with three sets of committees sequentially reviewing many of the same issues. Committees and staff are far too involved in the details of program management. This compounds the instability problem and seriously diverts the attention of both executive and congressional leadership from the larger issues of strategy, priorities, and the broad allocation of resources by mission that they should be addressing.

The fourth problem in defense management processes is that weapons requirements receive inadequate attention. Much effort and high-level attention are focused on the procurement process, but decisions on what weapons to develop get little attention by senior management. This is a critical shortcoming since it is virtually impossible to kill a program once it gets started. With too many programs underway, management is overextended and funds are spread too thin. Fifth, the weapons acquisition process tends to accentuate program instability. It has grown so complex that process tends to dominate substance. In a sense it is like the tax code, whose regulations are so arcane that only a few experts understand them, and their impact is difficult to predict. Moreover, there are too few incentives to control costs on the part of the contractors or the military departments.

Finally, one problem cuts across the entire DOD management picture: the extreme and growing complexity of the organization and key management processes. Over the years as problems develop, the answer invariably is to add a new organization or staff group in the hope of fixing the problem. In the same vein, the PPBS and weapons acquisition processes have been complicated in an effort to remedy shortcomings or avoid problems. As a result, it is difficult to fix authority and responsibility on anyone, and time demands on key decision makers make it virtually impossible to focus on broader issues or to give attention to effective program implementation. Figure 8–1 portrays, as an example, the players in DOD's development of its annual guidance for the service program and budget development.

Goals for Reform

If reforms are to make a real difference, a broad package of changes is needed, not just marginal tinkering or a single, simple change such as JCS reform. Procedures as well as organization must be improved, and all key players—the Congress, services, JCS, CINCs, and the secretary of defense and his staff (OSD)—will have to accept change. These reforms should have three primary objectives.

First, the government needs to improve the defense planning and resource allocation process to ensure that the nation develops the forces and buys the weapons and other equipment it needs to protect vital national interests and support key foreign policy objectives. The link between U.S. foreign policy and national security goals and its force structure and capabilities is weak at best. The United States cannot afford to acquire and maintain military forces that are inadequate or inappropriate in the light of the grave challenges to U.S. security. Nor, in view of the current and prospective budget deficits, can the United States afford to fund unnecessary defense programs. There are too many other pressing private and public claims on available resources.

Second, it is essential that the DOD execute the approved programs more effectively. Costs must be controlled, delivery schedules met, and new capabilities designed to meet emerging threats delivered to U.S. forces in a timely manner. To accomplish this, the military departments will have to be given greater responsibility and authority to implement approved weapon programs management processes. Reporting systems will also have to be improved.

Figure 8–1. Defense Guidance Development Process

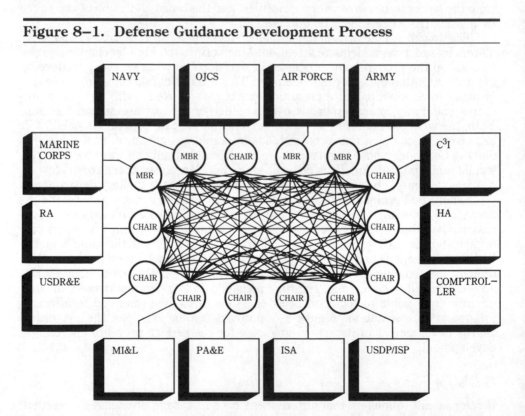

Finally, improvements should be made in the way the United States plans and prepares for military operations. Steps in this direction will strengthen the ability to employ military forces effectively and could augment the effort to deter those who might otherwise be tempted to challenge vital U.S. interests.

Program of Reforms

A broad range of improvements to DOD organization and processes is needed, together with changes in the way Congress deals with the department. The pieces of program outlined here are interdependent. Proceeding with only parts is unlikely to yield much value; however, if the full range of reforms is accepted, there should be significant improvement in the output the United States receives for the resources it allocates to defense, as well as more effective management. Moreover, it would be easier to make meaningful budget savings if the current deficit situation should force the government to allocate fewer dollars to defense.

Improved Planning and Priority Setting. The first area for reform is the policy direction provided to the services to shape the forces, weapons, and support programs they develop. Unless clear policy is provided and priorities identified, the forces of the four services are likely to be unbalanced and unable to work together effectively in the joint operations that dominate today's warfare. Moreover, U.S. capabilities are unlikely to match the national security needs as seen by the U.S. civilian leadership in the executive branch and the Congress. The needed reforms include providing more effective and relevant military advice to the civilian leadership. The current advice is either heavily skewed to views of one service or fiscally unrealistic. The current JCS structure needs to be revamped. The chairman should be given greater independent authority and control over the Joint Staff and should be required to provide advice on strategy and priorities that recognizes fiscal reality and is based on his independent judgment.

Second, greater priority should be given to the planning function by OSD and a strengthening of the staff of the under-secretary of defense for policy. This office should be organized on a mission basis to ensure that the major defense missions receive proper priority in the planning and resource allocation processes. One step that could be considered is to augment the policy staff with elements of the undersecretary of defense for research and engineering and the PA&E staff in order to give the office the ability to tie policy and priorities more closely to weapons, programs, and budgets.

Improved Resource Allocation. The way the United States allocates its scarce resources among missions and programs also needs to be revamped. The present system demands excessive time from the participants, encourages instability, and focuses too much on the inputs rather than outputs.

Shifting to a two-year budget cycle would be a welcome change. The present annual budget leads to excessive instability and turbulence since it encourages repeated changes as it undergoes a more than year-long review by OSD, OMB, and the Congress. Moreover, the process consumes so much time and energy that neither senior DOD officials nor key congressional committees are able to focus on longer-term issues, planning and strategy, or oversight of past program implementation. With a two-year cycle, DOD could focus on longer-term planning and program development in the nonbudget year, and the Congress could address such major issues as the draft versus the all-volunteer force, DOD's weapons acquisition process, or the strategic underpinnings of various major elements of the U.S. force structure.

If a two-year budget is not adopted, the programming and budgeting phases of the PPBS process should be combined into a single program-budget review and decision process. Combining them carries the risk that the longer-term program issues will be ignored, but the present approach jams both phases into a span of a few months, is duplicative and inconsistent, and consumes excessive amounts of senior officials' time. Regardless of the approach taken, the budget should be recast into program terms (that is, broken down by output or mission terms) rather than the current functional or input basis (personnel, operating costs, research, and procurement). This will ensure that the executive and legislative branches focus their review on the purposes of the spending and will understand more clearly the impact of budget changes on the major defense missions.

Increasing the emphasis within DOD on the requirements aspects of the weapons acquisition process would also improve matters. The government currently makes decisions to develop new weapons with limited critical consideration of their priority or responsiveness to essential security needs. Yet once a new system reaches the engineering development stage, the politics are such that it is almost certain to move into production. Little top-level attention from senior DOD officials or the Congress is given such weapons until after this decision point. Given the virtual political impossibility of killing a system, the government keeps them all going by uneconomic procurement rates or needlessly long development phases. The result is higher unit and total program costs and slower modernization. As one military procurement specialist puts it, "We need a rigorous process of weapons program infanticide."

Better Execution of the Program. Once Congress approves the budget, the next task is to execute the program effectively and efficiently. This critical area gets far too little attention by senior leaders, who are engaged in a never-ending effort to formulate and defend the budget. The result is far too little focus on implementation, leading to cost overruns, overpriced spare parts, and poor use of valuable personnel resources. One of the most vivid contrasts between the government and the private sector is the difference in emphasis on making decisions as opposed to executing them. The government spends 80 percent of its effort making decisions and 20 percent executing them. Large private-sector industrial operations reverse this allocation of effort. It is felt that any reasonable decision that is well executed will pay off far better than the most brilliant decision that is poorly carried out.

In this area, four reforms deserve priority attention. First, the military departments and their leaders should be made clearly responsible for implementing the approved program, and they must see this as their primary task. OSD and the Congress should focus on broad policy direction and appropriate follow-up to ensure that the service programs are consistent with the policy and priorities. To do this implies giving the military departments the necessary authority to manage well and reducing OSD and congressional interference in program detail. It also requires reducing the time and effort spent by the service chiefs and their staffs on joint military activities, freeing their energies for managing service programs.

Second, far greater emphasis should be placed on the evaluation of the results of program execution. At present little effort is spent determining how well policies and programs work—and where they do not work, in determining why not. This type of feedback should be an important element in decisions on future programs, as well as a critical aspect of ongoing program management.

Third, there is a priority need for better cost estimating. Overly optimistic cost projections lead to problems in the future when the real costs become evident, causing programs to be stretched out and delayed. One senior aerospace executive said that poor cost estimates are the greatest cause of problems in weapons acquisition. The solutions include wider use of independent estimates, parametric cost estimating procedures, and planning wedges and reserves to handle the almost certain cost growth over the life of a program.

Last, greater use of incentives is necessary to encourage program managers and contractors to hold down costs. Steps such as dual sourcing and continuous competition must be expanded. The focus of the procurement process should be on incentives, not regulations. The current acquisition process grows more cumbersome each year as the defense acquisition regulations are amended and complicated to fix this problem or solve that social or political imperative. As with the tax code, the time has come to consider a radical simplification.

Improved Means for Planning and Carrying Out Military Operations. While there are many explanations and rationalizations, recent experience in the use of military force has been less than satisfactory, to say the least. The costly *Mayaguez* rescue, the aborted Desert One attempt to rescue U.S. hostages in Iran, the peace-keeping mission in Lebanon all suggest weaknesses in the planning and direction of joint military operations. The problems appear to stem from a number of causes. These include the very limited amount of joint planning and training that actually takes place. Most of this activity is single service, and few senior officers have real expertise or experience in directing complex joint military operations. A cumbersome and bureaucratic command structure also afflicts planning and operations. The Long report on the Lebanon disaster pointed up the complexity of U.S. command arrangements and the resulting diffusion of authority and responsibility. Furthermore, joint military organizations from the CINCs to the Joint Staff are weak. This hinders the military in attracting the best officers to accept joint assignments.

The defense reforms of the 1950s instituted by President Eisenhower were directed in part at developing strong, independent joint military organizations. Eisenhower's goal was cross-services and independent advice for the civilian leadership and unified military direction of operations involving more than one service. His efforts were stymied in part by opposition in the Congress. In my view, the thrust of his reforms was correct. Further efforts to strengthen the joint military structures are needed. There are three primary areas for reform.

First, the chairman of the JCS must be given greater authority and independence. His role as the primary military adviser needs to be made explicit. In addition to the role he would play in strategic planning and resource allocation, the chairman, supported by the Joint Staff, should oversee the contingency planning, exercises, and training programs of the CINCs. In particular, working with the secretary of defense and other key executive branch officials, he must ensure that crisis planning and preparations are realistic and responsive to the priorities and political direction of the president and secretary.

Second, the CINCs should be given greater control over the service components in peacetime to make planning more effective and simplify the transition during a crisis or war. Current command relationships significantly circumscribe the CINCs' authority over the service component commands in peacetime. As part of this effort to give the CINCs a stronger role, they should be given control over funds for the readiness of their assigned forces to include the budgets for exercises, theater training, and the field operations of the forces. These changes would have the effect of providing a stronger voice for readiness in the defense establishment, counterbalancing the service view that tends to favor force structure and equipment modernization.

Third, joint military staffs need to be assigned better people. Steps must be taken to ensure that joint service helps rather than harms careers. A number of steps are needed to achieve this, including greater authority for the chairman and CINCs to select excellent officers and ensure that they are given appropriate consideration for later promotion and assignment. Other steps might include creating service specialties for officers who would periodically receive joint assignments and representation of the joint commanders on promotion boards.

Conclusion

Managing the defense establishment and directing complex joint military operations will never be easy or problem free. The tasks are difficult and the proper course of action seldom clear-cut. Moreover, issues of politics and ideology can never be separated from the task of running this vast department. Yet it can and must be run more effectively and, it is hoped, more efficiently as well. If this is to be accomplished, changes in defense organization and management processes are essential. The steps proposed here provide an outline of the reforms that are needed.

Changes in organization and procedures alone will not suffice. Sound management and effective military leadership depend primarily on the quality and experience of the civilian and military personnel who direct these sprawling organizations. A range of factors in recent years have combined to cause many of the best people to leave DOD and to deter others from taking up the challenge of leading this critical national institution. Included are inadequate pay for senior civilian and military executives, onerous conflict of interest rules that unnecessarily burden experienced executives who are considering service in defense, and the continued growth of bureaucratic procedures that deaden initiative and penalize innovation and drive. These issues, as well as issues of organization and process, deserve the highest-priority attention of the president, senior administration leaders, and the Congress. In this effort, these leaders deserve the input and critical support of interested observers, the media, and private citizens.

Chapter 9

Arms Control

Michael Krepon
Alton Frye

By every standard, 1984 was a poor year for arms control. The dominant event of the year was a nonevent: the absence of negotiations over intermediate-range and strategic nuclear forces. Washington and Moscow spent much of the year jockeying to place the blame for the demise of negotiations, as well as the burden of resumption, on the other side. The extent of the deadlock on nuclear arms control was reflected by the proliferation of compliance controversies throughout the year, suggesting that each side had grown increasingly uneasy over the other's intentions toward existing agreements.

Nevertheless, channels for dialogue remained open during 1984. The year saw a remarkable shift in the longstanding rhetoric of President Ronald Reagan, beginning in a temperate January statement on Soviet-U.S. relations and culminating in an October address to the United Nations, which set the stage for President Reagan's first meeting with Soviet Foreign Minister Andrei Gromyko. Together with a fresh formulation of the so-called linkage issue by Secretary of State George Shultz—specifically describing linkage as a tactical question that should not disrupt superpower negotiations of overriding importance—there emerged a more promising political context for resumption of the arms control process in a second Reagan term.

At year's end, the Kremlin agreed to plumb the meaning of the Reagan administration's concept of umbrella talks on a wide range of arms control subjects. Fresh from his overwhelming reelection victory, President Reagan named Paul H. Nitze as special adviser to Secretary Shultz for these talks, an appointment widely heralded as an indicator of the president's high priority on reaching an arms reduction agreement during his second term. At the same time, however, Reagan reaffirmed his pursuit of effective strategic defenses and expressed confidence in his divided team of national security advisers. The year ended on a note of cautious optimism about renewed superpower negotiations, although enduring conflicts in the president's official family and in his strategic objectives suggested that success in the talks would not come easily, if at all.

Strategic Arms and Intermediate Nuclear Forces

The year 1984 appears as a blank page in the history of nuclear arms control. For the first time since SALT began in 1969, an entire year passed without any negotiations between the superpowers over the control and reduction of nuclear armaments.

The roots of this impasse could be found in domestic U.S. politics and Soviet security policies. In the United States, skepticism toward arms control agreements had been growing throughout the SALT decade. Criticism of the SALT I accords was muted at first, in part due to the reputation of President Richard M. Nixon as a staunch anticommunist and tough negotiator. Opposition grew when it became apparent that the interim agreement governing offensive forces would have a negligible impact on Soviet strategic modernization programs. While the number of

Figure 9–1. Arms Control Agreements and Developments, 1959–1984

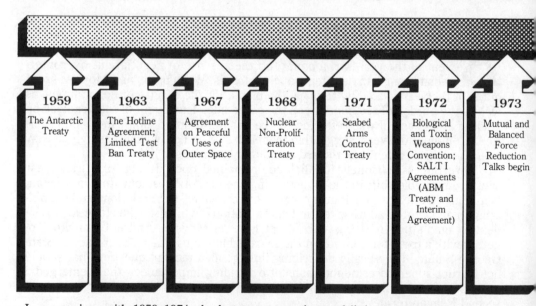

1959	1963	1967	1968	1971	1972	1973
The Antarctic Treaty	The Hotline Agreement; Limited Test Ban Treaty	Agreement on Peaceful Uses of Outer Space	Nuclear Non-Proliferation Treaty	Seabed Arms Control Treaty	Biological and Toxin Weapons Convention; SALT I Agreements (ABM Treaty and Interim Agreement)	Mutual and Balanced Force Reduction Talks begin

In comparison with 1959–1974, the last ten years witnessed little progress toward formal arms control agreements. 1985 and 1986 may produce results in dealing with intermediate-range, strategic, and "Star Wars" systems.

Sources: Caspar W. Weinberger, Secretary of Defense, Annual Report to the Congress Fiscal Year 1985 (Washington: U.S. Government Printing Office, 1984), p. 32; The New York Times, January 7, 1985, p. 5.

strategic launchers remained fairly constant, the Kremlin's nuclear war-fighting capabilities rose precipitously, due to the MIRVing of Soviet land-based missiles. Criticism of arms control gained momentum during the Carter administration, which was widely perceived as being unsteady in its handling of the superpower competition and lax in its appreciation of U.S. defense requirements. These concerns came to a head with the Soviet invasion of Afghanistan in December 1979 and forced President Carter to set aside his quest for Senate ratification of the SALT II treaty.

SALT II thus became the third consecutive nuclear arms control treaty that failed to achieve ratification. A similar fate befell the Threshold Test Ban Treaty signed by President Nixon in 1974 and the Peaceful Nuclear Explosions Treaty signed by President Ford in 1976. (See figure 9–1 for a portrayal of arms control developments since 1959.) This in itself did not signify a derailment of the negotiation process because each side could provisionally agree to honor the terms of unratified treaties contingent on corresponding restraint by the other. But the demise of the SALT II ratification effort was followed in short order by the election of a new president who, in contrast to his predecessors, was a staunch critic of prior accords. Ronald Reagan's advisers were similarly skeptical of the contributions of arms control to U.S. security, particularly SALT II.

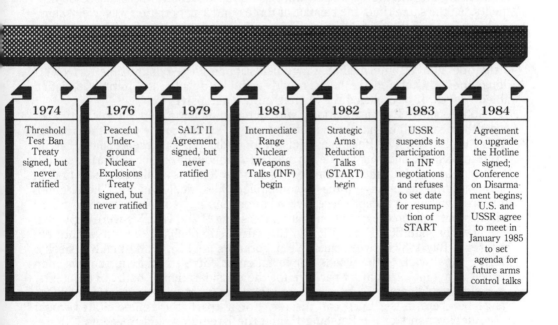

1974	1976	1979	1981	1982	1983	1984
Threshold Test Ban Treaty signed, but never ratified	Peaceful Underground Nuclear Explosions Treaty signed, but never ratified	SALT II Agreement signed, but never ratified	Intermediate Range Nuclear Weapons Talks (INF) begin	Strategic Arms Reduction Talks (START) begin	USSR suspends its participation in INF negotiations and refuses to set date for resumption of START	Agreement to upgrade the Hotline signed; Conference on Disarmament begins; U.S. and USSR agree to meet in January 1985 to set agenda for future arms control talks

Thus construction stopped in 1981 on the edifice of strategic arms control, an enterprise whose basic foundations were none too firm to begin with. Nor was Washington in any hurry to resume an arms control dialogue. The negotiations over INFs, called for by NATO's "dual track" decision mandating arms control efforts plus deployments, began in November 1981, prompted in good measure by large street demonstrations in Europe and strong entreaties by government leaders of the countries where Pershing II and GLCMs were to be based. The administration's opening proposal on strategic arms was not unveiled until May 1982, seventeen months after assuming office. START, as SALT was renamed, began one month later.

Intermediate-Range Weapons

The initial U.S. and Soviet negotiating positions in both START and INF were far apart. In the INF negotiations, the common thread in a succession of Soviet proposals was the exclusion of NATO intermediate-range missiles in Western Europe. While the Kremlin indicated a willingness to accept considerable reductions in its own forces to achieve such a result, its insistence on preventing the deployment of new NATO missiles precluded successful negotiation. The Reagan administration held an extremely weak hand in the INF talks. Administration officials were inclined to deploy the Pershing and GLCMs, but U.S. allies insisted on a strong negotiating effort and were reluctant to receive Euromissile deployments. At the same time, the balance of forces under negotiation was overwhelmingly in favor of the Soviet Union. The administration's opening bid masterfully collated these negatives to support its own preferences. The zero option—NATO's proposal to cancel its prospective deployments if the Soviet Union would agree to dismantle all of its intermediate-range ballistic missiles—bought time for NATO deployments, captured the high ground in public debate, and initially satisfied allied wishes. It also placed the Soviets on the defensive.

Subsequently INF negotiations, with one significant exception, recapitulated basic themes, with both sides indicating some flexibility in the pursuit of irreconcilable objectives. The Reagan administration indicated the acceptability of an interim agreement allowing the deployment of a politically, if not militarily, significant number of intermediate-range missiles as long as a sizable reduction in Soviet intermediate-range forces accompanied these deployments. The Kremlin appeared willing to accept successively larger cuts in its modern force of SS-20 missiles but only on the condition that no Pershing II and GLCMs were deployed.

The one significant exception to this ritualistic exchange was a private encounter in July 1982 between chief INF negotiators Paul Nitze and Yuli Kvitsinsky. During this "walk in the woods" undertaken at Nitze's initiative, the two men agreed to a joint exploratory package for the consideration of both governments: each side would deploy 75 intermediate-range missile launchers and 150 medium-range bombers in the European theater. For its part, the United States would forgo deployments of the Pershing II, and the Kremlin would freeze its INF deployments in the Pacific theater.

Both Washington and Moscow distanced themselves from the walk in the woods formula. After Nitze's return to Washington, President Reagan reaffirmed the need for Pershing II as well as cruise missile deployments, and Secretary of

State Shultz was reminded of the need for discipline within the bureaucratic ranks in a memorandum from national security adviser William Clark, a clear, if indirect, rebuke to Nitze. The belated Soviet reaction came just prior to the resumption of formal negotiations, with a harsh attack by Ambassador Kvitsinsky on the U.S. negotiating position.

In retrospect, it is difficult to see how the Kremlin could have accepted any buildup in NATO forces and reduction in Soviet intermediate-range forces to equal levels as the walk in the woods formula envisioned. In any event, the Reagan administration's reaction to Ambassador Nitze's efforts made the Soviet position academic. The president's advisers convinced him that forgoing a modest number of Pershing II deployments was an unacceptable price to pay for Soviet acceptance of equal levels in intermediate-range forces. In justification for their coolness toward the walk in the woods, administration officials later expressed concern that the Soviets would pocket Ambassador Nitze's concessions while bargaining on the remainder of the package. Both sides could employ these negotiating tactics, however. The walk in the woods presented a far better baseline for negotiations than the balance of forces then in being, a balance that could improve over time only with unilateral Soviet restraint.

The failure of the president and those around him to embrace Ambassador Nitze's handiwork provided clear testimony of the Reagan administration's priorities during its first term. New missile deployments rather than arms control agreements were deemed the safest way to provide for U.S. security and alliance leadership.

In one last effort to stop the deployments, the Soviets offered a proposal at the eleventh hour, which they later characterized as a U.S. offer. They proposed to reduce SS-20 deployments to approximately 120 launchers, a smaller number of deployed warheads within the European theater than before the SS-20 was introduced in 1977. Ambassador Kvitsinsky also hinted that the thorny problem of compensation for British and French nuclear forces could be deferred. But the price the Kremlin demanded in compensation remained the same: the complete cancellation of NATO missile deployments.

Even an administration predisposed to an arms control agreement would have had difficulty accepting this proposal after an acrimonious test of political wills over the Kremlin's insistence that not a single NATO intermediate-range missile be deployed. The Reagan administration was in no mood to accept Kvitsinsky's offer. By attempting to impose a veto over NATO deployments, the Kremlin effectively ensured the result it most wished to avoid.

Strategic Forces

The fate of START was always intricately linked to that of the INF negotiations, despite the formality of each side's having separate delegations to conduct the two parallel negotiations. For the Kremlin, any nuclear weapon able to land on Soviet soil constituted a strategic weapon. This definition led to Moscow's insistence throughout the SALT I and II negotiations on including British and French forces, as well as U.S. aircraft based in Europe or on its adjoining waters. The Kremlin eventually backed away from this position, accepting the U.S. stance that only intercontinental-range forces of the signatories should be subject to limitation.

In the INF and START negotiations, the Soviets reiterated their definition of strategic forces. With the introduction of Pershing II and GLCMs in Europe, their argument had much more force. The Kremlin's opening position in START clearly specified the linkage to INF: the Soviets suggested phased reductions from a SALT II framework to be carried out over a ten-year period. The proposed reductions varied from 9 to 20 percent below SALT II baselines—but only on the condition that reductions be tied to a settlement of outstanding INF issues.

The gulf between U.S. and Soviet opening positions in START was as wide as that in the INF talks. Reagan administration officials were not inclined to endorse the SALT framework as a basis for reductions; in their view, more drastic alterations were required. According to their critique, SALT II was deficient in numerous respects. The treaty did not bite deeply enough into Soviet MIRVed land-based missiles and was tied to the wrong unit of account—missile launchers and bombers instead of missile throw weight. Launchers were further deficient as a unit of account because they could be reloaded and refired. Thus, for those who thought that a nuclear war might be protracted, limitations in total missile inventories rather than launchers should be the object of an agreement. This objective in turn generated stringent requirements for intrusive verification measures, including on-site inspections of likely and potential missile warehouses, which stood in marked contrast to SALT's reliance on national technical means of verification.

Reagan administration officials conceded that these were ambitious negotiating objectives but argued that they were objectives worth waiting for. President Reagan's advisers, particularly Secretary of Defense Weinberger, Assistant Secretary of Defense Richard N. Perle, and START negotiator Lieutenant General Edward Rowny, insisted that agreements reached under their auspices, unlike those of previous administrations, would not simply codify the existing Soviet force structure or plans.

The Reagan administration's initial START offer called for deep cuts in nuclear forces to equal levels of land- and sea-based missiles. In a second negotiating phase, President Reagan called for equal levels of missile throw weight below current U.S. levels. In a public relations sense, the Reagan administration's START proposal, like its INF offer, had many attractive features since few would argue with the objectives of deep reductions and parity. In reality, the Reagan administration's offer required a radical restructuring of the Kremlin's strategic forces, given the preeminent position of land-based missiles and warheads within the Soviet arsenal. The U.S. offer called for reductions by two-thirds in Soviet missile types of most concern. Nor were the Soviets offered much by way of compensation for the reductions sought: U.S. bomber and cruise missiles, the primary growth stocks of U.S. strategic power, were excluded from the opening U.S. START proposal. The Kremlin's reaction was predictably negative, but few in the United States were willing to defend the Soviet position of what constituted equity. Nevertheless, informed members of Congress understood that the opening U.S. position was a nonstarter.

The one-sidedness of the Reagan administration's initial offers at START and INF placed the president in a poor position to defend his administration from congressional encroachment in the negotiations. The history of both his and his lieutenants' hostility to previous arms control agreements, the president's apparent lack of knowledge about the substance of negotiations, and a string of unfortunate public statements by high administration officials about nuclear war-fighting strategies and objectives did not inspire confidence on Capitol Hill. In search of a fail-safe agreement, the administration had incorporated numerous "fail-sure" provisions, ones that no Soviet leader could accept. Under the circumstances, the president could hardly claim the traditional deference by Congress to executive prerogatives.

Congressional interventions into the executive's negotiating positions were a constant feature during 1983, capped by the Reagan administration's endorsement of a "mutual guaranteed build-down" in October, two months prior to the collapse of the negotiations. In the intervening months, a small but critically important moderate block of votes in the House of Representatives succeeded in chipping away at several fail-sure provisions in the administration's START proposal, buoyed by strong congressional support for a mutual and verifiable freeze and continued stiff resistance in both houses of Congress to the administration's plans for deploying the MX missile.

The congressional coalition that brokered revisions in the administration's negotiating positions and adoption of the build-down was led by the so-called Gang of Six—Congressmen Les Aspin, Albert Gore, and Norm Dicks and Senators William Cohen, Sam Nunn, and Charles Percy. Together with the Scowcroft commission and its senior counselors—a collection of former secretaries of defense and state, CIA directors, NSC advisers, and other knowledgeable officials from past administrations—the Gang of Six attempted to steer the Reagan administration toward more constructive pursuits.

The mechanisms for doing so were many and varied. In part, these contacts provided the president with perspectives that were not given full due in the executive branch's prior deliberations on arms control and strategic modernization programs. Beyond that, the Scowcroft commission's prescriptions belatedly reaffirmed a strategic logic that was rejected by the executive branch during the SALT I negotiations when the Nixon administration refused to consider seriously limitations on MIRVs. To compensate for the instability this decision and subsequent MIRV deployments caused, the commission suggested orienting U.S. strategic forces over time away from MIRVed ICBMs and scaling back MX deployments from 200 to 100. The Scowcroft commission's final report, issued in March 1984, concluded with a strong endorsement for arms control and urged extreme caution in the pursuit of strategic defenses. The efforts of the Scowcroft commission and the Gang of Six were met with considerable skepticism from those who still viewed U.S. proposals as nonnegotiable, despite assurances from administration officials of new flexibility at the negotiating table.

Outside interventions by the Scowcroft commission and congressional moderates occasionally tipped the balance of presidential decision in an administration deeply divided over negotiating positions and objectives. Yet no outside power base, no matter how strong, can effectively carry out the responsibilities of the executive branch. When the power of the presidency is not felt in the execution of arms control policy, negotiating stalemate can easily follow.

The conditions for stalemate in the START and INF talks were always high during Ronald Reagan's first term in office. The Politburo was in transition during these four years, while the considerable power base of the Soviet Ministry of Defense and General Staff remained fairly constant. With the continued demise of what remained of détente, any U.S. president would have been hard pressed to pick up the pieces left from the SALT II debate. The Reagan administration was particularly ill suited to try, for it was led by a disengaged president and staffed by many advisers who saw little utility in resurrecting a cooperative superpower relationship anchored by strategic arms control agreements.

Strategic Defense and Antisatellite Weapons

The possibility of achieving the commonly stated U.S. and Soviet objective of radical reductions in offensive nuclear forces was severely complicated during President Reagan's first term in office by developments in strategic defense. In this area, the two superpowers adopted quite different but mutually reinforcing postures. The Soviets launched periodic peace offensives against the "militarization of space" while doubling their expenditures for space activities and positioning themselves to deploy conventional ballistic missile defenses (BMD). Soviet interest in BMD was reflected through a broad-gauged effort, including the upgrade of the Moscow ABM system; construction of new, large, phased array radars; testing of new surface-to-air missiles with some antitactical ballistic missile capabilities; and the development of rapidly deployable radars. In other words, Soviet officials continued to speak softly about space warfare while carrying a big stick.

Reagan administration officials, in contrast, talked loudly about the possibility of scrapping the Antiballistic Missile (ABM) Treaty and achieving the president's goal of rendering nuclear weapons "impotent and obsolete," but with no prospect of matching Soviet capabilities to deploy missile defenses in the near term. The scale of Soviet conventional and futuristic missile defense activities undoubtedly had considerable impact on the Reagan administration's deliberations, as did official U.S. pronouncements within the confines of the Kremlin.

The ABM Treaty is of unlimited duration, but it put to rest the quest for strategic defenses for only a single decade. In the intervening years, Soviet strategic offensive forces grew considerably due to the proliferation of MIRVed systems, while computing and sensing technologies that could be put to the service of defensive systems matured dramatically. The combination of these trends lent new force to the dilemma of deterrence by means of mutual vulnerability. The search for alternatives received official sanction when President Reagan announced in March 1983 his vision of saving lives rather than avenging them by means of a defensive shield over the United States and its allies.

Prominent scientists and former government officials soon joined the debate over the technical and political feasibility of defensive deployments of whatever kind. The Office of Technology Assessment and the Union of Concerned Scientists in the spring of 1984 issued technical critiques of what quickly became known as the president's Star Wars initiative. In the winter 1984–1985 issue of *Foreign Affairs*, McGeorge Bundy, George F. Kennan, Robert McNamara, and Gerard Smith argued that the president would have to choose between SDI and deep cuts in offensive forces; they urged the latter.

The year ended with all eyes focused on the impending umbrella talks in Geneva. Would the SDI be a bargaining chip for deep reductions in Soviet offensive nuclear forces, or would the Reagan administration attempt to pursue both objectives with the risk of achieving neither? Or worse, would the pursuit of U.S.

and Soviet defensive strategies mean the demise of SALT I and II limitations on both offensive and defensive systems? The president's SDI, however, was a long-term program whose payoffs, if any, were many years hence. The immediate issue for the arms control community in 1984 had nothing to do with futuristic technologies. On the contrary, the program in question was quite simple to perfect yet had profound implications for U.S. national security and arms control policies. It involved a system to destroy satellites in low orbits.

ASAT

Periodically, an impending weapons test program or deployment has a galvanizing effect on supporters of arms control. During these times, the benefits of an agreement appear clear-cut and the risks grave of failing to regulate the prospective military activity in question. Such was the case in 1984 regarding antisatellite weapons.

The United States began testing an advanced ASAT weapon system during 1984. Testing is a critical milestone for arms control, since tests of this nature cannot be concealed very well if they are to provide the user with confidence that the weapon will work as designed. If the U.S. test program continued, domestic opponents were confident that the Soviets would follow suit, breaking a self-imposed moratorium in place since 1983. Worse, the Kremlin might begin testing a more advanced system like the U.S. miniature homing vehicle carried under the wing of an F-15. Unlike the existing Soviet ASAT, which requires a large booster rocket with elaborate launch facilities and cumbersome operational constraints, a new Soviet system might have all the advantages in flexibility—and disadvantages of verification—of the U.S. ASAT program.

Supporters of the ASAT test program had a different set of concerns. To them, acceptance of an ASAT moratorium or ban would confer a free ride to Soviet satellites that could jeopardize U.S. forces and constrain U.S. military options. Nor would U.S. tests usher in a new phase of the competition. In this view, the existence of an operational Soviet ASAT system and the considerable growth in Soviet space activities over the past five years demonstrated that the militarization of space was already well underway. With both sides fully engaged in the competition, supporters of ASAT testing were confident that the United States would not be disadvantaged. Under an arms control regime, they were confident that the Kremlin would derive the benefits of interpreting its obligations loosely, while the United States adhered to the spirit as well as the letter of any accords.

The arguments for an unfettered U.S. ASAT program were contained in an administration report to the Congress in March 1984. Congress asked for the president's "arms control plans and objectives in the field of ASAT systems." Instead it got an arms control damage assessment. The report found that "no arrangements or agreements beyond those already governing military activities in outer space have been found to date that are judged to be in the overall interest of the United States and its Allies." The reasons for this pessimistic appraisal rested primarily on verification concerns and prospective Soviet compliance problems.

Specific verification problems included confirming the complete dismantlement or destruction of Soviet ASAT interceptors and boosters, detecting preparations for operational use of unauthorized ASAT systems such as ground-based lasers, and assessing damage and cause of damage for the objects of possible ASAT tests. The administration's report found these difficulties in detecting Soviet non-compliance of great significance since "cheating on anti-satellite limitations, even on a small scale, could pose a disproportionate risk to the United States."

The essence of the administration's position on ASAT limitations was that the possibilities of Soviet cheating were endless, while the prospects for solving negotiating problems or safeguarding U.S. security in the event of Soviet non-compliance were almost nil. The March report did not close the door entirely on ASAT arms control, however. The Reagan administration was reported to be considering a variety of negotiating options during the course of the year, including "rules of the road" compacts, moratoria on dedicated ASAT tests, and bans on high-altitude systems.

In July, the subject of negotiating options became more than an academic exercise when the Soviets again called on the United States to negotiate a ban on the use of ASAT weapons. On this occasion, their offer was quickly accepted by the White House, with the proviso that talks also resume on reducing strategic nuclear forces and INFs. A month-long exchange of notes and public statements followed, which clarified the improbability of any negotiation prior to the presidential election. In retrospect, the Soviet offer to begin ASAT talks appears to have been part of a well-orchestrated peace campaign and not meant to elicit a positive response from Washington.

After the presidential election confirmed Ronald Reagan as its negotiating partner, the Kremlin resumed its campaign for space arms control with renewed force. Heir apparent Mikhail Gorbachev played on this theme heavily during a trip to the United Kingdom in December, in concert with new public statements by General Secretary Chernenko. This time, however, the Kremlin was clearly willing to work on a new agenda for negotiations on offensive as well as space weapons.

Disputes over Compliance

The most important arms control story in 1984 was probably that of compliance controversies. While little evidence was available to indicate progress in arms control, there were substantial indications that previous accords were unraveling. For the first time, both the Soviet Union and the United States formally issued reports asserting violations of commitments undertaken in prior agreements. The mechanism SALT created to handle compliance questions, the Standing Consultative Commission (SCC), now appeared unable to resolve disputes. With the prospect of new agreements remote and with deepening suspicion about each other's long-term intentions toward existing accords, the list of unresolved compliance problems seemed likely to grow over time. The provisos in the SALT II Treaty limiting qualitative improvements in nuclear forces appeared increasingly in jeopardy. A central question at year's end was how long the United States and the Soviet Union would continue to adhere to numerical ceilings on offensive forces previously agreed to.

Evaluations of compliance controversies in the United States varied widely. For the extreme right wing, there was little new in Soviet behavior; what was novel was an administration that would not pull its punches. For the extreme left wing, the president and his advisers offered trumped-up charges and insufficient evidence. In this view, the Kremlin was merely taking its cues from the Reagan administration. For most of those who declined to adopt a dogmatic view, a pattern of systematic cheating by the Soviet Union remained unproved. Nevertheless, Soviet activities raised troubling compliance questions in a number of specific cases.

For its part, the Kremlin offered its own list of citations of U.S. noncompliance after the White House released two reports documenting Soviet misconduct. The substance of the Kremlin's countercharges was weakened by an obvious parallelism in its lists. Wherever the United States lodged a complaint, the Kremlin responded with a comparable citation of U.S. misconduct. Many Soviet countercharges were prospective (such as the inevitable incompatibility of the president's Star Wars vision with ABM Treaty limitations on testing and deployment); others dwelled on U.S. activities that were contrary to the spirit of a sound negotiating relationship. In contrast, the Reagan administration's presentations of Soviet compliance problems dwelled on actual practices tied to the letter rather than the spirit of the agreements in question.

The Reagan administration issued the first noncompliance report on January 23, 1984. It included seven citations of "violations and probable violations . . . of Soviet legal obligations and political commitments." Four of the seven citations related to unratified agreements; one related to a communiqué between heads of state, the Soviet failure to provide proper notification of a military exercise as the Helsinki Final Act suggested.

The most serious charges of noncompliance included in the January report dealt with chemical, biological, and toxin weapons use contrary to the 1972 Biological Weapons Convention and the 1925 Geneva Protocol; the construction of a radar that could be used for strategic defense in the interior of the Soviet Union contrary to the 1972 ABM Treaty; and the encoding of telemetry during Soviet missile flight tests, contrary to the unratified SALT II Treaty. In the last case, the Reagan administration deemed Soviet practices a violation of a political commitment rather than a legal obligation, since the White House had earlier declared that the United States had no moral or legal obligation to adhere to unratified agreements.

For these three cases, the Reagan administration could summon impressive evidence. On the matter of "yellow rain" use against antigovernment forces in Afghanistan, Laos, and Cambodia, much circumstantial evidence pointed to the use of prohibited toxins, either by the Soviet Union or by Soviet-equipped Vietnamese forces. The construction of a radar marginally suited for space-tracking purposes (an activity that would be permitted at the location in question) was undeniable, as was the extraordinary level of Soviet encryption during flight tests of new Soviet missiles.

In contrast, several of the citations in the administration's January report were extremely weak. Serious compliance questions could only be devalued when combined with tenuous ones, such as the citation of noncompliance with the Helsinki communiqué between heads of state (perhaps included to dampen enthusiasm for the Conference on Disarmament in Europe, then about to convene); the improper deployment of SS-16 missiles, contrary to the unratified SALT II Treaty (a finding for which the Reagan administration conceded the evidence was "somewhat ambiguous"); and the testing of underground weapons with yields over 150 kilotons, contrary to the unratified Threshold Test Ban Treaty (again with the caveat that the "available evidence is ambiguous").

The January report also included a citation that the Soviets were testing two new land-based missiles, contrary to the unratified SALT II Treaty. In this instance, there was little controversy over the newness of both missiles, the SS-X-24 and the SS-X-25. At issue was whether one of the two could be shoehorned into the permitted profile of a modernized older missile of dubious distinction and limited deployment. Predictably, U.S. and Soviet interpretations of the relevant treaty definitions and obligations differed.

The Kremlin's rejoinder to the Reagan administration's noncompliance report appeared quickly in the form of an aide-memoire delivered to the State Department. The core of the Soviet complaint related to the SALT II Treaty's protocol provisions governing cruise missiles and to the ABM Treaty. In these matters, as well as others, the Kremlin charged the United States with attempting to achieve military superiority, a goal that serious weapons initiatives and disingenuous negotiating proposals reflected.

On its cruise missile complaint, the Kremlin charged that U.S. deployments of sea- and land-based cruise missiles constituted violations of Article XII of the SALT II Treaty, in which both sides pledged not to circumvent treaty provisions through any other state or in any other manner. Moreover by "refusing to put [SALT II] into operation," the United States was in "non-fulfillment" of its commitment in the SALT II Joint Statement of Principles to pursue the resolution of issues included in the protocol, particularly the cruise missile deployment issue. The Reagan administration, according to the Kremlin, had no such intent, as reflected in its nonnegotiable INF proposals.

Several of the Soviet citations concerning the ABM Treaty paralleled U.S. concerns. Their most plausible complaint related to the construction of Pave Paws early warning radars, which could, in the Kremlin's view, serve as the basis for a territorial defense, contrary to Article I of the ABM Treaty. The Kremlin also resurfaced the charge that the United States impeded verification when it concealed its modifications of ICBM silos by using large environmental shelters. Another citation related to prospective U.S. testing and deployment of two new types of ICBMs, the MX and Midgetman.

This exchange of public reports on noncompliance dismayed supporters of arms control, who preferred to see such questions raised and resolved through private channels. In their view, previous administrations had been able to resolve satisfactorily compliance questions in the SCC. With the downturn in U.S.-Soviet relations and the politicization of compliance issues, the SCC was unlikely to repeat its earlier successes. Critics of SALT argued that the SCC's success stories constituted grandfathering the Kremlin's misdeeds. They were gratified that, at last, a president had publicly charged the Soviets with violations but were disappointed at the qualified language of the Reagan administration's report, as well as its limited scope.

For implacable opponents of past and prospective arms agreements, the release of the January report was merely the first step in what they hoped would be a series of public revelations of Soviet duplicity and cheating. Their efforts turned to the release of a more condemnatory report prepared by the General Advisory Committee (GAC) of the Arms Control and Disarmament Agency. The GAC membership appointed by President Reagan reflected, in the judgment of a Congressional Research Service assessment, "a focused ideological viewpoint." Its views toward the utility of arms control could best be evaluated by its chosen pursuits during the president's first term, which consisted primarily of the compilation of Soviet wrongdoing for a study entitled "A Quarter Century of Soviet Compliance Practices under Arms Control Commitments: 1958–1983."

The White House eventually released this study in October 1984, along with the disclaimer that "neither the methodology of analysis nor the conclusions reached in this report have been formally reviewed or approved by any agencies of the U.S. government." The GAC report listed seventeen "material breaches," which it defined as violations of treaties, unilateral commitments, and circumventions of the essential objects or purposes of agreements although not necessarily in explicit violations of their terms. Using this encompassing definition, the GAC listed six of the seven citations included in the administration's January report (excluding the citation on underground tests with yields over 150 kilotons) and found six additional material breaches during President Reagan's term in office. Among the breaches were four citations of instances in which Soviet officials said they would do one thing and then proceeded to do another. In another instance, the GAC report agreed with the Soviet aide-memoire that the venting of radioactive debris in the atmosphere, whether inadvertent or not, constituted violations of the Atmospheric Test Ban Treaty. The GAC included a citation of noncompliance to the Montreux Convention, a finding that signatories to the convention (the United States not being one) had declined to make. The GAC's conclusions were not entirely negative, however. The report found several areas of "apparent Soviet compliance," including accident avoidance and nonproliferation agreements. In contrast, the GAC found a recurring pattern of Soviet violations toward strategic arms control agreements, concluding that in some cases the Soviet sign and ratify treaties they are planning to violate.

The Soviet rejoinder to the GAC Report appeared in the form of a Tass statement questioning U.S. intentions toward existing nuclear arms control agreements. As in its aide-memoire, the Tass statement focused on SALT II Protocol and ABM Treaty compliance problems; however, the Kremlin seemed to downplay its response to the GAC report, just as the Reagan administration carefully distanced itself from the GAC's findings.

The significance of these noncompliance reports sanctioned by Washington and Moscow lay not so much in their content as in their political implications. The military significance of the compliance problems, while considered great by those least enthusiastic about continued treaty adherence, was deemed marginal by more dispassionate authorities. Indeed, Pentagon officials deleted funds for improved missile penetration aids in a self-imposed budget reduction exercise after repeatedly expressing concerns over Soviet ABM "breakout" capabilities.

Nevertheless, compliance controversies eroded domestic public support for arms control while elevating concerns over verification. These controversies also reflected genuine difficulties involved in building a long-term negotiating relationship with the Kremlin. As in the case of the two new types and radar controversies, the Kremlin could make a case for its interpretation of treaty obligations, but that case strained credulity. The resulting military advantages have been outweighed by their associated political costs. The Politburo could not be blind to these consequences, yet it appeared entirely willing to pay this price, particularly after the derailment of the SALT II treaty and the dismemberment of détente, events for which the Soviets also refused to accept responsibility.

At the same time, the Reagan administration's complaints over Soviet compliance practices have had a hollow ring. Numerous public statements have raised doubts about the commitment of administration officials to protect agreements they claim the Soviets have repeatedly violated or whose terms they themselves prefer not to see ratified. Under these circumstances, the Reagan administration has been poorly positioned to encourage strict Soviet compliance with existing agreements. Simple prudence could only reinforce the Kremlin's habitual instinct to define its treaty obligations loosely.

The defects of both Washington and Moscow's approach to compliance issues were complementary and reinforcing during 1984. At year's end, the prospects for ironing out these difficulties in mutually acceptable ways were inextricably tied to the fortunes of the umbrella talks on offensive nuclear forces and weapons in space. With progress in the new negotiations during 1985 and beyond, it is reasonable to expect progress in resolving compliance disputes as well. But if the new talks are as contentious as the INF and START negotiations, the list of unresolved compliance problems can only grow.

Nonnuclear Arms Control

In contrast to the stalemate on strategic and INF arms control, there was modest progress in a number of other negotiating venues.

Hot Line

The one concrete achievement relating to arms control during 1984 was an agreement signed in July to upgrade the hot line. In May 1983, during the height of the Euromissile controversy, President Reagan proposed several measures designed to improve direct communications between Washington and Moscow, including the addition of a facsimile transmission capability to the hot line for rapid exchange of messages, maps, graphs, and charts. In keeping with the Kremlin's desire to downplay the political significance of the agreement, the accord was initialed by the two sides without fanfare by Deputy Secretary of State Kenneth Dam and the chargé d'affaires of the Soviet embassy in Washington.

CDE

A new arms control negotiation began during 1984, the Conference on Confidence and Security Building Measures and Disarmament in Europe (CDE). The CDE promises to be long and complex, as might be expected from the progeny of the thirty-five-nation Conference on Security and Cooperation in Europe. The mandate of the CDE was to "undertake in stages, new, effective and concrete actions designed to make progress in strengthening confidence and security and in achieving disarmament." The first stage of the conference is devoted to "confidence and security building measures designed to reduce the risk of military confrontation" in Europe and its adjoining sea area and air space. The participants are committed to defining measures that are of military significance, politically binding, and adequately verifiable.

In prior years, multilateral negotiations on chemical weapons disarmament and mutual and balanced force reductions (MBFR) in Europe received little public notice. During 1984, the mere fact that the superpowers continued to engage in these negotiations was newsworthy. The United States tabled new negotiating initiatives in both forums during the spring, but little progress was made in subsequent months to narrow differences between U.S. and Soviet negotiating positions.

Chemical Weapons

On April 4, 1984, President Reagan unveiled a proposal for a comprehensive ban on the development, production, possession, transfer, and use of chemical weapons. Two weeks later Vice-President George Bush submitted the plan to the Committee on Disarmament. The U.S. proposal included "open invitation" verification provisions, requiring treaty signatories to allow inspections on twenty-four hours' notice of their military and government-owned or -controlled facilities, as well as privately owned factories working on government contracts. The Soviets immediately labeled the initiative a "propaganda trick." Their own proposal for a comprehensive ban on chemical weapons provided for verification by combined "national and international measures," which are largely undefined.

Despite the wide gulf that remained on verifying a comprehensive chemical warfare agreement, there were positive developments in this area. In November 1983, the United States invited representatives from the Committee on Disarmament to witness the operation of a chemical weapons disposal facility in Utah. This demonstration lent a degree of concreteness to discussions on how stockpile destruction treaty provisions could be implemented and provided credence to the U.S. position that on-site inspectors were needed to validate instrumentation data on the destruction of stockpiles. Eastern bloc countries declined to attend the demonstration, with the exception of Rumania. The Soviet Union followed this U.S. initiative with the announcement in February 1984 of its agreement in principle to permanent on-site verification of chemical weapons destruction.

Negotiations in the Committee on Disarmament then proceeded at a slow pace, typical in multilateral deliberations on topics of this complexity. The most difficult tasks facing the negotiators related to monitoring a complete ban (including the development) of chemical weapons and their precursors and coping with the problem of undeclared production facilities and stockpiles. The "any time, any place" inspection provision that the United States proposed was designed to address these concerns, but other Western nations were uneasy with this solution, and the Soviet Union remained adamantly opposed. Such a provision would mean that highly sensitive facilities, including the Central Intelligence Agency and the National Security Agency, would be open to foreign inspectors. Progress toward a chemical weapons ban in 1985 and 1986 will require alternative inspection provisions that address concerns over compliance while protecting the legitimate security interests of the signatories.

If further evidence were needed to reinforce customary international law and the Geneva Protocol's provisions against chemical warfare, it was provided during 1984 in the Iran-Iraq war. In March, the United States publicly accused Iraq of using mustard and nerve gas to counter an Iranian offensive. A United Nations fact-finding team later authenticated this conclusion. Unlike earlier multilateral inspection efforts to investigate claims of mycotoxin use in Southeast Asia and Afghanistan, the investigators could move expeditiously and were provided access to the sites in question. The U.N. mission in the Iran-Iraq case provided clear evidence of the utility of multinational inspections, at least when the issues in dispute are outside an East-West context.

MBFR

The MBFR talks in Europe marked their eleventh anniversary. The durability of these negotiations, usually a source of derisive commentary, became a welcome indicator of continuity when the Soviets walked out of the INF and START negotiations in the late fall of 1983. At first, the Eastern bloc also refused to set a date for the next round of MBFR, but negotiations later resumed on a business-as-usual basis.

Business as usual in an MBFR context is extraordinarily slow, marked over the years by a gradual convergence of positions between the two sides but also by an absence of the high-level political interest necessary to break the logjam over manpower baselines from which reductions to a common ceiling in Central Europe would begin.

During the course of negotiations, the East agreed to a common ground force manpower ceiling of 700,000 men in the zone of reductions and to the idea of a package of associated measures to provide confidence in compliance. In June 1983, the East made several concessions in principle on the associated measures deemed important by the West. The Eastern bloc agreed to allow observers of troop withdrawals, the designation of three or four permanent observation posts to monitor the entry or exit of troops after initial withdrawals have been completed, the possibility of on-site verification "with the observance of certain demands," the exchange of data and establishment of a consultative commission, and the noninterference with national technical means of verification. The West responded positively to the East's initiative on associated measures with the proviso that these proposals required considerable refinement in order to be satisfactory.

A major Western initiative at MBFR took place in April 1984. In an attempt to resolve the data issue, the West proposed to exchange data only on ground combat and combat support forces. The West would not demand Eastern figures precisely equal to Western estimates; however, the East's data would have to fall within an acceptable range of Western estimates, as yet undefined. To hammer out discrepancies, both sides would have to provide categories and counting rules for the troops in question, tackling ground combat forces first, where discrepancies were smallest and easiest to resolve. This procedure suggested a way in which more substantial data discrepancies—those involving combat service support troops—could be resolved later.

The East responded coolly to this initiative, and the talks proceeded at a languid pace. If previous patterns continue to hold, the next move in the negotiations is up to the East. Little progress appears likely in 1985 unless the data discrepancy problem is resolved by the Eastern bloc's either responding positively to the methodology proposed by the West or advancing a suitable alternative.

Arms Control and Domestic Politics

The events of 1984 demonstrated the depth of the domestic paralysis on arms control since the divisive national debate over the SALT II Treaty in 1979. The

U.S. public overwhelmingly desires to control nuclear weapons. It also has an abiding distrust of the Soviet Union. In theory, arms control agreements are supposed to bridge these two conflicting impulses. In practice, they have not. Instead, past agreements have sharpened domestic points of contention over how best to safeguard the nation's security in the nuclear age.

Both skeptics and supporters of arms control have powerful arguments at their command, but they are arguments that work far better in opposition than in implementing one's favored agenda. This mutual standoff is represented by highly tentative ground rules governing the strategic competition. The SALT I and II limitations on offensive forces remain only provisionally in place. Both superpowers have ratified only one treaty governing central strategic systems after more than twenty years of negotiating effort—the ABM Treaty—and that too is in jeopardy.

The centrifugal effects of U.S. policy debates over nuclear weapons and arms control were especially apparent during 1984. Earlier efforts by those outside the executive branch to reaffirm centrist principles could not be sustained during an election year in which no nuclear arms control negotiations were in progress. In the absence of active negotiations, congressional moderates lacked a forum to focus concerns and to encourage remedies. The Scowcroft commission's recommendations to move away from destabilizing offensive forces while reaffirming limitations on defensive deployments could not take root in the frigid climate near the end of the Reagan administration's first term.

A presidential election year is hardly an auspicious time to affirm a process of reconciliation essential to ameliorate the domestic divide over future steps for arms control and nuclear weapons. No presidential campaign, with the possible exception of the second Eisenhower-Stevenson contest, featured arms control so prominently as did the Reagan-Mondale campaign. The candidates' positions reflected domestic divisions, with the challenger championing a nuclear freeze and the incumbent supporting energetic pursuit of strategic modernization programs and the SDI. Walter Mondale placed the blame for failed negotiations on President Reagan's lack of command over his own lieutenants and the issues under negotiation. Ronald Reagan placed the blame for the breakdown on negotiations at the Kremlin's door, a plausible explanation under normal circumstances in U.S. politics and one given greater force in 1984 due to the Soviet walk-out from Geneva the previous year.

For its part, the Politburo continued to be absorbed in yet another year of leadership transition. Konstantin Chernenko appeared infrequently and unsteadily at ceremonial occasions, while his powerful colleague, Dimitri Ustinov, disappeared altogether from public view. Chernenko's health prevented him from appearing at ceremonies in which the long-time defense minister's ashes were buried in the Kremlin's wall. Before Ustinov's death, his top military deputy, Marshal Nikolai Ogarkov, a former SALT I negotiator, was suddenly removed from his position.

With senior officials in both the United States and the Soviet Union preoccupied with leadership questions, with nuclear arms control negotiations on hold, with verification and compliance problems steadily eroding the prospects for new agreements, and with weapons programs continuing their cyclical progression during 1984, an odd sense of complacency appeared to dominate U.S. politics.

Walter Mondale's messages of nuclear alarm, including political advertisements depicting the symbolic red telephone, had little impact. Demonstrations in Western Europe against deployment of the Pershing II and GLCMs were but a shadow of the mass outpourings of concern that preceded their deployment. Books and movies on nuclear apocalypse that attracted large audiences in 1983 gave way to escapist entertainment the following year. Western churches remained active in public education work about nuclear weapons and arms control, but the apogee of clerical involvement seemed to have been reached with the release of the Catholic bishops' pastoral letter in May 1983. With so many pressing concerns, religious institutions found it difficult to generate sustained involvement in the nuclear issue. Media interest turned to the Catholic bishops' activism on questions of social welfare and economic development. The nuclear freeze campaign, so central to U.S. political debates during 1982 and 1983, never became a prominent issue in the 1984 presidential campaign. No rallying cry appeared to take its place. In the absence of ill-advised statements by Reagan administration officials on nuclear questions, public interest in abstract questions of strategic doctrine or nuclear weapons employment policies waned considerably. The policy of no first use found no political constituency.

The public's sense of complacency seemed immune even to estimates from the scientific community that a nuclear war could mean global climatic catastrophe and perhaps human extinction. Subfreezing temperatures would be caused by a large cloud of dust and smoke that would encircle the earth, effectively blocking out sunlight and creating a nuclear winter effect. According to preliminary calculations, nuclear exchanges involving only a fraction of the superpowers' arsenals could trigger such effects if major urban areas were targeted. A report by the National Academy of Sciences, issued in December 1984, highlighted the unknowables associated with the nuclear winter theory but did not dispute it.

The Future

In key respects 1984 offered previews of the future of arms control. On the critical question of strategic defense and its relationship to possible reductions in offensive forces, both domestic and international positions began to take shape. Supporters and skeptics of new agreements clearly anticipated the features of impending debates and negotiations. Central questions relate to the longevity of the "interim restraint" or "no undercut" policy toward unratified or expired agreements limiting offensive forces and the Reagan administration's policies and objectives toward strategic defenses. Both questions are inextricably linked.

During the Carter administration, the United States and the Soviet Union agreed to respect the SALT I Interim Agreement's provisions limiting offensive forces beyond their expiration date in 1977 while negotiations for a follow-on agreement were underway. Then in 1981, the Reagan administration announced it would take "no action that would undercut existing agreements so long as the Soviet Union exercises the same restraint." Soviet officials responded with comparable statements.

The no undercut policy toward agreements only provisionally in place survived the Reagan administration's first term. Its continued viability during a second term depends primarily on the state of political relations between the superpowers and further developments on compliance controversies. In January 1985, President

Reagan indicated his intention to stay within SALT II ceilings when the seventh Trident submarine forces this issue in late summer or early fall; however, administration officials later qualified the president's position.

The staying power of SALT II numerical ceilings is closely linked to each side's plans to deploy strategic defenses. Much of the initial technical work in pursuit of the president's SDI indicated that early promise lay only in bolstering deterrence by defending strategic forces, not in escaping deterrence by affording comprehensive protection of populations. Knowledgeable voices, including former Secretaries of Defense Harold Brown and James Schlesinger, stressed the unworkability and exorbitant costs of more ambitious schemes. Others, notably McGeorge Bundy, George Kennan, Robert McNamara, and Gerard Smith, argued that many notions of Star Wars technology were clearly incompatible with the president's quest for early reductions in strategic offenses. British Prime Minister Thatcher conveyed European concerns directly to the president and reported his agreement that work on advanced defensive technologies must aim at enhancing deterrence, that it must be confined to research permitted by the ABM Treaty, and that actual development of such systems would be subject to negotiation with the Soviets.

On the other hand, Zbigniew Brzezinski and others were pessimistic that arms control could deal with the emerging problems of national security and took a more benign view of the prospects for technological breakthroughs in strategic defense. More tentative was the view of Henry Kissinger, but he shared the opinion of many others that, at the least, the SDI could help to energize diplomacy with Moscow.

On balance, the combination of further reflections and converging pressures seemed to have some impact on the administration. The president and his associates acknowledged that defense could not be pursued unilaterally and without regard to its impact on offensive forces. Although it remained unclear how far they would go in offering to restrain future defensive systems, they asserted a clear intention to abide by U.S. commitments under the ABM Treaty. A decisive majority of Congress shared that goal. Members made that apparent in one of the many provisions of the FY85 Defense Authorization Act. It required an annual report on the SDI specifically assessing how the effort comports with the ABM Treaty.

On other points as well, Congress used the prolonged stalemate in arms control to assess the relationship between various military programs and arms control possibilities. It slated a series of studies and reports from the executive designed to enable it to take a coherent role in the policy debates sure to come in 1985 and later. These included analyses on the role of tactical nuclear weapons, options for constraining SLCMs, the projected scale of U.S. counterforce capabilities and the definition of when such capabilities would constitute a first-strike potential, the implications of findings of the nuclear winter theory for strategy and arms control, and a number of other issues. Taken as a whole, the reporting requirements levied by Congress in 1984 constituted the most far-reaching effort yet undertaken to relate U.S. program needs and possible arms control arrangements. They set down markers for the likely legislative focus during the early months of the second Reagan administration.

On one major topic Congress went beyond an attempt to plan the analyses on which to base upcoming force posture and negotiating policy. In an effort to spur diplomacy, the Senate called on the president to request ratification immediately of the long-pending Threshold Nuclear Test Ban and Peaceful Nuclear Explosions Agreement and to seek prompt resumption of negotiations for a comprehensive nuclear test ban. The overwhelming support for these measures was an extraordinary sign of the Senate's desire to revive the languishing arms control process.

Through the closing months of President Reagan's first term, some observers detected what they thought was a genuine response to concerns of this nature. The president who came to office in 1980 amid allusions to the possibilities that nuclear war might be limited and denunciations of arms control approached his second term with quite a different tone. He now stressed time and again that "nuclear war can never be won and must never be fought." Having campaigned on a 1980 platform calling for "military superiority," he now discounted the goal as neither feasible nor desirable and urged the Republican Convention not to repeat the plank. Acknowledging that his initial proposals in START were unacceptable to the Soviets, he reiterated his commitment to making fair trade-offs between areas of U.S. strategic advantage and those of the Soviet Union. These altered perceptions appeared to mingle with the impulses of old in the president's mind—and certainly in some quarters of his administration—but they offered the main rays of hope that a second Reagan administration would pursue arms control with vigor and determination.

Given this new orientation in declaratory policy, President Reagan's close advisers pledged an agile decision-making process to replace the gridlock of the past. Secretary of State Shultz moved to place arms diplomacy at the center of the administration's foreign policy agenda and himself at the center of arms diplomacy. Both developments encouraged those who felt that the Reagan administration, building on its strong military record, was well positioned to carry the arms control process forward if it concentrated on the task. At the end of 1984 the record remained barren, but the outlook was less bleak.

Chapter 10

Special Supplement: The Strategic Defense Initiative

Albert Carnesale

"What if free people could live secure in the knowledge that their security did not rest upon the threat of instant U.S. retaliation to deter a Soviet attack, that we could intercept and destroy strategic ballistic missiles before they reached our own soil or that of our allies?" So asked President Reagan in a televised address to the nation on March 23, 1983. He responded in the same speech: "I am directing a comprehensive and intensive effort to define a long-term research and development program to begin to achieve our ultimate goal of eliminating the threat posed by strategic nuclear missiles." This announcement marked the birth of the president's Strategic Defense Initiative (SDI). The speech offered no hint of how the defensive task would be accomplished. It made no mention of space stations, lasers, or particle beams. The media, however, promptly applied the label "Star Wars" to the president's vision. The label has stuck.

Background

Strategic defense is not a new idea. Americans, like others, have always preferred an invulnerable homeland to a vulnerable one. While the goal is simple, its achievement is elusive. Against large modern nuclear arsenals, invulnerability has not been an option. Cities are vulnerable to attack not only by the traditional elements of strategic nuclear forces, including ICBMs, SLBMs, and long-range bombers, but also by the long-range cruise missiles that are being added to the Soviet arsenal. If these sophisticated vehicles for delivery were unavailable or ineffective, an adversary could resort to nuclear-armed torpedoes or to "smuggling" nuclear weapons in by other means. If the nation literally is to be invulnerable to attack, defense against all forms of delivery must be provided.

But the SDI is far less ambitious. It focuses solely on defense against ballistic missiles, which constitute the bulk of the Soviets' current long-range nuclear arsenal. Ballistic missile defense (BMD) is an essential ingredient of any comprehensive strategic defense and is, in the words of the president, "an important first step." Like the SDI, this chapter concentrates on BMD. It should be borne in mind, however, that even if the SDI were successfully to meet all of the challenges before it, there would remain many substantial obstacles to be overcome on the road to invulnerability.

BMD is a familiar subject. In the late 1960s, Americans debated intensely the question of whether to deploy the Safeguard ABM system. (To a large extent the acronym BMD has replaced ABM in the jargon of national security specialists, with the two terms being used interchangeably to refer to defense against ballistic missiles.) The subject arose again in 1972 with the signing and ratification of the ABM Treaty emerging from SALT I. Much has changed since then regarding BMD, especially in the realms of technology and military strategy.[1]

BMD Technologies

In principle, a ballistic missile could be countered during any of the four phases of its flight trajectory: the boost, postboost, midcourse, and terminal phases. (Destroying the missile before it is launched is not normally included under the rubric of BMD.) In the boost phase of a ballistic missile's flight, the multiple stages of the booster rocket thrust the missile up through and beyond the atmosphere. After the final booster stage has burned out, the missile enters the postboost phase of its flight, during which the postboost vehicle (also known as the bus) maneuvers through space, directs the nuclear-warhead-bearing MIRVs toward their targets, and releases any decoys and other penetration aids. During the midcourse phase, these objects travel through inner space on ballistic flight paths. In the terminal phase, they reenter the atmosphere, with the lighter objects, such as decoys, slowing down more than the heavier reentry vehicles. For a typical ICBM trajectory, the thirty minute flight time is composed roughly of three minutes of boost, five minutes of postboost, twenty minutes of midcourse, and two minutes of terminal phase. An SLBM flight could take much less time, with the difference lying primarily in the duration of the midcourse phase. Figure 10–1 shows an artist's rendering of how BMD could work.

To counter ballistic missiles in any phase of flight, a defensive system must perform the following functions: surveillance and acquisition, discrimination, pointing and tracking, interception and destruction, damage assessment, and battle management. Surveillance and acquisition refer to searching for and detecting any attacking ballistic missiles on their elements in flight. Discrimination means distinguishing the threatening objects from others (for example, identifying reentry vehicles among a host of accompanying decoys). Pointing and tracking refer to focusing sensors on a particular target, making a series of measurements of its position and velocity, and processing the data to estimate the target's future trajectory. Interception and destruction require directing an object or a concentrated energy beam (such as that emitted by a high-power laser) to the target—whether booster, bus, or reentry vehicle—and rendering it harmless. Damage assessment means determining whether the target has been destroyed or adequately damaged. Battle management encompasses all of the data transmission and processing, decisions, and communications involved in performing the defensive functions.

The SDI envisions a layered defense that would attempt to counter ballistic missiles in all four phases of flight. Each layer would serve as a backup to deal with the missiles or reentry vehicles that leak through the defensive layers directed at the earlier phases of flight. If the system were to consist of four independent layers, each 90 percent effective (that is, if each layer countered nine out of ten missiles or reentry vehicles reaching the phase of flight at which it was directed), then only 1 nuclear warhead out of an attacking force of 10,000 would arrive on target. For layer efficiencies of 75 percent and 50 percent, the number of penetrating warheads would be 39 and 625, respectively. The prospect of a four-layer defense is new because only recently have technologies emerged that offer any promise for conducting intercepts in the boost and postboost phases.

Boost-phase intercept is most attractive to the defense because it eliminates simultaneously all of the reentry vehicles, decoys, and other penetration aids carried by the missile. But boost-phase intercept poses enormous technological challenges. Given that the planet Earth is (roughly) round, that the boost phase portion of flight of Soviet ICBMs is brief and occurs well below the line of sight from beyond the borders of the Soviet Union, and that the Soviets hardly can be expected to permit deployment in their homeland of U.S. defensive systems, it follows that any attack on Soviet ICBMs in boost phase must be from space. (It follows also that the label Star Wars is not entirely undeserved.) The defensive system component that directs the object or energy beam toward the booster must either be stationed in

Figure 10–1. BMD and Antisatellite Weapons

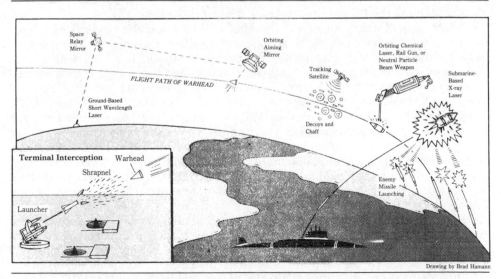

Source: © 1985/1984 by the New York Times Company. Reprinted by permission.

space or be popped up into space by its own ballistic missile upon warning from space-based sensors.

No one knows what a boost-phase intercept system would look like or what technologies it would use. It might employ directed energy weapons such as chemical lasers, X-ray lasers (which are powered by nuclear explosions), beams of neutral atoms or charged subatomic particles, or microwaves. The device might be continuously orbiting in space, or it might be popped up on warning. One concept uses ground-based chemical lasers and a network of space-based mirrors to reflect the energy back down toward earth to destroy booster targets. Kinetic energy weapons, such as rocket-propelled interceptors or high-velocity projectiles fired from advanced electromagnetic guns, also might have a role in boost-phase intercept. For the most part, these advanced concepts are little more than gleams in the eyes of defense scientists, but the gleams are coming more sharply into focus. And it is not enough to develop a system that would work against current Soviet missiles; it must be able to deal with responsive threats. The offense could use a number of countermeasures to limit the effectiveness of boost-phase defenses, including, for example, interfering with sensors and communications links, attacking space-based components of the defensive system, shortening the boost time and lowering the altitude of booster burnout, applying protective coatings, and increasing the number of boosters. It remains to be seen whether effective boost-phase intercept is possible.[2]

Destroying missiles in the postboost phase, before all of the reentry vehicles and penetration aids have been dispersed, also could have high payoff for the defense. The system concepts and technologies that appear to be applicable to postboost intercept are the same as those for the boost phase. But a bus is harder to track than a booster and is more readily shielded against the effects of directed energy weapons, so the BMD task in the postboost phase is likely to be even more difficult than in the boost phase, making it most difficult of all.

Midcourse BMD is something the United States and the Soviet Union have known how to do since the 1960s, at least under rather restrictive conditions, such as, a limited attack without sophisticated penetration aids. The U.S. Sentinel and Safeguard systems had huge ground-based radars and long-range nuclear-armed interceptor missiles for midcourse intercept, and so did (and does) the Soviets' Galosh ABM system around Moscow. The midcourse phase offers the defense more time (about twenty minutes) to do its job, but disadvantages lie in the large number of targets (each booster can carry multiple reentry vehicles and scores of decoys), in having to discriminate reentry vehicles from decoys and other penetration aids, in the enormous amount of data to be communicated and processed, and in penetrating the shielding already built into reentry vehicles to enable them to withstand the heat and stress of atmospheric reentry. More recent technological developments include infrared sensors (space, air, and ground based) to help with discrimination, and homing interceptor missiles capable of destroying the reentry vehicles in flight without resorting to a nuclear explosion (the latter capability was demonstrated by the United States June 1984 in the Homing Overlay Experiment). In addition, any space-based defensive weapons deployed for use against boosters and buses could also play a role in midcourse BMD.

Terminal defense is the oldest of BMD concepts. It takes advantage of the filtering performed by the atmosphere, which leaves the decoys and debris behind the heavier reentry vehicles, to simplify the problems of target identification. But the defense has little time in which to act because the reentry phase lasts only about two minutes and the intercepts must be conducted at high altitude to ensure that salvage-fused warheads (those designed to explode just before being destroyed) cannot carry out their destructive missions. (For this reason, among others, it is less difficult to defend a hardened military target, such as an ICBM silo, than a city or other soft target.) In recent years, the radars, interceptor missiles, and computers needed for terminal and late midcourse defense have been made much smaller and more capable than they used to be, and the prospect of highly accurate homing interceptor missiles has spurred interest in nonnuclear kill. Terminal defense, like midcourse defense, is something the United States and the Soviet Union can do. The technological questions relate to how well it can be done.

The challenge to defensive system designers lies not in hitting a bullet with a bullet; it lies in coping simultaneously with thousands of bullets and with potential countermeasures employed by a noncooperative adversary. As defensive technologies evolve, so too do the offensive systems with which they must deal, and the offense already enjoys an imposing head start.

SDI Funding

The SDI has been described by President Reagan as "a program of vigorous research focused on advanced defensive technologies . . . [that] will provide to a future President and a future Congress the technological knowledge required to support a decision on whether to develop and later deploy advanced defensive systems."[3] Responsibility for the SDI has been assigned to the DOD, under the direction of Lieutenant General James A. Abrahamson. DOD estimates that the SDI will cost about $26 billion over the period 1985 through 1989, of which $24 billion would be spent by DOD and $2 billion by the Department of Energy.[4] Before the SDI was announced, DOD was spending about $1 billion per year on strategic defenses and had planned to spend approximately $15 billion over the 1985–1989 period. Thus, the SDI calls for a fourfold increase over the current spending rate and an increase of about $9 billion, or 40 percent, over what had been planned for such research. In 1984, strategic defense accounted for 3.7 percent of the DOD's total budget for RDT&E; by 1989 it would account for 15.7 percent. The SDI, by any measure, is indeed "a program of vigorous research."

Central Questions

A program directed at defending the United States and its allies against missile attack and at reducing reliance on the threat of nuclear retaliation to deter aggression surely has strong emotional, ethical, and political appeal. Yet the SDI is controversial. Views differ widely on some of the most fundamental issues. The questions at the center of the SDI debate are these:

What are the objectives of the SDI?

Would it really work?

How much would it cost?

What would the Soviets do?

How would U.S. allies and others react?

How would it affect arms control?

How would it affect the likelihood and consequences of nuclear war?

Objectives of the SDI

In his Star Wars speech, the president unambiguously stated the ambitious goal of SDI: "I call upon the scientific community in our country . . . to give us the means of rendering these nuclear weapons impotent and obsolete." Four days later, Defense Secretary Weinberger reiterated this aim: "The defensive systems the President is talking about are not designed to be partial. What we want to try to get is a system that is thoroughly reliable and total. . . . I don't see any reason why that can't be done."[5]

It was not long before administration analysts and spokesmen began to discuss intermediate deployments of BMD, limited in capability and intended not to replace deterrence by threat of retaliation but to buttress it. The DOD strategy panel led by Fred S. Hoffman concluded (under the heading "The Preferred Path to the President's Goal: Intermediate Options"):

> The assessment in this study of the utility of intermediate systems is necessarily tentative. . . . Nevertheless, it indicates that, given a reasonable degree of success in our R&D efforts, intermediate systems can strengthen deterrence. They will greatly complicate Soviet attack plans and reduce Soviet confidence in a successful outcome. . . . Even U.S. defenses of limited capability can deny Soviet planners confidence in their ability to destroy a sufficient set of military targets to satisfy enemy objectives, thereby strengthening deterrence. Intermediate defenses can also reduce damage if conflict occurs. The combined effects of these intermediate capabilities could help to reassure our allies about the credibility of our guarantees.[6]

SDI director Abrahamson later offered a rationale intended to reconcile the two approaches:

> We are frequently asked whether the purpose of the Strategic Defense Initiative (SDI) is to defend people or military forces. Accomplishment of both missions is essential to the ultimate goal, which is to provide security for the people of the United States *and our allies.*[7]

The president's science adviser, George A. Keyworth II, picked up on the notion of the SDI's countering ballistic missiles not by intercepting them but by creating incentives for eliminating them. In fall 1984 he wrote:

> Although we cannot disinvent nuclear weapons, and although nations will continue to distrust one another, heavily defended countries could nevertheless realistically enter into treaties to reduce nuclear forces to zero. . . . Strategic defense therefore provides an option for a world effectively disarmed of nuclear weapons.[8]

And by the end of 1984, the president himself was speaking of near-term as well as long-term goals for his own initiative:

> In the near term, the SDI research program also responds to the ongoing and extensive Soviet anti-ballistic missiles (ABM) effort, which includes actual deployments. It provides a powerful deterrent to any Soviet decision to expand its ballistic missile defense capability beyond that permitted by the ABM Treaty. And, in the long-term, we have confidence that the SDI will be a crucial means by which both the United States and the Soviet Union can safely agree to very deep reductions, and eventually, even the elimination of ballistic missiles and the nuclear weapons they carry.[9]

In sum, the SDI is supposed to render nuclear weapons impotent and obsolete, to be reliable and thorough, to complicate Soviet attacks, to improve stability, to limit damage to military and civilian targets if conflict occurs, to extend to U.S. allies, to hedge against Soviet breakthroughs in BMD R&D, to discourage the Soviets from expanding their BMD deployments, and to bring about nuclear disarmament. All of these goals would be met by an impenetrable shield—a BMD bubble—covering the United States and its allies. But what if the best achievable defensive system were substantially less than perfect? Then U.S. cities, the most precious and the most vulnerable targets, would remain at risk, and U.S. security would continue to rest on deterrence by threat of retaliation. Defense of military assets, such as land-based strategic retaliatory forces and command and control centers, would reduce the effectiveness of Soviet ballistic missiles against those targets but would increase the effectiveness of U.S. ballistic missiles by improving their survivability. Comparable Soviet defenses would have the reverse effect. This strengthening of deterrence by threat of retaliation does not sound like what the president had in mind initially. A plan for eliminating deterrence by threat of retaliation can hardly be the same as a plan for bolstering such deterrence. The United States will have to decide what the SDI is for.

Technical Feasibility

Would a BMD work? The answer depends on many factors, including the number and nature of the targets to be defended, the level of protection required, and the characteristics of the attacking missile force. The notion that the SDI will come up with a perfect defense—that is, one that could intercept and destroy all ballistic missiles before they reach U.S. soil or that of its allies—is met with great skepticism. In a background paper prepared for the Office of Technology Assessment of the U.S. Congress, Ashton B. Carter put it this way:

> The prospect that emerging "Star Wars" technologies, when further developed, will provide a perfect or near-perfect defense system, literally removing from the hands of the Soviet Union the ability to do mortal damage to the United States with nuclear weapons, is so remote that it should not serve as the basis of public expectation or national policy about ballistic missile defense (BMD).[10]

Citing Carter's statement, scientists Hans A. Bethe, Richard L. Garwin, Kurt Gottfried, and Henry W. Kendall wrote, "Based on our assessment of the technical issues, we are in complete agreement with this conclusion."[11] And Stanford University physicists Sidney D. Drell and Wolfgang K.H. Panofsky concluded, "We see no practical prospect whatsoever of constructing a strategic defense that can—lacking prior *drastic* arms control restraints and reductions—enhance deterrence, much less render nuclear weapons impotent and obsolete."[12] The DOD's strategy panel was more optimistic, but guardedly so:

> In the long term, such [multilayered] systems might provide a nearly leakproof defense against large ballistic missile attacks. However, their components vary substantially in technical risk, development lead time, and cost, and in the policy issues they raise.[13]

Attractive as invulnerability to ballistic missile attack might be, it clearly should be viewed more as an aspiration than an expectation.

Defense systems intended to meet more modest goals are more feasible (or less infeasible, depending on one's point of view). Of the partial defenses, the kind most often considered is a defense of some or all of the ICBMs and long-range bombers and the critical command, control, and communications facilities associated with strategic forces. Such a defense would raise the attack price (the level of attack required to achieve a given amount of damage) and would decrease confidence in its success. An important question is how the cost of the defense would compare to the cost of offensive measures (such as additional ballistic missiles and penetration aids) sufficient to offset it. At the current state of offensive and defensive technologies, this cost-exchange ratio strongly favors the offensive. A vigorous program of research on defensive systems could conceivably lead to a change in that situation.

The question of whether BMD would work cannot be answered with a simple yes or no. A defense that would provide perfect protection against ballistic missiles is extremely remote. Defensive systems capable of achieving some of the more limited objectives, however, are more readily envisaged. The technological hurdles lying in the paths of such systems appear formidable but not necessarily insurmountable.

Economic Costs

No one knows how much a BMD would cost. What we do know is that the Reagan administration has requested authorization to spend $26 billion over the five-year period 1985 through 1989 on research required to support a future decision on whether to develop and deploy advanced BMD systems. The $26 billion is for research only. The cost of any defense that might eventually be developed and deployed probably would make the $26 billion figure seem small. To estimate the cost of such a system requires some knowledge of the technologies emerging from this research, the objectives of the defense to be deployed, the offensive threat to be countered, the characteristics of the major components, and the nature and extent of the overall system. None of these essential parameters is now known. Total cost figures of $500 billion and $1 trillion have been tossed around by interested observers, but these are guesses. No one knows what would be the cost of deploying a defense based on unknown technologies and intended to achieve unspecified objectives against an unidentified threat. Little is to gained at this stage by arguing about whether the hypothetical defense would be worth the unknown cost.

Soviet Actions

The Soviet BMD program got underway soon after World War II.[14] The first important development began with construction of the Moscow system in the early 1960s; it was fully operational by about 1970. At that time, it consisted of sixty-four ABM launchers and associated ABM interceptor missiles, one large modern battle management radar (with another soon to be added), four sets of smaller radars to guide the interceptors to their targets, and a network of early warning radars around the periphery of the Soviet Union. In recent years, the original interceptor missiles have been replaced by newer versions suitable for midcourse and terminal intercepts. Older mechanically steered radars have been supplanted by modern phased-array (electronically steered) ones. This upgraded system, even if expanded to the full complement of 100 interceptor missiles permitted by the ABM Treaty, provides some protection against small attacks but is of no military significance against the U.S. arsenal of about 7,500 ballistic missile warheads. (It is worth noting that the United States has no operational BMD. One site of the Safeguard system, at Grand Forks, North Dakota, became operational in 1974 and was ordered shut down in 1976 by a Congress that judged it not to be cost-effective.)

Additional developments in the Soviet BMD program have emerged in the past several years. These include a small, transportable phased-array radar that, if coupled with interceptor missiles of the types recently deployed as part of the Moscow system, could constitute an ABM system (designated by the West as the ABM-X-3) suitable for relatively rapid deployment.

The network of peripheral early warning radars also is being modernized. A matter of particular concern regarding Soviet compliance with the ABM Treaty is a new phased-array radar under construction near Krasnoyarsk in central Siberia. This radar appears to U.S. intelligence analysts to be designed to provide early warning of ballistic missile attacks. But the ABM Treaty prohibits the deployment of such radars by either country "except at locations along the periphery of its national territory and oriented outward."[15] Since Krasnoyarsk is more than 500 miles away from the border of the Soviet Union, the Reagan administration has charged that "the new radar under construction at Krasnoyarsk almost certainly constitutes a violation of legal obligations under the Anti-Ballistic Missile Treaty of 1972."[16] The Soviets maintain that no violation is involved because the new radar is not intended to be used for early warning. They hold that its purpose is to track objects in outer space, a function explicitly exempted (in agreed statement F) from the treaty limitations. This issue remains to be resolved.

Defenses against aircraft are widespread in the Soviet Union, with more than 10,000 launchers for antiaircraft surface-to-air (SAM) missiles currently deployed. Modernization takes place continuously. (The United States has no such systems in place.) The latest Soviet SAM systems are known as the SA-10 and the SA-12. The SA-10 is being widely deployed for defense against low-flying bombers and cruise missiles. The SA-12, which has become operational only recently, appears to have been designed to intercept not only aircraft and cruise missiles but also tactical ballistic missiles (which reenter the atmosphere at lower speeds than the longer-range strategic versions) and perhaps even SLBM reentry vehicles. Some analysts believe that further improvements in these systems, especially the SA-12, could enable them to conduct terminal intercepts against ICBMs as well. It is generally agreed, however, that penetration aids developed by the United States would, if deployed, enable U.S. strategic ballistic missiles to defeat these upgraded defensive systems.

The Soviets also are exploring advanced technologies with BMD potential, including research and development on directed-energy weapons such as lasers and particle beams. Although the Soviet effort in this area has been more intense than that of the United States, neither seems to be ahead.

While the Soviets have devoted enormous resources to strategic defense, their progress has been steady but slow. The United States, in sharp contrast, has placed little emphasis beyond research on defensive systems, generally regarding such efforts as futile. How would the Soviets react to a markedly invigorated U.S. BMD program? Not surprisingly the Soviet reaction to the SDI has been consistently and strongly negative. Rhetoric aside, however, there are a number of concrete steps they might actually take in response to a U.S. effort to develop and deploy an effective BMD system.[17]

The first-order military response would be to improve and, if necessary, expand offensive forces to ensure that they could defeat the defenses. For example, the Soviets might equip their ballistic missiles with decoys and other penetration aids, increase the number of MIRVs on their large missiles, deploy reentry vehicles capable of performing evasive maneuvers, shorten the burn time of their boosters, harden the boosters against directed energy weapons, and proliferate the number of boosters. They might deploy many bombers and cruise missiles, against which the SDI would provide no defense at all. (A nationwide air defense of the United States could be added, at an additional cost rivaling that of the BMD.) The Soviets could try to develop ASAT systems for destroying any space-based components of a BMD system. Of two technical programs, one aimed at designing a system for destroying ballistic missiles from a platform in space and the other charged with designing a weapon for destroying the platform before it could accomplish its mission, most engineers would judge the latter program to be more likely to achieve success.

In addition to measures designed to counter the defenses, the Soviets could intensify their own defensive efforts. A nationwide U.S. BMD system probably would be met by a Soviet one (though not necessarily of comparable quality).

We cannot foresee the Soviet military response to the American initiative, but there is bound to be one. Parts of it undoubtedly have already been set in motion.

Allies' Reactions

How would our allies view a shift in U.S. strategy toward greater reliance on defensive systems? The preliminary results are in, and they vary only within the narrow range between skepticism and opposition.

There are at least one hundred reasons U.S. European allies offer in opposition to a U.S. BMD program that goes beyond the research phase. The first 95 of these are variations on a single theme: widespread strategic defenses would change the status quo. For four decades Europe has seen neither nuclear nor conventional war. Why, the allies ask, should we try to fix something that isn't broken?

The 96th reason stems from the conviction that, if the United States were to have an extensive BMD, so too would the Soviet Union. This is of particular concern to the United Kingdom and France, each of which maintains its own independent deterrent force of ballistic missiles. The ability of these small forces to penetrate a much expanded Soviet defense could be seriously in question.

Argument 97 also relates to the Soviet defense. If the Soviets came to believe that their homeland were reasonably protected against a U.S. nuclear attack, they could adopt a far more adventurous and hostile foreign policy, perhaps one that would lead to conventional war in Europe or Asia. The next argument is the mirror image of its predecessor: if the United States were to feel significantly less vulnerable, it might act more adventurously and therefore increase the risk of conventional war.

The 99th argument maintains that if both superpowers were to find themselves substantially invulnerable to nuclear attack, they might view the rest of the world as safe grounds for conventional and nuclear wars. Reason 100 is a belief that, because a strategic defense would be enormously expensive, resources would inevitably be diverted from other, much more sorely needed defense programs, such as improvements in conventional forces.

These allied responses are preliminary ones. Like most Americans, U.S. allies are still trying to figure out what the SDI means.

Arms Control

The connections between the SDI and arms control are strongest in three areas: limitations on BMD systems, particularly those restraints embodied in the ABM Treaty, reductions in offensive nuclear arsenals, and constraints on ASAT weapons.[18]

From its inception in the Star Wars speech, the SDI was to be "consistent with our obligations of the ABM Treaty." This condition was reaffirmed by the president in December 1984: "The research that we are undertaking is consistent with all of our treaty obligations, including the 1972 Anti-Ballistic Missile Treaty."[19] To appreciate the constraints imposed on the SDI by the ABM Treaty, it is useful to review the relevant provisions of that agreement.

1. *Nationwide defense is prohibited.* Article I of the treaty states:

Each Party undertakes not to deploy ABM systems for a defense of the territory of its country and not to provide a base for such a defense, and not to deploy ABM systems for defense of an individual region except as provided for in Article III of this Treaty.

Article III begins, "Each Party undertakes not to deploy AMB systems or their components except that," and then goes on to specify the permitted deployments of ABM interceptor missiles, fixed land-based launchers for them, and ABM radars. Thus, unlike most other elements of international or domestic law, the ABM Treaty approach to governing deployments is based on the principle that what is not expressly permitted is prohibited. Moreover, the permitted deployments are severely constrained quantitatively, geographically, and qualitatively. Each side is permitted only one deployment area of 150 kilometer radius, within which it may have not more than 100 fixed land-based launchers, 100 interceptor missiles, and strictly limited ABM radars. No other ABM deployments are permitted.

2. *All ABM systems are covered by the treaty.* Article II provides the basic definition: "an ABM system is a system to counter strategic ballistic missiles or their elements in flight trajectory." The capability of weapons system determines whether it is to be considered as an ABM system. This interpretation is reinforced in Article VI:

> Each Party undertakes . . . not to give missiles, launchers, or radars, other than ABM interceptor missiles, ABM launchers, or ABM radars, capabilities to counter strategic ballistic missiles or their elements in flight trajectory, and not to test them in an ABM mode.

For example, an air defense system or an ASAT weapon that "could counter strategic ballistic missiles or their elements in flight trajectory" would be considered an ABM system. (Notice that the treaty limits only defenses against strategic ballistic missiles and not defenses against tactical ballistic missiles. The line between the two may prove difficult to draw in practice.)

3. *Only fixed, land-based ABM systems may be developed, tested, or deployed.* Article V includes an undertaking "not to develop, test, or deploy ABM systems or components which are sea-based, air-based, space-based, or mobile land-based." Only fixed land-based ABM systems or components can move beyond research and into development. Ambassador Gerard Smith, who headed the U.S. delegation to Salt I, provided the U.S. interpretation:

> The prohibitions on development contained in the ABM Treaty would start at that part of the development process where field testing is initiated on either a prototype or breadboard model. It was understood by both sides that the prohibition on "development" applies to activities involved after a component moves from the laboratory development and testing stage to the field testing stage, wherever performed. . . . Exchanges with the Soviet Delegation made clear that this definition is also the Soviet interpretation of the term "development."[20]

Despite this attempt to sharpen the distinction between research (permitted for all kinds of ABM systems and components) and development (prohibited for all but fixed land-based systems and components), the boundary remains somewhat fuzzy.

4. *Exotic ABM systems and components, even fixed land-based ones, may not be deployed.* Since Article III prohibits all ABM deployments other than the expressly permitted launchers, interceptors, and radars, any ABM systems or components

based on exotic technologies (such as lasers, particle beams, hypervelocity electro-magnetic guns, or other technologies capable of substituting for ABM launchers, interceptors, or radars) may not be deployed. A statement initialed by the U.S. and Soviet negotiators (agreed statement D) provided that such futuristic systems "would be subject to discussion in accordance with Article XIII [in the SCC] and agreement in accordance with Article XIV [by amendment] of the Treaty." The effect of this statement is to ban any deployment of exotic systems unless and until the treaty is amended to permit such deployment. It should be noted, however, that fixed land-based versions may be developed and tested at agreed test ranges.

5. *Verification is to be accomplished by national technical means.* The term *national technical means of verification* refers to methods of monitoring compliance with an agreement that are under the national control of the parties. These means can include data collection systems based in space, in the air, at sea, or on the ground. Article XII includes obligations "not to interfere with the national technical means of verification of the other Party" and "not to use deliberate conceal-ment measures which impede verification by national technical means of compliance with the provisions of this Treaty."

6. *A standing consultative commission is established.* Article XII created the U.S.-Soviet SCC in which the two sides will consider matters such as "questions concerning compliance," "possible changes in the strategic situation which have a bearing on the provisions of this Treaty," "possible proposals for further increasing the viability of this Treaty; including proposals for amendments in accordance with the provisions of this Treaty," and "proposals for further measures aimed at limiting strategic arms."

7. *The treaty is of unlimited duration.* While the two sides are formally to review the agreement at five-year intervals (Article XIV), it is of "unlimited duration" (Article XV) and remains in force unless one or both parties take positive action to terminate it. Either party can withdraw upon six months' notice "if it decides that extraordinary events related to the subject matter of this Treaty have jeopardized its supreme interests" (Article XV).

Clearly the ABM Treaty and the SDI are on a collision course. As long as the United States adheres to the agreement in anything like its current form, the obstacles to achieving the long-term objectives of the SDI are insurmountable. Amendment or withdrawal would have to come before even some of the shorter-term objectives could be met. Few can imagine an effective defensive system that does not employ space-based components for countering offensive missiles in the early stages of their flight and land-mobile components for intercepting nuclear warheads as they reenter the atmosphere; yet the treaty prohibits development and testing (as well as deployment) of such components.

The provisions of the agreement are subject to interpretation, and the line between permitted and prohibited actions is not always clear. At what point does permitted research become prohibited development? What distinguishes a component of an ABM system from a subcomponent of, or an adjunct to, such a system? To what extent may an ASAT system (or any system other than a dedicated ABM system) be capable of "countering strategic ballistic missiles or their elements in flight trajectory" before it is considered (for purposes of the treaty) to be an ABM system? Each of these questions is relevant to the SDI, and none can be answered precisely.

Calls for changes in the ABM Treaty come from all quarters. Those who believe that the treaty was a poor idea in the first place would terminate it as soon as possible. Some would prefer to maintain the treaty for now but would modify it to permit some defenses of ICBMs to relax the prohibition on development and testing of sea-based, air-based, space-based, and mobile land-based ABM systems and components. Others, who would prefer to see the treaty strengthened rather than weakened, would attempt to tighten the constraints on testing, to eliminate the ambiguities associated with dual-use systems, and perhaps even to ban all ABM deployment. Still others, concerned that attempts to amend the treaty might lead either to modifications far different from those originally intended or to the demise of the agreement, prefer to leave well enough alone and to rely on the SCC to work out individual problems as they arise.

The ABM Treaty is the only formerly enduring accomplishment of fifteen years of Soviet-U.S. strategic arms control negotiations. Its termination probably would signal the end of nuclear arms control, an enterprise whose future is clouded in any event.

How would the SDI affect the prospects for negotiated reductions in the offensive nuclear arsenals of the two superpowers? Proponents of the SDI maintain that strategic defense is just what is needed to pave the way to meaningful reductions. Effective defenses, they argue, would reduce the military utility of ballistic missiles and therefore weaken the resistance to eliminating some, or perhaps even all, of them. Others disagree, maintaining that the more likely Soviet response to a U.S. defense against ballistic missiles would include expansion of and improvements in offensive forces to counter the U.S. defense and probably also further deployments of Soviet defenses. They see the SDI as paving the way not to arms control but to an accelerated arms race.

This difference between the views of SDI proponents and opponents stems in part from differing assumptions about the effectiveness of BMD. The perfect or near-perfect defense envisaged by SDI supporters would tend to discourage further Soviet investment in offensive ballistic missiles. But the far less than perfect ABM systems seen by SDI opponents as available in the foreseeable future would permit a growing Soviet offense to maintain its decisive advantage over the defense. And, they believe, a growing Soviet offense is just what would be seen.

The BMD systems available for deployment for the next couple of decades are unlikely to be more than moderately capable. Such systems would contribute little to reducing the vulnerability of the nation unless the offensive forces of the other side were severely constrained. But each side, in its conservative planning, is likely to overestimate the effectiveness of the adversary's defensive systems and to underestimate the performance of its own. Thus deployment of defenses would heighten perceived needs to improve and expand, and not to reduce, offensive forces. Ironically the SDI may need a highly cooperative arms control environment far more than it would foster one.

The technologies associated with BMD and ASAT weapons have much in common. BMD systems designed to attack ballistic missiles in the boost phase and postboost phase offer great ASAT potential. These BMD systems face challenges even more formidable than the ASAT task because a ballistic missile attack would present a greater number of targets and would provide less time for their destruction. A boost phase or postboost phase BMD almost certainly would have some critical components operating in space, for that is the only way to have a direct line of sight to the missile boosters or buses to be destroyed. Thus, the ABM Treaty prohibition on development, testing, and deployment of space-based ABM systems and components in effect bans boost phase and postboost phase BMD.

After release by the bus, a warhead follows a trajectory quite similar to that of a satellite in orbit. Consequently BMD systems designed to destroy warheads in the midcourse phase naturally overlap with ASAT weapons. Indeed the Homing Overlay Experiment conducted by the U.S. Army in June 1984, which was heralded as having demonstrated a midcourse BMD capability, might almost as aptly have been described as a demonstration of an ASAT weapon.

BMD systems designed to destroy missile warheads as they reenter the atmosphere in the terminal phase of their flight have least in common with ASAT weapons. The overlap lies primarily in the radars employed for acquiring and tracking the targets and, in some types of systems, for guiding an interceptor missile to the target.

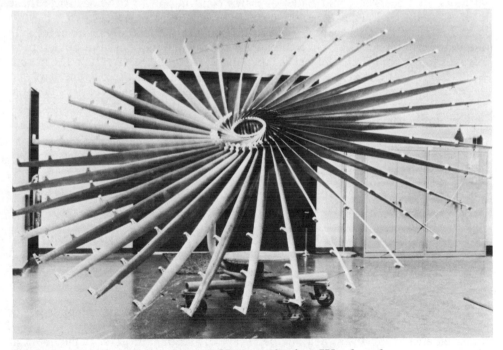

Homing Overlay Experiment Nonexplosive Warhead

This photograph depicts the nonexplosive "warhead" of the experimental flight vehicle in the Army's Homing Overlay Experiment (HOE) program. The device's metal ribs, approximately seven feet long and seeded with steel weights, are wound around the neck of the HOE homing-and-kill vehicle during flight. They unfurl seconds before the HOE vehicle collides with a target ICBM reentry vehicle and destroys it.

Source: U.S. Department of Defense.

The ABM Treaty inhibits, but does not preclude, continued development, testing, and deployment of ASAT weapons. Determining the threshold at which an ASAT weapon has sufficient BMD capability to count as an ABM system for purposes of the treaty remains a knotty problem. And even moderately capable BMD systems may serve as excellent ASAT weapons.

Without the ABM Treaty or other meaningful constraints on boost, post-boost, midcourse, and terminal BMD systems, ASAT activities would be essentially unconstrained. On the other hand, an agreement limiting the development, testing, and deployment of some or all types of ASAT weapons almost certainly would reinforce the ABM Treaty.

This cursory examination of some of the relationships between the SDI and arms control suggests that vigorous pursuit of the initiative would require (probably by 1990 or so) either substantial modification or termination of the ABM Treaty, would dim rather than brighten the prospects for significant reductions in offensive forces, and would reduce still further the chances for an agreement imposing meaningful constraints on ASAT weapons. To those who believe that such arms control accords could make a useful contribution to U.S. security, these aspects of the SDI argue strongly against it.

The SDI certainly got the Soviets' attention and undoubtedly contributed substantially to their renewed interest in arms control negotiations. But Soviet interest will wane if the United States is unwilling to place the SDI itself on the negotiating table. To be effective, a bargaining chip must eventually become part of a bargain. The question of whether the SDI is to be made available to U.S. negotiations for use as a potential bargaining chip will have to be decided before any serious progress can be made in nuclear arms negotiations.

Risk of Nuclear War

How would widespread BMDs affect the risk of nuclear war? The answer to this question depends on the effects of BMD on deterrence, on the incentives for preemptive attack in time of crisis, and on the level of damage suffered if nuclear war should occur.

Virtually all Americans would prefer a world in which the United States had meaningful defenses and the Soviet Union did not to one in which the situation were reversed. The Soviets, no doubt, hold the contrary view. In actuality, either both superpowers will continue to eschew widespread BMDs, or both will seek them. These are the alternatives worthy of serious consideration.

To the extent that deterrence rests on the U.S. ability to inflict high levels of damage on a potential aggressor, a substantial portion of U.S. strategic forces must be able to survive attack and penetrate to assigned targets. Deployment of BMD to defend U.S. land-based retaliatory forces and strategic command, control, and communication centers would improve their survivability, thereby strengthening deterrence. But a widespread Soviet BMD system would degrade the penetrability of surviving U.S. forces (ICBMs and SLBMs directly and bombers and cruise missiles indirectly by interfering with precursor ballistic missile attacks on Soviet air defenses) and in this way would weaken deterrence.

The net effect of increased survivability and reduced penetrability depends strongly on what is defended (and perceived to be defended) on each side. If the defensive networks unambiguously protect only retaliatory forces and not the targets against which a retaliatory attack would be directed, deterrence would be augmented. But if the defense protected a substantial portion of the national territory, including centers of population and industry, deterrence could be undermined. Unless a nationwide defense were almost perfect, cities would remain vulnerable. It is difficult to imagine a disarming strike so splendidly executed and a defense so effective that hundreds of nuclear warheads (of the many thousands in each superpower's arsenal) could not arrive on urban targets in a retaliatory attack. The ability to inflict unacceptable damage would not be affected by widespread deployments of the kinds of BMD system components currently available or likely to be over the technological horizon. No rational national leader could reasonably be convinced that his or her country would be better off with a nuclear war than without one.

Crisis conditions complicate the problem. Suppose the level of hostility between the superpowers (perhaps reflected in armed conflict somewhere in the world) were so high that one side or the other believed, rightly or wrongly, that the other intended soon to launch a nuclear first strike. The question then before the national leadership is whether the advantage gained by preemption would be sufficient to outweigh the alternative of waiting to see if nuclear war could be avoided. The choice is not between nuclear war and no nuclear war but between nuclear war initiated by one's own nation and a strong possibility (but not a certainty) that it will be started by the other side. Under these conditions, the effect of BMD on the incentive to preempt (or, in the jargon of the trade, on crisis stability) becomes important.

The conventional wisdom is that nationwide BMD favors the side that strikes first. It rests on the belief that a well-coordinated preemptive strike by a superpower drawing on its undiminished nuclear arsenal would be better able to counter defenses than would a ragged retaliatory attack launched by a crippled nation drawing only on those weapons that had survived the preemptive blow. The argument has merit, but it is not the whole story. Implicit in this logic is the assumption that increased survivability of the retaliatory forces would be more than offset by their decreased penetrability. This assumption does not reflect some inescapable law of nature, but it is consistent with most theoretical calculations of the outcomes of hypothetical nuclear wars. Indeed this assumption lies at the heart of the ABM Treaty. The burden of proof should rest on those who maintain that it is wrong.

Space-based BMD systems present a special challenge to crisis stability.[21] Imagine a world in which the United States and the Soviet Union, despite the technical, military, and political obstacles, had managed to deploy highly effective space-based BMD systems. Such systems are likely to be far more effective in an ASAT role than in a BMD role because the ASAT task is the easier one. Thus, each side's BMD satellites would be vulnerable to attack by those of the other side. It follows that a preemptive attack on the adversary's Star Wars satellites and other ASAT systems would render the adversary's homeland vulnerable to attack by ballistic missiles and, at the same time, ensure the continued relative invulnerability of one's own nation. In this imaginary world, preemption garners a great reward.

The instinctive appeal of the SDI lies largely in the hope that it might somehow reduce substantially the consequences of nuclear war. Perhaps in the distant future this might be achieved. In the nearer term, though more than a decade away, BMD might provide meaningful protection against small attacks, whether launched intentionally or by malfunctions of machines or minds, provided that the attacking weapons are ballistic missiles. This is of little comfort in dealing with the danger of possible future nuclear threats from terrorists or pariah nations, for they are most unlikely to have long-range ballistic missiles available to them if and when they acquire nuclear weapons. And even if they did, they need not choose to use the one form of nuclear delivery vehicle against which the United States had a defense. "Suitcase bombs" are the more likely threat from these quarters.

Against a large attack by a determined adversary with a nuclear arsenal comparable to that now in the hands of the Soviet Union, the United States will remain vulnerable for decades to come. The Soviet Union will remain vulnerable as well. Mutual assured destruction (MAD) describes the world as it is, not as we would like it to be. Each superpower can annihilate the other, and each will take the actions necessary to maintain that capability for as long as it can. For now, the primary objective is to ensure that these capabilities are not used. For the longer term, the United States must strive to replace this reliance on deterrence with a regime less subject to catastrophic failure. But unless the short-term objective is satisfied, there may be no long term.

Conclusion

This chapter is intended to deal primarily with the question of how to think about the SDI rather than what to do about it. Accordingly it has sought to raise questions rather than to answer them. The issues are complex and feature difficult trade-offs. Objective and knowledgeable individuals sharing the same information can arrive at different conclusions. Yet readers are justified in expecting the writer to disclose the general direction in which his own analysis leads him.

Decide what we are trying to do. The central questions associated with the SDI remain not only unanswered but largely unexplored. The SDI cannot simultaneously enhance and replace deterrence, be of clearly acceptable but inestimable cost, discourage and stimulate Soviet counteractions, calm and frighten U.S. allies, reverse and accelerate the nuclear arms competition, and lower and raise the risk of nuclear war. The implications of the SDI, favorable and unfavorable, are only barely perceived and certainly not understood. Further study, discussion, and debate are required if the United States is to make an informed decision on what it is trying to do.

Control the momentum. There is general agreement on the need for some research on strategic defenses. At a minimum, the United States should maintain a program adequate to hedge against Soviet breakthroughs in BMD technology, to reduce the Soviet advantage in lead time to deployment of BMD systems based on currently available technologies, and to search for an eventual replacement for deterrence by threat of nuclear retaliation. Disputes arise over additional objectives (and associated programs) and the intensity of the overall effort. Of particular concern is the political momentum being gathered by the SDI. The 1985–1989 SDI budget authorization requested by DOD calls for fiscal year 1989 funding of more than four times the 1985 level. And administration officials continuously remind us that the SDI is the president's initiative, with all the prestige of his office behind it. Left unabated, these political forces will generate great pressure to decide to develop and deploy something as a result of the SDI, even if the SDI research program uncovers no technologies and system concepts worthy of development and deployment. The alternative, doing nothing, might be interpreted as a waste of $26 billion and a presidential failure. To guard against the danger of being faced with such a choice, the rate of increase in SDI spending should be reduced. An expenditure of $15 billion between 1985 and 1989, as had been planned by the Reagan administration prior to the announcement of the SDI, seems more than adequate to meet the essential objectives of such a research program yet not so high as to generate uncontrollable momentum.

Reaffirm the ABM Treaty. Evaluations of the ABM Treaty all too often focus solely on the constraints it imposes on U.S. BMD, that is, on the costs to the United States of continued adherence. But one must also consider the benefits to the United States: the constraints on Soviet BMD. The United States has no BMD system now fully tested and ready for production and deployment. The Soviet Union has a BMD system deployed now and could increase the production rate for rapid deployment. The treaty clearly serves U.S. interests. Accordingly the United States should reaffirm its commitment to the ABM Treaty, should seek to reinforce the prohibition on giving ABM capabilities to air defense, ASAT, and other potential dual-capability systems, and should neither seek nor be receptive to amendments that would permit higher levels of deployment.

Counter Soviet BMD. The most effective military response to the threat posed by a widespread Soviet defense against ballistic missiles would be the deployment of countermeasures against that defense. To hedge against (and to deter) a significant Soviet BMD capability that might be achieved rapidly (by deployment of transportable BMD components and/or by upgrading non-BMD SAM systems to provide them with BMD capabilities), the United States should pursue a program of vigorous development and production of penetration aids suitable for use against such defensive systems.

Fortify deterrence. If there is one nuclear matter on which the political Left and Right agree, it is that deterrence by threat of nuclear retaliation is immoral, unsound, and unacceptable. One group would solve the problem by making nuclear weapons disappear, that is, by disarmament. The other group would neutralize these weapons with perfect defenses. Neither approach offers realistic solutions to the problems faced by the United States and its allies. We may be uncomfortable with deterrence as the shield between us and annihilation, but it is currently the only shield. Derogating deterrence serves only to undermine its credibility and impair its effectiveness; it does nothing to vitalize potential alternatives. Now and for the foreseeable future, U.S. interests would best be served by fortifying deterrence with words as well as with deeds.

Chapter 11

Special Supplement: Low-Intensity Conflict, the Strategic Challenge

Robert H. Kupperman
William J. Taylor, Jr.

lthough low-intensity conflict has not attracted the same degree of sustained attention in the United States as have the more violent and more obviously dangerous modes of warfare, there is growing recognition that it will be the most prevalent form of conflict confronting the nations of the world in the remainder of this century.[1]

A number of geostrategic factors have converged to produce this enduring reality. The rough military balance between East and West has made full-scale war between the blocs unlikely. But superpower tensions persist, evidenced by the continuing expansion of military arsenals, by frequently hostile and suspicious bilateral relations, and increasingly by political and economic competition in the developing world. In this overarching context of tension, volatile forces in the Third World have magnified the potential for instability and turmoil affecting the central U.S.-Soviet relationship. Pressure on immature governing institutions has become increasingly severe with skyrocketing population growth, the introduction of new technologies and associated alien values and modes of behavior, and the dislocating effects of economic, sociological, and political change. Regional interactions, frequently inflamed by ancient hatreds, hegemonism, and irredentist

John M. Oseth contributed to the first draft of this chapter; however, the coauthors are solely responsible for the contents in its published form.

hopes, are made even more combustible by the proliferation of advanced conventional weapons and war-fighting capabilities.[2] Finally, the Soviet Union continues to seek international advantage by encouraging and manipulating local revolution and regional strife, sometimes by direct means but usually through pliable surrogates. This overlays many localized struggles with long-term strategic implications for the United States. Washington cannot look on with equanimity as hostile machinations undercut the development of democratic values and free institutions around the globe.

It is true, of course, that direct Soviet challenges to U.S. interests have been and will continue to be subtle and careful. The most obvious challenges will continue to be manageable at levels of effort far below that of armed confrontation. It is also likely that political violence in the developing world will continue to be limited in geographic scope, duration, pace of combat, casualties incurred, and national resources devoted to the effort. Not every Soviet competitive drive, not every unstable regime, and not every small war will have a direct and adverse impact on U.S. interests.[3] But it is equally clear that some of these challenges will engage U.S. interests in ways that raise unarguable security concerns. Increasingly, however, questions have been raised both within and outside government about whether the United States has the capability to cope with the multidimensional future of conflict that lies ahead.[4]

Nature of the Challenge

The challenge is this: the Soviet Union will pursue low-cost–low-risk operations with high geostrategic payoffs. More specifically, the Politburo, in recognition of the unacceptable costs and risks of using nuclear weapons or major conventional force formations directly against the alliance interests of the world's industrial democracies, will press ahead with political-military initiatives in the Third World where the industrial democracies are most vulnerable, employing low-intensity conflict operations, which the democracies are least willing and prepared to counter. The costs for the USSR will be relatively low and will take the form of political support, military advice and training, and weapons sales. The risks will also be low because low-intensity scenarios have a low probability that Soviet and U.S. military forces will come into direct contact. The high geostrategic payoff that the Soviets envision is the capability to interdict the major sea-lanes of communication vital to the security of the industrial democracies. These sea-lanes are the lifelines for energy supplies, mineral and metal resources, and free trade without which the industrial democracies would face economic paralysis.

The Soviets will employ low-intensity operations to put in place advisers or proxy military forces near sea-lane choke points and at or near the sources of energy and mineral supplies. They will also seek to protect existing naval bases and acquire new ones in the Third World. Simultaneously they will continue to expand their blue-water power projections capability and numbers of ship operating days in Third World waters. The ways in which such Soviet capabilities might be used (beyond their psychopolitical uses) are legion. Many of them would fall under the heading of a scenario envisaging a Cuban missile crisis played in reverse. That is, the Soviets, with naval forces covered by local air, would block the entrance or exit through a vital waterway by the naval or maritime ships owned or chartered by a major industrial democracy allied with the United States. In an age of strategic nuclear parity between the superpowers, the question is, Who blinks first? The answer will make a significant difference in the geostrategic position of the United States for the long-term future.

Analysts have struggled endlessly, and not altogether successfully, with defining low-intensity conflict.[5] In part the problem is that the phenomena associated with such conflict transcend the traditional categories of peace and war that still dominate Western thinking about international politics. Defense specialists tend to focus almost exclusively on the warlike attributes and requirements of such conflict, neglecting its prior, less violent and nonviolent political and political-military aspects. Others tend to overlook the real security implications of the more subtle dimensions of conflict and therefore do not understand them to be fundamental strategic problems for the United States. Both sides, as Henry Kissinger reminded us, would do better to think of East-West peace not as a conflict-free condition but as a process of managing a variety of tensions and seeking to ameliorate and limit them.[6]

Superpower interests and activities continue to impinge upon one another directly and indirectly. Ideological hostility and political competition find many low-cost and low-risk outlets. The challenge to U.S. interests, and thus the need for a variety of political, military, and other tools for response, occurs during what many Westerners understand as peacetime. Conceptions of low-intensity conflict that are not part of that traditional reality can hardly support clear-eyed policy calculations in Washington or other Western capitals.[7]

A second factor that complicates defining low-intensity conflict is the blurred line dividing this category from higher levels of conflict. The spectrum of conflict has been formulated and reformulated; the ingredients of various levels of conflict have been packaged and repackaged. But it has been very hard to say authoritatively at what point a conflict becomes mid intensity rather than low intensity or which critical variables define the crossover point from one to the other. Former Army Chief of Staff General Edward C. Meyer once indicated that those who have operational defense responsibilities know that their higher-priority preparations for conventional war also prepare them for some lesser contingencies.[8] But until recently only a very few were interested in determining exactly what low-intensity capabilities have been left out of the U.S. readiness calculus. And a concept of that deficiency has not yet taken hold in either the public mind or the strategic community. While operational preparations cannot wait for concensus on definitions, there is certainly a need for more rigorous thinking and exposition about the problems we will encounter at the less violent end of the intensity spectrum.

This problem of definition has been addressed in great detail elsewhere.[9] For present purposes it is enough to outline a working concept as follows: low-intensity conflict includes any conflict between states and/or coherent political, economic, or ethnic groups that falls short of large unit engagement on a battlefield. Violence is implied but not essential. A wide range of conflictual contingencies is included: coercive diplomacy, propaganda and psychological operations, special intelligence operations, terrorism and counterterrorism, security assistance projects in relatively benign and varying degrees of hostile environments, insurgency and counterinsurgency, military and paramilitary deployments with limited goals, and limited conventional war. This concept posits a larger conflict environment that casts long shadows over seemingly localized political, political-military, and military strife. Such problems may not necessarily rise to the level of actual combat between identifiable forces, but where that is the case, it will fall at the lower end of a conceptual range of intensity of violence. It will involve many activities for which the great bulk of U.S. conventional military forces are unsuited or unnecessary for one reason or another.

The notion of low-intensity conflict can be given some empirical content with a survey of prominent events and trends that have raised policy challenges for the United States. This survey cannot be exhaustive, but it will lay groundwork for the ensuing discussion of relevant perspectives and policies of the Reagan administration.

Guerrilla Wars in Key Regions

The Central American situation is probably the best, though not the only, illustration. Nicaragua has become, in the words of the Kissinger commission, "a crucial steppingstone for Cuban and Soviet efforts to promote armed insurgency." Violence and counterviolence have increased rapidly throughout the region as the Sandinistas and their supporters execute a long-term design to export totalitarian revolution.[10] They have brought in large numbers of Cuban and other Soviet bloc advisers, developed sophisticated agencies of internal repression and external subversion, and sharpened polarizations both within individual countries and regionally. The armed strife in El Salvador is the most visible evidence of their efforts.

Expansion of Soviet Political-Military Pressure and Influence

In the Third World generally, the visible Soviet and Soviet bloc presence—advisers, bases, deployed forces, and so forth—is considerable.[11] Furthermore, Moscow has for years been the leading transferer of conventional arms to developing-world regimes.[12] Although not all such connections significantly magnify the military capabilities of the Soviet bloc, many do. Soviet cultivation of proxies in many troubled regions is a strategic reality that the United States ignores at its peril. Soviet material assistance and at least tacit approval of the specific policies has enabled one prominent ally, Cuba, to be involved actively on the African continent for two decades. The same point applies to ongoing Vietnamese adventures in Southeast Asia.[13] Soviet military involvement in Afghanistan is important by itself, but one must countenance a Soviet drive southeast through troubled Baluchistan to realize a traditional czarist objective: acquisition of a warm water port on the Indian Ocean.

Image-Shaping Competition

Incessant Soviet propaganda attacks on the United States and on specific U.S. policies constitute another dimension of the strategic problem. With regularity the Soviets and their fraternal regimes churn out attacks by all available means of communication. These attacks are aimed at specific concerns of often credulous, suspicious, and poorly informed foreign audiences. They actively propagate the image of the United States as militarist, aggressive, manipulative, deceitful, and disdainful of the needs and aspirations of others. Additionally Soviet disinformation programs—use of forgeries and staged events to shape the opinions and attitudes of foreign elites and publics—are a growing problem. Moscow has also emphasized long-term cultural and educational exchange programs that can build enduring links of understanding between peoples. The purpose (and effect) of this activity is a self-consciously strategic one: to reduce the material costs of preserving and advancing Soviet political aims, especially against the United States, by circumscribing and rolling back the spread of democratic values and institutions. It is an effort to win the strategic competition while minimizing the prospects for combat.[14]

Terrorism

Whether employed by radical subnational groups like the Palestine Liberation Organization, rogue nations like Iran and Syria, or Soviet-supported proxies, terrorism has become part of the arsenal of unconventional warfare. The bombings of the U.S. embassy and marine barracks in Lebanon, Colonel Muammar el-Qaddafi's recurrent public references to hit squad capabilities, and the clandestine mining of the Red Sea indicate the wide range of terrorist threats now confronting individual Americans, U.S. society as a whole, and U.S. interests and friends abroad. The threat is increasing worldwide, and U.S. authorities have taken careful note of its clear anti-U.S. bias.[15]

Even this partial survey of global realities outlines a wide array of low-intensity challenges and begins to sketch out a variegated list of policy instruments that decision makers in the United States may need to orchestrate in response. Some are clearly military or paramilitary: covert support for guerrilla fighters, peacekeeping missions, security assistance programs (including technical, logistical, and operational advice to foreign armed forces), and U.S. combat units capable of special missions ranging from Entebbe- to Grenada-style operations. Others are political-diplomatic in nature, such as participation with the Contadora group in accommodation efforts in Central America, the building of international norms on terrorism, and the promotion of democratic development abroad. Others are mainly economic, such as the Caribbean Basin initiative. The challenge for Washington might truly be seen not only as one of understanding the length and breadth of low-intensity conflict phenomena but also of understanding how the full policy repertoire might best be integrated and applied to meet the threat.

Low-Intensity Conflict and the Reagan Administration

In the last several years that realization has emerged fairly clearly in the declared policy of the Reagan administration, as well as in specific initiatives to revitalize U.S. capabilities to deal with the challenge. Perhaps the most prominent early evidence of administration strategies was the widely publicized concern about Soviet-Cuban-Nicaraguan expansionist tendencies in Central America. The result was a blend of policy approaches: political consultation and economic advice and assistance for the troubled regime in El Salvador; equipment, training, and operational advice for El Salvadoran armed forces; covert (though ultimately widely debated in public) aid for guerrillas opposing the Sandinista regime in Nicaragua; U.S. military construction and exercises in Honduras and elsewhere (clearly demonstrating larger U.S. interest and capabilities in the region); and a coordinated international information program intended, among other things, to expose and discredit Soviet, Cuban, and Nicaraguan manipulation.

Elements of that particular policy package remain controversial. There seems no way at present to escape divisive debate about the way the United States approaches conflict of any kind abroad (unless the Soviets do something cataclysmically foolish). But what is especially important here is the truly strategic approach taken: the orchestration of diverse policy instruments to deal with a localized situation perceived to implicate important U.S. national interests in the light of global realities and purposes. The Reagan administration has pursued a program with a number of components to revitalize a number of those key policy tools.

Intelligence

The administration has undertaken a general program of rebuilding and reenergizing the intelligence agencies in all facets of their capability: information collection, analysis, counterintelligence, and covert action meant to influence events abroad. This was an early administration priority. It was given special impetus by the Long commission's finding that correctible intelligence deficiencies had contributed to the vulnerability of the marines stationed at Beirut International Airport.[16] In addition, the former commander of U.S. trainers and advisers in El Salvador publicly drew attention to the importance of intelligence in dealing with low-intensity battlefield threats, and U.S. resources noticeably added to San Salvador's capability to deal with antigovernment guerrillas.[17]

Special Operations Forces Initiatives

Within DOD, there has been a revitalization of special operations forces designed for use in three situations:

1. Security assistance roles working with foreign armed forces to augment their defense capabilities.
2. Crisis situations requiring a flexible, tailored alternative where the use of conventional forces might not be appropriate or feasible.
3. Major conflict as an adjunct to conventional forces, utilizing special skills in unconventional warfare, psychological operations, intelligence, and surgical, direct action operations.

To improve cross-service coordination and to clarify command lines, the Pentagon has established the Joint Special Operations Agency in Washington, D.C. In each service high-priority initiatives were underway at the end of 1984 to amplify existing capabilities.[18] Perhaps the most visible of these was the addition of the new Army Special Forces Group, an Army Ranger Battalion (making a total of three battalions), and two navy SEAL (Sea-Air-Land) teams, along with associated special aircraft and communications facilities. There was also a concerted effort to upgrade the manning levels of these units and to improve training and career incentives for their personnel.

Security Assistance

The administration has expanded U.S. security assistance programs, especially military assistance (foreign military sales, grants, and training) to Third World nations. Prominent FY85 initiatives include increases in the training and grant aid elements of that effort, and region-specific objectives have been identified within the total program. The objectives are to assist countries in preserving their independence against direct and indirect aggression; to promote regional security; to help obtain access, overflight, and forward basing rights for U.S. forces; to contribute to interoperability among U.S. and other forces; to ensure U.S. and allied access to critical raw materials; and to provide a means of increasing U.S. influence abroad more generally.[19]

Combatting Terrorism

This has become a major priority, though a perplexing one. Defense measures at U.S. installations around the world have received greater attention (though bombings in Lebanon suggest that no installation may be made impervious to determined terrorists), as has the need for better intelligence. The administration has also sought to expand cooperation with other countries in developing both a common understanding of the problem and practical ways to deal with it. A training program for foreign law enforcement officers has been implemented. Beyond defensive postures, a more active strategy and capability is being sought to prevent or preempt terrorist attacks, as well as to retaliate against them by a variety of means (political, economic, and military).[20]

Strategic Military Flexibility

To a significant extent, deterrence and limitation of conflict around the world depend on a credible U.S. capacity to deliver forces rapidly to trouble spots and to sustain them when deployed. U.S. capabilities to project military power to regions outside Europe were emphasized in the Carter administration's response to the Soviet invasion of Afghanistan. They have been further amplified in the Reagan administration. The Rapid Deployment Joint Task Force became CENTCOM in 1983, with responsibility for contingencies in nineteen countries from the Horn of Africa to Pakistan. CENTCOM also oversees U.S. security assistance programs in that region. More generally significant airlift, sealift, and equipment prepositioning initiatives are underway. There has also been some attempt to accommodate the special requirements of Third World contingencies in the conventional force structure, notably in the army's movement to create several light infantry divisions—smaller and lighter than a standard division, with a higher percentage of combat troops, and tailored for quick reaction to low-intensity scenarios.[21]

Image Wars

The administration has taken an activist approach to the international image-shaping competition—the peacetime battle of words and ideas—as well. An interagency apparatus now directs U.S. public diplomacy programs, aiming for coordinated and innovative approaches to explain U.S. foreign policies, to promote greater understanding of U.S. society, and to counter Soviet propaganda and disinformation. The effort is animated by a true sense of mission: to foster development abroad of democratic institutions and to awaken foreign audiences to the reality of the manifold Soviet political and military threat.[22]

While these and other measures have appreciably improved Washington's ability to deal with low-intensity conflict in the future, important difficulties remain. They involve attitudinal and organizational impediments that complicate execution of the administration's overall design and undermine the effectiveness of specific programs. In the end, they could jeopardize the entire set of initiatives. Some may be irremediable because they stem from the nature of the United States' open society. But awareness and further analysis of them may enable us at least to moderate their effects, if not eliminate them entirely.

Inhibiting Factors

We have elsewhere pointed to the traditional, long-standing lack of a strategic approach in the United States to the problem of low-intensity conflict.[23] The Reagan administration has made great strides in that respect, but the problem is much wider than one of developing a strategic perspective within an administration. Much of the difficulty lies in other areas: in the Congress, whose purse strings and other forms of assent are essential to many programs (security assistance, for example); in the strategic analytical community, where recurrent debate about the meaning of world events and about the nature of U.S. interests complicates implementation of any policy; and in the larger body politic, where the traditional U.S. concept of peace blinds many to low-intensity conflict realities that need Washington's attention and resources even though they may not be immediately nation threatening for U.S. citizens. This more generalized lack of a strategic outlook is in large measure a product of the decline of the U.S. postwar foreign policy consensus: the dissolution of key beliefs and perceptions about the world and about the U.S.'s role in international affairs.[24]

One important aspect of this phenomenon is the widespread disagreement about the nature and implications of Soviet and Soviet-proxy activities. Few subjects can generate as much heat as does a discussion of Moscow's foreign policy intentions, despite an impressive and persuasive documented history of aggressive and manipulative Soviet actions around the world. Soviet conduct can be, and is, interpreted to support preconceptions, with the evidence arranged to align with preferred analytical outcomes. Ultimately this means that the rationale for U.S. low-intensity conflict competes against many contrary views. This debate at the most fundamental levels of analysis significantly undermines the attempt to deal with evident external challenges.

Another problem is that in the early, incipient stages of national liberation struggles and other types of political-military strife, many observers in the United States cannot be persuaded that such events are important enough to warrant a U.S. response. Other needs inevitably seem more pressing and their claim on overextended U.S. resources more compelling.

Yet another dimension of the problem concerns the complexity of the low-intensity conflict phenomenon itself, especially the roles and relationship of indigenous causes and external geostrategic factors. Some analysts find the major causes of Third World instability in purely local problems: poverty, widening rich-poor gaps, unresponsive elites, and so forth. They argue that if any U.S. policy is to address such instability, it must concentrate on those indigenous causes, not on dealing with assumed or asserted external forces. To complicate matters, some observers argue that many developing world difficulties stem from Washington's own prior interventionist policies. They are wary and critical of U.S. approaches that seem to reassert the U.S. controls or dominance they have found at the heart of the historical problem.[25] When such debates move to center stage in the policy process, as inevitably they do in the U.S. system, they immobilize it or significantly dilute and delay its product. The result, in the end, is a U.S. response that comes too hurriedly, too late, with too little.

Another factor inhibiting the U.S. approach to low-level conflict is the ten-dency—indeed the desire—of mainstream elements in the armed services to con-centrate their energies and resources on mid- to high-intensity contingencies. In consequence, U.S. military forces are relatively well prepared for high technology, mobile armored and mechanized combat against the Warsaw Pact in Europe (although many would debate this) but relatively poorly prepared for lesser contingencies elsewhere. This persistent disability is found in all key areas of preparedness: training, doctrine, equipment, manning, budgeting, and force structure.

A number of explanations have been offered for this tendency to focus on the least likely contingencies at the expense of the most likely. Edward Luttwak has argued essentially that the military services actually, though mistakenly, believe that the violent aspects of low-intensity conflict constitute a lesser-included case of conventional, European-style war. Therefore preparation for the latter is preparation for the former.[26] General Meyer, by contrast, has suggested that the problem is one of myopia about threats, uncertainty about which truly unique, special capabilities are required, and the real need in a resource-constrained world to get maximum use out of mainstream forces.[27] One Reagan administration of-ficial, Principal Deputy Assistant Secretary of Defense Noel Koch, points to another facet of the problem: obstinate bureaucratic resistance in the military, especially in the Army, to directives from DOD's political leadership requiring more emphasis on special warfare capabilities (psychological operations, counterinsurgency, and unconventional warfare).[28] The armed forces' suspicion of elite or special units is a widely noted historical phenomenon.[29] The present ef-fect of this suspicion is visible not only with respect to unconventional forces but also regarding those flexibility initiatives that broaden U.S. conventional capabilities. In the Army, for instance, some observers have not been content to let the light infantry initiative stand on its Third World rationale. They have in-stead searched for ways to orient it on more familiar European contingencies.[30] In other words, mainstream lines of thinking find it hard to accept the merits of the Third World rationale, and they work to conventionalize a capability that seemed to them in danger of sliding too far toward unconventionality.

Other kinds of constraints have impeded the U.S. effort to deal with ter-rorists. A truly threshold difficulty has been the profusion of definitions of ter-rorism in academic circles, among legal experts, in U.S. official councils, and in diplomatic forums, with important practical consequences. It has given rise to an unfortunate semantic pollution in international discourse; charges and counter-charges of terrorism are issued indiscriminately to denounce political enemies. It has also complicated the instructing and training of counterterrorist forces.[31] Additionally uncertainty about who is a terrorist, plus reluctance to trust the judgment of U.S. officials about such a determination, has led to criticism of recent proposals for preemptive or retaliatory capabilities.[32]

Operational constraints on intelligence agencies have also been important limitations, although the Reagan administration undertook early to revitalize the intelligence agencies and restore the public faith in them that was lost in the 1970s debate about abuses. The terrorist menace figured prominently in the rationale for that revitalization, but informed opinion has been divided as to whether sufficient capacity has been restored.[33] Even beyond the problem of self-imposed constraints, moreover, the nature of the operational challenge with respect to terrorism is such that the timeliness and reliability of intelligence will always be a major concern.[34]

An innate U.S. suspicion of and aversion to manipulative, influence-seeking activities abroad also impedes certain U.S. responses to low-intensity conflict. Although covert manipulation and psychological operations are standard practice for determined adversaries, many Americans believe that the United States should not indulge in such activities, even though it has no other way to answer low-level, subtle, and indirect challenges. The public outcry about CIA support for the contras in Central America, and especially about the mining of Nicaraguan ports and the coaching of guerrillas in techniques of psychological warfare, illustrates the point, as does the suspension of congressional funding for such programs. In the arena of public diplomacy—the image-shaping competition—U.S. efforts have traditionally been constrained by the prevalent sentiment that the worth of democratic values and institutions is self-evident: they need no additional and contrived promotion and can flourish abroad on the strength of that appeal alone. History shows that this assumption is tenuous at best. Worlds are not easily made safe for democracy.

General Orientations for the Future

One lesson emerging from the review of inhibiting factors is that any administration seeking to increase low-intensity conflict capabilities will bear an immense burden of persuasion, both outward and inward. The strategic underpinnings of such programs will have to be explained to and accepted by large segments of the public, by key elements of Congress and the bureaucracy, and by the military services themselves. If the job of explanation falters, there will be great difficulty in enacting and implementing any such programs. And even when put into place, such programs are unlikely to have much endurance if their rationale is not widely understood. This public information effort will probably require at least as much energy as has been devoted to justifying the extensive modernization of the defense establishment at conventional and strategic levels of war-fighting capacity. The Pentagon in particular has been successful in building support for its defense modernization programs; the challenge now is to widen that support to embrace all the policy instruments applicable to low-level conflict.

Administration officials must avoid the tendency, evidenced in the Nicaraguan port mining episode, to say as little as possible, even to responsible oversight authorities in the Congress, about what they are doing or want to do.[35] Not everything can be examined in public, but where key authorities outside the executive have make-or-break power over U.S. security policies, there is no excuse for slighting the job of explaining and convincing them of the reasonableness of those policies. In the U.S. political system, leadership must articulate purposes and rationales and join in the essentially political process that produces informed and involved assent. If it does not, policy achievements can be quickly undermined later when dissent emerges belatedly and questions the analytical groundings of government programs.

In part this is a matter of more widely disseminating information—and not just argument—about the nature and extent of Soviet influence and activity in the world, especially in regions of geostrategic importance to the United States. The administration must seek to promote greater awareness of the U.S. interests abroad that are or may be affected by regional instabilities, terrorist tactics, and Soviet advances. It is not just the domestic audience that needs convincing. Allies and their publics need similar attention. Washington must be conscious of the need to aggregate strength worldwide for low-level competition and conflict. The United States should not be content to undertake the necessary tasks alone; coalition building at the lower end of the spectrum of conflict can greatly magnify U.S. strategic capabilities. This is, after all, in the larger interests of the West, not just the United States. The Soviets understand this implicitly, as their proxy-cultivation activities have shown all too clearly.

As for more specific initiatives, the Reagan administration has pursued many good ones, but there are still significant shortfalls and other promising avenues yet to be explored. Activist strategies to combat terrorism are under scrutiny. Public diplomacy and security assistance programs are on the rise. Intelligence capabilities, especially in the analytical and human source collection realms, have been upgraded. All of these projects deserve the best efforts of the U.S. government, but there is still more to be done.

In some respects the report of the Kissinger commission has pointed the way toward better capabilities across the full array of U.S. policy instruments. Although their analysis was focused on the Western Hemisphere, they usefully identify three general principles that should guide U.S. policies more generally and can assist policymakers in publicly explaining them.

The first principle is devotion to democratic self-determination. The United States benefits from the spread of political pluralism, freedom of expression, respect for human rights, independent and effective systems of justice, and elections conducted free from repression, coercion, and foreign manipulation. U.S.—and Western—efforts together must, as a matter of national and collective interest, seek the legitimation of governments by free consent, rejecting violence and murder as political instruments and the use of state power to suppress dissent. The overriding imperative is to nurture democratic development.

The second principle is the encouragement of economic and social development that fairly benefits all. Poverty must be stopped. Prosperity must be advanced, and the basis must be laid for sustained economic growth. The incentives that energize free economies must be put in place, and popular hopes for a better future must be revived. Any policy package must address these problems, or it will be fundamentally flawed.

Finally, meeting security threats must be a collective endeavor. There is no real security without economic growth and social justice. But there can be no prosperity, and no justice, without security. Democratic and economic development must be nurtured and then protected. No nation is immune from the threats of terrorism and external aggression (direct or indirect) from forces inimical to democratic values, economic growth and social justice. There are, then, authentic incentives, and indeed, imperatives, for collective security cooperation in the low-intensity conflict arena.[36]

These principles might well be taken as the overarching national objectives that strategists must serve and for which the policy instruments available must be carefully integrated and deployed. How the various instruments—political, economic, and security—ought to be orchestrated will depend on the circumstances of each particular case. But at the outset an understanding of all of them as relevant to the low-intensity challenge is central to any strategic approach. Limitations of space preclude extended discussion of each category of policy instruments here. There are, however, a number of points one should highlight concerning what has clearly become the most pressing operational problem for Washington: how to use its policy arsenal sensibly in coping with the use of terrorism as an unconventional weapon to achieve conventional political ends.

The Toughest Case: Terror as a Strategic Tool

International terrorism is a new class of violence that exploits advanced technologies, especially jet transport and instantaneous global communications, and is now well established as a global, steady-state phenomenon. With media coverage amplifying its impact, terrorist violence has paralyzed Western governments and undermined their credibility. In an international environment rife with instability, the terror instrument offers significant advantages to radical nations or to others willing to pursue foreign policy objectives by any and all means. It has become a low-cost, low-risk, high-leverage tool of low-intensity warfare, difficult to combat because uncertainty about the origin of the threat limits the full range of diplomatic and military responses.

In a piquc of understandable frustration, Secretary of State Shultz has implored the U.S. public to authorize preemptive or retaliatory attacks against international terror—whether the perpetrators are known or presumed, whether or not innocent lives may be lost.[37] There can be little question that the measured use of force is justifiable on occasion. But the United States cannot behave like Israel, a small beleaguered state that stands poised to retaliate in kind for every attack. U.S. policy toward terrorism must reflect both the changing forms of international warfare, as well as the moral and legal tradition of the United States.

There are at least two reasons to be wary of such an approach to counterterrorism. First, it may not succeed. The United States has had relatively few unequivocal successes against international terrorism; preemptive or retaliatory actions require an extraordinary degree of political cunning, intelligence, and operational precision that the United States has yet to demonstrate. Rhetoric without substance will succeed only in making the United States look foolish or, worse, incompetent. Second, if the United States succeeds too well, it runs the risk of granting the terrorists their real objective by overreacting and subverting its own principles in the process. If it falls into the trap of paranoia, the cure for terrorism may be far worse than the disease.

It is not enough for the government to bemoan U.S. vulnerability to terrorist attack when so little appears to have been done to shore up U.S. defenses. The attack in September 1983 against the U.S. embassy in Beirut suggests an unwillingness to learn from previous errors, just the existence of crude barriers (such as dump trucks laden with sand) would have sufficed. The United States has been slow to learn how to protect itself against similar modes of attack even when the targets are clearly identifiable. This should not be surprising given the paucity of resources, particularly intellectual resources, devoted to the problem. There are few first-rate minds engaged in developing counterterrorism policy.

No one would deny that the United States has the right, in fact the duty, to defend itself against terrorism. The government must realistically assess all of its policy options, overt and covert, against the full spectrum of potential threats. But it should be the first to recognize that U.S. society is resilient. Although society can absorb the effects of terrorist acts, it can be undermined in subtle but far reaching ways by an ill-conceived counterterrorism campaign.

Government officials and law enforcement and intelligence agencies must guard against overreaction. The most insidious aspect of terrorism is that it is intended to produce such an overreaction. No terrorist truly expects that a bombing incident will bring the United States to its knees. The real target is the public: to undermine its confidence in government and in its elected officials. As terrorist acts occur, however, there is a tendency to reach for simplistic and constitutionally corrosive solutions.

To illustrate the potential risks to which counterterrorism policies are subject, one need only examine the administration's recent antiterrorism proposals to Congress. Parts of the package were innocuous, largely because they are also irrelevant to any long-term solution. But at least one provision was truly dangerous: a bill to grant the secretary of state unilateral authority to brand groups and nations terrorists (without meaningful definition of the term) and to provide for criminal punishment of Americans involved with those groups or nations. Although this piece of the package was quickly rejected by the Congress, it was a revealing indicator of administration perspectives. If this kind of suggestion can be made at a time of relative tranquility, the public must be especially alert when the going gets rough.

The United States must also weigh carefully the advantages of clandestine actions against the potential political and constitutional drawbacks. Given its track record, it is not clear that the United States can keep an operation covert in any case. More important, perhaps, it is not clear that the United States has the capability to execute these kinds of operations successfully or to deal with the consequences of failure. If bungled (amateur operations) or mistargeted (poor intelligence), such covert actions have disastrous potential for political overreaction in both the United States and abroad.

Consider the potential for escalation had the United States retaliated against Syria for its involvement in the Beirut marine massacre. A successful counterattack—the deployment of an elite team to assassinate the Syrian officials in charge of planning and logistical support—would likely not have gone beyond international condemnation. But suppose the team had failed, and some of the elite forces were caught, publicly tried, and hanged. The United States would then have faced the equally unpalatable options of appearing politically and militarily impotent or returning with a larger force, leading to military confrontation with Syria and a risky debacle with the Soviet Union.

If the danger of escalation in covert operations is real, so too is the risk that their secrecy will open the door to unacceptable behavior. Even ignoring the recent CIA psychological operations manual, which has been disclaimed as the work of a contractor poorly supervised at midlevel in the agency, the mining of Nicaraguan harbors provides a case in point. Some would—and did—argue that this was itself an act of state terrorism. Whether one agrees with that position, it is clear that the U.S. position against international terrorism is undermined when Washington is accused of engaging in the tactics of terror. To this end the U.S. government must do a better job of explaining foreign policy objectives and the means employed to achieve them, in addition to confining its own behavior within acceptable, or defensible, limits.

There is a danger, moreover, that an overly aggressive counterterrorism policy will hasten the migration of terrorism to U.S. shores. An abrupt shift to aggressive military tactics could provoke retaliation in kind, placing U.S. leaders and those of allied governments in even greater jeopardy than they are at the moment. Islamic fundamentalists, with their determined, even maniacal viciousness and their enclaves of extremist support in the United States, are the best illustration of this threat. It is possible that such cells could be activated were the United States to become a primary target of attack, and it is not clear that officials have thought out the ramifications of responding in kind to their acts.

International terrorism is far more subtle and complex than U.S. officials have yet acknowledged in their rhetoric. We must not lump together, under the rubric of terrorism, everything from airline hijackings to embassy bombings. All may be important, but the United States cannot realistically defend itself against every attack anywhere in the world. The hijacking of an airliner by a frustrated Cuban refugee does not represent the same level of threat as an attack against elected U.S. officials or diplomatic and military representatives abroad. Consequently the U.S. government must determine priorities for its antiterror efforts and imaginatively vary its tactics if it is to distinguish between nuisance incidents and devastating blows.

Any workable counterterrorism strategy must assess the phenomenon in its larger diplomatic and military context. The days in which terrorism was limited to isolated instances of disruption are over. Increasingly it has become part of the spectrum of international conflict, one way among others in which states and other groups make war on one another in peacetime, at low cost, and with low risk.

Military force may well be required to counter this emerging form of international conflict, but there are no sure solutions. First, it is questionable whether the government can readily identify and eliminate suspected terrorists. A policy of active preemption requires reliable penetration and corruption of terrorist organizations, an uncertain business at best. Given the numbers of different groups—estimated at more than one hundred worldwide—and in most cases their tightly knit cell structures, the United States will always be forced into a position of looking for a needle in a haystack. Second, even if the perpetrators are identified after an event, it is not at all clear against whom one should retaliate. We might line up a group of terrorist proxies against the nearest wall, but that would not necessarily deter the state (perhaps even the Soviet Union) that sponsored the event. Finally, U.S. success in Grenada notwithstanding, the United States is a long way from the reliable use of surgical strike teams.

The traditional teachings of the military academies may not apply in an era dominated by low-intensity warfare. The United States must not define its readiness strictly in terms of ships, aircraft, tanks, and missiles; terrorism does not adhere to the well-understood conventions of warfare. And although errors on the battlefield by small units generally have limited impact, such errors in an unconventional warfare setting could ultimately topple a president.

The knowledge that nations rather than individuals are likely to sponsor major terror events should have profound implications for U.S. threat assessment and response calculations. Hostile acts that might have been beyond the scope of a radical organization are certainly within the grasp of new tactics of terror that will evolve in response to emerging capabilities.

Although it is popular to talk of nuclear or biological threats of mass destruction, these are not likely even for the intermediate future. On the other hand, there is ample evidence of terrorist interest in other modes of attack: assassinations of world leaders, an adaptation of the big truck bombings to airplanes, small chemical or radiological attacks that deny access to key facilities, and attacks on the technological infrastructure, including electric power grids, oil and natural gas pipelines and the microchip-based communications and data networks on which the public increasingly depends.

That attacks on the soft technological underbelly of U.S. society are probable is not mere speculation. Since 1970, over 200 attacks have been directed against electrical utilities from California to Puerto Rico, from France to the Philippines. Groups as diverse as the Shining Path in Peru, the ETA in Spain, and the New World Liberation in the United States have targeted the new Achilles' heel of Western civilization. For systems like electrical power, the damage control options are inadequate; there is no way to halt cascading failures of other energy networks. The financial community moves the equivalent of the entire annual federal budget through its electronic fund-transfer networks every two to four hours. The gas and oil pipeline networks are so centrally interconnected as to be catastrophically vulnerable to attack.

The United States must begin to explore the full range of its vulnerability to attack, or even to accident. But there is no national-level emergency preparedness mechanism capable of controlling bureaucratic battles at a time of crisis, buffering the president from minute-to-minute decisions, or dealing with the policy and operational problems. If the lights go out in the Northeast for several weeks, putting handcuffs on the perpetrators of the act will be the least concern.

U.S. counterterrorism policy must not be intellectually limited by "gunslingers and locksmiths." The government needs to orchestrate a comprehensive program of physical security that limits access to important installations and protects key officials; intelligence collection that does more than assess ambiguous trends; covert and overt military options that should be sparingly used; and incident management machinery that can cope with events far more varied and serious than any experienced to date. The greatest protection from attack is not violent preemption but substantive knowledge, imaginative planning, and a well-run crisis management machinery. Seldom recognized is that the image of a forewarned nation (even if only partially true) is itself a powerful tool. The United States needs to develop and organize its visible and invisible resources and then test them.

The problem of countering terrorism is not new. The United States has been engaged in the business since the Munich massacre of 1972. Over the past three administrations, U.S. responses have varied from paranoia to apathy, with little, if any, real progress. The Reagan administration has made useful strides in the area of counterterrorism, but it is time to stop thinking in terms of tactics and start thinking in terms of long-term, multidimensional strategies.

The United States needs to develop the contingency plans, procedures, logistics, and technologies to support the president in advance of crises. It cannot rely on panic to produce a well-thought-out range of policy and tactical options. The Special Situation Group, under the direction of the vice-president, must become more than a reactive organization and begin to do the substantive and creative planning in the areas of terrorism and unconventional warfare. The vice-president has a prime opportunity to oversee the effort of putting a new crisis management apparatus in place. Left to the bureaucracy, with its internecine fights even in the Office of the President, the necessary level of strategic planning and intragovernmental coordination may never occur.

Conclusion

The foregoing evaluation of the U.S. response to terrorism illustrates the sort of analysis needed across the entire policy repertoire: a top-to-bottom review of all U.S. low-intensity conflict capabilities in the light of well-articulated strategic goals. Those goals must, as a prior matter, be formulated in the light of a clear appreciation of conflict futures, notably the gathering prospect of proxy wars, internal insurgencies, transborder revolutions, psychological warfare, and terrorism sponsored by nations hostile to U.S. and Western values.

The United States will have much going for it in the rest of the 1980s. Its major competitor, the Soviet Union, will likely have only one comparative advantage, in military assistance. In all other fields of international relations, the United States will continue to realize benefits, as clients and would-be client states express preference for U.S. economic assistance, culture, and political traditions. It will, nonetheless, be a challenge-filled period, requiring responses quite unconventional for U.S. planners.

Planning for conflict in disparate areas of the developing world is not an insuperable task. A useful step would be to establish a forum where academics and others with specific country and regional knowledge could come together with government officials to assess the current state of thinking and planning for low-intensity conflict. This would include evaluating probable trends and the instrumentalities the United States and its allies might have available for affecting them. Allied foreign policy planners should be brought in to assess mutual interests and capabilities and to discuss possibilities for combined unconventional operations.

The initial study could be followed by annual reviews that would reevaluate the trends and provide near-term (say, one to two year) details for planners. Such a forum could not substitute for the formal planning machinery within the national security system, either at the top or in the several departments, but it would provide an approach to this problem that would routinely integrate thinking and planning about policy with more detailed thinking and planning for execution. Such arrangements, while complex and cumbersome, are no more complex than the world in which the United States must make its way during the years ahead.

Defense
Chronology
1984

January

1   The first sixteen Tomahawk ground-launched cruise missiles delivered to the United Kingdom become operational.

1   The Joint Chiefs of Staff establish the Joint Special Operations Agency to coordinate special forces operations and counterterrorism.

6   President Reagan signs National Security Decision Directive 119 calling for a research program to evaluate the technical feasibility of strategic defense.

11   The National Bipartisan Commission on Central America presents its report to the president, recommending that the United States provide the Central American countries with $8 billion in economic and military aid over the next five years.

11–13   A second round of negotiations between the United States and the Soviet Union on upgrading the hot line is held in Washington. The previous session took place in August 1983.

17   The Conference on Disarmament in Europe (CDE) opens in Stockholm, attended by the thirty-five members of the Conference on Security and Cooperation in Europe.

17   The Soviet news agency Tass reports that tactical missiles of an "enhanced range" have been deployed in East Germany. These are believed to be Soviet SS-21, SS-22, and SS-23 missiles, with respective ranges of 60, 600, and 300 miles. Tass claims the new missiles are a response to the deployment of cruise and Pershing II missiles in Western Europe.

18   Secretary of State George Shultz and Foreign Minister Andrei Gromyko meet at the CDE to discuss U.S.–Soviet relations and arms control developments.

21   The U.S. Air Force conducts the first test of an antisatellite weapon, launched from a high-flying F-15.

22   Secretary of State Shultz announces that the United States has agreed to a Soviet proposal to resume negotiations on the mutual reduction of forces and armaments in Central Europe (MBFR) on March 16.

23   President Reagan submits a classified report to Congress on suspected Soviet arms control violations. The findings involve seven case studies of claimed or probable violations. An unclassified fact sheet is also issued.

29–30   Tass reproduces a diplomatic note presented to the State Department charging the United States with violations of both the SALT I and SALT II arms control agreements, which the State Department rejects as "baseless."

February

1   Secretary of Defense Caspar Weinberger presents the Fiscal Year 1985 *Annual Report to the Congress*. Budget requests total $305 billion.

4   Secretary of the Navy John Lehman announces a "substantial surge" in the number of Soviet ballistic missile submarines in the Atlantic.

6   President Reagan orders the use of U.S. air and naval fire against antigovernment forces near Beirut to protect marines and U.S. embassy personnel shelled the previous day.

7   President Reagan orders 1,600 U.S. Marines in Lebanon relocated to U.S. ships offshore. The president also authorizes a less restrictive use of naval gunfire and air strikes against Syrian-controlled positions in Lebanon.

9   Soviet General Secretary Yuri V. Andropov dies at age sixty-nine.

11   The U.S.S. *Georgia,* the fourth Trident missile submarine of the United States, is commissioned.

13   Konstantin Chernenko is elected general secretary of the Soviet Communist party.

20   Assistant Secretary of State Richard Burt announces that new SS-20 bases are under construction in the eastern and western Soviet Union. He adds that 378 SS-20s have been deployed, 243 of which are within range of Western Europe.

21   A State Department report, presented to the United Nations on the use of chemical weapons in 1983, declares that there is no confirmed use of chemical weapons in Afghanistan that year. The report notes that chemical weapons are used in Laos and Cambodia and are reportedly employed in the Iran-Iraq war.

21   U.S. Marines begin their evacuation from Beirut International Airport to U.S. naval vessels.

21   The Pentagon's inspector general releases a report criticizing waste and excess profits in defense contracts. It cites poor management and failure to penalize companies that overcharge.

26   U.S. Marines complete their withdrawal from Beirut. The battleship *New Jersey* opens fire on Syrian antiaircraft batteries in the Lebanese mountains.

March

1   The Defense Department notifies Congress of the administration's intent to sell 1,613 shoulder-fired Stinger antiaircraft missiles to Jordan at an estimated cost of $133 million. An additional 1,200 Stingers are to be provided to Saudi Arabia.

1   Nicaraguan contras declare that they have mined the Nicaraguan ports of Corinto and El Bluff to prevent the arrival of military supplies from Soviet bloc countries. They declare the coasts of Nicaragua a war zone.

16   The first round of the CDE ends, with the next session scheduled to begin on May 8.

16   MBFR negotiations resume in Vienna.

19   Two airborne warning and control radar aircraft (AWACs) are sent to Egypt. The AWACs are to assist Egypt, Sudan, and Chad monitor increased Libyan military movements.

20   The Reagan administration, facing strong opposition in Congress, cancels the proposed sale of Stinger missiles to Jordan and Saudi Arabia.

20   The U.S. Air Force begins airlifting Egyptian personnel and equipment to Sudan in response to a Libyan air raid against Sudan.

20   An explosion from a mine laid by Nicaraguan contras damages a Soviet tanker at the port of Puerto Sandino, on the Pacific coast of Nicaragua. Tass states that five crewmen of the tanker *Lugansk* are hurt in the blast.

22   The Defense Department announces that a joint navy, marine corps, air force, and army exercise will begin on April 20 and continue for fifteen days in the Caribbean. According to the Pentagon the exercise, "Ocean Venture 84," is designed to demonstrate and improve the capability to protect and maintain sea-lanes of communication in the Caribbean Basin and the Gulf of Mexico.

23   The chairman of President Reagan's Commission on Strategic Forces, retired Lieutenant General Brent Scowcroft, submits a final report to the president. The report stresses the need for arms control, an agreed-on methodology for measuring the strategic balance, and the deployment of the MX and Midgetman missiles.

23   The Pentagon announces that as part of its upcoming military exercises in Honduras, Granadero I, two assault airstrips will be constructed near the borders of El Salvador and Nicaragua. The exercise begins on April 1.

24   U.S. paratroopers of the Eighty-second Airborne Division land near an airfield in Honduras in exercise Kilo Punch, designed to test the ability of U.S. and Honduran forces rapidly to assault and hold airfields. About 350 U.S. personel and 130 Honduran airborne infantrymen participate.

26   An international team of military and medical experts conclude in a United Nations' report that chemical weapons, including mustard gas and nerve agents, have been used in Iran.

27   Lieutenant General James A. Abrahamson, head of the U.S. Space Shuttle Program, is selected as the first director of the Strategic Defense Initiative effort of the Reagan administration.

30   The U.S. Air Force conducts a fourth test launch of the MX or "Peacekeeper" missile from Vandenberg Air Force Base and reports the test a success.

April

1   Exercise Granadero I begins in Honduras.

2   In a letter to Congress, President Reagan declares his intent to proceed with the development of antisatellite weapons and restates his position that any comprehensive ban on such weapons with the Soviet Union would be impossible to verify.

3 President Reagan signs National Security Decision Directive (NSDD) 138, a counterterrorism directive endorsing the principles of preemptive strikes and reprisal raids against overseas terrorists.

3 In an unannounced exercise, more than fifty Soviet ships and submarines enter the Norwegian Sea for maneuvers. The exercise is the largest ever conducted in the seas bordering Northern Europe.

3 The first U.S. cruise missiles in Comiso, Sicily, become operational.

3 The U.S. Strategic Air Command begins an annual major ten-day exercise, Global Shield 84, to provide missile and bomber crews with realistic training for nuclear war.

5 A congressional study critical of U.S. military planning and execution during the invasion of Grenada is released. The report criticizes Pentagon coordination and its efforts to involve elements of all four services in the operation.

18 Vice-President George Bush introduces the new U.S. draft treaty on chemical weapons at the Conference on Disarmament in Geneva. A major feature of the draft calls for on-site inspection within twenty-four hours of the filing of a request for inspection. Eight days later, the USSR rejects the draft as discriminatory.

19 The U.S. and its NATO allies introduce a new proposal to the MBFR talks as the thirty-second round comes to a close. The proposal calls for exchanging new data on force levels, excluding service personnel and air forces previously counted in the totals.

20 The United States begins Ocean Venture I, a military exercise in the Caribbean involving 350 ships and 30,000 servicemen.

23–27 A third round of negotiations on upgrading the hot line is held in Moscow.

25 A report prepared for the Congressional Office of Technology Assessment on the Reagan administration's Strategic Defense Initiative concludes that successful missile defense will be extremely difficult to achieve and susceptible to Soviet countermeasures.

26 President Reagan arrives in China on a six-day visit. The agenda consists of discussions on economic and strategic cooperation between the two nations, as well as discussions on the development of nuclear energy.

26 The twenty-member Joint Task Force-Lebanon, established following the departure of U.S. Marines from Lebanon in February, is disbanded.

28 The battleship U.S.S. *Iowa* is recommissioned, the second of the navy's four Iowa-class ships scheduled to reenter service.

30 A panel of military officers and retired journalists set up to study relations between the media and the military submits its report to the chairman of the joint chiefs, General John W. Vessey. The panel was headed by retired Army Major General Winant Sidle and was set up following the barring of reporters from the U.S. invasion of Grenada.

May

3   Defense Secretary Weinberger submits a list of $13.9 billion in military budget cuts to Congress. The revised defense budget requests $291.1 billion for fiscal 1985, down from the original request of $305 billion.

6   Costa Rica formally requests an emergency military aid package from the United States to support its border security forces.

7   Secretary of Defense Caspar Weinberger leaves on a six-day trip to South Korea and Japan to discuss regional defense problems there.

7   The United States and West Germany reject a proposal made by Italian Prime Minister Bettino Craxi for a moratorium on further NATO missile deployments if the Soviets return to the intermediate-range nuclear arms negotiations.

8   Lieutenant General James A. Abrahamson, director of the Reagan administration's Strategic Defense Initiative, remarks that the possibilities of early deployment of defensive measures are being examined should a Soviet break-out from the ABM Treaty occur.

8   The second session of the CDE opens. The Soviet Union introduces its proposals consisting of the following: (1) a no first-use agreement; (2) a treaty on the nonuse of force; (3) limitations on military expenditures; (4) a European chemical-weapons-free zone; (5) nuclear-free zones in the Balkans, Nordic area, and Central Europe; (6) confidence-building measures.

8   U.S. officials announce that 1,000 U.S. troops are being sent to Honduras on May 23 to participate in joint maneuvers along its borders.

10   A General Accounting Office report states that the new Peacekeeper ICBM may be incapable of accomplishing its mission of destroying hardened Soviet missile silos.

12   Defense Secretary Weinberger states that the United States opposes a compromise plan for deployment of cruise missiles in the Netherlands whereby the missiles would be stored outside the country and brought in during a crisis.

12   The U.S. Navy commissions a *Los Angeles*–class attack submarine, the *Salt Lake City*.

13   A Congressional Research Service study finds that the United States was the leading exporter of arms to developing nations in 1983, followed by the Soviet Union.

14   The United States, Australia, Canada, New Zealand, and Japan begin a six-week naval exercise, RIMPAC '84, in the Pacific. The exercise involves more than 50,000 sailors and marines from the participating countries.

14   The Soviet Union announces it is deploying an "additional number of Soviet enhanced-range theater missile complexes" in East Germany in response to U.S. missile deployments in Western Europe.

14 The Defense Department issues a report on combat readiness, "Improvements in U.S. Warfighting Capability, 1980–84." The report states that substantial progress has been made over the years, but that shortages in such areas as ammunition and spare parts still remain.

14 A Pentagon report outlining plans to spend $149 on military construction in Central America and the Caribbean over the next four years is released.

19 The sixth U.S. Trident ballistic missile submarine, the *Alabama*, is christened in Groton, Connecticut.

20 Soviet Defense Minister Dimitri Ustinov announces that the Soviet Union has increased the number of ballistic missile submarines off of U.S. shores to "counterbalance" U.S. missiles in Europe.

22 The air force and army chiefs of staff announce a Memorandum of Agreement designed to coordinate budget priorities and eliminate duplication of functions between the two services.

29 The Reagan administration announces that it has sent 400 Stinger antiaircraft missiles and 200 launchers to Saudi Arabia. The president uses his emergency powers to sell the missiles in response to increased attacks against shipping in the Persian Gulf.

29 NATO begins its annual spring meeting in Washington. The agenda includes U.S.–Soviet relations and the growing tension in the Persian Gulf. The meeting concludes on May 31.

June

1 About 160 U.S. Special Forces troops join Honduran and Salvadoran troops in heliborne assault exercises in the Cucuyagua region of Honduras.

1 The Dutch government announces that it will cancel deployment of NATO cruise missiles on its soil if the Soviet Union freezes its SS-20 missiles at existing levels.

1 The U.S. Army reports that a Pershing II test carried out on May 16 suffered a guidance failure late into its flight.

11 Pentagon officials announce that a ballistic missile interceptor successfully intercepted an incoming dummy warhead 100 miles above the earth. The test is part of the army's Homing Overlay Experiment (HOE) on ballistic missile defense.

12 The Senate votes sixty-one to twenty-eight to halt full testing of a U.S. antisatellite weapon until President Reagan certifies to Congress that he is seeking strict negotiated limitations with the Soviets on such weapons.

13 The Defense Department releases a preliminary study indicating that Soviet military spending increased significantly in 1983 over previous years.

15 The U.S. Air Force successfully conducts the fifth flight test of the Peacekeeper ICBM from Vandenberg Air Force Base, California.

19   The Pentagon announces the sale of twelve C-130 military transports along with support equipment and training to the government of Taiwan at an estimated cost of $325 million.

20   The United States and Israel hold a joint exercise to practice evacuating wounded U.S. troops to Israeli hospitals.

20   The Senate defeats an amendment to begin the withdrawal of U.S. troops from Europe in 1987 should European NATO members fail to increase annual defense spending 3 percent a year after inflation, as originally agreed under the Carter administration.

21   The Department of Defense issues its response to an earlier congressional report, authored by William S. Lind, critical of U.S. military performance during the Grenada invasion. The response was commissioned by chairman of the Joint Chiefs of Staff, General John W. Vessey, Jr., and refutes the findings of the Lind report in a point-by-point rebuttal. The report concludes that U.S. forces demonstrated "initiative and flexibility" and that planning was effective in achieving the objectives sought by the invasion.

21   NATO publishes a revised estimate of comparative NATO and Warsaw Pact troop strengths. The number of troops considered immediately available to the Warsaw Pact is reduced from a previous 1982 estimate of 173 divisions to 115.

25   A. Ernest Fitzgerald, deputy to the assistant air force secretary for financial management, testifies under subpoena before a Senate subcommittee on poor management and waste in weapons procurement at the Pentagon.

28   Kenneth L. Adelman, director of the U.S. Arms Control and Disarmament Agency, announces that the United States and the Soviet Union have resumed talks on how to verify a treaty banning chemical weapons.

July

6   President Reagan signs a National Security Decision Directive ordering the preparation of a detailed arms control agenda for space weaponry and other nuclear force-related issues.

9   Greek officials warn that failure by the United States to allow the sale of F-5 fighter aircraft by Norway to Greece could result in the closing down of two Voice of America relay stations in the country.

12   The United States and West Germany sign an accord calling for a $2.9 billion upgrading of the European air defense systems of the two countries. U.S. Patriot missiles and European-built Roland missiles will be used in the improvement.

13   The State Department releases its biannual report to Congress on political developments in El Salvador. The report notes that there has been a decline in the number of deaths attributed to political violence and that the country is demonstrating "prog-

ress toward land reform, free elections, freedom of association, the establishment of the rule of law and an effective judicial system." The report also states that the Salvadoran military continues to suffer from equipment shortages and sporadic guerrilla assaults.

13   The United States, thirteen NATO allies, and the government of Japan sign an accord extending and broadening export controls over computer and telecommunications equipment sold to the Soviet Union and Eastern Europe.

15   New Zealand Prime Minister–elect David Lange announces his firm commitment to the ANZUS pact with Australia and the United States but stands by his party's pledge to ban nuclear-armed or nuclear-powered ships from New Zealand's waters.

17   U.S. and Soviet officials sign an agreement to expand the capabilities of the hot line between Washington and Moscow.

18   Secretary of State George Shultz announces that Vietnam has agreed to resume talks on U.S. missing-in-action personnel in mid-August. A U.S. delegation is sent to Hanoi on August 15.

19   MBFR talks recess for the summer. No progress is reported.

19   In a speech before the Federal Procurement and Trade Conference in Indianapolis, Secretary of Defense Caspar Weinberger reports that Pentagon and Justice Department officials have nearly doubled the number of convictions related to fraudulent defense contracts in the last fiscal year.

22   A congressional study conducted by the House Appropriations Committee states that the "United States Army cannot be sustained in combat for any extended period of time." It also questions the ability of the navy and air force to carry out prolonged operations. Shortages of equipment and personnel are cited as principal causes.

23   Secretary of Defense Caspar Weinberger holds a press conference rejecting the findings of a House Appropriations Committee report on the state of U.S. combat readiness. He states that U.S. forces are much stronger now than when the administration assumed office.

25   The Defense Department successfully conducts the first live test of a Tomahawk cruise missile with a high-explosive warhead. The missile is launched from a submerged submarine and travels more than 400 miles before hitting its target.

30   The last of the marine combat troops in Lebanon begin their final withdrawal from the U.S. embassy compound in West Beirut. Roughly one dozen troops are to remain behind to protect the new U.S. embassy in East Beirut.

August

1   The Defense Department sends a mine warfare survey team to Egypt following a series of explosions in the Gulf of Suez. The team is requested by the Egyptian government.

7   The U.S. Army Missile Command announces the successful 980-mile test of a Pershing II missile. Prior to its launch, the missile was subjected to harsh environmental tests for five months, designed to simulate battlefield conditions in Europe.

7–13   The United States sends mine-sweeping helicopters to Egypt and Saudi Arabia to search the Gulf of Suez and Red Sea for explosives.

20   The Defense Department announces the opening of a counter-insurgency exercise in Honduras involving U.S. Army Green Berets. The exercise, named Operation Lempira, is to continue throughout the month of August.

20   The Greek government announces it has cancelled a two-week joint military exercise with the United States scheduled to begin September 1. A spokesman for the government states that the exercise is "pointless" given that it does not acknowledge the danger posed to Greece by Turkey.

25   The Soviet Defense Ministry announces that it is conducting tests of long-range ground-launched cruise missiles in response to the deployment of such weapons by the United States.

29   U.S. Air Force officials announce that a prototype of the B-1 bomber crashed in the Mojave Desert during a test flight. One crewman is killed and the two others are injured.

September

3   Warsaw Pact and NATO forces begin two months of autumn military exercises in Europe. Designated Shield 84 and Autumn Forge, respectively, the two exercises involve more than 300,000 troops.

4   The first production model of the new B-1B bomber rolls off the assembly line at Rockwell International's Palmdale plant in California.

11   The U.S. Army announces the creation of two additional light infantry divisions, bringing the army's total to four.

13   An unarmed Minuteman-III ICBM is successfully test launched from Vandenberg Air Force Base, California.

17   A U.S. Army spokesman announces that the service's new Patriot antiaircraft missile system has successfully completed its operational tests.

17   The Reagan administration announces that U.S. Navy mine-sweepers sent to the Gulf of Suez will soon be withdrawn. The source of the explosions in the gulf remains unknown.

17   President Reagan signs National Security Decision Directive 145 establishing a high-level group to combat electronic surveillance of sensitive U.S. information by external powers.

20   House and Senate leaders reach agreement on a $292.9 billion defense appropriations budget. The House goal was $285 billion, the Senate's $299 billion.

20   The U.S. embassy annex in the eastern sector of Beirut is bombed by an explosive-packed van. Two Americans and an undetermined number of Lebanese are killed. A group calling itself the Islamic Jihad claims responsibility.

24   In a speech before the thirty-ninth session of the United Nations General Assembly, President Reagan calls for "a better working relationship" with the Soviet Union and "constructive negotiations" toward arms control agreements.

24   The State Department requests $372 million in emergency funds from Congress to improve security at U.S. embassies. The funds are to be used to upgrade physical protection measures.

27   MBFR talks resume in Vienna.

28   President Reagan and Soviet Foreign Minister Andrei Gromyko meet at the White House to discuss relations between the two countries.

30   U.S. Special Forces and Honduran Army troops begin a series of counterinsurgency exercises in Honduras. The exercises are expected to last about three weeks.

October

10–11   The Defense Department establishes a press pool to cover surprise military operations. It includes the Associated Press, United Press International, and a daily newspaper. The pool is set up in response to criticism over secrecy during the Grenada invasion.

10   President Reagan sends Congress a seventeen-page unclassified summary of a report prepared by the General Advisory Committee on Arms Control and Disarmament charging the Soviet Union with repeated "violations, probable violations, or circumventions" of past arms control agreements.

11   Secretary of Defense Caspar Weinberger states that the Soviet Union has substantially increased deployment of its SS-20 missiles beyond the public figure of 378. The statement comes at the end of the first day of a NATO defense ministers' meeting on nuclear strategy.

13   The Soviet Ministry of Defense announces that it has begun deployment of long-range cruise missiles in response to the "massive deployment" of such weapons by the United States. The missiles are being deployed aboard Soviet aircraft and submarines.

18   President Reagan orders an investigation into the possibility of improper conduct by employees of the CIA stemming from the publication of a guerrilla operations manual supplied to Nicaraguan resistance forces. Portions of the manual advocate the use of violence against the opposition.

19   President Reagan signs a defense spending bill totaling $292.9 billion for the upcoming year.

20   U.S. employees of the U.S. embassy in Beirut begin leaving the country amid growing threats directed against them.

21   President Reagan and presidential candidate Walter F. Mondale meet in a ninety-minute televised debate on U.S. foreign policy in Kansas City. Key defense issues include the U.S. military role in Central America, progress on arms control, and the prospects for ballistic missile defense.

22   Defense Secretary Caspar Weinberger states that a new Soviet ICBM, the SS-25, "is very close to being fully operational."

27   The fourth *Nimitz*-class aircraft carrier, the *Theodore Roosevelt*, is launched at Newport News, Virginia.

31   Assistant Secretary of Defense Lawrence J. Korb reports that the 1984 fiscal year yielded the highest-quality recruits for the armed services. More than 90 percent of the recruits were high school graduates.

31   India's Prime Minister, Indira Ghandi, is assassinated by her Sikh bodyguards.

November

1   Ships and aircraft of the U.S. Second Fleet begin Composit Training Unit Exercise 1-85 (Comtuex 1-85), a military exercise in the Caribbean involving twenty-five naval vessels.

1   The General Accounting Office releases a report claiming that the armed forces' plans for training troops during a wartime emergency mobilization are insufficient for the task.

5   Egypt and the United States begin a three-day military exercise code named Sea Winds. The exercise is designed to test Egypt's ability to repel air and naval attacks.

6   The United States and the Soviet Union agree to hold talks on nuclear proliferation in Moscow. The talks begin on November 28.

7   The Pentagon releases a new directive signed by Secretary of Defense Caspar Weinberger designed to prevent the disclosure of technical information having military applications. The directive applies to information generated by the Department of Defense or those working under contract to it "that would make a significant contribution to the military potential of any country."

7   President Ronald Reagan is reelected as president of the United States.

9   The NATO's Defense Planning Council approves a plan calling for deep conventional bombing strikes into Eastern Europe in the event of a Warsaw Pact attack. The new approach is designated Follow-On Forces Attack (FOFA).

9   U.S. officials announce that a Soviet ship docked in a Nicaraguan port and suspected of carrying MIG-21 aircraft has not unloaded any Soviet jet fighters.

10   President Reagan agrees to discipline CIA employees linked to the development and publication of a manual for Nicaraguan rebels. The recommendation to do so comes from the CIA inspector general and the Intelligence Oversight Board.

13 The air force announces the second test firing of an antisatellite rocket from an F-15 fighter. Test results remain classified.

17 Secretary of Defense Caspar Weinberger states that the speed and size of the Nicaraguan military buildup is "far beyond anything they need to protect themselves."

22 The United States and Soviet Union announce that Secretary of State George Shultz and Soviet Foreign Minister Andrei Gromyko will meet in Geneva January 7 and 8 to negotiate an arms control agenda.

26 The United States and the government of Iraq resume full diplomatic relations, originally broken following the 1967 Arab-Israeli war.

26 Chinese Communist party General Secretary Hu Yaobang states that U.S. warships will be permitted to visit China's ports on ceremonial calls.

26 Soviet President Konstantin Chernenko states that the Soviet Union wishes "to start negotiations on the entire complex of interconnected questions of nonmilitarization of outer space, reduction of strategic nuclear arms and medium-range nuclear weapons."

27 The Supreme Soviet meets and approves a 12 percent increase in Soviet defense spending for 1985.

28 In a major address to the National Press Club, Secretary of Defense Caspar Weinberger outlines six tests for determining the use of U.S. combat forces: (1) forces should be committed only when vital interests are at stake; (2) forces should be committed wholeheartedly and with the objective of winning; (3) political and military objectives should be clearly defined; (4) the relationship between the use of force and those objectives must be constantly reassessed and altered if necessary; (5) reasonable assurance of congressional and citizen support for any commitment must exist; (6) forces should be committed only as a last resort.

30 The Pentagon announces that a centralized U.S. space command is to be created in order to make "more effective use of military space systems." The Pentagon states that the new command "may be viewed as an operational parallel to the Strategic Defense Initiative Organization."

December

4 Defense Secretary Caspar Weinberger announces the creation of a new post, deputy assistant secretary of defense for spares program management. The deputy assistant is responsible for all aspects related to spare parts purchase and maintenance.

4 The State Department announces that the Soviet Union has deployed at least 387 SS-20 missiles and that given ongoing construction the number is expected to increase. Assistant Secretary of State Richard Burt later estimates (December 20) that an additional 60 to 110 SS-20 missiles will enter the Soviet inventory.

4   The U.S. Navy successfully test fires an unarmed Trident ballistic missile from the submerged U.S.S. *Henry M. Jackson,* the latest U.S. Trident submarine.

4   NATO defense ministers approve a $7.85 billion increase in defense spending over the next six years to upgrade various communications facilities, aircraft shelters, and equipment dumps. Emphasis is to be placed on maintaining a capacity to fight prolonged wars without resorting to nuclear weapons.

5   NATO defense ministers issue a statement at the close of their annual winter meeting declaring that the alliance "is willing to reverse, halt, or modify" current missile deployments if an "equitable and verifiable agreement" can be reached with the Soviet Union. It adds that in the absence of such an agreement, NATO will continue its own deployments.

18   Defense Secretary Caspar Weinberger announces an $8.7 billion reduction in the proposed defense budget for the next fiscal year. Much of the savings are to be derived from a reduced military pay increase and a 5 percent pay cut for civilian employees of the military. Military growth is also to be scaled back by $9.2 billion in 1987 and $10.2 billion in 1988.

20   Soviet Defense Minister Dimitri F. Ustinov dies at age seventy-six. He is replaced by First Deputy Minister of Defense Marshal Sergei L. Sokolov.

Worldwide U.S. Security Commitments, 1985

Figure B–1. Worldwide U.S. Security Commitments, 1985

 North Atlantic Treaty

Signed in 1949, 12 (later 16) countries united in an alliance for the common defense of Western Europe and North America. France does not participate in NATO's integrated command structure.

Belgium, Canada, Denmark, France, Federal Republic of Germany, Greece, Iceland, Italy, Luxembourg, Netherlands, Norway, Portugal, Spain, Turkey, United Kingdom, United States.

The Rio-Treaty

In 1947, the Inter-American Treaty of Reciprocal Assistance committed the United States and 21 Latin American nations to the defense of the Western Hemisphere. Cuba was suspended from the pact.
Argentina, Bolivia, Brazil, Chile, Columbia, Costa Rica, Cuba, Dominican Republic, Ecuador, El Salvador, Guatemala, Haiti, Honduras, Mexico, Nicaragua, Panama, Paraguay, Peru, Trinidad and Tobago, United States, Uruguay, Venezuela.

Bilateral Defense Treaties

The U.S. government has signed bilateral defense treaties with three Asian nations that provide mutual protection from aggression. (Year of signing in parentheses.)

Philippines (1951)
South Korea (1953)
Japan (1960)

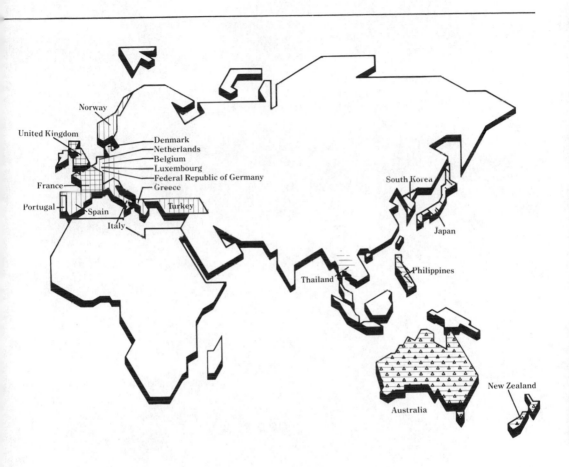

Norway

United Kingdom

Denmark
Netherlands
Belgium
Luxembourg
Federal Republic of Germany
Greece

France

South Korea

Portugal

Spain

Turkey

Italy

Japan

Philippines

Thailand

New Zealand

Australia

 Southeast Asia Treaty

In 1954, a treaty was signed for the collective defense of Southeast Asian nations and any regional territory that those states might designate. Pakistan withdrew in 1973. The treaty's organizational apparatus was dissolved in 1975, but the obligations of the treaty remain in force. France is inactive.

Australia, France, New Zealand, Philippines, Thailand, United Kingdom, United States.

ANZUS Treaty

Signed in 1951, this mutual defense pact provides security in the Pacific.

Australia, New Zealand, United States.

Other Security Commitments

The United States maintains strong but informal defense ties with a number of other nations.

East Caribbean nations (Antigua and Barbuda, Barbados, Dominica, Grenada, Jamaica, St. Lucia, St. Vincent), Egypt, Israel, Pakistan, Persian Gulf states (Bahrain, Kuwait, Oman, Qatar, United Arab Emirates), Saudi Arabia, Taiwan.

Defense Bibliography 1984

A List of Books on U.S. Defense Published during 1984 (with a Cross-Index by Author)

The Abolition, by Jonathan Schell. New York: Knopf, 192 pp. In a sequel to *The Fate of the Earth*, the author attempts to prescribe alternatives to current methods of nuclear deterrence.

America's Volunteer Military: Progress and Prospects, by Martin Binkin. Washington, D.C.: Brookings, 63 pp. Evaluates the performance and future of the all-volunteer service, noting several difficulties that lie ahead.

Arming the Heavens: The Hidden Military Agenda for Space, 1945–1995, by Jack Manno. New York: Dodd, Mead, 256 pp. A peace activist examines the space program and its relationship to military activities.

Arms Control: Myth versus Reality, edited by Richard F. Starr. Stanford: Hoover Press, 211 pp. A collection of articles focusing on past, present, and future arms control questions by some of the leading experts in the field.

Arms Control and International Security, edited by Roman Kolkowicz and Neil Joeck. Boulder, Colo.: Westview Press, 157 pp. Recordings of a conference on the subject of arms control at UCLA's Center on International Security and Arms Control.

Ballistic Missile Defense, edited by Ashton B. Carter and David N. Schwartz. Washington, D.C.: Brookings, 455 pp. A comprehensive examination of current prospects, problems, and proposals surrounding the subject of ballistic missile defense.

The Bishops and Nuclear Weapons: The Catholic Pastoral Letter on War and Peace, by James E. Dougherty. Hamden, Conn.: Archon Books, 255 pp. A critical look at the 1983 pastoral letter by a Catholic college professor in international relations.

Caveat: Realism, Reagan and Foreign Policy, by Alexander M. Haig, Jr. New York: Macmillan, 367 pp. The former NATO commander and secretary of state assesses the foreign policy of the Reagan administration in which he served from January 1981 to July 1982.

Central America: Anatomy of Conflict, edited by Robert S. Leiken. New York: Pergamon Press, 351 pp. A collection of essays focusing on the current situation in Central America exploring, among other subjects, the ramifications of U.S. military intervention and the prospects for negotiated settlements.

The Cold and the Dark: The World after Nuclear War, by Paul R. Ehrlich, Carl Sagan, Donald Kennedy, and Walter Orr Roberts. New York: Norton, 229 pp. Conference report on the long-term biological effects of nuclear war, with special emphasis on the prospects for a nuclear winter.

Combat Fleets of the World, 1984/85: Their Ships, Aircraft, and Armament, edited by A.D. Baker III. Annapolis: Naval Institute Press, 1035 pp. A reference work containing information on naval vessels and equipment in use throughout the world.

For the Common Defense: A Military History of the United States of America, by Allen R. Millett and Peter Maslowski. New York: Free Press, 621 pp. A comprehensive account of military events and institutional developments in the United States from the earliest days to the present.

Conventional Deterrence in NATO: Alternatives for European Defense, edited by James R. Golden, Asa A. Clark, and Bruce E. Arlinghaus. Lexington, Mass.: Lexington Books, 245 pp. Examines the emerging technologies and tactics that may make conventional defense of Europe possible and their economic and political ramifications.

The Counterfeit Ark: Crisis Relocation for Nuclear War, edited by Jennifer Leaning and Langley Keyes. Cambridge: Ballinger, 368 pp. A series of articles commissioned by the Physicians for Social Responsibility critical of civil defense planning for nuclear war.

The Day after World War III: The U.S. Government's Plans for Surviving a Nuclear War, by Edward Zuckerman. New York: Viking, 407 pp. Examines federal emergency planning measures designed to maintain government integrity following a nuclear attack.

Deadly Gambits: The Reagan Administration and the Stalemate in Nuclear Arms Control, by Strobe Talbott. New York: Alfred A. Knopf, 380 pp. Examines the arms control process under the Reagan presidency by focusing on the bureaucratic battles taking place within the administration.

The Defense Reform Debate: Issues and Analysis, edited by Asa A. Clark, IV, Peter W. Chiarelli, Jeffrey S. McKitrick, and James W. Reed. Baltimore: Johns Hopkins, 370 pp. A volume containing a wide variety of views on virtually all aspects of the current military reform movement.

Defining Defense: The 1985 Military Budget, by Earl C. Ravenal. Washington, D.C.: Cato Institute, 48 pp. Analysis of the defense budget in the light of extensive U.S. commitments and military challenges abroad.

The Economics of National Security, by Lee D. Olvey, James R. Golden, and Robert C. Kelley. Wayne, N.J.: Avery Publishing Group, 404 pp. A textbook about national security economics, including an assessment of the strengths and weaknesses of current economic techniques the defense community uses.

From Gunboats to Diplomacy: New U.S. Policies for Latin America, edited by Richard Newfarmer. Baltimore: Johns Hopkins, 254 pp. A look at the Latin American world with an emphasis on diplomatic and economic solutions as the vehicles for meeting U.S. security needs.

From H-Bomb to Star Wars: The Politics of Strategic Decisionmaking, by Jonathan B. Stein. Lexington, Mass.: Lexington Books, 118 pp. Contends that political decisions drive technological developments in weaponry rather than the reverse. Utilizes the decision to build the hydrogen bomb and the recent Strategic Defense Initiative as case studies.

Grenada: Revolution and Invasion, by Anthony Payne, Paul Sutton, and Tony Thorndike. New York: St. Martin's, 233 pp. Divides the subject into a history of Grenada and a review of the U.S. invasion in 1983.

The Gulf and the Search for Strategic Stability: Saudi Arabia, the Military Balance in the Gulf, and Trends in the Arab-Israeli Military Balance, by Anthony H. Cordesman. London: Mansell/Boulder, Colo.: Westview Press, 1041 pp. An exhaustive study of the strategic aspects of the Persian Gulf region by a former Defense Department official.

The Illogic of American Nuclear Strategy, by Robert Jervis. New York: Cornell University Press, 240 pp. A critical appraisal of war-fighting nuclear strategies and what the author views as the "conventionalization" of nuclear weapons.

Industrial Capacity and Defense Planning: Sustained Conflict and Surge Capability in the 1980s, edited by Lee D. Olvey, Henry A. Leonard, and Bruce E. Arlinghaus. Lexington, Mass.: Lexington Books, 192 pp. Ten essays examine the inadequacy of the U.S. industrial base for wartime demands.

International Security Dimensions of Space, edited by Uri Raanan and Robert L. Pfaltzgraff, Jr. Hamden, Conn.: Archon Books, 324 pp. A Fletcher School of Law and Diplomacy conference examines superpower competition in space and concludes that the United States must increase its efforts.

International Security in the Southeast Asian and Southwest Pacific Region, edited by T.B. Millar. New York: University of Queensland Press, 317 pp. A collection of papers resulting from a 1982 conference held by the Strategic and Defence Studies Centre at the Australian National University.

International Security Yearbook, 1983/84, edited by Barry M. Blechman and Edward N. Luttwak. New York: St. Martin's Press, 337 pp. An annual publication designed to present and analyze international military developments of the year.

The Iron Triangle: A U.S. Security Policy for North-east Asia, by A. James Gregor and Maria Hsia Chang. Stanford: Hoover Press, 160 pp. Argues for a very limited military association with the People's Republic of China and a bolstering of other countries in the region, notably Taiwan, Japan, and South Korea.

The Making of America's Soviet Policy, edited by Joseph S. Nye, Jr. New Haven: Yale University Press, 416 pp. Several authors analyze the factors driving U.S. policy toward the Soviet Union and why consistency is so elusive.

Managing Moscow: Guns or Goods? by Harry Rositzke. New York: Morrow, 243 pp. A former CIA operative's evaluation of how best to contain Soviet influence, with an emphasis on nonmilitary options.

Maritime Strategy or Coalition Defense? by Robert W. Komer. Cambridge, Mass.: Abt Books, 116 pp. Argues for a well-balanced force structure based on strategic considerations rather than inherited service preferences and advocates coalition defense as opposed to independent efforts.

The Military Balance: 1984–1985. London: International Institute for Strategic Studies, 159 pp. The institute's annual data book on national military forces around the world.

Military Leadership: In Pursuit of Excellence, edited by Robert L. Taylor and William E. Rosenbach. Boulder, Colo.: Westview Press, 253 pp. An interdisciplinary examination on the subject of leadershp by twenty-two authors with distinguished backgrounds in the military, industry, and education.

Military Lessons of the Falkland Islands War: Views from the United States, edited by Bruce W. Watson and Peter M. Dunn. Boulder, Colo.: Westview Press, 181 pp. Seeks to determine the elements of British success and places emphasis on military discipline and training.

Military Strategy in Transition: Defense and Deterrence in the 1980s, edited by Keith A. Dunn and William O. Staudenmaier. Boulder: Westview Press, 225 pp. Examines the concept of retaliatory deep strike operations into Eastern Europe as a NATO defense strategy.

Missiles for the Nineties: ICBMs and Strategic Policy, edited by Barry R. Schneider, Colin S. Gray, and Keith B. Payne. Boulder, Colo.: Westview Press, 176 pp. The authors address the role of the MX in deterrence strategy, the impact of new technologies on strategic planning, and likely Soviet responses.

The Morass: United States Intervention in Central America, by Richard Alan White. New York: Harper, 319 pp. Evaluates the U.S. position in Central America in the context of U.S. involvement in counterinsurgency warfare.

NATO: A Bibliography and Resource Guide, by Augustus Richard Norton, Robert A. Friedlander, Martin H. Greenberg, and Donald S. Rowe. New York: Garland Publishing, 252 pp. An extensive compilation of books and articles organized under a variety of subject headings, including individual member-state sections.

NATO Under Attack: Why the Western Alliance Can Fight Outnumbered and Win in Central Europe without Nuclear Weapons, by F.W. von Mellenthin and R.H.S. Stolfi, with E. Sobik. Durham, N.C.: Duke University Press, 161 pp. The authors challenge current doctrine in examining the strengths of NATO and Soviet weaknesses.

The 1985 Defense Budget, by William W. Kaufmann. Washington, D.C.: Brookings, 54 pp. Examines the 1985 budget in terms of the force planning assumptions of the Reagan administration and its emphasis on new weapons programs.

Nuclear America: A Historical Bibliography, Santa Barbara: ABC-Clio Information Services, 184 pp. An annotated research guide containing over 800 abstracts of the literature on nuclear weapons and energy from 1973 to 1982.

Nuclear Arms: Ethics, Strategy, Politics, edited by R. James Woolsey. San Francisco: Institute for Contemporary Studies, 289 pp. A series of articles by several prominent defense analysts covering a variety of perspectives on nuclear weapons and arms control.

Nuclear Forces in Europe: Enduring Dilemmas, Present Prospects, by Leon V. Sigal. Washington, D.C.: Brookings, 181 pp. NATO's dual track decision and its implications for future arms negotiations are addressed.

Nuclear Weapons Databook, vol. 1: *U.S. Nuclear Forces and Capabilities*, by Thomas B. Cochran, William M. Arkin, and Milton M. Hoenig. Cambridge: Ballinger, 340 pp. An extensive catalog of U.S. nuclear forces, including assessments of capabilities, weapons design, and manufacturers.

Nuclear Weapons in Europe, by William G. Hyland, Lawrence D. Freedman, Paul C. Warnke, and Karsten D. Voigt. Edited by Andrew J. Pierre. New York: Council on Foreign Relations, 118 pp. Essays on the debate surrounding the deployment of cruise and Pershing II missiles in Europe cast in the larger context of East-West relations.

The Nuclear Weapons Freeze and Arms Control, edited by Steven E. Miller. Cambridge: Ballinger, 208 pp. Examines the nuclear freeze in depth.

The Nuclear Weapons Industry, by Kenneth A. Bertsch and Linda S. Shaw. Washington, D.C.: Investor Responsibility Research Center, 405 pp. A look at the current industrial groups involved in nuclear weapons development and production in the United States and their prospects for the future.

The Reagan Strategic Defense Initiative: A Technical, Political, and Arms Control Assessment, by Sidney D. Drell, Philip J. Farley, and David Holloway. Stanford: Stanford University

Press, 147 pp. Examines the political implications of the Strategic Defense Initiative and concludes that it will have a negative impact.

The Report of the President's National Bipartisan Commission on Central America, foreword by Henry Kissinger. New York: Macmillan, 158 pp. The twelve-member commission's assessment of the economic, political, and military problems facing Central America and their recommendations for future U.S. policy in the region.

Rift and Revolution: The Central American Imbroglio, edited by Howard J. Wiarda. Washington, D.C.: American Enterprise Institute, 392 pp. A primer on the current problems facing Central America by former UN Ambassador Jeanne Kirkpatrick and ten other scholars.

The Russians and Reagan, by Strobe Talbott. New York: Vintage Books, 140 pp. An analysis of Soviet perceptions of the first Reagan administration and prospects for future negotiations between the two powers.

Small Nuclear Forces and U.S. Security Policy: Threats and Potential Conflicts in the Middle East and South Asia, edited by Rodney W. Jones. Lexington, Mass.: Lexington Books, 285 pp. Evaluates potential problems and U.S. responses to a Middle East and South Asia consisting of nuclear-armed states.

Strategic Requirements for the Army to the Year 2000, edited by Robert H. Kupperman and William J. Taylor, Jr. Lexington, Mass.: Lexington Books, 541 pp. Examines the types of conflict the United States is likely to encounter over the next fifteen years, with emphasis on low-intensity operations and how to prepare for them.

Strategic Responses to Conflict in the 1980s, edited by William J. Taylor, Jr., Steven A. Maaranen, and Gerrit W. Gong. Lexington, Mass.: Lexington Books, 527 pp. Addresses the types of U.S. strategies required to face the diverse conflict conditions of the 1980s.

Strategic Stalemate: Nuclear Weapons and Arms Control in American Politics, by Michael Krepon. New York: St. Martin's Press, 191 pp. Examines the last four decades of U.S. debate over nuclear weapons and strategy and offers guidelines for consensus building in the future.

Strategy and the Defense Dilemma, by Gerald Garvey. Lexington, Mass.: Lexington Books, 137 pp. Argues that the United States faces a basic crisis in its strategic concepts and needs to reevaluate what is required to protect its vital interests.

The Tattered China Card: Reality or Illusion in United States Strategy? by Robert L. Downen. Washington, D.C.: Council for Social and Economic Studies, 128 pp. Argues for a limited number of concessions to the People's Republic of China on strategic grounds.

Technobandits, by Linda Melvern, David Hebditch, and Nick Anning. Boston: Houghton Mifflin, 305 pp. Examines Soviet efforts to acquire U.S. high technology illegally.

Thinking about the Unthinkable in the 1980s, by Herman Kahn. New York: Simon and Schuster, 250 pp. A revised edition of the late author's original work on nuclear war and strategy incorporating the political, technical, and moral developments of the past two decades.

Trouble in Our Backyard: Central America and the United States in the Eighties, edited by Martin Diskin. New York: Pantheon, 264 pp. A series of essays examining the problems of the region in general and those of El Salvador, Nicaragua, Guatemala, and Honduras in particular.

The Troubled Alliance: Atlantic Relations in the 1980s, edited by Lawrence Freedman. London: Heinemann/New York: St. Martin's, 170 pp. Series of papers presented at a Chatham House conference focusing on the traditional subject of problems and prospects among the NATO members.

The 25-Year War: America's Military Role in Vietnam, by General Bruce Palmer, Jr. Lexington, Ky.: University Press of Kentucky, 236 pp. The author critically analyzes the Vietnam experience in the field and at the strategic level of decision making, drawing on his experience as deputy to General William Westmoreland.

The Unstable Gulf: Threats from Within, by Lenore G. Martin. Lexington, Mass.: Lexington Books, 232 pp. A look at internal sources of instability within the gulf and their applications for U.S. strategy in the region.

Up in Arms: A Common Cause Guide to Understanding Nuclear Arms Policy, by Sandra Sedacca. Washington, D.C.: Common Cause, 130 pp. A primer on nuclear weapons and strategy for the interested layperson.

The Verification of Arms Control Agreements, edited by Ian Bellany and Coit D. Blacker. London: Cass, 95 pp. Examines the growing number of gray areas in arms control verification and the trade-offs between reaching an agreement politically and the technical certainty of establishing compliance.

Vietnam as History: Ten Years after the Paris Peace Accords, edited by Peter Braestrup. Washington, D.C.: Woodrow Wilson International Center for Scholars and University Press of America, 184 pp. Fifty leading historians and analysts of the U.S. involvement in Vietnam take a retrospective look at the strategies behind the war and the lessons learned.

The Wars in Vietnam, Cambodia and Laos, 1945–1982: A Bibliographic Guide, by Richard Dean Burns and Milton Leitenberg. Santa Barbara, Calif.: ABC-Clio Information Services, 290 pp. A revised edition containing extensive references on the wars under a variety of cross-referenced subject headings.

Weapons and Hope, by Freeman Dyson. New York: Harper/Bessie, 340 pp. An examination of the assumptions behind the various positions on nuclear arms along with recommendations for moving to a defense-dominated world.

Western Interests and U.S. Options in the Caribbean Basin: Report of the Atlantic Council's Working Group on the Caribbean Basin, edited by James R. Green and Brent Scowcroft. Boston: Oelgeschlager, 331 pp. Stresses the strategic threats posed to the region and potential U.S. responses.

Cross-Index by Author

ABC-Clio Information Services, *Nuclear America: A Historical Bibliography*
Anning, Nick, *Technobandits*
Arkin, William M., *Nuclear Weapons Databook*, vol. 1: *U.S. Nuclear Forces and Capabilities*
Arlinghaus, Bruce E., *Conventional Deterrence in NATO: Alternatives for European Defense*
Arlinghaus, Bruce E., *Industrial Capacity and Defense Planning: Sustained Conflict and Surge Capability in the 1980s*
Baker, A.D., III. *Combat Fleets of the World, 1984/85: Their Ships, Aircraft and Armament*
Bellany, Ian, *The Verification of Arms Control Agreements*
Bertsch, Kenneth A., *The Nuclear Weapons Industry*
Binkin, Martin, *America's Volunteer Military: Progress and Prospects*
Blacker, Coit D., *The Verification of Arms Control Agreements*
Blechman, Barry M., *International Security Yearbook, 1983/84*
Braestrup, Peter, *Vietnam as History: Ten Years after the Paris Peace Accords*
Burns, Richard Dean, *The Wars in Vietnam, Cambodia and Laos, 1945–1982: A Bibliographic Guide*
Carter, Ashton B., *Ballistic Missile Defense*

Chang, Maria Hsia, *The Iron Triangle: A U.S. Security Policy for North-East Asia*

Chiarelli, Peter W., *The Defense Reform Debate: Issues and Analysis*

Clark, Asa A., IV, *Conventional Deterrence in NATO: Alternatives for European Defense*

Clark, Asa A., IV, *The Defense Reform Debate: Issues and Analysis*

Cochran, Thomas B., *Nuclear Weapons Databook*, vol. 1: *U.S. Nuclear Forces and Capabilities*

Cordesman, Anthony H., *The Gulf and the Search for Strategic Stability: Saudi Arabia, the Military Balance in the Gulf, and Trends in the Arab-Israeli Military Balance*

Disken, Martin, *Trouble in Our Backyard: Central America and the United States in the Eighties*

Dougherty, James E., *The Bishops and Nuclear Weapons: The Catholic Pastoral Letter on War and Peace*

Downen, Robert L., *The Tattered China Card: Reality or Illusion in United States Strategy?*

Drell, Sidney D., *The Reagan Strategic Defense Initiative: A Technical, Political, and Arms Control Assessment*

Dunn, Keith A., *Military Strategy in Transition: Defense and Deterrence in the 1980s*

Dunn, Peter M., *Military Lessons of the Falkland Islands War: Views from the United States*

Dyson, Freeman, *Weapons and Hope*

Erlich, Paul R., *The Cold and the Dark: The World after Nuclear War*

Farley, Philip J., *The Reagan Strategic Defense Initiative: A Technical, Political, and Arms Control Assessment*

Freedman, Lawrence D., *Nuclear Weapons in Europe*

Freedman, Lawrence, *The Troubled Alliance: Atlantic Relations in the 1980s*

Friedlander, Robert A., *NATO: A Bibliography and Resource Guide*

Garvey, Gerald, *Strategy and the Defense Dilemma*

Golden, James R., *The Economics of National Security*

Golden, James R., *Conventional Deterrence in NATO: Alternatives for European Defense*

Gong, Gerrit W., *Strategic Responses to Conflict in the 1980s*

Gray, Colin S., *Missiles for the Nineties: ICBMs and Strategic Policy*

Green, James R., *Western Interests and U.S. Options in the Caribbean Basin: Report of the Atlantic Council's Working Group on the Caribbean Basin*

Greenberg, Martin H., *NATO: A Bibliography and Resource Guide*

Gregor, James, *The Iron Triangle: A U.S. Security Policy for North-East Asia*

Haig, Jr., Alexander, *Caveat: Realism, Reagan and Foreign Policy*

Hebditch, David, *Technobandits*

Hoenig, Milton M., *Nuclear Weapons Databook*, vol. 1: *U.S. Nuclear Forces and Capabilities*

Holloway, David, *The Reagan Strategic Defense Initiative: A Technical, Political, and Arms Control Assessment*

Hyland, William G., *Nuclear Weapons in Europe*

International Institute for Strategic Studies, *The Military Balance*

Jervis, Robert, *The Illogic of American Nuclear Strategy*

Joeck, Neil, *Arms Control and International Security*

Jones, Rodney W., *Small Nuclear Forces and U.S. Security Policy: Threats and Potential Conflicts in the Middle East and South Asia*

Kahn, Herman, *Thinking about the Unthinkable in the 1980s*

Kaufmann, William W., *The 1985 Defense Budget*

Kelley, Robert C., *The Economics of National Security*

Kennedy, Donald, *The Cold and the Dark: The World after Nuclear War*

Keyes, Langley, *The Counterfeit Ark: Crisis Relocation for Nuclear War*

Kissinger, Henry, *The Report of the President's National Bipartisan Commission on Central America*
Kolkowicz, Roman, *Arms Control and International Security*
Komer, Robert W., *Maritime Strategy or Coalition Defense?*
Krepon, Michael, *Strategic Stalemate: Nuclear Weapons and Arms Control in American Politics*
Kupperman, Robert H., *Strategic Requirements for the Army to the Year 2000*
Leaning, Jennifer, *The Counterfeit Ark: Crisis Relocation for Nuclear War*
Leiken, Robert S., *Central America: Anatomy of Conflict*
Leitenberg, Milton, *The Wars in Vietnam, Cambodia and Laos, 1945–1982: A Bibliographic Guide*
Leonard, Henry A., *Industrial Capacity and Defense Planning: Sustained Conflict and Surge Capability in the 1980s*
Luttwak, Edward N., *International Security Yearbook, 1983/84*
Maaranen, Steven A., *Strategic Responses to Conflict in the 1980s*
McKitrick, Jeffrey S., *The Defense Reform Debate: Issues and Analysis*
Manno, Jack, *Arming the Heavens: The Hidden Military Agenda for Space, 1945–1995*
Martin, Lenore G., *The Unstable Gulf: Threats from Within*
Maslowski, Peter, *For the Common Defense: A Military History of the United States of America*
von Mellenthin, Frederick W., *NATO under Attack: Why the Western Alliance Can Fight Outnumbered and Win in Central Europe without Nuclear Weapons*
Melvern, Linda, *Technobandits*
Millar, T.B., *International Security in the Southeast Asian and Southwest Pacific Region*
Miller, Steven E., *The Nuclear Weapons Freeze and Arms Control*
Millett, Allen R., *For the Common Defense: A Military History of the United States of America*
Newfarmer, Richard, *From Gunboats to Diplomacy: New U.S. Policies for Latin America*
Norton, Augustus Richard, *NATO: A Bibliography and Resource Guide*
Nye, Joseph S., Jr., *The Making of America's Soviet Policy*
Olvey, Lee D., *The Economics of National Security*
Olvey, Lee D., *Industrial Capacity and Defense Planning: Sustained Conflict and Surge Capacity in the 1980s*
Palmer, Gen. Bruce, Jr., *The 25-Year War: America's Military Role in Vietnam*
Payne, Anthony, *Grenada: Revolution and Invasion*
Payne, Keith B., *Missiles for the Nineties: ICBMs and Strategic Policy*
Pfaltzgraff, Robert L., Jr., *International Security Dimensions of Space*
The President's National Bipartisan Commission on Central America, *The Report of the President's National Bipartisan Commission on Central America*
Raanan, Uri, *International Security Dimensions of Space*
Ravenal, Earl C., *Defining Defense: The 1985 Military Budget*
Reed, James W., *The Defense Reform Debate: Issues and Analysis*
Roberts, Walter Orr, *The Cold and the Dark: The World after Nuclear War*
Rosenbach, William E., *Military Leadership: In Pursuit of Excellence*
Rositzke, Harry, *Managing Moscow: Guns or Goods?*
Rowe, Donald S., *NATO: A Bibliography and Resource Guide*
Sagan, Carl, *The Cold and the Dark: The World after Nuclear War*
Schell, Jonathan, *The Abolition*
Schneider, Barry R., *Missiles for the Nineties: ICBMs and Strategic Policy*
Schwartz, David N., *Ballistic Missile Defense*

Scowcroft, Brent, *Western Interests and U.S. Options in the Caribbean Basin: Report of the Atlantic Council's Working Group on the Caribbean Basin*

Sedacca, Sandra, *Up in Arms: A Common Cause Guide to Understanding Nuclear Arms Policy*

Shaw, Linda S., *The Nuclear Weapons Industry*

Sigal, Leon V., *Nuclear Forces in Europe: Enduring Dilemmas, Present Prospects*

Sobik, E., *NATO under Attack: Why the Western Alliance Can Fight Outnumbered and Win in Central Europe without Nuclear Weapons*

Starr, Richard F, *Arms Control: Myth versus Reality*

Staudenmaier, William D., *Military Strategy in Transition: Defense and Deterrence in the 1980s*

Stein, Jonathan B., *From H-Bomb to Star Wars: The Politics of Strategic Decisionmaking*

Stolfi, R.H.S., *NATO under Attack: Why the Western Alliance Can Fight Outnumbered and Win in Central Europe without Nuclear Weapons*

Sutton, Paul, *Grenada: Revolution and Invasion*

Talbott, Strobe, *Deadly Gambits: The Reagan Administration and the Stalemate in Nuclear Arms Control*

Talbott, Strobe, *The Russians and Reagan*

Taylor, Robert L., *Military Leadership: In Pursuit of Excellence*

Taylor, William J., *Strategic Requirements for the Army to the Year 2000*

Taylor, William J., *Strategic Responses to Conflict in the 1980s*

Thorndike, Tony, *Grenada: Revolution and Invasion*

Voigt, Karsten D., *Nuclear Weapons in Europe*

Warnke, Paul C., *Nuclear Weapons in Europe*

Watson, Bruce W., *Military Lessons of the Falkland Islands War: Views from the United States*

White, Richard Alan, *The Morass: United States Intervention in Central America*

Wiarda, Howard J., *Rift and Revolution: The Central American Imbroglio*

Woolsey, R. James, *Nuclear Arms: Ethics, Strategy, Politics*

Zuckerman, Edward, *The Day after World War III: The U.S. Government's Plans for Surviving a Nuclear War*

Notes

Chapter 2
U.S. Defense Doctrine: A Debate

1. Caspar Weinberger, *Annual Report to Congress*, FY84 (Washington, D.C., February 1, 1983) (hereafter cited as *Annual Report*).

2. Eugene Rostow, "The 'Lessons' of Vietnam and Presidential Powers," *Strategic Report* (Fall 1984).

3. Norman Podhoretz, *The Present Danger* (New York: Simon and Schuster, 1980).

4. Readers should consult the DOD *Annual Reports*, the annual *Military Posture* reports of the Joint Chiefs of Staff, and the three editions of *Soviet Military Power*. At the same time, they should be aware that competent independent analyses still regard those reports as understatements of the situation and overstatements of the likely improvements to come through existing military programs. See, for example, Committee on the Present Danger, *Has America Become Number 2?* (1982) and *Can America Catch Up?* (1984); and frequent analyses in *Armed Forces Journal International*, such as Anthony Cordesman, "Strength without Strategy, Programs without Purpose?" (March 1984).

5. See DOD, *Annual Reports*; Committee on the Present Danger, *Has America* and *Can America*.

6. Earl C. Ravenal, *Defining Defense: The 1985 Military Budget* (Washington, D.C.: Cato Institute, 1984) (emphasis added).

7. Library of Congress, Congressional Research Service, "The Defense Spending Debate," Report No. 84-97F (May 29, 1984).

8. Committee on the Present Danger, *Is the Reagan Defense Program Adequate* (March 17, 1982), p. 5 (emphasis added). The committee's executive committee includes former secretaries and deputy secretaries of the treasury and reknowned economists.

9. Poll contained in Charles Tyroller II, ed., *Alerting America: The Papers of the Committee on the Present Danger* (New York: Pergamon Press, 1984).

10. Dean Acheson, *Power and Diplomacy* (New York: Atheneum, 1962), p. 66.

11. Harold W. Rood, *Kingdoms of the Blind* (Durham, N.C.: Carolina Academic Press, 1980), p. 285.

12. DOD, *Annual Report*, FY85, p. 56.

13. Committee on the Present Danger, *Has America*, p. 12.

14. "The Soviet Armed Forces shall be provided with all resources necessary to obtain and maintain superiority in outer space sufficient to deny the use of outer space to other states and to assure maximum space-based military support for Soviet offensive and defensive combat operations on land, at sea, in air, and in outer space." Defense Intelligence Agency, *Soviet Military Space Doctrine*, 1984, quoted in *Soviet Aerospace*, October 22, 1984, pp. 160–161.

15. For an evaluation of the Reagan administration and arms control, as well as an overall assessment of the arms control record, see William R. Van Cleave, "The Arms Control Record," in Richard Starr, ed., *Arms Control: Myth versus Reality* (Stanford, Calif.: Hoover Institution Press, 1984).

16. *Time*, December 13, 1984. Quoted in *Can America Catch Up?* Other examples of the negligence of constraints are from Secretary of Defense Weinberger's description of the nature of defense spending: "Defense spending is unique, being the only part of the total U.S. budget determined solely by factors external to our nation. The continued Soviet military buildup, as well as the growing menace of international terrorism, regional instabilities, and geopolitical uncertainties around the world, dictate that our nation maintain its commitment to rebuild its deterrent capability." *Annual Report*, FY86, p. 3.

17. *New Republic*, October 14, 1981.

18. This point is illustrated by the cardinal example of the aircraft carrier battle group. I have demonstrated that to put one such group steadily into forward waters, over its thirty-year lifetime, including all support and overhead costs, takes $400 billion, in 1985 dollars. See Ravenal, *Defining Defense*. The carrier battle group is a force, or a major weapons system, that works. But its military output is only about thirty-five individual sorties, or individual flights, of fighter-attack planes a day.

19. "Nuclear Weapons and the Atlantic Alliance," *Foreign Affairs* 60, no. 4 (Spring 1982):753–768.

20. Leonard Sullivan, Jr., "The FY84 Defense Debate: Defeat by Default," *Armed Forces Journal International* (May 1983).

21. These are my estimates, derived by a strict and consistent methodology from Secretary of Defense Weinberger's FY86 "Posture Statement."

22. See the remarks on allocating the cost of major geographical commitments, below; and Earl C. Ravenal, "Defending Persian Gulf Oil," *Intervention* (Winter 1985), and *Defining Defense*. The figures there must be updated to FY86.

23. Lest anyone think that I am negligent—deliberately or otherwise—of the fact that Reagan's military budget has not really exceeded Carter's planned expenditures, I cite this passage from my book *Defining Defense*: "As early as November 1981, *Armed Forces Journal International* could conclude that 'Ronald Reagan's program to rearm America now adds up to less than a one percent increase in actual defense spending over the Pentagon budgets proposed by former President Jimmy Carter last January for the next three years.' (In fact, in terms of outlays, the military budget for 1983 that Jimmy Carter projected in his last month in office, January 1981—admittedly for political effect—was $205.3

billion; Ronald Reagan's actual outlays for 1983 were $205.0 billion.) What is striking is that, far from being able to fulfill its alleged wish-list of expansive military programs, the Reagan administration has had trouble maintaining a defense budget that is just about at the level that Jimmy Carter might have attained."

24. "Fiscal Year 1984–1988 Defense Guidance," leaked to and summarized by *New York Times,* May 30, 1982.

25. Robert Komer, *Maritime Strategy or Coalition Defense?* (Cambridge, Mass.: Abt Books, 1984).

26. *Annual Report,* FY86, p. 39.

27. From a 1980 campaign speech by Ronald Reagan to the Ohio Conference of the International Brotherhood of Teamsters.

28. A more ample definition appears in Ravenal, *Defining Defense.*

29. Charles Krauthammer offers a fine discussion of the "new isolationism" in *New Republic,* March 4, 1985.

30. See *Defense and the Deficit,* released March 8, 1985, by the Committee on the Present Danger. See also Herbert Stein, "Cutting the Lean Out of Defense," *Wall Street Journal,* February 27, 1985, p. 30.

31. "The Passionate State of Mind," interview by Eric Sevareid, CBS, September 1967.

32. Brian Crozier, *Strategy of Survival* (London: Temple Smith, 1978), pp. 150, 154–155.

33. "Lessons," p. 31.

34. *Annual Report,* FY85, p. 203.

35. Professor Frederick A. Lindemann, letter to the *London Times,* August 8, 1934, quoted in R.V. Jones, *The Wizard of War* (New York: Coward, McCann & Geohegan, 1978), p. 13.

36. *New York Times,* February 16, 1984.

37. John G. Kester, "War and Money," *Washingtonian* (January 1983).

38. Pentagon budgeteers complain that attributing particular units to particular regional missions distorts the picture. But the allocation of forces to regions of the world (along with "full-slice" costing of combat forces) is necessary to making defense costs intelligible—that is, relating the primary inputs to the ultimate outputs. A full account of the methodology by which I arrive at these force allocations and costs appears in Ravenal, *Defining Defense.*

39. "A Requiem for 'Rearmament'," *The Wall Street Journal,* February 19, 1985.

Chapter 3
The Defense Budget

1. Tables and graphs were prepared by the author from open source data supporting FY86 and prior defense budgets. These include secretary of defense and chairman of the Joint Chiefs of Staff posture statements and Office of the Secretary of Defense reports on manpower, training, readiness; operations and maintenance overview; RDT&E (R-1); procurement (P-1); national defense budget estimates; and allied commitments to defense spending. Trends in federal nondefense spending are from current Congressional Budget Office reports.

Chapter 5
Theater Forces: U.S. Defense Policy in NATO

1. William Drozdiak, "NATO Agrees to $7.8 Billion in Improvements," *Washington Post*, December 5, 1984, p. 1.

2. Henry Kissinger, "A Plan to Reshape NATO," *Time*, March 5, 1984, p. 24.

3. There was a slight drop in 1968, when the United States withdrew two-thirds of a division (two brigades) and four tactical aircraft squadrons from Europe, or about 33,000 personnel. The United States then redeployed two brigades to Europe in 1975.

4. *Department of Defense, FY 1983 Annual Report to Congress*, p. III–91.

5. For the air force, the goal of forty tactical aircraft wings has been scaled back. For the army, new light divisions will be created from existing personnel bases and thus is not an expansion in force structure in the traditional sense.

6. NATO sources report that 102 missiles are now based in Western Europe: 54 Pershing-II missiles in West Germany, 32 GLCMs in Britain, and 16 GLCMs in Italy. William Drozdiak, "Missile Freeze Idea Divides NATO," *Washington Post*, November 29, 1984, p. 18.

7. The original list of technologies was reduced to thirty-three and submitted for U.S. and European consideration at the Spring Conference of the National Armaments Directors meeting in 1984. Of these, the group selected eleven possible projects that could be developed cooperatively.

8. Deborah Kyle, "AFJ Interview with General Billy M. Minter," *Armed Forces Journal International* (January 1984):47.

9. David Fairhall, "Trident Programme Cost Rockets Past £10 Billion," *Guardian*, December 29, 1984, p. 3.

10. As reported in William Drozdiak, "NATO Warned of High-Tech Arms 'Dazzle,' " *Washington Post*, November 15, 1984, p. 30.

11. This section draws on a working paper prepared for the Georgetown Center for Strategic and International Studies Group on Strategy and Arms Control, "Reducing the Risk of Nuclear War in Europe," by J.A. Thomson (June 1984).

12. For a description of the operational concepts behind forward defense, see P. Karber, "In Defense of Forward Defense," *Armed Forces Journal International* (May 1984).

13. R.W. Komer, "A Credible Conventional Option: Can NATO Afford It?" *Strategic Review* (Spring 1984).

14. Donald R. Cotter, "Potential Future Roles for Conventional and Nuclear Forces in Defense of Western Europe," in *Strengthening Conventional Deterrence in Europe*, report of the European Security Study (New York: St. Martin's, 1983), pp. 209–253.

15. A comprehensive review is B.D. Sutton et al., "Deep Attack Concepts and the Defense of Central Europe," *Survival* (March–April 1984).

16. Cotter, "Potential Future Roles," gives a life cycle figure of about $10 billion.

17. Komer, "Credible Conventional Option."

18. If, for example, the Warsaw Pact has ninety divisions and NATO thirty (these are representative figures, although NATO divisions are generally more capable than pact ones), about forty and twenty of these, respectively, might be committed to the first offensive and defensive echelons, respectively. Taking into account terrain and other factors, the twenty NATO divisions could stand off the pact forty. This leaves fifty and ten in reserve, a 5:1 ratio. This ratio concerns Western analysts and has led to the deep strike

concepts. The deployment of five new operational reserve divisions would reduce this ratio to 3.3:1. Whether this ratio is satisfactory is beyond the scope of the analysis, but to make a similar improvement, the deep strike capabilities would have to be capable of destroying roughly seventeen Warsaw Pact divisions completely; delaying their arrival would not make the same improvement.

19. Because of the current interest in improving NATO's conventional defense, we have not provided an analysis of NATO's nuclear needs. One of us has previously done so (James A. Thomson, "Planning for NATO's Nuclear Deterrent in the 1980s and 1990s," *Survival* 25 [May–June 1983]) arguing that NATO needs to modernize its battlefield nuclear capability and find a replacement for tactical air power in nuclear missions. These capabilities are especially important for maintaining the credibility of the first nuclear use threat. In the current European political environment, it seems unlikely that significant modernization that includes the deployment of new weapons can occur. Although the so-called Montebello decision of NATO's Nuclear Planning Group mandated both a reduction and a modernization of NATO's nuclear stockpile, it is likely that only the reduction will occur. Nevertheless, NATO will face the problem on an increasingly obsolescent or obsolete nuclear capability with a declining deterrent value unless some action is taken in the future.

Chapter 7
Manpower

1. "Weinberger Calls AVF 'Huge Success,' " *Army Times*, November 21, 1983. This chapter draws on the author's *America's Volunteer Military: Progress and Prospects* (Washington, D.C.: Brookings Institution, 1984).

2. The widely accepted slogan—"As goes the Army, so goes the all-volunteer force"— is not intended to minimize the importance of recruit quality to the other services. The army, however, is the largest and generally has had the greatest difficulties since the end of conscription meeting quantitative and qualitative goals.

3. Reenlistment rates should be interpreted with some caution. Since they are the proportion of eligibles who reenlist, any redefinition of eligible will affect the rates. The army, for example, tightened reenlistment criteria in 1982, and the air force did so in 1984 to reduce the number of eligibles. See Larry Carney, "Re-up Bar Tightened for 18-Year Troops," *Army Times*, January 4, 1982, and "Small Decline in Reenlistment 'Not a Concern,' " *Air Force Times*, November 12, 1984.

4. The selected reserve is composed almost exclusively of organized units, whose members drill periodically and are paid.

5. The 1979 figure is from Robert B. Pirie, "The All-Volunteer Force Today: Mobilization Manpower," in Andrew J. Goodpaster, Lloyd H. Elliott, and J. Allan Hovey, Jr., eds., *Toward a Consensus on Military Service* (New York: Pergamon, 1982), pp. 126–127. Current figure obtained from Department of the Army.

6. The dramatic growth in the proportion of blacks during the 1970s, especially in the ground combat forces, raised questions about the equitability of imposing an unfair burden on a segment of society that has not enjoyed a fair share of the benefits that the state confers. For further discussion of the issues raised by fielding military forces manned by a disproportionate number of blacks, see Martin Binkin and Mark J. Eitelberg with Alvin J.

Schexnider and Marvin M. Smith, *Blacks and the Military* (Washington, D.C.: Brookings Institution, 1982).

7. This is not meant to imply that racial discrimination exists. But under current entry standards, a great deal depends on aptitude test scores. As matters stand, if cutoff scores are set at a point at which 50 percent of whites qualify, then only about 16 percent of black Americans will qualify. See Binkin, *America's Volunteer Military*, p. 26.

8. Department of Defense Authorization Act, 1985, Conference Report, 98th Cong., 2nd sess., September 26, 1984, pp. 286–289, 294–295.

9. It is unlikely that many will qualify for the maximum entitlement. First, the chances that the secretary of defense will authorize the maximum supplementary payments are remote, given the administration's opposition to the program. Second, while the basic benefit is to be funded by the Veterans Administration, the fact that supplementary payments are to be funded by the individual services on an accrual basis will be a disincentive.

10. "Army Reports Downturn in Recruiting," *Washington Post*, February 3, 1984.

11. Walter Andrews, "Drop in Top Recruits Worries Army Brass," *Washington Times*, November 14, 1984.

12. U.S. Department of Labor, Bureau of Labor Statistics, *Employment and Earnings*, October 1984, p. 7.

13. Robert H. Baldwin and Thomas V. Daula, "The Cost of High-Quality Recruits," *Armed Forces and Society* 11, no. 1 (Fall 1984):96.

14. "Services, DOD Argue over Cost of Recruits," *Navy Times*, September 3, 1984, p. 7.

15. Comments of Lawrence J. Korb, assistant secretary of defense for manpower, installation, and logistics, in *Atlanta Constitution*, November 23, 1984.

16. Comments of General Frederick J. Kroesen, commander in chief, U.S. Army, Europe, in *U.S. News and World Report*, August 9, 1982, p. 23.

17. John W. Woodmansee Jr., "Blitzkreig and the Airland Battle," *Military Review* (August 1984):37.

18. Omnibus Defense Authorization Act, 1985, Senate Armed Services Committee, 98th Cong., 2nd sess., May 31, 1984, p. 918.

19. The differences are even greater in the high-skill occupations. For example, about 51 percent of white males (ages 18 to 23) would be expected to qualify for entry into training to become an electronics technician in the navy, compared to 8 percent of black males and 21 percent of Hispanic males in the same age group. See Martin Binkin and Mark J. Eitelberg, "Women and Minorities in the All-Volunteer Force" (paper prepared for a conference on The AVF after a Decade: Retrospect and Prospect, Annapolis, Md., November 1983), table 15.

20. The calculation is restricted to males inasmuch as the number of female enlistments is demand constrained because of the limited positions they are allowed to fill by law or policy.

21. For a fuller discussion of this methodology and underlying assumptions see Binkin, *America's Volunteer Military*, p. 33.

22. The number of male recruits needed each year is not solely a function of the size of the armed forces but involves a variety of other factors, such as length of enlistment, attrition rates, retention rates, and utilization of women. For simplicity, the calculation here assumes that accession needs are proportional to end strength.

23. The current differences between army and air force entrance standards are substantial. By best available estimates, about 77 percent of the male youth population would

meet the army's minimum aptitude and education standards compared to only 63 percent for the air force. See Mark J. Eitelberg et al., *Screening for Service: Aptitude and Education Criteria for Military Entry* (Alexandria, Va.: Human Resources Research Organization, 1983), pp. 3-27, 3-30.

24. For a description of the challenge to the higher education community, see David W. Brenemen, *The Coming Enrollment Crises: What Every Trustee Must Know* (Washington, D.C.: Association of Governing Boards of Universities and Colleges, 1982).

25. Department of Defense Authorization Act, 1985, p. 292.

26. Thomas V. Daula and D. Alton Smith, "Recruiting Goals, Enlistment Supply and Enlistments in the U.S. Army" (paper presented at U.S. Army Manpower Economics Conference, Williamsburg, Va., December 1984), p. 22.

27. Gary F. Johnson, "Rating Balance Adjustments" (Center for Naval Analyses, July 1984).

28. For a fuller discussion of the potential for civilian substitution and of the domestic and bureaucratic politics involved, see Martin Binkin, Herschel Kanter and Rolf H. Clark, *Shaping the Defense Civilian Work Force: Economics, Politics, and National Security* (Washington, D.C.: Brookings Institution, 1978).

Chapter 8
Organization and Management

1. *Armed Forces Journal* (February 1984):10.

2. U.S. Senate, Armed Services Committee, *Hearings, Organization, Structure and Decisionmaking Procedures of the Department of Defense*, 98th Cong., 1st sess., 1983. The witnesses included Mr. Weinberger, former Defense Secretaries Harold Brown and Eliot Richardson, chairman the Joint Chiefs General John Vessey, all of the other service chiefs and service secretaries, as well as other retired senior military officers and former civilian officials of the DOD.

3. House, Armed Services Committee, "Joint Chiefs of Staff Reorganization Act of 1983," Report 98-382 (September 1983). This bill (H.R. 3718) was incorporated into the House-passed 1985 DOD Authorization Bill in its entirety.

4. Department of Defense Authorization Act, 1985, 98th Cong., 2d sess.

5. U.S. House, Committee of Conference, "Department of Defense Authorization Act, 1985, Report 98-1080, 98th Cong., 2d sess., pp. 330-331.

6. Ibid., pp. 331-334.

7. The ideas included in this section draw heavily on the deliberations of the Georgetown Center for Strategic and International Studies (CSIS) Defense Organization Project, which the author chaired. For further information, see the committee report *Toward a More Effective Defense: The Final Report of the CSIS Defense Organization Project* (Washington, D.C.: CSIS, February 1985).

Chapter 10
Special Supplement: The Strategic Defense Initiative

1. Soon after President Reagan's March 23, 1983, announcement of the SDI, two studies were commissioned, one on technology and one on strategy. James C. Fletcher

directed the technology study, and Fred S. Hoffman chaired the strategy panel. Unclassified summaries of the findings of these panels (known as the Fletcher panel and the Hoffman panel) appear in "The Strategic Defense Initiative: Defense Technologies Study" (U.S. Department of Defense, March 1984) and "Ballistic Missile Defenses and U.S. National Security: Summary Report," prepared for the National Security Strategy Study (U.S. Department of Defense, October 1983). For a comprehensive independent treatment of BMD issues, see Ashton B. Carter and David N. Schwartz, eds., *Ballistic Missile Defense* (Washington, D.C.: Brookings Institution, 1984).

2. See Ashton B. Carter, "Directed Energy Missile Defense in Space: Background Paper" (Office of Technology Assessment, U.S. Congress, April 1984).

3. See "The President's Strategic Defense Initiative" (Washington, D.C., January 1985), p. i. (The presidential forward is dated December 28, 1984.)

4. U.S. Senate, Committee on Foreign Relations, James A. Abrahamson, "Statement on the President's Strategic Defense Initiative," April 25, 1984.

5. Interview with Secretary of Defense Caspar Weinberger on "Meet the Press," NBC, March 27, 1983.

6. "Ballistic Missile Defenses and U.S. National Security," p. 2.

7. Abrahamson, "Statement."

8. George A. Keyworth II, "The Case for Strategic Defense: An Option for a World Disarmed," *Issues in Science and Technology* (Fall 1984):43–44.

9. "President's Strategic Defense Initiative," p. i.

10. Carter, "Directed Energy Missile Defense," p. 81.

11. Hans A. Bethe, Richard L. Garwin, Kurt Gottfried, and Henry W. Kendall, "Space-Based Ballistic-Missile Defense," *Scientific American* (December 1984):49.

12. Sidney D. Drell and Wolfgang K.H. Panofsky, "The Case against Strategic Defense: Technical and Strategic Realities," *Issues in Science and Technology* (Fall 1984):64.

13. "Ballistic Missile Defenses and U.S. National Security," p. 2.

14. For an excellent discussion of the role of BMD in Soviet forces and doctrine, see Sayre Stevens, "The Soviet BMD Program," in Carter and Schwartz, "Ballistic Missile Defenses," pp. 182–220.

15. The quote is from Article VI. The full name of the ABM Treaty is Treaty between the United States of America and the Union of Soviet Socialist Republics on the Limitation of Anti-Ballistic Missile Systems. The treaty is accompanied by Agreed Statements initialed by the heads of the U.S. and Soviet negotiating teams and Common Understandings supported by the negotiating record.

16. See "The President's Report to the Congress on Soviet Noncompliance with Arms Control Agreements" (Washington, D.C., January 23, 1984), p. 4.

17. See Sidney D. Drell, Philip J. Farley, and David Holloway, "The Reagan Strategic Defense Initiative: A Technical, Political, and Arms Control Assessment" (Stanford: Center for International Security and Arms Control, Stanford University, July 1984), pp. 27–29.

18. The discussion that follows is adapted from Albert Carnesale, "The Strategic Defense Initiative and Arms Control," *Harvard International Review* 7, no. 4 (January/February 1985):29–31.

19. "President's Strategic Defense Initiative," p. i.

20. U.S. Senate, Committee on Armed Services, *Military Implications of the Treaty on the Limitations of Anti-Ballistic Missile Systems and Interim Agreement on Limitation of Strategic Offensive Arms, Hearings*, June 6, 20, 22, 28, July 18, 19, 21, 24, 25, 1972, p. 377.

21. See U.S. Senate, Committee on Foreign Relations, "Prepared Statement of Albert Carnesale," in *Strategic Defense and Anti-Satellite Weapons, Hearings*, April 25, 1984, p. 212.

Chapter 11
Special Supplement: Low Intensity Conflict, The Strategic Challenge

1. See Bruce Russett, "Security and the Resources Scramble: Will 1984 Be Like 1914?" *International Affairs* 58 (Winter 1981–1982):42; Zbigniew Brzezinski, *Power and Principle: Memoirs of the National Security Adviser, 1977–1981* (New York: Farrar, Straus, Giroux, 1983), pp. 530–533; William J. Taylor, Jr., *The Future of Conflict: U.S. Interests*, Washington Papers 94 (New York: Praeger Publishers, 1983), pp. 39–58.

2. This threat to Western security is analyzed in Barry M. Blechman and Edward W. Luttwak, eds., *International Security Yearbook 1983/84* (New York: St. Martin's Press, 1984), p. 281. See also Rodney W. Jones and Steven Hildreth, *Modern Weapons and Third World Powers*, CSIS Significant Issues Series, volume 4, no. 4 (Boulder, Colo.: Westview Press, 1984).

3. See George C. Herring, "The Vietnam Syndrome and American Foreign Policy," *Virginia Quarterly Review* 57 (Autumn 1981):594; Robert E. Osgood, "American Grand Strategy: Patterns, Problems and Prescriptions," *Naval War College Review* (September–October 1983):5; and Norman A. Graebner, "Coming to Terms with Reality," *Naval War College Review* (September–October 1983):91. See also Gregory D. Foster, "On Selective Intervention," *Strategic Review* 11 (Fall 1983):48.

4. For insider perspectives on U.S. capabilities, see the address by Noel C. Koch, principal deputy assistant secretary of defense, International Security Affairs, in *Congressional Record-Senate*, April 3, 1984, p. S3660; Donald R. Morelli and Michael M. Ferguson, "Low-Intensity Conflict: An Operational Perspective," *Military Review* 64 (November 1984):2. For the outsider perspective, see Neil C. Livingstone, "Fighting Terrorism and Dirty Little Wars," *Air University Review* 35 (March–April 1984):4; and Eliot A. Cohen, "Constraints on America's Conduct of Small Wars," *International Security* 9 (Fall 1984):151. The report of the Kissinger commission on Central America raised a number of capability issues in the context of a specific policy challenge: U.S., National Bipartisan Commission on Central America, *Report of the National Bipartisan Commission on Central America* (Washington, D.C.: Government Printing Office, January 1984) (hereafter cited as Kissinger Commission, *Report*).

5. The definitional problem as seen by scholars is surveyed in Sam C. Sarkesian, "American Policy and Low-Intensity Conflict: An Overview," in Sam C. Sarkesian and William L. Scully, eds., *U.S. Policy and Low-Intensity Conflict: Potentials for Military Struggles in the 1980s* (New Brunswick, N.J.: Transaction Books, 1981), pp. 2–5. For an official definition, see the U.S. Army's Field Manual 100-20, *Low Intensity Conflict* (January 16, 1981), pp. 14–15.

6. Henry A. Kissinger, "Ronald Reagan's Great Opportunity," *Washington Post*, November 20, 1984, p. A15.

7. Yet another treatment is offered in Morelli and Ferguson, "Low-Intensity Conflict," p. 5.

8. Edward C. Meyer, "Low-Level Conflict: An Overview," in *Terrorism and Beyond: An International Conference on Terrorism and Low-Level Conflict*, R-2714-DOE/DOJ/DOS/RC (Santa Monica, Calif.: Rand Corporation, December 1982), pp. 38, 39.

9. See, for example, William J. Taylor, Jr., Steven A. Maaranen, and Gerrit W. Gong, "U.S. Strategic Responses to Conflict in the 1980's," in Taylor, Maaranen, and Gong, eds., *Strategic Responses to Conflict in the 1980s* (Lexington, Mass.: Lexington Books, 1984), pp. 483, 496–498.

10. Kissinger Commission, *Report*, p. 91. See also Robert S. Leiken, *Soviet Strategy in Latin America*, Washington Papers 93 (Washington, D.C.: Praeger Publishers, 1982).

11. Moscow's global reach is described in U.S. Department of Defense, *Soviet Military Power 1984* (Washington, D.C.: Government Printing Office, 1984), pp. 113–127.

12. U.S. Arms Control and Disarmament Agency, *World Military Expenditures and Arms Transfers, 1972–1982*, Publication 117 (Washington, D.C.: Arms Control and Disarmament Agency, April 1984), p. 95.

13. On proxy operations generally, as well as the Cuban dimension, see William J. Taylor, Jr., and James J. Townsend, "Soviet Proxy Warfare," in William J. Taylor, Jr., and Robert H. Kupperman, eds., *Strategic Requirements for the Army to the Year 2000* (Lexington, Mass.: Lexington Books, 1984), p. 209. On the Vietnam problem, see W. Scott Thompson, "Invasion and Sustainability in Southeast Asia," in William J. Taylor, Jr., and Steven A. Maaranen, eds., *The Future of Conflict in the 1980s* (Lexington, Mass.: Lexington Books, 1982), p. 293.

14. Soviet activities are described in Richard H. Shultz and Roy Godson, *Dezinformatsia: Active Measures in Soviet Strategy* (New York: Pergamon-Brassey's, 1984).

15. See, for example, U.S. Department of Defense, Organization of the Joint Chiefs of Staff, *Military Posture FY 1985* (Washington, D.C.: Government Printing Office, 1984), p. 89.

16. The early Reagan perspective was made clear in the president's intelligence charter: U.S. President, Executive Order 12333, "United States Intelligence Activities," *Federal Register*, December 9, 1981, p. 59943. The Long commission's findings were reported in U.S. Department of Defense, *Report of the DOD Commission on Beirut International Airport Terrorist Act, October 23, 1983* (Washington, D.C., December 30, 1983), esp. pp. 63–66, 130–33.

17. See Alvin Bernstein and John D. Waghelstein, "How to Win in El Salvador," *Policy Review* 27 (Winter 1984):50; and Robert J. McCartney, "U.S. Reconnaissance Helps El Salvador Increase Bombing," *Washington Post*, April 12, 1984, p. A37.

18. *Military Posture, FY 1985*, pp. 65–66; U.S. Department of Defense, *Annual Report to the Congress, Fiscal Year 1985, February 1, 1984* (Washington, D.C.: Government Printing Office, 1984), pp. 54, 276. See also Joseph C. Lutz, "Special Forces to Help Others Help Themselves," *Army* (October 1983):246; and Ian V. Hogg, "Special Forces Update," *Jane's Defense Weekly*, November 17, 1984, p. 900.

19. Noel C. Koch, principal deputy assistant secretary of defense for international security affairs, "Third World Problems and International Security," *Defense/84* (February 1984):16. See also *Military Posture FY 1985*, pp. 82–83, and *Annual Report to the Congress, Fiscal Year 1985*, pp. 203–224.

20. See Ambassador Robert M. Sayre's address, "International Terrorism: A Long Twilight Struggle," in U.S. Department of State, Bureau of Public Affairs, *Current Policy*, August 15, 1984; and Secretary of State Schultz's speech, "Terrorism and the Modern World," *Current Policy*, October 25, 1984.

21. Force projection programs are described in *Annual Report to the Congress, Fiscal Year 1985*, pp. 175–184. See also Raphael Iungerich, "U.S. Rapid Deployment Forces— USCENTCOM—What Is It? Can It Do the Job?" *Armed Forces Journal International* (October 1984):88. On the army's light infantry division, see Michael R. Gordon, "The Change of the Light Infantry—Army Plans Forces for Third World Conflicts," *National Journal*, May 19, 1984, p. 968.

22. The rationale for this energetic approach was outlined in John Lenczowski, "A Foreign Policy for Reaganauts," *Policy Review* 18 (Fall 1981):77. An overview of administration initiatives was provided by USIA director Charles Wick in U.S. Senate, Committee on Foreign Relations, *USIA: Recent Developments, Hearings*, 98th Cong., 1st sess., 1983, pp. 2–5.

23. See, for example, Taylor and Maaranen, *Future of Conflict*, pp. 86–87.

24. See the papers by Zbigniew Brzezinski and Henry Kissinger in *Forging Bipartisanship*, a *Washington Quarterly* White Paper (Washington, D.C.: Center for Strategic and International Studies, 1984).

25. See, for example, Walter LaFeber, *Inevitable Revolutions: The United States in Central America* (New York: W.W. Norton, 1983).

26. Edward Luttwak, "Notes on Low-Intensity Warfare," *Parameters: Journal of the U.S. Army War College* 11 (December 1983):11.

27. Meyer, "Low-Level Conflict," pp. 40–41.

28. *Congressional Record—Senate*, April 3, 1984, p. 3660.

29. See, for example, Albert H. Paddock, Jr., *U.S. Army Special Warfare: Its Origins* (Washington, D.C.: National Defense University Press, 1982).

30. See David H. Petraeus, "Light Infantry in Europe: Strategic Flexibility and Conventional Deterrence," *Military Review* 64 (December 1984):35.

31. Brent L. Smith and James Fraser, "Countering Terrorism: The Development of an Instructional Model for Appropriate Military Involvement," *Conflict Quarterly* (Winter 1982):30.

32. See the editorial view in the *Washington Post*, May 9, 1984, p. A30.

33. Compare the upbeat views of Charles P. Monroe, an FBI professional, in "Addressing Terrorism in the United States," in Marvin E. Wolfgang, ed., *International Terrorism, The Annals of the American Academy of Political and Social Science* 463 (September 1982):141, with James B. Motley, *U.S. Strategy to Counter Domestic Political Terrorism* (Washington, D.C.: National Defense University Press, 1983).

34. See the official reservations described in George C. Wilson, "Get Tough Policy on Terrorism Seen," *Washington Post*, November 27, 1984, p. A1.

35. See "Casey Apologizes to Hill for Lapse on Port Mining," *Washington Post*, April 27, 1984, p. A1.

36. Kissinger Commission, *Report*, pp. 12–14.

37. See, for example, "Terrorism and the Modern World," U.S. Department of State, Bureau of Public Affairs, *Current Policy*, October 25, 1984. See also Robert H. Kupperman and David Williamson, Jr., "Let's Calm Down and Get Smart About Terrorism," *Washington Post*, Dec. 2, 1984.

Index

About the Contributors

Martin Binkin is a senior fellow, foreign policy studies, at the Brookings Institution. He has had extensive experience working in systems analysis for the Department of Defense and the U.S. Air Force. In addition, he has served as a consultant for the U.S. Senate, the General Accounting Office, and the Joint Center for Political Studies. Martin Binkin has written or coauthored ten books on military manpower issues, including, most recently, *America's Volunteer Military: Progress and Prospects.*

Nanette C. Brown is assistant to the director of national security programs at the Rand Corporation. She previously worked for the United Nations Education, Scientific and Cultural Organization. She is currently working on two manuscripts dealing with nuclear deterrence and Europe and with political issues behind the U.S. Strategic Defense Initiative.

Albert Carnesale, professor of public policy at Harvard University and dean at Harvard's John F. Kennedy School of Government, has been chief of the Defensive Weapons Systems Division at the Arms Control and Disarmament Agency and senior adviser to the head of the U.S. delegation to the SALT I talks. He is the author or coauthor of many articles on nuclear issues in collected works and such journals as *Arms Control Today, Foreign Affairs,* and *International Security.* He is also a coauthor, most recently, of *Hawks, Doves, and Owls: An Agenda for Avoiding Nuclear War.*

Alton Frye is Washington director and senior fellow of the Council on Foreign Relations and a member of the Mershon Center Board of Visitors. He has been legislative assistant to Senator Edward W. Brooke and a fellow at the Woodrow Wilson International Center for Scholars. Among his many publications are *A Responsible Congress: The Politics of National Security* and *Nazi Germany and the American Hemisphere,* a Pulitzer Prize nominee. He has contributed to all major national newspapers and to many journals, including *Bulletin of the Atomic Scientists, Foreign Affairs,* and *Foreign Policy.*

Alexander L. George is the Graham H. Stuart Professor of International Relations at Stanford University and chairman of the Mershon Center Board of Visitors. He worked for twenty years as a research analyst with the Rand Corporation. He is author or coauthor of eight books, including the classic study *Woodrow Wilson and Colonel House,* written with his wife, Juliette L. George; *Deterrence in American Foreign Policy* (a Bancroft Prize winner in 1975); and, most recently, *Managing U.S.-Soviet Rivalry: Problems of Crisis Prevention.* He is the author of many articles in journals and books and is a recipient of a MacArthur Foundation Fellowship.

Michael Krepon is a senior associate at the Carnegie Endowment for International Peace where he serves as director of its Verification Project. As a legislative assistant to Congressman Norman Dicks he worked on defense issues. He has also been director of defense program and policy reviews at ACDA. He is the author of *Strategic Stalemate: Nuclear Weapons and Arms Control in American Politics, Treaty Verification and Compliance,* and articles in many national newspapers and in *Foreign Affairs* and *Foreign Policy.*

Robert H. Kupperman is a senior associate and the executive director for science and technology at the Georgetown University Center for Strategic and International Studies. Dr. Kupperman is a specialist in the field of counterterrorism and advises both the U.S. and foreign governments in this area. He has served as chief scientist for the Arms Control and Disarmament Agency and assistant director for government preparedness in the Office of Emergency Preparedness. He is the author or coauthor of numerous publications, including *Strategic Requirements for the Army to the Year 2000.*

Philip A. Odeen is regional managing partner of Coopers and Lybrand's Management Consulting Group in the mid-Atlantic area and managing partner for its Washington, D.C., operations. He has served as director of programs analysis for the National Security Council. He has also been principal deputy assistant secretary of defense for systems analysis, having been responsible for defense planning and program issues, manpower and equipment requirements, and a broad range of matters affecting the U.S. posture overseas. He recently directed a study for the Georgetown Center for Strategic and International Studies on defense organization.

Earl C. Ravenal, former director of the Asian division (systems analysis) in the Office of the Secretary of Defense, is a professor of international relations at the Georgetown University School of Foreign Service. He is also an adjunct scholar of the Cato Institute of Washington, D.C. Dr. Ravenal's 135 articles have appeared in many major professional and popular publications in the United States and abroad, including *Foreign Affairs, Foreign Policy,* and the *Atlantic Monthly.* He is the coauthor and editor of two books and the author of seven others, including *Defining Defense: The 1985 Military Budget* and the forthcoming *Foreign Policy in an Uncontrollable World.*

Walter B. Slocombe is a member of the Washington, D.C., law firm of Caplin and Drysdale. He has been deputy under secretary of defense for policy planning and the principal deputy assistant secretary of defense for international security affairs. He is the author of an Adelphi Paper, *The Political Implications of Strategic Parity* (no. 77), as well as articles in journals such as *International Security, Strategic Review,* and *Washington Quarterly.*

Leonard Sullivan, Jr., is an independent, Washington-based consultant on matters of national security policy and resident consultant for the Center for National Security Research within the System Planning Corporation. He has served as assistant secretary of defense (program analysis and evaluation) and has been a consultant to a wide variety of defense-related firms and organizations. Mr. Sullivan is currently a director of the Atlantic Council, a director of the Committee on the Present Danger, and a member of the Defense Science Board. He was project director for a two-year Atlantic Council study, *Securing the Seas.*

William J. Taylor, Jr., is executive director of the Georgetown University Center for Strategic and International Studies. Until retirement in 1981 as a U.S. Army colonel, he served in Germany, Korea, and Vietnam, completing his final ten years of military service as director of national security studies at West Point and as a visiting professor at the U.S. Naval War College. Dr. Taylor is author or coauthor of seven books and over fifty publications, including *Strategic Responses to Conflict in the 1980s* and *American National Security: Policy and Process.*

James A. Thomson is vice president of Rand for Project Air Force, director of national security studies at Rand, and senior researcher on defense issues related to Europe. He has been a member of the National Security Council staff and has served at the Pentagon as an operations research analyst in the office of Program Analysis and Evaluation. He has published *The Future of Nuclear Arms Control* and articles in journals such as the *Washington Quarterly* and *Survival.* He has also published sixteen articles on nuclear physics in scientific journals.

Harlan K. Ullman is senior fellow and director of several major programs, including the Maritime Studies Program at the Center for Strategic and International Studies, Georgetown University. He is also a senior partner of Ullman-Bristol Associates, a Washington-based consulting firm. He has served as an officer in the U.S. Navy with lengthy operational and staff experience. He has published numerous journal and newspaper articles and is the author of *Crisis or Opportunity? U.S. Maritime Industries and National Security* and *White Paper on Forecasting U.S. Maritime Industries.*

William R. Van Cleave is professor of international relations and director, Defense and Strategic Studies Program at the University of Southern California, and senior research fellow for national security at the Hoover Institution, Stanford University. Dr. Van Cleave has been a member of the SALT I delegation, senior defense adviser for Ronald Reagan during the 1979–1980 presidential campaign, and director of the Department of Defense Transition Team. He is the author or coauthor of many publications on defense, international security, and arms control in journals such as *Orbis, Survival,* and *Armed Forces Journal* and in national newspapers, magazines, and collections. His latest book is *Reflections on Nuclear Testing,* coauthored with S.T. Cohen.

R. James Woolsey, a partner in the Washington law firm of Shea and Gardner, has served as under secretary of the navy, general counsel to the U.S. Senate Committee on Armed Services, and member of the National Security Council Staff. He has also been an adviser to the U.S. SALT I delegation and a program analyst in the Office of the Secretary of Defense. He has written for *Foreign Affairs* and is a frequent contributor of articles on defense and foreign policy to the *Washington Post, Armed Forces Journal,* and other publications.

About the Editors

George E. Hudson is associate professor of political science, Wittenberg University, and senior faculty associate at the Mershon Center, The Ohio State University. During 1983–1984 he was visiting professor of social sciences at the U.S. Military Academy, West Point. Between 1978 and 1979 he was a Council on Foreign Relations International Affairs Fellow in the U.S. Department of Defense, where he specialized in Soviet affairs and European security issues. Professor Hudson is the author of numerous papers and articles on Soviet and U.S. national security.

Joseph Kruzel is associate professor of political science, The Ohio State University, and senior faculty associate at the Mershon Center. He was a member of the U.S. delegation to the Strategic Arms Limitation Talks (SALT I) and has served as a consultant to the Department of Defense, the National Security Council, and the U.S. Senate. Professor Kruzel taught previously at Harvard and Duke Universities and has written extensively on arms control and U.S. defense policy.